Gone the Dark Night

Gone the Dark Night

The Story of 488(NZ) Squadron, RAF

New Zealand's first Night Fighter Unit in the UK and Europe, June 1942 to April 1945.

Graham Clayton

First published in the United Kingdom in 2019 by Mention the War Ltd. Merthyr Tydfil, CF47 0BH, Wales.

Copyright 2019 © Graham Clayton

This book is copyright. Except for the purpose of fair review, no part may be stored or transmitted in any form or by any means, mechanical, including recording or storage in any information retrieval system without permission in writing from the publisher.

The right of Graham Clayton to be identified as author of this work is asserted by him in accordance with the Copyright, Design and Patents Act 1988.

Cover design: Topics – The Creative Partnership
www.topicdesign.co.uk

Cover image: Des Knock B.Sc.

A CIP catalogue reference for this book is available from the British Library.

ISBN 9781911255383

KA NGARUE RATAU (WE SHAKE THEM)

Dedication

*From the far corners of the earth they came;
From the great people, Lincoln loved and led;
No land refused the urgent call and claim
that spoke the tongue of Milton, and was bred
on freedom's air. From the Antipodes, they came,
 and where was Britain's need, they stood;
No desert, forest, mountain range nor seas
could separate them from that brotherhood
where none is after or before another;
Best youth of every freedom-loving nation,
who offer all to aid one common mother,
spread your bright squadrons for the world's salvation
Wing-tip to wing, a brave and lovely sight,
Morning has come and **gone the dark night.**

A Sonnet by W.A.G. Kemp   1946

For Ron Watts, Peter Hall, John Gard'ner, Chris Vlotman, Norman Crookes, Ray Gager and Reg Mitchell.

My "oldies" who sadly passed on during the research stages for this story.

Their lives were long and illustrious and what personal contact I had with them was truly rewarding. They had done more than most to ensure lives for countless millions of people around the world were enhanced with the coming of peace and that the tyranny that they fought against with the utmost bravery was firmly and clearly put in its rightful place.

The world is a much better place for their sacrifices and we of the following generations owe them so much.

Each of their families have every reason to be proud of them

*For my Grandchilden,
Luke, Olivia, Ruby, Isla, Liam and Pippa*

So they and countless children around the world can come to understand what sacrifices were made so their world would be safe and free from tyranny.

Tribute

Flying Officer Reginald Walter Mitchell
RNZAF 416812

488 (New Zealand) Squadron RAF

15th March 1921 – 5th September 2013

Reg Mitchell – The catalyst for the telling of the 488 Squadron story. It was Reg who brought a very human dimension to the fine young men who served the Allied cause in the night skies over the UK and Europe during the course of the Second World War. Reg was passionate about the need for the 488 story to be told and having the squadron's history preserved for posterity. This narative is dedicated to him.

Rest in Peace – 'Mosquito Man'

Contents

Dedication 5

Tribute 7

Foreword by Air Vice Marshal G. B. Lintott 11

Preface 13

Acknowledgements 22

Author's Notes 28

Introduction 33

Chapter One: Church Fenton - Yorkshire, England 59

Chapter Two: Ayr - Ayrshire, Scotland 75

Chapter Three: Drem - East Lothian, Scotland 107

Chapter Four: Bradwell Bay - Essex, England 114

Chapter Five: Zeals - Wiltshire, England 190

Chapter Six: Colerne - Wiltshire, England 223

Chapter Seven: Hunsdon - Hertfordshire, England 250

Chapter Eight: Amiens-Glisy - Amiens, France 260

Chapter Nine: Gilze-Rijen - Breda, Holland 308

Chapter Ten: 322

The Aftermath 338

Squadron Combat Victories 341

The Men of 488 Squadron 344

Epilogue 347

Roll of Honour 349

Honours and Awards	351
Those Who Served	353
The Pilot Speaks	375
488 Squadron Aircraft	377
Bibliography	395
Squadron Memorabilia and Items of Interest	399

Foreword

Former Chief of the Royal New Zealand Air Force, Air Vice Marshal G.B. (Graham) Lintott, ONZM, FRAeS

Serving as part of the Royal Air Force, 488 Squadron was New Zealand's only night fighter squadron of the Second World War, and yet the outstanding service given by the squadron has until now been mostly forgotten.

Flying low over enemy territory on moonlight sorties against enemy ground targets, or flying offensive or defensive patrols against enemy aircraft, the night-fighter crews had a difficult and demanding task. Always alert to the dangers of ground and air attack, the nearly 200 men who served as aircrew and the many more who served as ground crew on this squadron deserve to have their story told.

In their three short years 488 Squadron's crews flew nearly 3,000 sorties, destroyed at least 67 aircraft, 40 trains and countless ground installations. Squadron members earned twenty-three gallantry awards and sadly thirty-six men lost their lives.

Nearly half of the aircrew that served with 488 Squadron were New Zealanders. Young men, far from home, who were prepared to face whatever danger was necessary to do the job they had volunteered for. The rest of the crews were from Britain and other Commonwealth countries and a few were American. Whatever their origins, all were united in their war service.

This spirit of service, of doing the right thing, is part of the intangible traditions that are passed between generations of the RNZAF. It is perhaps fitting then that the Squadron's badge features a Taiaha and Tewhatewha, both prized and effective ancient weapons of war which were passed from one generation of Maori warrior to another. The men and women of the modern RNZAF can learn a great deal from the history of 488 Squadron, and those that have served before them.

I can only congratulate Graham Clayton for taking on the challenge of bringing this story to life. In telling it, he brings a very human dimension to the statistics and finally puts the proud record of 488 Squadron clearly into the spotlight.

Royal New Zealand Air Force Headquarters
New Zealand Defence Force
Wellington, New Zealand
May 2011

Preface

The history of No. 488 (NZ) Squadron of the Royal Air Force is not well known in this country. Long known as the "forgotten" squadron it was the first New Zealand based Fighter squadron, originally formed at Rongotai in Wellington, New Zealand on 2nd September of 1941. The squadron initially saw service in what was colloquially known as the *"Far East"*[1] in Singapore and the Netherlands East Indies before being officially disbanded on 2nd March 1942. This was the day they arrived safely in the port of Fremantle in Western Australia. They had escaped from Singapore following the defeat of the British and surrender of Singapore to the Japanese on 15th February 1942. The surviving squadron personnel were repatriated back home to New Zealand after a fighting retreat that allowed them to escape the Japanese onslaught by the skin of their teeth. These squadron personnel were posted on to other RNZAF squadrons to be retained for the defence of New Zealand and the Pacific.

In the meantime, the British High Command saw the need to form further Dominion squadrons to help protect Britain from the German invasion on the other side of the world. They had anticipated an influx of newly trained aircrew from training courses being set up for that purpose. Rather than setting up a new bureaucracy to recreate a new squadron they retained the same squadron classification number and reformed a completely newly manned 488 Squadron some three months later on 25th June 1942 at RAF Church Fenton in Yorkshire, England.

The Air Ministry in London had the upper hand in this affair. The so-called Dominion squadrons were to be fully funded by the British Government so the New Zealand Government was forced to acquiesce and after some discussion relinquished control of the squadron identity to the Air Ministry in the UK, albeit retaining the link with New Zealand. Unlike the predecessor squadron which was fully manned by New Zealanders the newly formed squadron had a majority of its aircrew selected from New Zealand air-crew mostly serving in the UK but drew on ground-crew personnel from Britain and the Dominions. As with the earlier squadron the new squadron was to be identified as No. 488 (New

---

[1] *The expression "Far East" is derived from an old Northern Hemisphere expression and perspective meaning all the Asian territories to the east of the continent of India.*

Zealand) Squadron of the Royal Air Force. All command appointments for both squadrons were made by the RAF

There was however, considerable disappointment in New Zealand that a second 488 Squadron was being formed, as the original 488 Squadron, despite its ignominious ending in retreat from the Far East, was very well regarded and had in its short operational life gained a unique identity and respect all of its own. The composition of the new 488 could not have been more different.

In a wonderful turn of events in recent times, the RNZAF on 8th December 2010, raised the 488 flag once again by forming a new operational Wing at RNZAF Base Ohakea as part of a re-vitalised defence system for the New Zealand military. The occasion was marked with a parade and attended by some of the surviving wartime personnel. It must have been a real thrill for them to at long last gain some recognition for their valiant efforts all those years ago.

None of the original "Far East" squadron personnel served in the re-formed UK squadron but the same brave and resolute reputation of the original squadron, badly mauled by the Japanese earlier in 1942 was to be continued by the new squadron. Thus, the squadron, even if it was in name only, had the distinction of being one of the very few operational air force units in the Allied services that fought in two different theatres of war, fighting both the Germans and the Japanese. The majority of the newly formed UK squadron aircrew were to be New Zealanders, either already serving with the RAF, seconded from RNZAF aircrew attached to other RAF squadrons, or straight out of aircrew training courses. Most of the crewmen that is non-pilots, and almost all of the ground-crew were from the Royal Air Force supplemented by personnel from other Dominion forces. The reason for this will be discussed later.

The history of the original *"Far East"* squadron was covered in my earlier book *"Last Stand in Singapore"* published with the support of the RNZAF by Random House in August 2008. It was therefore inevitable that the history of the re-formed squadron should follow on. With further support and encouragement from the RNZAF I started research in early 2009 to complete the sequel to the 488 Squadron history. It turned out to be a very interesting story.

We do not do Military history very well in this country. Sources for research information on this particular squadron were scarce and I had long pondered why this was so. The original 488 Squadron suffered some indignity by being part of one of the Allies greatest defeats in the

Second World War when the Japanese over-ran Malaya and Singapore forcing the British to surrender. The original squadron members were re-posted to new squadrons, eventually being scattered far and wide over New Zealand and the Pacific immediately after their escape from Singapore. It was perhaps easy to understand that a comprehensive history was never going to be easily compiled. When the war with Japan ended, these men returned home, many with the stigma of surrender still on their minds and in most cases, went back to civilian jobs and simply got on with their lives.

The latter re-formed squadron, the subject of this story, operated on the other side of the world during the hours of darkness, using top secret night radar equipment that was largely experimental at the time. The public acclaim that other day fighter and bomber squadrons were receiving daily in the worlds media meant little or no coverage of 488 Squadron's activities were in the public arena. Hence little available contemporary public information existed. In my view, they deserved better recognition.

Conversations with a wide group of New Zealand ex-servicemen during the research stage for this project revealed the widespread belief among them that 488 was the "forgotten" squadron and that beyond RNZAF circles not a lot was known of their achievements. The rapid re-deployment of the manpower from the original squadron to other squadrons on their return from Singapore was an obvious factor plus the fact that they were under control of the Royal Air Force during both of their deployments. One would have thought that publicity would by way of compensation have been forthcoming from British sources after the war but nothing of any note has been found. In fact, the official report commissioned and gazetted by the British Government after the Singapore debacle and presented to the British Parliament made no mention at all of the original 488 Squadron other than a listing in the index showing they were based at Kallang on Singapore Island. This was despite the fact that they were the last surviving Airforce squadron, still operational with the Japanese Army moving in and around the perimeter of their airfield at Kallang. In fact, for several days they were literally in "No Mans Land" with the British Army behind them defending the City and the Japanese army encircling them. All the other air force units were long gone having been evacuated off the Island.

Just to emphasise the paucity of local knowledge, I was taken into the Officer's Mess at RNZAF Base Whenuapai by the then Officer

Commanding 485 Wing, Group Captain Edward Poot, and shown the squadron boards displayed on the walls. It was an impressive display of all the squadrons that served this country but one of the boards was bereft of photographs and text; that of 488 Squadron. He wanted that changed.

Another example was the surprise expressed by aviation Forum writers commenting on the recent passing of Norman Crookes who with his pilot, "Jamie" Jameson performed one of the greatest night-fighter exploits of the Second World War by downing four enemy aircraft, at night in just thirty minutes. When Norman's obituary was published in national newspapers in the UK it was quite ironic reading of the number of aviation commentators and Historians who expressed surprise that they knew nothing of the feat.

Only one account of the squadron's history of any note was written, that of Leslie Hunt's *"Defence until Dawn"* published in 1949 in England with help from public subscriptions and Hunt's appeals to fellow squadron members for financial assistance. Hunt was 488 Squadron's Intelligence Officer for some time and noted himself that the nature of the squadron's secret nocturnal work could not be revealed publically. His account, even though published four years after the war was still short on detail, due I am sure to the secret Radar equipment carried on board their aircraft as presumably these radar systems were still in use post war.

There were however, many other unpublished anecdotal accounts produced after the war, mostly for family and friend's consumption and some of the higher profile RAF squadron members who continued with air force or public service careers produced autobiographical memoirs, sections of which covered the period that they served with 488. These were very helpful in compiling this narrative. There were magazine and newspaper articles printed in this country during the war but without exception any of those written focussing on 488 Squadron were written in very ambiguous terms by anonymous authors and the squadron number was never mentioned.

A New Zealand War Correspondent, Alan Mitchell did spend some time with the Squadron in the UK and Europe but even he, despite having full access to the New Zealand members of the squadron was restricted from reporting on anything that would identify the squadron

F/L Leslie Hunt, Author of 'Defence until Dawn' (Reg Mitchell)

or its whereabouts. Mitchell wrote accounts of New Zealand air force personnel and squadrons that were published late in 1945. Even though this was after the end of the war as with Leslie Hunt's narrative, he was also unable to comment on the Radar equipment in use at that time as any details were still classified information.

Being one of the squadron's operating under the command of the Royal Air Force also caused significant research difficulties in that official information was kept in files locked away in archives in London after the war. These were difficult to access without some effort on the part of any New Zealand based researcher mainly due to the distance involved to carry out personal research or lacking the local contacts to research the files.

The war had been going very badly for Britain in early 1942. The call had gone out to the Dominions to take up the call to arms and assist the "Mother" country. The power balance in Europe had shifted dramatically with the German land forces having "Blitzkrieged" their way across Europe, enveloping France and swinging north to tip the British forces literally into the sea at Dunkirk on the north-western coast of Europe. The fall of France on 25th June 1940 brought the German forces to within thirty-four kilometres of the south coast of England at Dover, well within striking distance of the Luftwaffe bombers. It was in all probability that narrow stretch of water known as the English

Channel that saved Britain from the final push from the initial momentum of the Nazi land-based onslaught.

It was this scenario that faced the young airmen from New Zealand and the other Dominions, sent northwards from their homes in a desperate attempt to save the British Empire. For them the defence of Britain was vital, as capitulation to the German forces would mean the Dominions losing their sovereignty and, in all probability, having to come under German rule, even though geographically we were literally placed at the other end of the world. Some New Zealanders had already travelled north in the years preceding the start of hostilities in Europe to join up with the RAF in Britain. For many however that were looking to the air force as a career, the warning signs of the pending conflict was enough to consider joining locally and it was these men that formed most of the personnel that would eventually end up in RAF air force squadrons based in the UK.

Selected airmen were sent to Canada as part of the Dominion Training Scheme funded by the British Government. This scheme was instituted by the respective Allied governments to boost the aircrew numbers needed to form squadrons in the UK. These squadrons were to be known as Article XV Squadrons and eventually consisted of airmen from Australian, New Zealand and Canadian air force flying squadrons that graduated from the British Commonwealth Air Training Plan (BCATP). Canada was selected as the ideal training venture for this training due to the facilities available, proximity to the USA and far enough away from the conflict in Europe to ensure safety of the personnel and programs.

Six New Zealand Article XV Squadrons were formed from this scheme although a big percentage of the training school graduates were sent directly into RAF squadrons. The six new RNZAF Squadrons thus formed were 485 (Fighter), 486 (Fighter/Bomber), 487 (Fighter/Bomber), 488 (Night Fighter), 489 (Torpedo Bomber) and 490 (Flying Boat) squadrons. All of them were under the direct command of RAF Operational control for the duration of the war. The scheme was hugely successful and when combined with the training schemes already underway in New Zealand and other counties, eventually formed an oversupply of airmen. The BCATP scheme trained a total of 131,553 aircrew, 7002 of whom were New Zealanders. Most of these airmen were trained in Canada. The excess numbers of trained airmen eventually formed a serious glut in the numbers of crews needed for the available aircraft and equipment and these surpluses caused the suspension of the training scheme by the end of 1944.

The setting up of these squadrons under this scheme was not without problems. For a start the British High Command gave little advance warning of their formation and initially finding suitable qualified manpower was a problem for the participants until trained personel came on stream. Qualified and experienced ground crew technicians were in very short supply and most of the so called New Zealand Dominion squadrons formed consisted of up to 75% RNZAF aircrew but rarely more than 5% RNZAF ground crew technicians. The RNZAF in particular simply did not have the numbers of trained technicians required to service these new "kiwi" manned squadrons. Of immediate concern to the authorities was the manpower composition of the two-man night-fighter aircraft, particularly the Beaufighter, where trained observers were required to team up with a pilot to work the very new Radar units installed on these aircraft. The lack of notice with the re-formation of 488 Squadron did not allow the RNZAF time to train Observers or Radar operators for these very specific operational crews.

[2] It has been suggested in more recent times that the RAF had not been overly keen on setting up autonomous "Dominion" squadrons as they would have much preferred that all personnel under their command be treated as a pool of trained individuals that could be posted anywhere at any time without constant reference to Dominion governments, particularly those of Canada and Australia who were particularly vociferous in this respect. Canada was for instance keen to set up its own administrative group of both Bombers and Fighters but the RAF was seriously opposed to any suggestion that the setting up of autonomous groups within their command structure was going to happen. They did not mind permitting a proportion of their squadrons to bear Dominion titles but anything beyond that would in their view cause serious disruption in planning and provisioning the group as a whole.

The influence of politicians from the three dominions and the British parliament was also seen as counter productive to their attempts to set up a single command and the proposed Article XV set up was a concession of sorts to the respective participating countries. It was thought that the "mixing" and "matching" of personnel would negate any influence being brought by any of the respective countries involved. So, Article XV squadrons were in the end a political construct.

---

[2] *Squadron set up comments and information from notes by David Duxbury.*

All personnel known to have served with the UK based 488 Squadron are listed at the end of this book. This is my personal acknowledgement to these men who served so bravely, with little reward at a time when our way of life in the troubled times of the Second World War was under serious threat. These squadron members, and I have included ground crew and support staff in the listings, played a big part in defending Great Britain from the terror of German night bombing in early 1942 and continued their good work on the Continent as the months unfolded until eventually the Nazi regime was crushed and forced into surrender in 1945.

The squadron was an integral part of the D Day invasion of Europe, protecting ground troops from air attack at night, eventually following up with intruder missions deep into Germany. The contribution of 488 Squadron can never be overstated as they played a vital part in the Allied counter attack that led to the German invaders being driven back to where they came from, and to their eventual defeat and surrender.

This narrative has been compiled by a very enthusiastic amateur with apologies for any indiscretions in advance. I make no apology for the use of material from many different and sometimes controversial sources that add to the telling of their story. There has been no intention to infringe copyright. Where sources are able to be identified, I have done so and where quotations have been used, the source of those quotations are fully acknowledged and listed in the Endnotes and Bibliography.

Any opinions advanced are personal and as a good amount of the material I have used is sourced from anecdotal information from the surviving veterans themselves, the passage of time may have dimmed its accuracy somewhat.

Access to the official Squadron Operations Records forms the basis of this narrative and for these I have to acknowledge the assistance of research staff in both the UK Archives at Kew in London and our local National Archives in Wellington NZ, who between them provided me access to enough information to allow the compilation of a complete set of documentations covering the squadron's existence. These original records were compiled on a daily basis and signed off each day by the squadron's Commanding Officer so those sources of information are impeccable.

The other major source has been the book published by Leslie Hunt way back in 1949 which captured much of the more personal aspects of squadron life during their time on active service and has proved invaluable in the compilation of this story.

Some of you reading this narrative may have access to further information that adds to the story of 488 Squadron and the author welcomes any contributions that build on what is known of the squadron's time in the Far East, UK and Europe.

I make no claim that this is the complete story.

Graham Clayton
Auckland, New Zealand
Email: gacn@xtra.co.nz

1st February 2019

Acknowledgements

The late Reg Mitchell on the right and the author, Graham Clayton framed in the nose section of a Mosquito rebuild being constructed by Glynn Powell in Auckland, New Zealand (Peter Wheeler)

Most researchers have found when embarking on a project that there is usually one event or one personality that initiates the research or gives it the impetus to start the ball rolling. In my case, it was a veteran and surviving air crew member of 488 Squadron by the name of Reginald Walter Mitchell. Group Captain Edward Poot, then as a Senior Commander of RNZAF Base Whenuapai, linked me with Reg Mitchell late in 2008 following the publishing of my earlier work *"Last Stand in Singapore'*.

Edward Poot felt strongly that the follow-on history of 488 Squadron should be continued. With his encouragement, and a considerable amount of arm twisting, I was asked to follow up a contact that Reg Mitchell had made earlier offering the RNZAF the use of memorabilia and photographs he had in his possession. The sample photographs and notes I viewed offered an insight and a great starting point to continue with the research on the second stage history of the squadron. This led to an ongoing friendship and huge respect for Reg, who despite his great age recalled vividly and articulately his time with the squadron all those years ago. Reg Mitchell had compiled a wonderful photographic record and his written notes describing those troubled times back up his commitment to see the squadron history recorded for posterity. Sadly, Reg passed away on 5th September 2013 aged 92 and to my great disappointment did not see the results of countless hours of my collaboration with him to put this story of his beloved 488 Squadron together.

Reg Mitchell had been heartened by the response he had been given, by young school children after he gave a talk to them on ANZAC day some years ago and following encouragement and prompting from his Grand-daughter, Alika, the contents of his wartime 'shoebox' were emptied and from it the stories flowed. Reg was a quiet, unassuming man who unlike many of our returning servicemen, took the time after the end of the war to maintain contacts and involve himself in reunions with his fellow squadron members that gave these young men something to hold onto as the years advanced. He had been a tireless worker in publicising the work done by his old squadron, in fact one of his close friends gave him the name *"Mosquito Man"* and I thought that was entirely appropriate. Reg gave me access to many contacts and his support enabled the story of 488 Squadron to be expanded into a narrative that reflected its part in the military aviation history of this country.

The many photographs in his collection were collated, edited and affixed into an album and Reg Mitchell's eldest son, John produced a memorable memoir of his Fathers service life. My thanks therefore go to the late Flying Officer Reginald Walter Mitchell, NZ 416812 of the RNZAF and his family for their input into this story of 488 Squadron.

Reg's son, John Mitchell spent countless hour's proof reading the manuscript and making changes to tidy my amateur grammar structure, something I have struggled with since my school years. His tidying up of the manuscript has made the Publishers job much easier and is much appreciated.

To the family of the late Ron Watts, Wing Commander RNZAF, and the last Commanding Officer of 488 Squadron, specifically to his daughter, Judy Anderson, my thanks for the copy of the memoir she was compiling on her Father and notes from Ron's collection and the family support for this project. Ron sadly passed away during the early research stage but what contact I had with him proved very productive and valuable and gave me an early insight as to why this man had been so widely respected by the squadron members under his command. Ron was respected for his honesty and integrity and the skilful manner in which he controlled the morale of a squadron thrown into frontline action in the air at night and during the very worst of weather related conditions. The squadron suffered continually from logistical problems and it was his skilled handling of these adverse situations that made life very much easier for the men under his command.

My thanks go to Dave Homewood, the author and driving force behind his many International Web Sites and Forums. Dave had early contact with the late Ron Watts and the posting of his interviews with Ron and the publication worldwide of Ron's wartime photographs certainly made my job a lot easier and opened the way for me to make contact with other ex squadron members or their families around the world. Dave has a passion for our air force history and has been wonderfully supportive during the research stage of this story.

To Carol Jeffs, the wife of the late Wing Commander Raymond Jeffs, O.B.E., one of the more successful but unrewarded aircrew pilots whose skill and daring in the night skies over the UK and Europe was legendary. Carol was a valuable source of contacts for me, particularly with some of the UK based aircrew. She also allowed me access to a very rare and much sought-after autobiography of one 'Jock' Cairns, one of 488 Squadrons most successful navigator/crewman.

My research overseas and the seeking out of contacts were assisted greatly by the use of 'go betweens'. In most cases these were younger people, not necessarily family members, who took it upon themselves to be the contact points between myself and the veterans, usually with the email or internet medium that my 'oldies' would have found difficult to master. The age and varying degrees of wellness of these veterans did not preclude them from enthusiastically providing anecdotal information that formed the back-bone of this narrative.

I particularly want to offer my thanks to Jenny Windle in Chesterfield, England, my link to Flying Officer Norman Crookes, M.B.E. D.F.C. Norman sadly passed away on 17th April 2012 aged 91 and would not see this tribute to him and his mates published.

To Soren Hawkes in Ypres, Belgium, who was my link to Corporal George Sutherland, a ground-crew member of the 6488 Echelon which provided technical support for 488 Squadron.

To Alastair Gager for photographs and documentation from his late father Ray Gager, a skilled Radar Technician who was with the squadron from its inception right through to the end of the war.

To Ann MacPherson of Cambridgeshire, England, the daughter of Chris Vlotman, who on one of her many regular trips to visit her ailing father living in Huizen in Holland, brought back much information. Chris also sadly passed away before completion of this project.

My thanks also to Steve Whiteley of London, England, grandson of the late Flight Sergeant Edgar (Ron) Rayner RAF for photographs and anecdotal accounts of his grandfather's time in the very early days of the squadron and to Adam Forrest in Bristol, England, the grandson of the late Pilot Officer Andrew Broodbank RAF, and the link to Peter Hall. Both Steve and Adam were patient providers of material sourced in the UK and the enthusiasim that these two had for my project dragged me out of a dark hole following the death of Reg Mitchell who had been my mainstay through the long days and nights of research.

To Dharan and Brett Longley, the sons of the late Flying Officer Harold Longley RNZAF who left 488 Squadron to fly single seater Typhoons and Tempests with No. 3 Squadron.

To Piers Wood, son of the late Flying Officer Johnny Wood, D.F.C. who shared with me memories and photographs of his late father.

To Len Wyman and his son Chris, from Middlesex in England for the use of their photographs and Len for his recollections of his many interesting moments during his time with 488 Squadron.

To James Jameson my thanks and congratulations in having the foresight to gift his father's memorabilia to the Air Force Museum at Wigram in Christchurch, New Zealand. It is an extensive collection dedicated to the memory of F/L George "Jamie" Jameson, known as "Bill" to his family and friends. He was the leading New Zealand night fighter ace of World War Two.

To Murray Richardson one of the Fleet Air Arm Navigators, seconded to the squadron, who gave me the background story on the Royal Navy flyers that joined 488 for night-fighter training.

All of whom being patient but enthusiastic providers of photographs and log book information.

My thanks also to Therese Angelo QSM, the Director of the Air Force Museum of New Zealand, for her support, along with Simon Moody and Darren Hammond from the archives section of the Wigram Museum; who co-ordinated and assisted my early access to 488 related material, many samples of which appear in this narrative. Therese and her team were instrumental in pushing for the latest squadron Wing that was set up by the RNZAF at Base Ohakea on 8th December 2010 to be named No. 488 Wing out of respect for those that had gone before.

I would like to acknowledge the efforts of Archivists at both the National Archives at Kew in London and Archives New Zealand in Wellington for their help in sourcing the squadron's official record books, also John Ross a volunteer Archivist at the Armoury of the Auckland War Memorial Museum. Their work allowed me to compile a complete and accurate daily record of the squadron's activities.

It is necessary to record the support and encouragement of the RNZAF, particularly that of Group Captain Edward Poot who had the foresight to keep the whip cracking following the publishing of my history of the earlier 488 Squadron. The more the research developed the more important the need to complete the history seemed to become. Both of us felt most strongly that we at least owe these young men that much.

My thanks to Air Vice Marshall Graham Lintott, then Chief of Staff of the RNZAF before his posting as the New Zealand Defence Attache to the United States, for his interest and support of this project and the earlier "Far East" project which culminated in "Last Stand in Singapore" being published. He is a man totally involved and committed to the current military security of New Zealand but has never lost sight of the sacrifices of the men who formed the foundations of our modern Air Force. It was an honour to have him write the Foreword for this book.

To Peter Wheeler, the Co-ordinator and mainstay of the Bomber Command Association of New Zealand who linked me on many occasions with contacts that made valuable inputs into the 488 story.

To Jonathan Pote, for his assistance with the early chapters of my manuscript and his knowledge of things 'Air Force'.

My thanks once more to David Duxbury for his vast wealth of knowledge on things Air Force particularly relating to RNZAF history but also aviation knowledge from around the world and to Larry Hill who provided valuable sources particularly encouraging me down the publishing path.

To F/O Terry Clark of York England, who still mourns the loss of his flying companions of those earlier years and has constantly supported efforts in the UK to commemorate and celebrate anniversaries of significant aviation events during WW2. The recounting of some of his stories added to the telling of this narrative.

Leslie Hunt is not forgotten although he and his publishers of *"Defence until Dawn"* have seemingly disappeared into the mists of time. His narrative published in 1949 has been an important source of information for this project. Hunt went on to become a leading expert in vintage aircraft following his retirement from the RAF in 1959. He was a prolific author and letter writer to many different aircraft publications until well into the late 1970's.

I would also like to acknowledge the owners of photographs, drawings and graphics used throughout this publication. I have listed these in chronological order in the appendices and where humanly possible have acknowledged my sources.

To the surviving veterans, themselves, seemingly diminishing on a monthly basis – It was difficult not to be humbled by the very polite carefully handwritten letters, written with faltering hands that arrived in my mail box. Many very poignant letters were written by proud widows, pleased that their husband's stories were at long last about to be told and expressing the hope that the full extent of those wartime experiences was now to be revealed. If nothing else is achieved at least the children and Grandchildren of these heroes will know of their sacrifices.

To the team at Mention the War Ltd., specialist publishers of aviation history books, especially the RAF in World War Two; Des Knock B.Sc. for his stunning cover image and the cover designers, Topics Design – The Creative Partnership. The aircraft on the front cover is Tony Agar's Mosquito HJ711, resident at the Lincolnshire Aviation Heritage Centre, East Kirkby.

Lastly it is traditional to thank spouses and family for having to suffer the physical and mental absences of the "man about the house" during the research stage but my wife Judy, readily acknowledges that she has had by way of compensation, unlimited and unencumbered use of the television remote during the course of this project.

To my wonderful family for their support and encouragement over the many, many months it took to compile this narrative.

Author's Notes

The Chapter headings throughout this narrative are set according to the chronological sequence of the various airfields that the squadron was stationed on. Each and every posting had its own particular set of circumstances and the shift to a new airfield usually involved changes in the movement of personnel and the upgrading of aircraft and equipment that set the scene for quite different happenings during the life of the squadron. The new locations seemed to create situations unique to that area that added to the overall story of the life of 488 Squadron. Sadly, each posting also meant leaving behind fellow crew members, many who died in training accidents during their time there and were often buried in local cemeteries, buried, in most cases far from home and loved ones.

There appears to be no official designation or consensus on the title for the second crew member on board both the Beaufighter and Mosquito Night Fighters. This crewman's functions were multi-tasked in that he had to navigate the aircraft, operate the on-board Radar detection equipment, operate the radio communications with the ground control, direct his pilot via radio telephone and on the early model Beaufighters reload the cannon ammunition drums. The notation "Radar Operator" was banned by Air Operations as any airman captured by the enemy wearing this designation on his uniform would be in for special treatment given the secrecy surrounding this newly developed function. This crew member has been variously described as crewman, radar operator, navigator, gunner and observer by many publications but for this narrative I have chosen the designation as *"crewman"*. It is worth noting that a good number of these men were qualified in all the trades listed and in many cases were qualified pilots as well.

As the 488 story progresses the reader will note numerical items in a dialogue box alongside reports on aircraft listed as 'Kills' by the squadron.

(27) 23/06/1944 – 00.12hrs - Ex Zeals - McCabe and Riley - Ju 188 - East of Bayeux

The format for these is *"Kill No. – Date - time of destruction – home airbase – Pilot and Crewman – Type of aircraft destroyed – where shot down.*

These are guides to the so called 'score'and in no way are these intended to glorify the killing of German air crews. I have found without exception that most, if not all the veterans I have interviewed for this project expressed a sadness and distaste at having taken the lives of their opponents during the course of their operational work against the enemy. There was I have found a mutual respect between these airmen and both sides are on record of having reported some relief when the crews of damaged aircraft falling to the ground were seen to escape by parachute from the inevitability of sudden death.

At the start of operations against Britain the Luftwaffe was using three main types of bomber aircraft, all classed as "light" bombers, the Dornier Do 17, the Heinkel He 111 and the Junkers Ju 88, all twin engined aircraft. With no four engined bombers available for its bombing campaign the Luftwaffe thankfully were incapable of airlifting a big weight of bombs on any one raid. The Do 17 was phased out with the introduction of the improved model Do 217 and later Junkers upgraded the aging Ju 88 to give a faster more manoeuvrable light bomber, the Ju 188. In early 1943 the Me 410 replaced the aging Bf 110 and together with the Focke Wulf Fw 190, the Luftwaffe had two night-fighter aircraft that were capable of countering the speed and manoeuvrability of the best of the Allied Night-fighters. They were to find out later, at great cost and loss of life, that the Mosquito technology in the end would more than counter the introduction by the Luftwaffe of the newer night-fighters they employed to defend their bomber aircraft. The German High Command also failed to develop a heavy bomber and this cost them dearly in the end. A belated attempt was made by Heinkel with the He 177 but this design was a disaster with many of the aircraft suffering serious engine problems and, in many cases, crashing due to engine failure sometimes after having just left their own airfields.

The Luftwaffe aircraft coding system looked complicated with a series of numbers and letters painted either side of the black cross on the aircraft fuselage. The first two characters on the left of the cross was the code for the aircraft "Gruppe" with the first letter to the right of the cross being the individual aircraft identification number and the last letter the Squadron code. The individual aircraft factory number unique to each aircraft was prefixed Wnr (Werknummer) followed by the

Luftwaffe Ju 88 coded 4N+EH
Aufklärungsgruppe 22 (4N) + E for "Emil" of 1 Staffel (H)

production number and was generally only shown on written records or documents. [3]

The following Glossary [4] lists some of the slang or service jargon in use during the period of the Second World War, many words that are still in use today. As I have included in this narrative a number of verbatim reports compiled during the squadron's time in the UK and Europe, this list may prove helpful to decipher accurately the actions described in these reports. German and Luftwaffe terms used throughout this narrative are listed also:

AI: **Airborne interception units** – the top-secret radar detection equipment portable enough to be fitted into aircraft and operated by the second crew member on board Allied aircraft.

Baedeker: The name given by the Luftwaffe to the bombing raids against Britain in the summer of 1942. Taken from a well-known tourist Guide book compiled by Karl Baedeker.

Bandit: Unidentified enemy aircraft

Bogey: Unidentified aircraft that needs to be checked visually to establish whether or not it is friendly or enemy.

Coned: Being caught by a searchlight beam followed closely by others locking on from other areas on the ground. Rapid and evasive action was the only way to escape the light beams that set you up as a target for anti-aircraft gunfire.

---

[3] *Notes sourced from the Fishponds Local History Society of Bristol, compiled by Paul Johnson.*

[4] *The Author acknowledges items in the above Glossary extracted from 'Aircrew' compiled by Bruce Lewis and published by Cassell in 2000.*

Dispersal: The area of an airfield where squadron aircraft are parked up when not in use. Usually protected from bomb blast and generally dispersed well apart to minimise loss or damage from air raids.
Dispersal Hut: The building used by air-crews while waiting for call to get their aircraft airborne.
Duppel: Anti Radar metal foil known to the Allies as *"Window"*
E/A: Enemy aircraft
Feldwebel: Luftwaffe rank equivalent to Sergeant (Fw)
Flak: The resulting explosion in the air of a shell, generally at a preset height activated by either a timer or pressure switch after being fired by Anti Aircraft gunnery. Shortened form of the German word *Fliegerabwehrkanone.*
Flieger: Luftwaffe rank equivalent to Aircraftsman Second Class (Flg)
F/L: Flight Lieutenant – rank of British Air Force
F/O Flying Officer – rank of British Air Force
F/Sgt.: Flight Sergeant – rank of British Air Force
Freya: Luftwaffe code for German ground radar to detect approaching Allied bombers.
Gefreiter: Luftwaffe rank equivalent to Aircraftsman First Class (Gefr)
Grp. Capt.: Group Captain – rank of British Air Force
Gruppe: An operational Luftwaffe unit similar to an RAF Wing. Normally with three squadrons totalling approx thirty aircraft.
H2S: The first Allied self-contained airborne navigational radar system needing no ground stations.
Hauptmann: Luftwaffe rank equivalent to Flight Lieutenant (Hptm)
IFF: "Identification, Friend or Foe": An electronic device fitted to all allied aircraft that emitted a continual signal able to be picked up on radar of Allied planes and anti-aircraft defences.
Knickebein: A precision German VHF radio beam navigation and bombing system.
Leutnant: Luftwaffe rank equivalent to Pilot Officer (Ltn)
Lichtenstein: Luftwaffe code for the German version of airborne (AI) interception equipment.
Luftwaffe: German Air Force
    Luftwaffe Aircrew abbreviations:
        Pilot (F)
        Observer / Navigator / Bomb Aimer (B)
        Wireless Operator (Bf)
        Flight Mechanic (Bm)

Gunner (Bs)
Major: Luftwaffe rank equivalent to Squadron Leader (Maj)
Oberfeldwebel: Luftwaffe rank equivalent to Flight Sergeant (Ofw)
Obergefreiter: Luftwaffe rank equivalent to leading aircraftsman (Ogefr)
Oberleutnant: Luftwaffe rank equivalent Flying officer (Oblt)
Oberst: Luftwaffe rank equivalent to Group Captain (Oberst)
Oberstleutnant: Luftwaffe rank equivalent to Wing Commander (Oberstlt)
Perfectos: Radar detection equipment fitted in Allied aircraft that triggered the IFF identification units on board German aircraft and identified them as enemy.
P/O. Pilot Officer – rank of RAF.
Radar: Radio Detection and Ranging – An American term originally.
RAAF: Royal Australian Air Force.
RAF: Royal Air Force.
RCAF: Royal Canadian Air Force.
RNZAF: Royal New Zealand Air Force.
Stabsfeldwebel: Luftwaffe rank equivalent to Warrant Officer (Sfw)
Sgt.: Sergeant – Non-comissioned officer (NCO) rank of RAF.
S/L: Squadron Leader - rank of RAF.
Staffel: The smallest Luftwaffe operational unit – generally of nine aircraft - the equivalent of an Allied squadron.
Stall: When the slow speed of an aircraft loses the airflow around the wing surfaces and the lack of supporting air pressure literally causes the aircraft, to drop from the sky under the force of gravity
Trade: Potential airborne enemy targets
Unteroffizier: Luftwaffe rank equivalent to Corporal (Uffz)
W/C Wing Commander - rank of British Air Force
Window: Small metallic strips dropped in bundles from aircraft to give distorted and confusing radar readings to hide and shield attacking aircraft from detection from enemy radar.
X-Verfahren: A German VHF multi-beam precision bombing system.
Y-Verfahren: A German VHF single beam range measuring precision bombing system.

Introduction

Dawn was just breaking over the airfield perimeter. The faint drone of an aircraft engine could be heard approaching from the south east. Fingers of light were silhouetting buildings and trees on the eastern horizon. A small group of men stood huddled, with arms clasped across their chests stamping their feet in the early morning cold. Clustered alongside an unlit concrete walled building, a flash from a struck match or the soft glow of a lighted cigarette from the group the only light showing in the darkness. The engine noise increased with every second that passed and could now be clearly recognised as that of a twin engined aircraft flying low down and approaching rapidly. The runway lights flickered briefly and clicked on, a green Aldis light flashed, reflecting in the glass window of the control tower and the distinctive shape and sound of a Mosquito Fighter aircraft came out of the darkness, the roar of the twin Merlins suddenly ceasing as the aircraft throttled back as it cleared the boundary fence, tail up, dropping onto the concrete runway and seemingly gathering speed as it sped towards the waiting group. As it hurtled on past, several men left the group and jogged off into the darkness towards the moving aircraft which by this time was bouncing in a wide arc over the grass towards its dispersal area. A quick sharp turn, a rapid stop, and another safe return for one of 488 Squadron's night fighters.

The twin Rolls Royce Merlins roared one more time then shut down and the propellers spun noisily to a stop. The only sound heard was a low humming and crackling as the hot engines met the cold early morning air. The pungent smell of hot oil attacked the nostrils. The ground crew, crouching low dragged chocks under the wings and kicked them against the steaming tyres. A hatch, low down in the fuselage and forward of the Crewmans position swung open and a small steel ladder clunked onto the frosty ground. There was a brief conversation between one of the ground crew and an unseen person up in the darkness of the cockpit through the open hatch. Moments later two bulky figures descended, stretching before moving stiffly off towards a small truck waiting with engine running. Both crewmen made a rather ungainly leg-over onto the tray of the truck after throwing parachute and dinghy packs onboard and the truck spluttered away in a cloud of exhaust smoke towards some dimly lit buildings in the near distance. The ground crew started their work to replenish fuel and munitions to ready the aircraft for its next "sortie". The distant noise of twin engined Merlins from the south east again heralded the approach of more returning aircraft much to the relief of the rest of the waiting ground-crew.

By now the air-crew of the landed aircraft had reached the de-briefing hut ready for a session with the squadron's Intelligence Officer and looking forward to having a hot meal and to be able to put their heads down and sleep off the night's work. Their working day had started early in the afternoon the previous day with aircraft and systems testing in the air, followed by an on-call wait during the early evening until the order came to 'scramble'. Their average flight time in the air varied depending on *'trade'* but was generally two to three hours of actual operational flying.

This was the scene the squadron personnel faced nightly or in the early morning hours before dawn during the periods that they were on operational work. Most returned safely after their night's work but many did not. The ground crews of those that did not return would wait in vain for the sound of their aircraft, often until well after the known fuel loads were expended, returning slowly and sadly to the shelter of their work areas hoping in their hearts that their crew had somehow managed to reach the safety of another airfield or had bailed out to safety somewhere. The bond between the pilot, his crewman and the ground crew service unit for his aircraft was a strong one with the safety and serviceability of each aircraft being put in the hands of the ground crew senior NCO and his small select group of technicians. The aircrew fighting for their lives in the night skies over Britain and Europe had to put the utmost trust in these men to provide an aircraft with equipment that worked when it was needed. They in turn felt an obligation to return with the news that their sortie had been successful and one less German bomber would be returning at night over the cities and towns of Britain to threaten the lives of those living there.

Although vastly outnumbered the day fighters had turned back the Luftwaffe and forced the German High Command to reconsider their plans to conquer Britain. As a result of the brave and tenacious defence of Britain by these Allied airmen, the German High Command were forced to change their pre-invasion tactics from daylight bombing to night attacks and the British struggled to counter this measure. London, Plymouth, Coventry, Bristol and Glasgow in the far north suffered heavy casualties and extensive damage as a result of these raids. Fighter Command began setting up counter measures and the formation of specialist night fighter squadrons began, to try and prevent the losses from the sustained after dark bombing that England was enduring early in 1942. This was the scenario that set the scene for the re-establishment of 488 (NZ) Squadron of the RAF. The new squadron was to be one of sixteen specialist night-fighter squadrons set up to protect the southern shores of England.

The 488 Squadron story had started much earlier as recounted in the Preface section of this narrative. The original squadron was set up at Rongotai air base in Wellington, New Zealand on 2nd September of 1941 but was disbanded on 2nd March 1942 after being mauled by the invading Japanese in Singapore and Java. Unlike their inexperienced but gallant predecessors in the Far East squadron, these UK based men were handpicked for the task from a mixed pool ranging from very experienced fighter and bomber pilots to new recruits coming out of the Dominion Training Scheme with no combat experience whatsoever. Most of the experienced aircrew had served in single seat fighter aircraft and some were fighter pilots who had fought in the Battle of Britain in 1940. A good number of New Zealand airmen had joined the RAF early in the war and fought with distinction alongside their British and Dominion counter parts. The ground crew component of the squadron was composed of a separate servicing echelon, predominantly composed of RAF technicians.

The aircraft and equipment available for these early night fighter squadrons was very rudimentary and a huge effort was made to develop night fighting defences that could at least compete with the Luftwaffe bombers in the air after dark but success was to be a long way off. These young New Zealanders were right there at the forefront of this struggle against impossible odds and this narrative sets out to tell the story of a New Zealand night fighter squadron, from those early days struggling to survive not only the enemy attacks but the dangers of flying at night in adverse weather conditions and struggling to use new technology that seemingly changed on a weekly basis. They showed a determination that ultimately gained them success and victory in Europe. The pathway to victory however was paved with a life and death struggle to gain ascendancy over a skilful and wily enemy and much personal tragedy was encountered on the way.

A German bombing campaign known as the *Baedeker Blitz* or *Baedeker raids* started in direct retaliation for the Allied bombing raids on the city of Lubeck in late March 1942. The Allied High Command had earlier authorised saturation bombing of Lubeck, not a vital target but it signalled a change in tactics by the RAF to try and affect the morale of the civilian population rather than concentrate on solely military targets. The city of Lubeck had large areas with medieval timbered buildings so this gave the British the opportunity to experiment with bombing techniques using a high proportion of incendiaries.

The first retaliatory night raid by the Germans was carried out on the English city of Exeter on 23rd April 1942 and it was against this scenario that the re-formed 488 Squadron came into being just two months later on 25th June 1942. Interestingly the name, *Baedeker* was chosen by the Germans from the German Baedeker Tourist Guide to Britain and it was the avowed aim of the German bombers to target every cathedral town marked in Britain with three stars in the Baedeker Guide.

These raids by the Luftwaffe were carried out by light to medium fighter bombers such as the Heinkel 111, the Junkers Ju 88, the Dornier 17 and its later replacement the Dornier 217. Their tactic was to literally hit and run, travelling in at high speed to unload quite light bomb loads but dangerous all the same, and return to their bases as quickly as they had arrived.

The role of the Allied night fighter was a new concept developed in the early stages of the Second World War. Initially the only defence capability against German night bombing raids over Britain and Europe were the use of searchlights, combined with anti-aircraft artillery or the simplistic use of black-out over what was considered potential target areas. It was a very hit and miss concept and not altogether successful.

Radar was in its infancy at the start of the Second World War and a massive effort was made to develop systems that would give some advantage over the enemy. In 1935 experiments, had been conducted by Robert Watson-Watt and Arnold Wilkins in the UK to establish if an intense beam of radio waves could be used to incapacitate an enemy aircraft and its crew, effectively a large-scale ray gun. It soon became very clear that a massive amount of power would be needed to concentrate the beam at that particular moment and this would have been impossible with the limited resources and equipment that Watson had available. It was however noticed that when an aircraft or object passed through the beam it created an echo. Further refinement of this discovery led to the implementation of radar detection which did not rely on good visibility or daylight conditions to effectively indicate the position of an aircraft. It became a relatively simple task to develop the electronic mechanisms to interpret height, speed and direction of the targeted object.

After a period of prolonged experimentation, warning of approaching bombers was obtained with the use of the newly designed and built ground-based radar systems known as CHI stations (Chain Home Interception). These first twenty stations were scattered along the east coast of Great Britain and Scotland and set up at regular intervals around key areas that needed defending from attack from enemy bombers. They were each given code names or call signs to identify one from the other. They were often housed in quite primitive situations in rural areas using old farm buildings, derelict houses or even caravans.

The CHI stations consisted of transmission / reception masts of considerable height massed around the on- ground communication building. In one of the more bizarre twists to the allied radar story, the German's for some reason did not target these for destruction and most remained undamaged and in constant use for the duration of the war. They must have formed a very distinctive profile on the landscape as they were set up at regular intervals around the coastline of England and Scotland around areas that needed defending from the Luftwaffe bombers.

Each station had a controller who was responsible for his particular area or "sector" as it was known. The controller sat in front of a cathode ray tube that had the perimeters of his sector superimposed on it and any aircraft crossing those perimeters showed up as a green image and could be tracked across the screen. The speed, height and direction could be established by simple calculation. The key to the success of this system was to be able to identify friend from foe and have the means to transmit this information to the patrolling defending aircraft. The stations had a range of up to 180 miles and could actually pick up images over the Continent well before they reached the coast of Britain.

In the early days of the war the "warning" of approaching aircraft was just that. There were no means of countering these attacking bombers as night defence was largely ineffective simply due to there being no adequate means of vision enhancement available to defending aircraft after dark. The German night bomber had a huge advantage in that simple navigation plotting could have them over targets around London and the south coast, unload their payload of bombs and return back to base on a reversed course. The lack of night vision was not much of an

CHI Stations down the east and south-east coasts of England and Scotland

Chain Home Interception towers (Ex Dover Museum)

impediment to them as the course to their target and return to base could be worked out on a chartroom table before they even got into the air.

The Luftwaffe had developed an incredibly simple radar system known as *"Knickebein"* which projected two separate UHF radar beams from stations set apart; say one on the coast in Holland and the second one on the coast in France. The direction of the beams was calculated to intersect over the projected target for the night. The German bombers left from bases on the continent and flew in the general direction of the target until they reached one of the beams. The beams were set at differing frequencies so the attacking aircraft followed the first beam with its audio tracking until the second beam was heard. When the two sounds converged into one constant sound the bomber simply dropped its load and turned for home. Visibility was not an issue as bombing could be carried out in cloud, fog, rain or snow with the target sight unseen. The Allies did find a counter to *Knickebein* fairly early on in the war but the Germans' developed an up graded version called *"X-Verfahren"* which superseded *Knickebein* and this was used to devastating effect against Coventry and other English cities.

Much later in the war the Allied technicians working in counter radar found an electronic method of "bending" these beams and many a farmer in the Cotswolds, on the eastern slopes of the Pennines or the mountain areas in Wales found flocks of sheep or cattle blasted by wayward bombing attacks by Luftwaffe bombers, cunningly diverted by the bending of their electronic flight paths. There must have been some scratching of heads by German navigators trying to plot the trip home after being fooled into diverting so far off their planned flight path.

The finding of moving targets by Allied night-fighters after dark in the air as a defending aircraft was a different story altogether. It would be purely good luck to chance upon an attacking bomber during a routine patrol without the help of Radar. There were huge frustrations at Fighter Command for many months as the Luftwaffe bombed the English cities with impunity. However, the research and development of a new airborne radar system, specifically a small compact direction indicator unit known as AI (Airborne Interception) changed the defence previously limited to systems solely located on the ground, to units compact enough to be installed in aircraft. These installations, due to weight and size were better suited for twin engined aircraft hence the choice of the Bristol Beaufighter and later the De Havilland Mosquito as the main recipients of the newly developed units.

The development and use of the AI system was one of the best kept secrets of the Second World War. The Allies, when trying to play down the eventual success and obvious impact of these units, spread the rumour that their pilots were being fed carrots and vitamins to give enhanced night vision rather than have the Luftwaffe know that they were being beaten by newly developed technology. One of the earlier very successful night fighter pilots, Group Capt. John Cunningham featured in the popular press as one of these supposedly organically treated aircrew and quickly became known as "Cats Eyes" Cunningham. This propaganda myth was unknowingly spread far and wide by the news media much to the chagrin of Cunningham who despised the tag and had to live with that nick name for the rest of his life.

The AI units were very much a mystery to the aircrews when they were first fitted. This new technology was a huge learning curve for the young men who were expected to use it. They of course had no experience in electronics unlike the young people of today in the Computer age with cellphones and electronic items in daily use around the globe. Training for these young pilots and crewmen was very basic and it was obvious to many of those learning to operate the system that those supposedly teaching the use of the equipment were struggling with the concept themselves.

Due to the secrecy surrounding their development they were never referred to as AI units but given nicknames such as *"The Gubbins"* or most often *"The Black Box"*. There were of course no manuals so any instruction was verbal and it took many hours of usage to develop the units as useful tools in the fight against the enemy. Once entrenched in a crew's operating 'modus operandi' these systems gave the allied night fighter a huge advantage in the air war, defending the south coast and the frontline cities that were facing continuous bombing by the Luftwaffe.

These AI units were fine if you were on our side of the Front Line under the direction of the land-based CHI stations but the down side was that they would not give any assistance to the crews flying over enemy territory while out of range of their controllers. They were only of use as a 'stand alone' defensive system against enemy aircraft if the target aircraft presented itself close into the radar beam of the individual night fighter carrying the AI equipment. The airborne AI range was never more than four kilometres. The normal application was for the CHI or as they were later known, "Ground Control Interception" stations to contact the AI carrying aircraft and advise it of the approx. speed and direction of the target and at this point the defending aircraft was directed by the Ground Controller towards the target. When within range and locked on to the target, the airborne crewman / radar operator was able to take over from Ground Control and direct his pilot closer in to affect a visual sighting and get confirmation that the target aircraft was in fact the enemy.

When the war situation changed and the allied aircraft found themselves on the offensive, they left the assistance of the fixed CHI stations well behind and even a brief excursion off the coast of England generally meant loss of contact with their Ground Controller. For a long time, any aircraft carrying an AI system was forbidden from flying over enemy territory to prevent the units being stripped from any allied aircraft shot down behind the lines and being copied by the enemy. This presented some frustration for the night-fighter crews as many times badly damaged Luftwaffe bombers about to be dealt to finally by the pursuing fighter, had to be left to limp over the frontline into France and into German controlled territory and escape certain destruction.

The AI systems onboard the aircraft had a very limited range, around four kilometres so a new concept of off-shore radar detection needed to be developed. When the Allies eventually invaded the Continent, they were able to set up mobile ground control systems that linked up with the aircraft overhead. One of the answers to the problem was a new Radar system known as 'Serrate' which also went some of the way towards providing a means of detecting enemy aircraft when on operations away from the ground control systems. Radar in its simplest form works by sending a radio beam and then picking up a reflection bounced off the target. Cleverly the 'Serrate' system picked up the German night fighter and bomber transmissions targeted at allied aircraft and allowed the Allied night fighters to home in on them. There were problems however in that this system was unable to deduce just exactly how far away the target aircraft might be so a certain amount of guess work was still needed in order to apprehend a potential target.

It was a common occurrence for night fighter crews over or approaching enemy held territory to hear in their headsets the German radar signals searching for them. An electronic buzzing would gain in intensity in their earphones and go past them, returning a little latter seemingly going back in the opposite direction before returning again. It was as they said an unnerving experience and it made them feel quite vulnerable being all alone up in the night sky as they were being targeted by the enemy unseen on the ground far away down below them.

One further radar system developed early in 1942 was a simple box known as the 'Gee' system, fitted with a cathode ray tube that received radio pulses from ground stations in the UK that allowed navigators to pinpoint their position from intersecting points and transpose those on to a grid to help determine the actual position of their returning aircraft. This was to save many lives as lost units; particularly damaged heavy bombers struggled back over the channel in darkness and adverse weather unable to determine exactly where they were. It was of course a comfort for those night-fighter crews in bad visibility situations but was never able to be used as tool to apprehend or defend against enemy aircraft.

One system that was perfected by the Luftwaffe later in the war was a means of giving early warning to its aircraft with a radar system that scanned rearwards, known as the *"Naxos system"*, to indicate an attack from the rear, something that the British were slow to develop. When the first Allied rear facing, systems known as *"Monica"* were set up for their heavy bombers they were quickly countered by the Luftwaffe who developed signal seeking radar which picked up the *"Monica"* transmissions and led their night-fighters right on to the rear end of the transmitting aircraft. After considerable bomber losses from attacks from the rear the units were scrapped after a defecting Luftwaffe crew and their aircraft containing the *"Monica"* seeking Radar landed in the UK. The removal of the "Monica" unit from all Allied aircraft stopped the losses almost immediately. Some Allied night-fighter crews however did perfect the use of *'Monica'* by carrying out a manoeuvre known as the "Whiting" move which consisted of a series of changes in direction that looped them around in a tight turn and quickly put them onto the tail of any aircraft that was picked up by their rear facing radar units. There was no margin for error though as you were basically offering your aircraft as 'bait' for an intruder and instant reflexes had to be the order of the day as an early or even late turn would put your aircraft in range of the following aircrafts weapons.

The technology of radar systems was so new and innovative that modifications and upgrading meant continual changes to the systems by both sides in the conflict as counter measures were put in place.

Technology perfected one week could easily be obsolete by the end of that same week as changes were made. It was a constantly changing scene.

The use of twin engined aircraft allowed the new radar systems and heavier armaments to be fitted and this development initially included a limited capacity for bombs to be carried. Later developments saw modifications made to the Mosquito 'fighter-bomber' that allowed bombs as big as 4000 pounders to be fitted and carried over long distances to their targets. What was originally intended to be a 'fighter' unit was quickly turned into a very successful 'fighter-bomber'. Now the allies had aircraft suitable for attack and defence and able to be used at night or when conditions of poor visibility would normally keep aircraft on the ground.

One significant development made by the Luftwaffe and not copied by the Allies was the installation into their night-fighters of upward firing cannon. These weapons known as *'Schrage Musik'* were simplicity in themselves. They were installed in the fuselage behind the pilot but still controlled by him. This gave him the ability to fly under a targeted bomber and when lined up by the special gun-sight, fire at an upward angle of 70 to 80 degrees, a burst of tracer-less cannon fire that struck the target in its most vulnerable regions, either loaded bomb bay or wing fuel tanks. The Allies at no stage in the war developed anything as successful as these units. There was simply no defence for the attacked aircraft as the attacker was below and rearward, unseen and sufficiently far away to avoid any damage from the inevitable destruction of its target. There were many months of tragic losses to Allied bombers before anyone realised just what was happening. I often wonder if the installation of the 'Schrage Musik' system used by the Luftwaffe might have changed things in the night skies if the Allies had fitted something similar into their night-fighters.

The heavier armaments or fire power of the Allied twin engined night fighters was an important component as there was usually only one chance at night – the first burst of fire had to be destructive as there was seldom a second chance unlike a day fighter. An overshoot or swinging away by either aircraft meant visual separation and the chances of picking up the target again in the dark was not good as it took skilful reading of the radar image following that separation to pick up the target again for another attack.

It took great skill to convert the initial information picked up on the ground-based radar and to transmit this by way of radio telephone to an aircraft already mobile on patrol and in the air. The first task was to identify the radar image as either friend or foe. Some electronic assistance was available with Allied aircraft being fitted with an emission system known as IFF to indicate its *"friendliness"* that could be picked up by the controller but more often than not he was able to make a judgement of who was who on his screen by knowing through radio contact the position in the sky of his own patrolling aircraft. There was never a 100% certainty though by using this method.

Invariably the final responsibility for confirming the identity of the *"bogey"* [5] was passed on to the airborne aircraft. The crewman on the aircraft would seek identification via his cockpit radar system to try and establish this status. A lack of response or wrong identification however never guaranteed the identification of the target image as being the enemy so the uncertainty and concern about apprehending and destroying what may well turn out to be a *'friendly'* aircraft was never far from the minds of the crew.

The airborne crews patrolled in designated areas or *'sectors'*. From the individual aircraft radar system, the crewman / radar operator would give his own pilot information on the speed, direction and height of the target aircraft and direct his pilot to allow him to home in to close proximity. At this point the crew would seek visual identification before commencing an attack. Most often the only means of finally identifying their target was a brief glimpse, a silver flash highlighted in the passing beam of a searchlight or the momentary flash from an exploding anti aircraft shell. A decision to attack needed to be made instantaneously or the target would escape into the darkness or the defending crew would come under fire from the target aircraft.

The teamwork between the two crew members was a vital ingredient in a successful contact as a missed opportunity would very quickly allow the enemy aircraft to achieve its purpose and unload its payload of bombs and escape back to the safety of its base ready for another opportunity on another night. A highly stressful game of cat and mouse would invariably follow with the defending aircraft stalking its prey with on-board radar to get into position for an attack or at the very least try and divert the attacker from its destructive purpose. To be effective

---

[5] *"Bogey" – unidentified aircraft that needs to be intercepted and identified.*

they had to close to within two to three hundred metres for a visual sighting to be successful and to bring their armaments to bear. That was only half the battle. If their quarry sighted them, evasive tactics or doing a *'runner'* was adopted by the target aircraft and the dogfight would then begin. *"Dogfight"* was probably not the best description for the action. Leslie Hunt described it as more a *"scientific stalking"*. The pilot was under the direction of his crewman right up until the point of contact. When the pilot had visual contact then his skill was fully tested as he sought to get into a position to bring his armaments to bear. If he lost contact at any point, then the crewman guided the pilot from the images on his AI screen until visual contact was made once more.

Alan Mitchell, the author of "New Zealanders in the Air War", published way back in 1945 commented:

> *The work of a night-fighter pilot was once described to me by the commanding officer of a night-fighter squadron as "something between blind-man's-buff and hunt-the-thimble". The pilots, he said "are groping for their man all the time, and it's as though somebody were saying to them, you're getting warmer...warmer...now can you see him? Now shoot him down quickly".*

Mitchell then goes on to comment on the status of what he calls "the scientific aids" employed by the Allied night-fighters but he seemed not able to elaborate on these for security reasons.

Imagine if you will, the analogy drawn by one of the most successful night fighter navigators, C.F. Rawnsley. *'Jimmy'* Rawnsley started his career as an air gunner in the Auxiliary Air Force prior to the advent of the Second World War. He partnered his pilot, John Cunningham as a team that worked together for nearly all the duration of the war. They eventually progressed to a night-fighter role and together destroyed over twenty German aircraft as one of the most enduring and successful night fighter crews of the war. Rawnsley used an analogy that to me epitomised the environment that night-fighters operated in:

> *Some of the faith that a night-fighter pilot had to have in his navigator during the seek and destroy mission on a nightly basis might be explained by suggesting that a car*

owner should try driving a very fast car, with no lights and no brakes, on a dark night down a winding, unlit road close behind another equally fast car with no lights driven by an armed desperado who is swerving violently and making unsignalled crash stops. Let the car driver then shut his eyes and keep them shut and let him rely entirely on his passenger's instructions to keep him out of trouble and at the same time he must keep closing in on the car he is chasing. So far as the navigator was concerned, he was in the position of the passenger, breathlessly trying to keep the blinded driver on the road, to hide the fact that at every bend he kept losing sight of the other car, and all the time doing his best not to imagine what would happen if he found their quarry broadside across the road just around the corner. [6]

Jimmy Rawnsley spoke at length of the shortcomings of his AI unit particularly when close to the ground. The screens would be full of green *grass* in place of the single blip that represented a potential target. The radar images simply bounced back when in close proximity to the ground and swamped the screen with distorting images. Later the Germans perfected jamming devices that had the same effect and caused no end of trouble for the AI equipped night-fighters.

Rawnsley had a rare experience when on one occasion the 'blip' that he had latched on to suddenly split and became two 'blips'. "Dive" he shouted to John Cunningham but despite his pilot's quick reaction the contact was slipping away at an incredible speed. He then noticed that the first 'blip' was still in its original position and fast receding away from them as they dived at high speed. He then realised that they were in fact trying to intercept the bomb load dropped by their target and by the time they had pulled out of their dive and desperately tried to gain altitude their original target was well gone and the bombs had done their damage somewhere below them.

Sometimes the night was so black and the clouds so dense the only visuals apparent were the glowing exhaust stubs of the target. The patterns glowing in the night were very often used to identify a particular model of aircraft without any other visible means of doing so.

---

[6] *Notes taken from "Night Fighter" by C.F. Rawnsley and Robert Wright.*

The approach from the rear needed to be stealthy and generally made from below and behind the target in the so called *"blind spot"*. Many times, the two aircraft were alongside one another before identification was confirmed and the one with the quickest reaction was often the winner. These German aircraft were not lumbering, slow moving bombers but fast fighter-bombers that had the firepower and turn of pace to outrun or out manoeuvre both the Beaufighter and Mosquito aircraft used by our night-fighter squadrons. On the odd occasion that one of the slower bombers was encountered a different set of skills were needed. Many a time our night fighter pilots were forced to attack at stalling speed just to match speeds with the target. There was considerable danger with the low speed approach as the aircraft could lose up to twenty-five kilometres per hour in airspeed with the recoil of all cannons firing and this was often enough to critically affect the stability of the aircraft. You just did not have the chance to pull up and go around as the target would be immediately lost in the darkness. You had to firstly drop back to a safe distance to ensure separation in case of striking debris or flaming fuel from a strike on your target and to also ensure that you could present your target with a sustained burst of cannon fire to cause its destruction. It was then a case of full flaps, nose up and try to align with the target without your own aircraft dropping from the sky in a stall situation.

The skills needed to achieve a successful intervention were honed through countless hours of team training and the relationship between the pilot and his crewman was vital to the success of these night fighter units. Depending on the type of AI radar unit fitted to the aircraft and operated by the second crew member, the earlier Mk IV units usually consisted of two screens showing two lines, one vertical and the other horizontal which individually indicated the height, distance away and speed of the target aircraft. The skill needed to interpret this information required considerable concentration but the ultimate test came when those readings needed transferring by voice instruction to the pilot, who flying blind was directed into a position, firstly of visually sighting the target, then when sure of its identification getting in position to attack. Given the vast areas of sky being patrolled, the lack of available vision and the evasion tactics used by the enemy, the high number of after dark interceptions and combats that happened were a tribute to the skills and expertise developed by these crews.

The later Mk VIII AI model was developed as a single screen tube with a revolving arc which reverted to a full circle when the target was directly ahead. It was known as the centimetric variety. The Radar beam, narrow in itself, scanned a cone ahead of the aircraft 45 degrees from the centreline in all directions. This was achieved by a rotating reflector in the nose, which not only rotated about its axis at high speed, but also constantly swung out to 45 degrees and back again. The significant thing of this was that, at the lowest point of scan, the Radar beam picked up "ground returns". These were reflections from the ground or the sea. Consequently, as the beam scanned out and back again a green wash of light moved up and down at the base of the display unit, which was essentially a basic cathode ray tube.

One of of the squadron's Navigators, F/O Andrew Broodbank commented on what he called the "soporific" effect that the green wash had on you when you spent a good part of your time on patrol looking intently into your AI screen. [7]

Graham White, in his book *"Night Fighter over Germany"* provided a commentary that typified the relationship between the two crew members "going it alone" when he described a "contact" situation high in the night sky over Belgium after crossing the coast at Ostend:

> *An hour after Ostend we suddenly get a contact. Dagwood (His navigator) is brooding quietly over his electronic box and I am mentally calculating the fuel consumption, when he gives a shout.*
> *'Contact! Twelve thousand feet, ten degrees at three o'clock'*
> *I turn slightly starboard so that the blip of light slides to the centre of the radar tube.*
> *'Steady! Dead ahead, coming down fast.... looks like a head-on, prepare to turn thirty degrees starboard'.*
> *It's the Whiting manoeuvre, the only thing to do in a head-on, when you have a maximum range of no more than sixteen thousand feet and a combined closing speed of around six hundred miles an hour. The little green light charges down the screen like a Formula One glow-worm.*
> *'Four thousand feet! Turn starboard now' And as we complete it, 'turn hard port two hundred and ten degrees....'*

---

[7] Comment on the Mark V111 AI unit from Flg.Off. Andrew Broodbank provided by his grandson Adam Forrest.

> *The green hands on the blind-flying panel clocks lurch to one side and we are pushed deep into our seats. There is no up, no down, no horizon; we rotate slowly in a world of black velvet, the only things in the universe. There is nothing out there anymore- the radar echoes are blanked out by the turn – only the slowly spinning gyro compass seems to be moving. One ninety, two hundred, and we start to come out of the turn. We should be right behind him.*
> *Dagwood sings out in triumph. 'Got him! Two thousand feet and closing. Climb five hundred, turn ten degrees' port'.*
> *I see nothing, but totally trusting, I follow the directions blindly. We creep slowly in to twelve hundred feet.*
> *Where the hell is he?*
> *'He's diving – turn port – hard port'*
> *Damn! He must have picked us up on his Naxos rear warning device, and he's running for the electronic shelter of the ground returns. The little green numbers whirl again as I jam the stick forward and a great unseen hand tries to prise us from our seats.*
> *'He's pulling away – increase speed – keep turning hard port.'*
> *Increase! What speed are we doing, anyway? The altimeter seems to be racing round faster than the propellers. Then suddenly it's over.*
> *'We've lost him' He disappears into the expanding glare of electronic interference that floods the radar tube as we plunge towards the earth. There is nothing more we can do. We slowly climb back to height.*

The nature of the work and the detection equipment used meant most night fighters worked alone, patrolling pre-planned sectors to avoid contamination of radar images by other aircraft. It became a very intense situation with each crew being aware that they were defending their *"patch"* in the sky, very much alone with little chance of seeking backup if it was needed. The expression *"freelance "*or *"poaching"* was used to describe a defending night fighter going it alone outside of his designated sector looking for targets randomly in the night sky. Permission to do this needed to be sought from the sector ground controller to avoid crossing on to a fellow defender *"patch"* and running the risk of being shot down by *"friendly fire"* or compromising an attack mission already underway by another team.

Given that very few of the crews were career servicemen but had come into the air force on the outbreak of war, the results obtained against an enemy that had years of training and battle hardness speaks volumes for the characters of these young men. Even a brief glance at the list of pre-war occupations of these men shows little compatibility with the reality of piloting a war machine but instead confirms the high standard of commitment, dedication and bravery they somehow found in themselves. It must always be remembered that these men were volunteers and at any time could walk away from the constant stress and pressure put on them sometimes on a nightly basis. Very few did. Flying an aircraft in that same situation during daylight hours was traumatic enough without flying in conditions of nil visibility. They flew for hours on instruments alone on the darkest of nights, the only light being that shining from the instrument panel or the soft green light of the cathode ray tubes in the AI unit.

Ron Watts, later to become Commanding Officer of the squadron, spoke of the strain of flying for a two to three hour stretch without the use of the yet to be designed "Auto Pilot". It was hands on flying continuously, staring fixedly at the dials in front of you and fighting the urge to correct the flight of the aircraft. At times, he said he was sure the plane was flying with one wing down despite the evidence on the instrument panel and he found himself leaning sideways to stay upright. He had to make a conscious effort to sit up straight and believe his instruments. Outside of the cockpit window everything looked the same, up, down or either side, just like heavy dark fog.

Teamwork was vital to ensure the success of each operation and more importantly to ensure survival in the night skies. It was an occupation fraught with continuous danger as the hunter could very quickly become the hunted and the possibility of being shot down by your own side was also a very real possibility.

There was a time limit set for crews on operations. Unlike Bomber Command the night fighter limit was a calendar period of eighteen months rather than the number of sorties flown although three hundred hours became accepted as the top limit when crews were despatched for a rest period. The time period was set up as the standard due to the sometimes-lengthy periods between contacts with enemy aircraft because of bad weather or simply no Luftwaffe aircraft being in their patrol area. The stress factor was always there however as all squadrons had a 48 hour on call and 48 hour stand down period and for some personnel the waiting around during down time had them wishing they were in action despite the obvious dangers involved.

When selected for an operation on any particular night the aircrew would generally take their aircraft off around mid afternoon for systems testing. This occurred before each and every night operation with the only exception being when additional aircraft were needed urgently at short notice. These test flights were usually carried out by two aircraft working in tandem testing their AI gear on one another and carrying out full testing of every aircraft system. Only when the crew were fully satisfied would they return to base, leave the aircraft with ground crew for fuel top ups and any adjustments needed before heading for the relative comfort of the crew room for a feed and some relaxation before the standby call-up came later in the evening.

The crew room or dispersal huts varied in size and type from station to station. There was a basic setup however that hardly varied. Centre table with dilapidated couches or camp beds around the perimeter walls, rudimentary bookshelves and walls covered in notice boards supplemented with hooks holding apparel of all types. Smoking was extant in those days and every photograph taken at that time showed a smoker's haze. Some crews played cards, some slept but most seemed to sit and talk quietly, generally about anything other than the upcoming nights work. Takeoff times were preset and mostly regular and the only arbiter was the weather conditions over their patrol areas. They were seldom called to get off the ground in a hurry unless some Luftwaffe bomber or intruder had strayed into their sector. Unlike their bomber command colleagues there was no group takeoff but individual aircraft took off at regular intervals and were directed by control until a safe altitude was reached and they reported to Control that they were "on station".

The crew rooms had limited sleeping areas within them or in huts close by. They had cots or makeshift beds or even just mattresses on floors for those that were either on standby awaiting the call to get airborne or those who had returned from a sortie but were still required to be on call. This resulted in a sort of sharing arrangement when sometimes returning crews climbed into still warm beds recently vacated by crews heading out to replace them into the cold night air. This situation led to a humorous incident recounted by Len Wyman. He had reported for duty but seeing he was not listed until much later in the evening he decided to catch up on some sleep. He had recently had some dental work done and as a result had been fitted with a partial plate. He found the plate very uncomfortable so slipped it under his pillow and drifted off to sleep. When he was woken for his turn to take off on patrol he completely forgot about his dental plate. The next morning, he was greeted by his C.O. Ron Watts with, *"Hey Wyman! Was that your bloody teeth biting my arse all night?"* Just the sort of humour needed at that time.

The waiting on "call out" or even the scheduled patrol times must have weighed heavily on those on duty. There was little chance to relax as a call could come at anytime and many of those aircrew interviewed commented that the call to get airborne was a relief despite the inherent dangers that they were inevitably going to face. Those dangers were increased markedly if the weather conditions were bad as they often were.

When the call finally came, the crews were taken by out to their aircraft and dropped close to their machine for that night's operation. They generally flew their own machine, in this case a Mosquito so there was a familiarity built up with the comfort of knowing the idiocyncrasies of a particular aircraft even though when the other flight was on duty their machine would be shared with another crew so "ownership" was never exclusive.

The ground crew would have their machine ready, often with the motors already warmed up and they would be standing at the ready for the startup. Getting into the Mosquito was always difficult with the door access nothing but a relatively small hatch low down against the cockpit floor on the crewmans side of the aircraft. The Pilot would enter first after throwing his dinghy and parachute pack up into the cockpit and seat himself in his crewmans seat while he stowed the packs into his area. Once he was settled the crewman would climb the small steel ladder and sit himself down on his dinghy pack which was in effect the 'cushion" for his seat and position his parachute on the floor under him. Then the strap struggle started. Within the confines of this tiny cabin they would would find the hooks on their web harness and snap the dinghy clamps onto them. The crewman would assist his pilot with his seat straps before strapping himself. Once done there was very little room for much activity at all.

When they were settled the ground crew NCO would unhook the ladder and with help from the crewman stow it onto its clips, slam the hatch shut and latch it from the outside. There was no time for claustrophobia but if it was to happen it would be then. When the pilot was ready he would check that the ground crew were ready with the battery accumulator trolly and would fire up both engines in turn. There always seemed to be a great deal of vibration, a lot of noise and smoke until both engines settled down and eventually ran smoothly. The pilot checked with the Tower for clearance to taxi and the aircraft lurched forward, out of the dispersal area and onto the taxiway. The outside around them was in complete darkness but eventually they would reach the runway flarepath running away from them into the distance. A quick check with the Tower and they were moving forward, slowly at first and as the pilot pushed forward the throttles with his left hand they gathered speed down the runway.

The speed increased until the flarepath lights became a solid white line, the tail would lift and suddenly they would be airborne into the darkness. The undercarraiage lever was operated by the pilot almost immediately and the raising of the wheels seemed to throw off the shackles of the ground connection and the engines settled into a vibration free steady roar as they climbed into the night sky. A slow turn towards their planned flight path and they were on their way to the always uncertainty of what lay ahead of them for the next few hours of their lives.

Once the patrol area was reached they came under the control of the Ground based Radar stations and could do nothing but keep a watchful eye out and await instructions from their Controller. The following description of a typical night's operation gives some idea of the nature of the work [8] :

> *When Jerry stays at home a patrol is a dull enough affair – especially when the night is cold and unfriendly, the horizon an indistinct smudge and the stars but fleeting blobs of light between the clouds. You are hurtling along with all lights out through a dark tunnel. You take comfort in the array of phosphorescent dials in the cockpit, in the*

---

[8] *This commentary was reprinted from 'New Zealanders with the Royal Air Force (Vol.II) by Wing Commander H.L. Thompson, published by the Historical Publications Branch, 1956, Wellington, part of 'The Official History of New Zealand in the Second World War 1939 - 1945*

steady pulsating of your motors and in, perhaps, a thought or two of a bright fire waiting for you when you get down, a cup of steaming cocoa and a cigarette – unless there is business about, and that is different.

There are nights though when every moment of the trip is a sheer joy, when there is magic in the air; nights clear and frosty when the stars are near and in clusters like primroses; blue – green summer nights with far-away pinpoints for stars; nights of the moon when the surface of the earth shows up in sharp relief, cold, stark, mysterious and still, and the sea has a sheen whose loveliness no brush can paint.

You come across Huns, a dark shape darting across your bows, a suggestion of a swastika caught in the glance of a tail, a silhouette against stars, and you could hit them but often never know if the blow had been fatal. But tonight, is full moon. We are going to fasten on till he falls out of the sky with both engines on fire.

On patrol the minutes drag by slowly. The cloud is breaking in a strong wind and scurrying across the moon. We watch and listen. Then suddenly orders come over the R/T: 'Climb to operational height and steer due west. 'Hostile aircraft approaching position D from south – east.'
A mixture of fear and elation and we increase speed and steer for interception. Each second – miles and distance matter no longer – each second draws us nearer to the enemy. We make a quick speed calculation. How many seconds now and in what part of the sky will he appear? We strive to pierce the darkness, eyes straining, anticipation and exasperation struggling with one another. For a moment, the moon gleams on some object entering the cloud half a mile to starboard and we realise we are on his track. We increase speed, skim under the cloud, estimating the position at which he is likely to emerge. Or is he an old hand, and will he, sensing our presence, dodge

us by changing his direction in cloud? In a moment, he is slap- bang in front of us, like a silver fish. A Dornier, with his high wing and twin fins; no mistaking him. His tracer is passing above us like a trail of elongated sparks. The rear gunner has got us against a background of cloud. We do a quick check turn, dive a little and pull our nose up right under him and give him a long burst. He begins to do a steep climbing turn prior to evasive dive. But we've got his starboard engine. A piece of cowling blows off, there is a long plume of grey-white smoke and then a tongue of flame, a further half-hearted stream of tracer, again gloriously above us, and now he is dropping like a plummet line. There is a deep red glow in the cloud below us and a spiral of smoke.

We pull out a thousand feet above a sea, placid in the evening. There is no sign of the Dornier.

This account more than anything encapsulates the nature of the business and gives an idea of what was involved in a typical night's work for our night-fighter crews even to the point of uncertainty, as to whether the contact had been successful or not. Against this background the story of No. 488 (NZ) night-fighter squadron of the Royal Air Force will be told. It is a very interesting story.

Dornier 17Z bomber (Golden Press Pty Ltd - Richard Townshend Bickers)

A 488 Squadron Dispersal hut or crewroom with duty aircrew waiting on a callout. Flg.Off. Scott (sleeping) and Sqd.Ldr. Watts both under blackboard. (Ron Watts)

Another typical crew-room scene, with Plt.Off. Norman Crookes on left facing camera, Harry Watkins and Jimmy Concannon playing cards (Reg Mitchell)

Lining up for yet another "sortie" into the night skies

Lining up on that flare path (Leslie Hunt - from Defence until Dawn)

The damage to Exeter Cathedral following the 23rd April 1942 night raid (Reg Mitchell)

The Dornier 17Z Luftwaffe bomber that carried out raids over England in the early months of the War (Ron Dupas)

Chapter One

Church Fenton, Yorkshire, England

25TH June 1942 to 1st September 1942

Church Fenton, a small village in northern Yorkshire was established as an RAF airbase in 1937. The village and its surrounding area are very old and even mentioned in the Domesday Book dating back to the tenth century.

Church Fenton was a grass airfield and set up as a fighter base with a pre-war expansion scheme as part of No.12 Group, Fighter Command. When the war with Germany finally broke out in 1939 the original squadrons on base were replaced by RAF squadrons 245 and 242 both using Hurricanes. For this early part of the war Church Fenton was responsible for the protection of the East coast of England and surrounding towns, particularly the industrial cities of northern England. The base got very busy during the time of the Battle of Britain when battle weary and fatigued squadrons were taken off the defensive line and sent to the area for rest and re-equipping. Church Fenton's one claim to fame was the awarding of the Victoria Cross to one of the squadron members on the base (F/L J.B. Nicholson) – the only Victoria Cross awarded to Fighter Command during the Second World War.

When the first primitive airborne radar systems were under development and allowed night intercepts to be made more successfully a need for specially trained aircrew was identified. Church Fenton took on this roll of training specialist night fighter crews.

It was to Church Fenton that 488 Squadron was to come into being. Orders from RAF Air Operations were promulgated and air force personnel from all over the UK were posted and travelled in varying degrees of transport, overland and by air to the base in the northern Yorkshire village. Most would have been posted sight unseen but there is plenty of anecdotal evidence to suggest that a good number of the crews sought a posting to the new 488.

A significant link to the earlier 488 Squadron was re-established on 25th June 1942 when the New Zealand squadron arrived to set up camp. No. 242 Squadron RAF, a mainly Canadian manned squadron, had left from Church Fenton in December 1941 to reform in Singapore a few weeks after the original 488 "Far East" squadron arrived there. They were hastily shifted on to Palembang airfield on the island of Sumatra just as the Japanese invasion force reached the outer reaches of Singapore Island. The squadron, as with the original 488 squadron was ill-equipped and stood no chance and was eventually swallowed up by the momentum of the Japanese advance. Most of the personnel spent the rest of the war in the Japanese death camps on the islands of Sumatra and Java. Some of the 242 air-crew meantime had flown on to Batavia in Java and joined forces with some of the Far East 488 air-crew to fight a rearguard action.[9]

Surviving aircrew from both squadrons were eventually re-formed into a composite squadron designated as No. 605 RAF after retreating to Batavia and saw action together until the final capitulation to the Japanese just a few weeks later on Java in March of 1942. Both squadrons were disbanded following the surrender, with No. 242 being re-formed by RAF Air Operations at Turnhouse in the UK on 10th April 1942, followed by the UK version of No. 488 at Church Fenton on 25th June 1942. Both squadrons were linked with their predecessor squadrons by number designation only and were reformed with completely new and unconnected personnel.

The re-formed 488 Squadron had a very disjointed start to its formation at Church Fenton. By the end of day one, the squadron strength was just fifteen – P/O. Turner RNZAF NZ405644, who as it turned out was already serving at Church Fenton, being joined by fourteen airmen from a signals branch on station on the first day. Turner enjoyed for the first few days, the distinction of being the de facto Commanding Officer of the squadron. In fact, it was a very haphazard

---

[9] *The connection and the relationship between the two original squadrons is detailed in the narrative "Last Stand in Singapore", the story of the original 488 RNZAF Squadron based in the Far East, written by this author and published in New Zealand in 2008 by Random House.*

start to operations with aircraft and personnel arriving in dribs and drabs right through to the middle of August.

The first four aircraft - Beaufighter IIF models arrived on the second day, the 26th June and further aircraft were delivered singly or in small groups over the next six weeks flown in by air transport pilots. It would not be hard to imagine the situation with just a few squadron members watching as the first of their aircraft arrived on delivery flights and wondering just what they were going to do with them. The first week of July was chaotic and by the end of that week an office administration was set up to try and bring order to the situation. Pleas to the Group administration to speed up the manpower formation process seemed unsuccessful so that when the new commanding officer arrived at Church Fenton on 9th July he would have been totally dismayed at the scene in front of him. He had at that stage a squadron consisting of P/O. Turner, fourteen signallers, P/O. Amor, an Engineering Officer, an Adjutant, F/O Westcott, a Flt. Sgt. Armourer and ten Beaufighter IIF aircraft, with assorted crates of spares and equipment in unknown and questionable condition. No ground crew reached Church Fenton until 17th and 18th of July but the situation slowly improved with the squadron strength recorded as 137 by 22nd July, still well short of the 300 personnel needed to effectively support a normal fighter squadron's operation. The condition of the aircraft was frankly well below the standard required for safe flying, reportedly having been handed down from a Polish squadron which were to be re-equipped with later model Beaufighters.

The squadron was visited on the 15th July by the A.O.C. of No.12 Group, Air Vice Marshall Saul, CB, D.F.C. who no doubt would have been well informed by squadron personnel of the frustrations they were facing. Aircraft acceptance inspections were carried out by skeleton ground-crews and the first Beaufighter to pass scrutiny was personally tested by the new Commanding Officer.

The new and first Commanding Officer of the re-formed 488 Squadron was Wing Commander Richard M. Trousdale, DFC and bar of Auckland NZ and his Flight Commanders were later to be S/L Johnny Gard'ner, of Nelson, NZ who arrived on 14th August from 409 Squadron as had Trousdale, and Acting Sqd.Ldr Paul Rabone DFC, of
Palmerston North NZ who reported for duty on 22nd August. All three were very experienced airmen who fought during the Battle of Britain

in 1940 and had already been involved in night fighting operations since that time.

Trousdale, although a New Zealander, had joined the RAF before the war and was already an ace. He was one of the youngest Wing Commanders to attain that position and his promotion coincided with his posting to take command of 488 Squadron. He arrived at 488 having just been awarded a bar to his DFC. At the completion of his posting with 488 he was transferred to a Staff position then on to an experimental establishment at Boscombe Down. He had considerable night flying experience with five of the eight he had already shot down being victories at night. He had flown Spitfires and Defiants during the Battle of Britain. He then progressed on to Beaufighters.

Trousdale, among other postings, flew with 266 Squadron when his squadron during one of the days when the coastal airfields were under sustained attack, was forced to land at Manston to refuel. Unbeknown to them they were being watched from above and when they grouped their squadron Spitfires together for refuelling they were attacked by Messerschmitt 109s from 1st Gruppe of Fighter Geschwader 52. The Me109s came in low and fast over Manston and with cannon shells bursting around them the 266 Pilots hurled themselves to the ground. Whilst others ran or rolled around on the ground to escape the bursts of cannon fire Trousdale, still wearing his parachute pack could not run or even lie down. He simply dropped down on his knees, pointed his rear end and the parachute pack towards the enemy and huddled on the ground. One of his fellow pilots, F/L Dennis Armitage remembered that he looked *'Just like a Mohammedan at prayer'*. Miraculously Trousdale escaped injury from the bullets striking all around him. [10] Ironically the Me 109s had come from their base in Amiens in France, one of the airfields that 488 was to have as their base later in the war. He survived the war, returned to New Zealand and joined up with the RNZAF in 1946. Trousdale returned to England in early May to collect two Mosquitos and ferry them back to New Zealand, but was killed on 16th May 1947, when his aircraft suffered engine failure on takeoff at RAF Pershore.

---

[10] *From Battle of Britain: The Hardest Day by Alfred Price*

Johnny Gard'ner had spent all his earlier war years on night fighting operations and had been shot down over the English Channel and badly injured as a result. His badly damaged aircraft pan-caked into the sea six kilometres from Dover and sank immediately. He luckily was picked up about fifteen minutes later. He spent the next three months in Hospital with severe head injuries before returning to his old squadron. Gard'ner left 488 for Staff College in November 1942 but did eventually return to his old Flight Commanders position in October 1944 staying on until 488 was disbanded in April 1945.

Wing Commander Richard M. Trousdale, DFC & Bar, 488 Squadron's first Commanding Officer, 25th June 1942 to 14th February 1943.

Sadly, Johnny passed away on the 6th of May 2011 before this book was published at the good old age of 92. He was at the end of his life one of only three New Zealand airman left that had flown against the Luftwaffe in the Battle of Britain.

Paul Rabone with six bailouts from crippled aircraft in his career gave every indication that this was a man not afraid to "mix it" with the enemy. His first escape while serving with an earlier squadron was probably the most eventful in that he bailed out with his crew over German occupied Belgium and walked for five days in civilian clothes to Dieppe on the French coast. They had hidden among the crowds of refugees on the march. When they reached the coast, he found three damaged Hurricanes abandoned by the retreating Allies. He was able to get one airworthy using parts and fuel from the remaining two and successfully flew back to England.

His second escape occurred when a Me109 got the jump on him and he was forced to bail out with his crew at quite a low altitude. They landed behind the British lines this time and commandeered a French lorry to take them back to their airfield. Four days later they were evacuated back to the UK in the general retreat from France. His third escape was made at a better altitude when after despatching a Me109 he was jumped by another enemy aircraft and parachuted to safety landing in Dungeness *"too close to the sea"* as he commented. Jump number four was from a Hurricane night-fighter and was caused by extreme weather conditions that forced him to abandon his out of control aircraft coming down near Selsey Bill again unharmed. Later the same month, he had engine failure over London and parachuted into Green Park in the centre of London. His sixth and last jump was nearly his undoing as engine trouble at very low altitude meant a quick escape. His crewman got out immediately but Rabone got hooked up while trying to clear the cockpit and by the time his parachute opened he was almost at ground level.

Rabone was born in Salisbury in the UK but travelled with his family to live in New Zealand in his younger years before enlisting in the RNZAF in July 1938. He saw service with numerous squadrons and had been used as an instructor with two OTU units. He was still only twenty-four years old. He was later to earn the DFC with 23 Squadron flying Mosquito night intruder operations but sadly was lost over the North Sea while heading on a mission into north-west Germany on 24th July 1944. His body washed ashore three months later on Heligoland Island and buried there the next day. He was re-interred in the Hotton British Military Cemetery in Belgium. [11]

The squadron Operations Record Book from this time paints a dismal picture of a squadron trying to set up training programs in a very piecemeal fashion given that aircraft, spares and air-crew and ground-crew alike were simply not available to move forward with a proper training program. The squadron records show manpower shortages, particularly of N.C.O.s and notes that W/C Trousdale took the opportunity whenever Group, or Fighter Command Staff officers visited, to emphasise the shortage of trained personnel. The Record book amusingly notes the delivery of 150 Sten Guns [12] being delivered on 7th August and equally ridiculous the arrival of twenty A.T.C. Cadets

---

[11] *Information on Sqd.Ldr. Paul Rabone sourced from Auckland Museum Cenotaph records*

[12] *Sten Guns were a form of light machine gun designed and adapted for use by land-based army units as a personal weapon. They had an effective range of approximately twenty-five metres and were known colloquially as "Jam tin specials".*

for instructional work on 10th August. Training began with Bristol Beaufighter Mk 11f aircraft. The Beaufighter was a relatively new aircraft although it had been derived from a pre-war Bristol Beaufort torpedo bomber. Its design came about with the British Air Ministry realising that its current fighter aircraft such as the Spitfire and the Hurricane lacked the endurance and the firepower to effectively defend the land areas of Britain let alone carry out sorties over the continent away from their bases in the UK. The call went out for the development of a heavy duty, well armed fighter aircraft that had the fuel capacity to remain airborne for a long period in the air, travel long distances at speed and have an arsenal of weaponry to deal with any fighter or bomber that the enemy could send Britain's way. This specification could only be met by developing either a new design of twin engined aircraft or upgrading from an existing proven machine.

  The Bristol aircraft factory took up the challenge and produced the first prototype on July 17th 1939 only eight months after being given the go ahead by the Air Ministry and by October 1940 the first RAF squadron took delivery of the *Mk. If Beaufighter*. As mentioned earlier, this aircraft was largely based on the design of the Bristol Beaufort torpedo bomber, in fact a large proportion of the components used in the earlier Beaufort's were used. These included the wings, tail assembly and undercarriage. The main fuselage and engines being the only major components that were new. Any aircraft buff would see that clearly this was a composite or hybrid aircraft with questionable parentage! This was however a huge advantage for the Bristol production team and the use of already manufactured components greatly sped up the construction and development process.

  The Beaufighter was powered by twin Hercules radial engines. As production continued many modifications were made to develop machines that were compatible with the particular duties they were being asked to perform. Whilst they were never considered a high-speed aircraft, they had a long range and formidable firepower. A total of 5,562 aircraft were built and they were manufactured until late in September 1945. They were used in all theatres of the Second World War. The Beaufighter earned itself a 'nick name' being called the 'Whispering Death' by the Japanese in the Far East.

The German Messerschmitt Bf 110 had been developed earlier as a heavier long-range fighter / bomber than most of those put into production by the Luftwaffe and was creating havoc in the night skies over Britain in the early days of the war. The Beaufighter was the perfect foil for these attacks and when fitted with the new AI airborne interception radar its speed and firepower negated the early advantage gained by the German aircraft.

The Beaufighter aircraft allocated to 488 Squadron in June 1942 were the much-improved Mk. 11f models. The Pilot and his crewman / navigator sat in a fore and aft configuration in separate compartments with no visual contact and reliant on RT contact only.

The Beaufighter had a pugnacious bulldog look about it. The obvious features that struck you right away were the size of the twin engines and the heavy looking undercarriage that seemed all out of proportion with the rest of the aircraft. The crewman / navigator entered the aircraft through the same under belly hatch behind the pilot's seat but had to make his way down the fuselage to the rear using a catwalk with the breech blocks and ammunition drums for the Hispano cannons on either side. His flying position was about halfway down the main fuselage and located under a fixed Perspex dome. When reached, the seat was found to be on a swivel and the AI set was fitted beyond the dome so that the operator faced to the rear of the aircraft under normal operations but could swivel to the front if a visual outlook was required. The crewman / navigator in the earlier models also had responsibility for the reloading of the ammunition drums as needed but later models used automatic feeds, much to the relief of the crewmen as handling the 25kg drums, in confined space and in a twisting, turning, bucking aircraft in a combat situation was no joke!

The pilot by comparison had a roomy compartment with good visual outlook due to the very high seating position and the broad expanses of bullet proof Perspex. He was separated from his crewman by two armour plated bullet proof doors and only able to communicate by radio telephone. Getting into the aircraft was a bit of a mission but getting out during emergency situations was even more difficult as will be seen later.

Most pilots enjoyed flying the Beaufighter despite its sluggishness and it did have a propensity for lurching savagely to the left during takeoff but both conditions were soon tolerated and the necessary compensation made by the pilots as they gained more experience with these machines.

The Beaufighter 11f had a formidable arsenal of weaponry. It was fitted with four 20mm Hispano cannon in the fuselage nose and six

0.303in machine guns, three in each wing. It had a maximum speed of 540 km/h and a range of 2,380 kilometres.

The Bristol Hercules Mk.111 radial engines that powered the early Beaufighters were massive fourteen-cylinder air cooled engines of 2,360 cubic inches and they were completely different in construction and principle of any radial engine of its time. The later model Beaufighters were fitted with a much smaller capacity Rolls Royce Merlin twelve-cylinder engines where the weight difference was used to power the fighter version rather than the bomber. It was the Merlin engined 11F model that was issued to 488 Squadron for night fighter operations although the Hercules unit was reintroduced into the Mk.VI and later model Beaufighters.

The early days of the squadron at Church Fenton, once aircraft and men alike were tuned and trained, were calm and orderly with few incidents reported despite the personnel being new to one another and the aircraft being totally alien to most of the aircrew and ground-crew. They were stationed well away from the action that was occurring in the night skies over Britain and in this quiet training period the opportunity was taken to mould together the various crews that would stay together in many cases for the duration of the war. At the end of a three-month orientation period the squadron was advised that they were to be moved across the border into Scotland for further training and to take up *"guard"* duties on the coast.

It was an American pilot, Sgt. D.M. Bush, of the U.S. Airforce who had the honour of damaging the first 488 aircraft when hydraulic failure was stated as the cause but the extent of the damage was not recorded. There were three U.S. Air-Force personnel serving with 488 at this early stage but the three were sent back to the American Air Corps on 28th September 1942.

On 27th August four Beaufighters were sent northwards to Ayr Air force base on the west coast of Scotland followed the next day by a further four aircraft. An advance party of two officers two, senior NCO's and twenty-two airmen followed by train on 31st August.

Sqd.Ldr. Paul Rabone DFC," A" Flight Leader, Wng.Comm. Richard Trousdale DFC & Bar, 488 Commanding Officer & Sqd.Ldr. Johnny Gard'ner, "B" Flight Leader. (John Gard'ner)

The late Group Captain John Gard'ner pictured in 2011 Battle of Britain hero and long serving member of No. 488 Squadron (Dave Homewood)

S/L Paul Rabone DFC (shown on left in second photo).

Top: The Bristol Beaufighter (The Whispering Death) model 1f shown with the characteristic nose bulb housing the AI airborne radar equipment (from Defence until Dawn – Leslie Hunt} Centre: Early model Beaufighter (From Bristol Aircraft Collection). Bottom: RAF Church Fenton, 1942.

Above: A Beaufighter with the plexiglass nose bulb housing removed showing details of the Mk. VIII AI unit fitted into the nose cone. (Chris Poole) Below: A navigator's view of his pilot which gives a good indication of the all-round Beaufighter cockpit visibility.

A pilot's view of the navigator sitting under his perspex dome half way down the fuselage, in this case a very young looking Flg.Off. James Affleck (Ex Mike McBey from Adam Forrest)

Above: Cockpit of early model Beaufighter 1F (Andrew Thomas Collection, from Beaufighter Aces of World War 2). Below: A squat pugnacious machine – note the crewman's position under the Perspex dome halfway down the fuselage.

A photograph that gives a good indication of the size of the Hercules 14-cylinder radial engine (From "Beaufighter Squadrons")

Chapter Two

Ayr - Ayrshire, Scotland
1ST September 1942 to 3rd August 1943

The main party of the squadron left Church Fenton on 1st September 1942 by rail for what would turn out to be a twelve month stay at Ayr on the south west coast of Scotland. Eleven of the squadron's Beaufighters and one lonely Tiger Moth were flown up the same day and immediately went on to an operational footing that same night. (The Beaufighters and not the Tiger Moth!) The squadron was to take over from No. 410 Squadron, a Canadian unit in a move that linked them with that squadron, the contact being made that continued until the end of the war. They seemed to end up as neighbours on most of their future operational bases. Sqd.Ldr Davison, with P/O. Cutfield, brought one of the remaining aircraft northwards the next day with the rest of the ground-crew party following by rail. When S/L Gard'ner and P/O. Kemp arrived with the last aircraft on 5th September the squadron was well into its operational program with day and night test flying being carried out by all aircraft.

Ayr is a port town on the Firth of Clyde. It was an area of significant Scottish history with Robert the Bruce holding the first Parliament of Scotland there in 1315. It was despite its historical interest a bit of a backwater in terms of action! Training continued at Ayr and although most of the aircrew had vast experience in single engined aircraft the flying of a twin engined aircraft brought for them the need to develop new skills. By the middle of September, the crews were carrying out calibration tests with the local G.C.I. station at Rosemount, exercising with anti aircraft batteries and trying out cine gun testing during live firing exercises. Most flights were recorded as being in late afternoon and early evening so the gradual emersion into night flying was now underway. For most of the crews this was a very new experience and considerable time would be needed to become comfortable with this new method of doing things.

The squadron had the first of what would be many visits by the New Zealand High Commissioner in London, Mr. W.J. Jordan on 27th September. Bill Jordan spent many hours visiting the various sections and spoke with most of the New Zealand personnel on the base. This contact was to prove very beneficial for the squadron especially when problems were to be encountered a little later in the year. He provided a valuable link between the Kiwi's in the squadron and families at home. This ensured a constant supply of goodies cherished by the squadron members away from the comforts of home. At this time, there were twenty-one RNZAF air crew personel attached to the squadron, all but three being pilots.

The first operational Control ordered scramble was made by F/L Athol McKinnon and his navigator F/L Robert McChesney, both New Zealanders at 18.45 hrs on 2nd October 1942 when they were ordered to intercept an enemy aircraft plotted at 128 kilometres north east of Drem air force base and coming southwards. Nothing came of the alert as the "bandit" turned east and the crew were ordered back to base. This pattern was to happen for the rest of October with lots of optimism from the crews but very little action resulted.

Operations decided to send a flight over to the base at RAF Drem on the East coast of Scotland following several radar contacts in the area but the night skies around Ayr remained quiet and the situation somewhat tedious for the crews on standby. There was some excitement particularly for the ground-crew on the last day of the month when W/O. Reed and Sgt.McQueen both separately thumped their aircraft into the ground more heavily than recommended while landing and damaged tail units. W/O Reed's accident report listed engine failure as the cause in mitigation but no such comment was recorded for Sgt.McQueen. It was noted that this was the first serious aircraft damage recorded after two months of flying so some leeway was obviously given for the incidents.

W/C Trousdale was summoned to the Palace on 3rd November to receive a Bar to his DFC from the King followed by F/L Westcott the squadron Adjutant on 16th November to receive an M.B.E. Both awards were for work done prior to their posting to 488 Squadron. Westcott particularly had vast experience, being a veteran of the First World War and was to take over the role of Chief Administration Officer also known as the Squadron Adjutant. Contemporary photographs of the time showed him as a fatherly figure and his influence in the activities of the squadron would have benefitted the younger members immensely.

The squadron training continued through the month of November with a lot of work being done working with the G.C.I. (Ground Control Interception) stations in the area. Sgt. Gordon Patrick learnt the hard way on his first solo takeoff in a Beaufighter at Ayr when he lost control during takeoff on 2nd December, badly damaging his machine fortunately without injury to himself. He had an earlier whoops in late November when a tyre burst on landing causing some damage but again no injury.

This learning process was fraught with danger and nothing brought home to the squadron more tragically the terrible cost involved when two of the squadron's aircraft collided just after midnight on 6th December 1942, killing both F/L Athol McKinnon RNZAF and his crewman F/L Robert McChesney RNZAF and also the second crew of F/O Raleigh Peacocke RNZAF, and his crewman P/O. Spence RAF. Both aircraft had been working with the local G.C.I. station and were returning to base at a height of 8,000 feet when they collided and the two aircraft broke up on impact. This scenario was feared more than any other by most of the air crews. There were only vary rare occasions where airborne collisions took place in operational situations with enemy aircraft but the risk increased tenfold, particularly at night when training exercises were held with their own squadron aircraft or there were aircraft freelancing, either on approach or leaving base on practice flights.

These were the first fatalities for the squadron and the loss very quickly highlighted the perilous nature of the work they were involved in. There was some irony in the situation as the McKinnon / McChesney combination were also the first 488 Squadron Beaufighter crew to take part in an operational flight on 2nd October 1942 and as it turned out the first to die as the result of an accident.

The bodies of the four airmen were interred in the local Ayr Cemetery with full military honours on the 10th of December with the parents of P/O. Spence, and the wife of F/L McKinnon attending.

The flight from 488 that had been sent over to the east coast to Drem, the sea coast closest to Edinburgh on interception patrol duty, reported little or no action. There was a continual German presence off the coast but the 488 boys were disappointed that none came close enough for the scramble order to be given by Air Operations. Most of the detachment sent to Drem, were very experienced airmen with battle experience so the sitting and waiting must have been a constant source of boredom. There was cause for excitement on one occasion when a fully bomb laden USAF Liberator Bomber crash landed on the edge of the airfield and burst into flame. Members of 488 Ground-crew managed to save four members of the crew from the blazing bomber despite the incredibly dangerous circumstances. One of the ground-crews, Lac. Phillips was *"Mentioned in Despatches"* for his bravery at the time.

January 1943 was a relatively boring month for all squadron members. There were plenty of opportunities presented for interceptions but except for a Luftwaffe flight of seven aircraft crossing the coast on 13th nothing came close to cause any excitement.

On 14th February 1943 W/C Trousdale was replaced as Commanding Officer by W/C Nesbitt-Dufort, DSO who was to be 488 Squadron's second Commanding Officer. Nesbitt-Dufort had earlier replaced S/L Johnny Gard'ner as 'A' Flight Commander on first joining 488.

On the 15th February 1943, another group of crews consisting of S/L Rabone, F/O Browne, F/O Gunn, P/O. Broom with F/O MacLachlan of the medical unit all left for RAF Coltishall on the Norwich coast and two nights later, three of the Beaufighters flew independently from Coltishall out across the channel and over enemy territory for the first time into Belgium airspace. One of the three aircraft piloted by S/L Paul Rabone with W/O Longhorn as his navigator was forced to return due to heavy icing on his wings as they crossed the coast but the second aircraft piloted by P/O. Jimmy Gunn and his crewman P/O. Broom, pressed on through deteriorating weather conditions and made 488's first *kill*, attacking two barges on the coast and strafing a passenger train and three railway engines a little further inland at Nieuport. The third Beaufighter piloted by Wing Commander Trousdale, returning briefly from an Air Operations posting and with a borrowed 488 aircraft caused serious damage to a train at Courtrai. He and his crewman, P/O. Affleck also had a bonus strike on two barges just off the coast while returning to base later that night. These may well have been the same two barges dealt to by Jimmy Gunn and Paul Broom. Ever the opportunist Trousdale would have relished the chance to have a go at attacking anything that looked like the enemy. This was to be the start of 488 Squadron's wartime offensives with the so called *"Ranger"* operations.

These Ranger operations were a new phase in the allied tactics and were designed to disrupt movement of troops and munitions on the continent during the night hours. Operations were scheduled over the *"Moon"* period which was usually a period of one week of the full moon in the middle of the month. The moonlight gave just enough light to allow low flying aircraft to pick out hazards during the hours of darkness. It was inconceivable to me that these aircraft were capable of flying over strange territory at night. So- called instrument flying was taught to aircrews as part of their basic training for situations of low visibility such as cloud or fog. This was fine if you were flying at altitude and well above any obstructions arising from the ground. There were no instruments capable of setting a course around ground obstructions at night so the visual capabilities of crews became vital for the safety of the aircraft and especially important as they would be travelling at high speed and as close to the ground as they as they safely could. Too much moonlight and they would be the target of every anti-aircraft gun crew. Not enough moonlight and they would be forced to fly at higher altitudes and become easy pickings for enemy night fighters. These were pioneering operations in every sense and the bravery of these men under these circumstances was worthy of the highest praise. Three crews would regularly travel down from Ayr to the south coast airfields such as Coltishall and operate from there before returning back to Ayr until the next full moon a month later.

The Beaufighter was perfectly designed for the task with its quiet approach, low altitude capability and firepower. It carried four 20mm Hispano Cannon under the Fuselage nose and six .303in machine guns in the wings. With an operating range of over 2000 kilometres it could probe deep into enemy territory, usually by skirting around well defended areas to reach its target. It usually flew solo as a lone raider at very low altitude to avoid detection by ground-based radar that easily fixed on to formations of aircraft well before they arrived over their intended target. The Beaufighter was later to be known as the *"Whispering Death"* due to its quiet, steady low-level approach, sudden and massive burst of fire and high speed turning climb away to disappear over the horizon from which it had seemingly just appeared. Being twin engined the Beaufighter was able to carry large quantities of armaments and with night radar installed, operated against ground and airborne targets alike.

Throughout occupied France and Belgium, the German army ran their railway systems after dark and once the *Ranger* squadron aircraft picked up the network of rail tracks behind the Front Line it was relatively easy to follow a rail system in the moonlight at low level until the inevitable troop or munitions train came into view. Even on the darkest night the steel rails would shine and the plume of white locomotive smoke gave away its position well before those on the train were aware they were about to be hit. Most trains carried formidable anti aircraft defences usually on open decked wagons but the surprise factor of the low-level attack caught most unawares. The damage and destruction inflicted by these low-level night fighter attacks caused huge disruption to the German war effort.

Given that the Germans in occupied territories generally imposed after dark curfews on the civilian population, any vehicle or transport moving at night was considered fair game by the night fighters and even individual trucks were stopped dead in their tracks by the impact of a single burst from the Beaufighters arsenal. Most were caught by surprise by the suddenness of an attack but any that chanced to spot their attacker usually ended up overturned in ditches or over banks on the side of the road in their haste trying to escape the onslaught.

It is easy to under estimate the complex situation and the danger to the attacking crews during these train busting raids. Just getting to and from the attack areas was fraught with danger. The approach across the channel had to be at very low altitude and fast, sometimes just metres above the waves to get under the German radar defences on the coast of France. This was night flying right on the limit of prudence and foolishness. When the coast was reached the 488 Beaufighter night fighters climbed steeply once beyond the radar sites but almost immediately dived at top speed to run through the anti-aircraft batteries set up behind the radar units. Once clear of these, the patrolling continued at a more sedate pace until the telltale column of smoke or the rail lines shining in the moonlight revealed the presence of a potential target.

These train busting operations were something new to aerial warfare so there were no text book methods available. It was a learning curve for most pilots and you had to feel sorry for the poor crewman who was reduced to being a redundant passenger due to the low altitude destroying any possibility of using his on-board radar to assist his pilot. All he could do was keep as much of a lookout as he could from his position halfway back down the fuselage towards the tail. The usual technique once the train was sighted was to approach from the rear to run the lines as low as possible. Once the fire box in the locomotive was sighted the attack was made in a dive. On firing the cannons there was always a time lag until the first of the tracers revealed the line of fire. There was little time to adjust at that speed and altitude and with no crewman to keep watch on the instruments it was a very dicey situation all round. Many of the crews found themselves having to suddenly climb out of railway cuttings and flying below the treetops and the power lines was not a healthy thing to be doing at speed and at night.

Bridges and tunnels were a real problem. Judgement had to be near perfect as the tendency of an aircraft to "squash" down in the transition from diving to climbing was a time lag that needed to be factored in to avoid landing in the locomotive cabin. The other important factor was the anti-aircraft defences that most trains carried. This usually took the form of flat top wagons fitted with large calibre quick firing cannons. One of the *"Ranger"* air-crews commented on the embarrassing possibility and extreme irony of being shot down by a train!

Further sorties out of Coltishall over the succeeding days proved successful for 488 Squadron. These night time strikes were good for the morale of the squadron members involved and made up for what seemed to be endless days waiting around for the enemy to come to them. It could never be as good as the feeling of shooting down an enemy aircraft in a more competitive situation but they at least felt they were doing their "bit" and at the same time working on the skills necessary for night time work over unfamiliar territory. The success rate of these crews was very high and the tally of over forty trains destroyed on the ground over a six-month period was nothing less than spectacular. This tally did not take into account numerous motor vehicles, mainly trucks and also included railway infrastructure around the train strike areas. Many opportunities were taken, generally when on return from inland sorties when they encountered barges or shipping off the coast and these were also given a going over for their trouble.

Building a rapport with your fellow crew member was a vital ingredient in this mix and these combinations and partnerships were crucial for the crew's survival when things really got tough over the coming months. Several combinations really stood out with high strike rates as their techniques and confidence in one another improved with each sortie. Make no mistake this was very dangerous work, flying deep into enemy territory totally alone with no backup if things went wrong. They were many kilometres from safe territory and the chances of getting a malfunctioning or crippled aircraft back safely across the large expanses of water between the continents was never going to be easy. Even reaching and crossing the coast back over England was no guarantee of safety as the crews could never be sure that the local night defences would recognise them as friend rather than enemy. So-called friendly fire was an ongoing problem for the returning crews and evasion was sometimes a better option than trying to provide radio or visual identification.

One of the more successful crews on these ranger missions was the combination of P/O. Graeme Reed RNZAF and his crewman, Flt. Sgt. Ralph Bricker RAF. This crew destroyed or put out of commission thirteen Locomotives including triple strikes on the same mission on two occasions.

The acknowledged "train busters" Reed and Bricker, were soon to be posted away for their operational break to an O.T.U. unit with the full expectation that they would soon return to 488. They were to eventually be posted on to 219 squadron and all efforts by the squadron leadership to rectify the situation and have them back with 488 came to nothing. Such was the intransigence of the Royal Air Force High Command despite endless requests from Reed and Bricker they were ignored. To say they were disappointed was an understatement as they desperately wanted to continue their operational work with their old squadron.

Other successful crews at the time were S/L Frank Davison and his crewman, P/O. Arthur Cutfield, with strikes on ten locomotives. P/O. Edgar Watt claimed six locos destroyed including four on one mission alone. Close behind on the honours board F/Sgt. Douglas Bergemann and Sgt. Bishop with three locos, Sgt. Douglas Robinson also with three trains and after stopping one of the trains literally in its tracks, made a second run and destroyed the water tower alongside the destroyed train. To add to the success of the same mission they managed to blow a lorry off the road and watched it being enveloped in flames as they turned for home. Many of the attacked trains stopped and shut down steam knowing that the plume of smoke from the smokestack was a dead giveaway at night. On one occasion Robinson got cunning and stooged around close to the horizon for about ten minutes until the engine got up steam again thinking the coast was clear and gave away its position. Robinson swooped and added another victim to his tally.

The crew of F/L Allen Browne with W/O Tom Taylor scored four trains with Sgt. Keith Fleming with his crewman, F/O Ken Nagle seriously damaging one. [13] Not one single aircraft was lost during these "Ranger" missions and that was a significant result given the risks and potential for disaster the crews on each night of operations.

On 27th March, P/O. Edgar Watt and his crewman, Sgt. Cheetham were diverted when on patrol from Ayr to investigate a burning aircraft carrier sinking eight kilometres off the coast at Great Fell. They were over the burning carrier HMS Dasher for over two hours directing rescue boats to pick up survivors floating in patches of oil on the sea surface. They remained overhead until the carrier eventually sank before they returned to base. An internal explosion caused the sinking and not enemy action as was first thought.

Towards the end of the period of incursions into German territory the Ranger section of the squadron was based at RAF Middle Wallop in the South of England while their operational base and Headquarters still remained at Ayr on the South West coast of Scotland. Flights of six aircraft were based at Middle Wallop and sent at regular intervals over North West France. The inexperienced crews however were kept back at Ayr for further training and it was from this base that tragedy intervened again when P/O. Rupert O'Gara RNZAF and Sgt. D.G. Masters were killed in a training accident late in the afternoon of 2nd April 1943. Their Beaufighter VIF X8263 crashed into high ground at Ballig Farm on the Ayr – Dunure Road some five kilometres south of Ayr. They had only just taken off from Ayr a few minutes earlier.

The parents of Sgt. Masters requested that he be buried locally and both men were buried together at Knighton Radnorshire, the home town of the Masters family, on the 7th April. Sgt. Rawlings and Sgt. Roe attended as 488 squadron's representatives and photographs were taken to send to P/O. O'Gara's parents back home in New Zealand. O'Gara had received his commission posthumously, news of which was received by the squadron just days after his death.

---

[13] *Account of successful tallies sourced from "Defence until Dawn" published by F/L Leslie Hunt, who was 488 Squadron's Intelligence Officer at that time.*

Rupert O'Gara was a product of the Empire Training Scheme receiving his "wings" on 27th March 1942 while at his training school at Saskatchewan in Canada and was posted on to the UK in May of 1942 with the rank of Sergeant. He underwent advanced training on Beaufighters before being despatched to 488 Squadron on the 3rd of November 1942. Not a lot is recorded of the accident that killed O'Gara and his crewman Derrick Masters. Early records indicate that they hit high ground in conditions of limited visibility. O'Gara had a total of 413 hours flying time, 100 hours on Beaufighters so he was far from being inexperienced. An attempt was made to locate the aircraft after the war but no trace was found of the crash site. [14]

The week of 16th to 20th April proved to be a busy week for the detachment at Middle Wallop with W/O. Graeme Reed and F/Sgt. Ralph Bricker flying Beaufighter EL148 attacking and stopping three trains and on the same night S/L Davidson with P/O. Cutfield in V8588 shot up the marshalling yards at Mesidon damaging one locomotive in the process. The following night F/Sgt. Bergmann with Sgt. Bishop derailed a goods train also at Mesidon. On the 18th April, Reed and Bergmann in Beaufighter EL148 attacked three trains damaging two of them so badly that they were brought to an abrupt halt with clouds of steam issuing out of punctured boiler tubes. Similarly, Bergmann and Bishop dealt to an engine and tender on the night of the 19th April with the crew of Reed and Bricker attacking three trains with 100% success, one of which burst into flames while the others were literally stopped on their tracks with steam billowing away into the night air. The following night all three crews were in action and the night's tally was five locomotives, a water tower and a lorry. Two of the trains were attacked beam on, that is from the side rather from down the length of the train which gave some indication of the growing skills of this group remembering that these attacks were made in darkness and at a very low altitude.

The 27th April saw the arrival of S/L Dudley Hobbis DFC and P/O. Terry Clark DFM at the squadron. Hobbis and Clark were a very experienced combination having been together almost continuously since October 1940. Both had four victories at night already and were decorated during a very successful spell with 219 Squadron RAF. Both would figure prominently in the 488 story over the coming months.

---

[14] *Information on Rupert O'Gara provided by his nephew Mr. Peter O'Gara*

Early May 1943 saw the continuation of the ranger operations into north western France with successful night strikes to rail traffic in Fleurs, Montanton and along the banks of the River Loire. As the month progressed the successes came over a wider region of France which must have severely disrupted the movement of enemy material and troops during the night time hours. May 17th saw S/L Davison with P/O. Cutfield attacking two trains and also destroying two cars near Rennes, both left burning on the side of the road. This last success brought an end to the months "Ranger" missions over Europe until the next new moon period in mid June.

On 21st May 1943 Sgt. Chris Vlotman and Sgt. John Wood, who would turn out to be the top scoring NCO unit joined 488 Squadron. Chris Vlotman was from the Dutch Free Forces and had moved from Holland in advance of the German invasion and ended up serving his country from the allied side of the Channel. Sgt John Wood, his navigator at eighteen years of age was the youngest air-crew member to serve on the squadron.

Some air / sea rescue work was carried out at the end of the month from the contingent still based at Ayr with F/L Gunn and P/O. Bishop, being directed to an aircraft reported to be down in the sea north of Arran. They located a dinghy with three survivors and orbited overhead until the rescue launch arrived from Troon to pick up what would have been three very grateful airmen.

Wng. Com. Nesbitt-Dufort relinquished command of the squadron on the 22nd of May 1943 and was succeeded by Wng. Com. P.R. Burton-Gyles DSO, DFC, 488 Squadron's third Commanding Officer who came from 418 Squadron of the Royal Canadian Air Force. Nesbitt-Dufort did not have a happy time with the squadron but despite the negative picture painted by an official communiqué of his time at 488, he had a long and distinguished flying career culminating with over 10,000 hours of flying time and experience with around a hundred different types of aircraft. He was heavily involved in aircrew training both before and after his tenure with 488. Reading through his autobiographical work *"Black Lysander"* he gives little away about his time with the New Zealand squadron and despite four months in command he only offers *"I was lucky and given command of No. 488 New Zealand Night-Fighter Squadron stationed at Ayr for the defence of Glasgow"* Obviously, he did not rate his time there as this is the only mention of his time with the squadron in his entire autobiography.

There were clearly indications that squadron morale was suffering during their time at Ayr as archival material dated 21st May 1943 shows concerns expressed by the RNZAF Air Officer Commanding, Air Commodore Neville, in a confidential memo [15] on behalf of himself and the New Zealand Minister of Defence, reporting on concerns raised by the Ayr Station Commander Wng Comm. Chalmers-Watson, AFC during a visit to the squadron on Tuesday 18th May 1943. Chalmers-Watson had been posted from Group Headquarters to Ayr Station with the object of reorganising the squadron and improving its general morale. He had stated that:

> *Conditions at the station were, prior to his arrival, most unsatisfactory, that the existing Squadron Commander, Wng. Comm. Nesbitt-Dufort, DSO, should be relieved, and that the RAF Medical Officer was unsatisfactory. Wng Comm Nesbitt-Dufort has had considerable operational experience but is apparently tired and has no capacity for organisation and administration. As a result of the arrival of the new Station commander last month, the two Flight Commanders, who are New Zealanders (Sqd.Ldrs. Rabone and McIntyre) have been removed, and the Station Commander is now endeavouring to replace the present Squadron Commander by another officer, possibly W/C Burton-Gyles, DSO, DFC. Wng Comm. Chalmers-Watson mentioned that the Group Commander Air Vice Marshall Henderson (Commanding No. 13 Fighter Group) was well acquainted with the situation. No.488 Squadron has since its arrival at Ayr in August/September 1942 been in a back sector with very little activity and indifferent equipment. The Beaufighter IIs have now been replaced with Beaufighter VI's, but these aircraft have mostly been received from the Polish squadron and were in bad condition. They have only three new Beaufighter VI's. The squadron was promised new equipment about December last, but the North African campaign had higher priority, and they are unlikely to get replacement equipment until early next year'.*

---

[15] *Confidential Memo 85/410.14 from RNZAF Museum Archives dated 21/5/43 from Air Commodore Neville RNZAF following visit to Ayr RAF Base*

The New Zealand Minister of Defence would have got from this visit a very clear understanding of the situation and changes were made to improve things just a few weeks later. It could not have escaped his attention that this situation was almost identical to the predecessor 488 Squadron in Singapore that was faced with the same problem relating to sub standard aircraft and equipment, a situation that eventually impacted on its operational efficiency and lead to its eventual demise as a fighting unit. With the support of the New Zealand High Commissioner, Mr. Jordan and his approaches on Burton-Gyle's behalf directly to Winston Churchill things changed rapidly.

The Ranger patrols had compensated in some way for the boredom but most of the squadron felt they were being left out of the action completely. The aircrews from New Zealand particularly felt that the commitment they had made and the distance they had travelled should have entitled them to a larger share of the action than they were currently getting. They despaired at having to fly the by now obsolete Beaufighters and were clamouring to have a crack at the new Mosquito fighters

The month of June 1943 finally saw major changes to the resources of the squadron. Air Operations finally decided to single out 488 Squadron to make the change-over from Beaufighters to the radically new Mosquito fighter. This changeover was done in advance of all the established squadrons operating in the south of England and was considered a real coup for the squadron given the intense rivalry between the squadrons that had been underway since the beginning of the war.

On the night of 6th June Sgt C.W. Collins with P/O. H.J. Evans as his crewman, and Cpl. Rodgers flying as a passenger, as if to sheet home to the authorities the bad habits of their old Beaufighters, swung badly on takeoff and crashed into the signals hut of "A" Flight dispersal. In the subsequent pandemonium, the occupants of the signals hut threw themselves out fortunately escaping with only minor injuries. The three on board had to be rescued and were dispatched to the station sick quarters for assessment. Just minutes after they were removed from the wreckage the aircraft burst into flames and was completely destroyed. The three were then sent on to the Bangour Military Hospital in Broxburn for further treatment.

The "Moon" period in the middle of the month was well utilized by the four crews sent to Middle Wallop with Jeffs and Spedding recording good hits on a Goods train in the early morning hours at Rennes in north west France. Jeffs made three attacks on his target and reported light flak on his return over Guingamp on the way home. An hour or so later Fleming and Nagle attacked two trains, the first two miles east of Guingamp which came to an abrupt halt and the second near Caulnes, twenty-three miles North West of Rennes. They reported a spectacular fiery display from two of the wagons on this train, the flames being seen from a good distance away as they gleefully sped away in the night back to base.

Two nights later, S/L Davison and P/O. Cutfield (V 8590) stopped a goods train two miles south of Gace. They followed up their first attack with a second that saw flames pouring from the disabled engine. They had some drama on the way home when they were *"coned"* by searchlights near Rouen and had to climb very fast to escape. Taking evasive action away from their planned route home used more fuel than they had allowed for and they eventually had to land at RAF Hurn to refuel before returning to base. F/L Browne with Sgt. Taylor, not to be outdone attacked three trains sheltering in a siding at Coutances. For the first time, they were subject to some spirited resistance with light but very accurate flak forcing them give what would have been a very good target a miss. They flew on to attack a train south of Tinteniac which they stopped with their first run but a failure of their firing mechanism cut short what had promised to have been a very productive night.

Fleming and Nagel had further success in the early morning hours of 19th June when they stopped passenger train fifteen miles north of Vendome. The next night saw Jeffs and Spedding (E.L. 154) having some visual difficulties and being forced to return to base and just to compound their frustration, crashing on landing fortunately without injury to either of the crew. With the weather deteriorating and the moon period over, the four crews returned back to Ayr on the 23rd June.

The 23rd June was also notable for the wedding of F/L Jimmy Gunn to S/O Daphne Beatrice Bell, W.A.A.F. The ceremony was held at the Holy Trinity Church in Ayr with the wedding reception being held at the Officers' Mess on station. Neither of them would have thought for one moment that their marriage tragically was going to be a short one.

There were to be a number of weddings between squadron members and local WAAF personnel stationed on bases where 488 were stationed.

There was great excitement when notice was received on the 30th of June that the first of the squadron Mosquitoes would be arriving soon. These first aircraft were to be the Mk. 13 model equipped with Mk. 8 AI radar units in the nose. By comparison with the stocky, snub nosed Beaufighter they were elegant slim and more streamlined looking. The Mosquito was soon known to all as the *'Wooden Wonder'*.

The De Havilland Mosquito was a unique aircraft in many ways. It was first developed as a bomber aircraft, starting on the drawing board as an original design in 1938, rather than a development or modification of an existing aircraft. Its originality stemmed from the extensive use of timber in its construction. Its development started during the time that Great Britain was under huge defensive pressure following the fall of France and the evacuations from Dunkirk. Production of existing designs was given first priority by Ministry production programmers to build up stocks of desperately needed aircraft to defend a beleaguered Britain. Vast quantities of metallic materials were poured into factories to boost production. Despite the Ministry halting the design and development programme at De Havilland on more than one occasion, after having given tentative approval earlier for its implementation, De Havilland pushed ahead to produce a prototype and only then did the Ministry sit up and take notice. The De Havilland design concept was to produce a light weight, twin engined bomber aircraft made from wood, to take advantage of a furniture industry with huge capacity but grossly under-utilized machinery and material stocks. The main selling point for De Havilland being that the production of their aircraft would not take away any material sorely needed by existing aircraft manufacturers.

The first prototype bomber made its maiden flight on 25th November 1940 flown by Geoffrey De Havilland Junior after being built at Salisbury Hall, London Colney. This flight took place just eleven months after detailed workshop drawings had been produced. Further development was needed when the Ministry requirements changed and pressure was brought to bear to produce a fighter aircraft version. The design changes were duly made and the first prototype fighter was flown on 15th May 1941. Just four months later the first Mosquito sortie was flown over France on a reconnaissance flight. The Mosquito legend was born.

The aircraft construction was based on the use of 10mm sheets of Ecuadorian balsawood forming a sandwich between Canadian Birch plywood sheets. The plywood layers were literally glued together with the fuselage shape being formed by bending and shaping around concrete moulds. The fuselage sections were formed in right and left side combinations which allowed for the easy installation of internal components before the two halves were glued and bolted together. The entire structure was then covered in doped Madapolam fabric. The wings were also made of wood and formed into a single piece construction for maximum strength. There was little metal used in the construction except for mounting brackets and fittings necessary to fix the engine and control components.

De Havilland perfected radio frequency drying of the glues used in the construction which later revolutionised the production of furniture making and timber construction generally in the years after the war.

The use of Madapolam cloth was also a clever move that utilised a cotton / linen fabric easily produced in quantities by an under used cotton industry stalled by the effect of the war on its production. The veneer used for the plywood was sourced from a manufacturing plant in the United States and shipped to De Havilland. [16]

This was a very resourceful project, carefully thought out to maximise the use of materials that would have no impact on raw supplies destined for the conventional makers of aircraft who were at that time fully stretched in their efforts to source raw materials to produce large numbers of fighting aircraft badly needed to ensure the survival of the British people. The work was farmed out to over four hundred sub-contractors who produced separate parts in workshops all over England, the parts being brought into the De Havilland factories for final assembly. As the war progressed manufacturing plants were set up in Canada, the United States and Australia. Over seven thousand Mosquitoes in their various forms were produced.

Three prototypes were originally built for presentation to the Air Ministry, the bomber version taking to the air on 25th November 1940, the night fighter on 15th May 1941 and the photo reconnaissance version on 10th June 1941. The outstanding feature of all the versions was its speed, which negated the need for defensive armour with its subsequent saving in weight. The Mosquito was faster than every other aircraft built at the time with the exception of the fastest of the German day fighters. The first photo reconnaissance and bomber versions were

---

[16] *The Mosquito construction information was sourced from "The Pathfinder Museum" website*

unarmed relying on their superior speed to outrun German defensive fighters.

The crew configuration was based on two men – a pilot and a crewman navigator sitting side by side rather than the fore and aft situation of the Beaufighter which it eventually replaced. The crewman sat on the pilot's right hand slightly to the rear on what was effectively a shelf sitting on top of the main spar of the starboard wing. Several of the crewmen commented on the fact that as most of the dangers they faced in the air came up from underneath the aircraft mainly in the form of shrapnel from anti-aircraft fire they found the plywood protection under their *"wedding tackle"* a bit disconcerting. They had two layers of plywood while the Pilot had armoured plate to protect his *"jewels"*.

A further form of discrimination was in place with the installation of the "pee" tube which had a sort of funnel and a tube running out to the exterior of the aircraft. There was only one on the aircraft and it was tucked away under the pilot so the poor crewman was unable to make use of the facility. De Havilland did take a bit of stick over that one but I have yet to be able to confirm that later models were fitted with this piece of comfort apparatus for the crewman as well as the pilot.

The crewman had additional duties to perform compared with the old Beaufighter cockpit in that he had to be responsible for the instrumentation and switches on the right-hand side of the cockpit, namely the petrol taps, oxygen supply controls and lighting switches as these were inaccessible to the pilot from his position. He was though spared the job of reloading the cannon as the four on board the Mosquito together with their automatically loaded ammunition belts were immediately under the cockpit floor.

The Mosquito carried 600 rounds of 20mm cannon ammunition and 2,000 rounds of .303 for the four Browning machine guns. When the AI Radar units were fitted the Brownings were removed and the nose cones modified to accommodate the units. Tracer and incendiaries were used to help monitor fire paths and when fired at night the butt ends of the 20mm cannon shells would be lit up by the following shell and they looked like small disks floating away into the distance. Some of the low-level attacks though created added danger when the aircraft flew through ricochets from their own guns when the cannon fire bounced back up from hard surfaces and these were seen flying past as they pulled up from their attack. Not a nice feeling knowing that it was possible to shoot yourself down!

The 20mm cannons were armed with semi-armour-piercing incendiary rounds and high explosive incendiary alternate rounds. A strike from just one of these rounds could shatter an engine block to pieces with the incendiaries setting fire to any fuel or oil vapour in the area of the strike. They were very lethal. They were set up or registered at two hundred metres so that the flight paths of each cannon coned at that point.

Teamwork was again the feature of these machines as a clear understanding of who did what was imperative in the close confines of the very confined space. It was a tight cockpit situation with all the additional equipment required but was a vast improvement on the old Beaufighter set up. Access in and out of the aircraft was through a small side entry panel a little lower down from the crewman's position. A small retractable ladder was supplied and this was handed up to the crewman-navigator as the ground-crew latched the hatch. The AI unit was hinged to allow access in and out of the cockpit and was able to be pulled back into position once the aircraft was airborne. It was a very tight squeeze to get into and out of the cockpit wearing all the necessary flying gear.

The engine noise from the Mosquitos twin Merlins was horrific compared with the earlier Beaufighters, with the exhaust outlets close to the cockpit side panels. There was though some advantage with the close proximity of the exhaust system with the heating effect meaning most crews could fly in relatively light clothing which was somewhat of an advantage in the confined space. The downside was during the summer hours when the heat induced drowsiness, not a good thing when flying at a height above the ground.

Access out of the aircraft in an emergency was something that worried a lot of the aircrew. The main access was through that small hatch low down on the starboard side of the aircraft. Each crewman sat on his deflated dinghy pack and generally kept his parachute on the floor at his feet. Getting out quickly was a problem and you had to remember to jump towards the back of the aircraft as going forward put you straight into the starboard side propeller. One recorded incident of this had a New Zealander, Ken Sutton who was forced to bale out of his Mosquito after being hit by friendly fire. He was struck by the starboard propellor as he jumped and lost his left arm and and lower left leg. He survived making a remarkable recovery and actually flew again with a special arm attachment. [17] The upper hatch in the canopy could only be used when on the ground as ejection from it when airborne meant you had to contend with the tailplane. Not a happy situation. Later model aircraft had a mechanism that allowed the canopy top above the crew's heads to detach to allow escape from the cockpit.

The development of this aircraft was one of the biggest success stories of the war. This machine was easily adapted for tactical bombing, pathfinder missions, day or night fighting, fighter / bomber, intruder, maritime strike or photo reconnaissance. It truly was a wonderful machine. It could out climb and turn more quickly than the best of the Allied single seater aircraft, the Spitfire. The bomber version could carry a 4000-pound blockbuster bomb in modified bomb bays. The night fighter version used by 488 Squadron was armed with four 20mm Hispano cannons mounted in the lower front fuselage and four 7.7mm Browning machine guns in the nose alongside the AI Mk. IV radar unit. The later introduction of centmetric AI radar systems greatly improved the search and destroy capability of the Mosquito but meant the removal of the Browning's and the addition of a fairly unsightly nose cone. Some of the later machines were fitted with an additional single 57mm cannon which was capable of stopping any armoured vehicle with complete devastation.

Most pilots enjoyed flying the Mosquito, variously describing it as very light on the controls except for the takeoff. It had the same propensity as the Beaufighter to lurch sideways under power at takeoff time with the pilot needing to give the port engine full boost but just have half throttle and feed in the starboard engine until airborne. When up to safety speed it became very light at the touch and could be flown with finger tip control. When flying at night it was smooth and steady enough to feel slight turbulence when you crossed over the path of another unseen aircraft in the air, not unlike crossing the wake of a passing boat at sea.

By the end of the war, the Mosquito had emerged as probably the most versatile and successful aircraft developed by the Allies. It could out speed and out manoeuvre the best of any aircraft pitted against it. It carried as big a bomb load as the best of the British bombers and could

---

[17] *From "Day after Day" by Max Lambert*

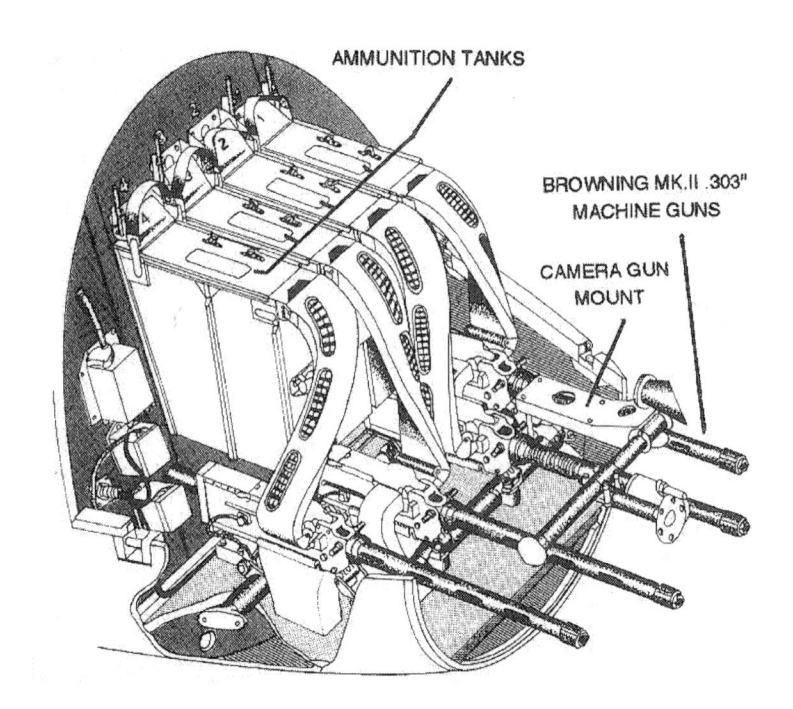

Above: The nose mounted machine gun set –up similar to that in the model used by a 488 Squadron Mosquito but these were removed to allow installation of the AI Radar unit. Below: The set-up for the 20mm Hispano cannon installed under the cockpit floor (De Havilland)

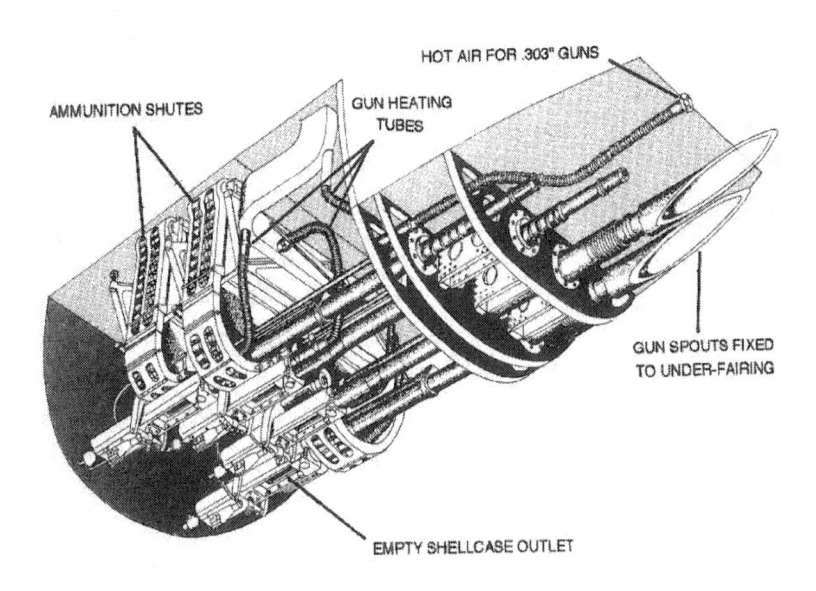

94

outrun the fastest of the fighter aircraft. The Luftwaffe pilots developed an incredible fear of the Mosquito, particularly at night when what was known as *"Mosquito Panic"* developed towards the end of the war. Contemporary German reports of the time related incidents and reports, blaming the Mosquito night-fighter for large scale losses among Luftwaffe squadrons when none were even close to the area to cause any damage. The obvious conclusion drawn from this was that the Luftwaffe aircrews were very fearful of the AI equipped night-fighters they knew to be lurking in the night skies and feared having them suddenly appearing out of the darkness like the proverbial "bogeyman".

It was easy then to appreciate the excitement of the 488 aircrew when they were told that the first of these superb units were going to be delivered progressively to them at Ayr Air Force base soon after 30th June 1943.

In the early days of July 1943, the preparation for the arrival of the new Mosquitos intensified with new crews arriving from squadrons all over the UK. The Air Ministry was determined to outfit the squadron with the best pilots and this move showed the confidence that they had in the developing worth of the mosquito as a night fighter. The new aircraft were however slow to arrive despite W/C Burton-Gyles, the squadron C.O. travelling to London on 1st July to meet with the High Commissioner of New Zealand and report on the squadrons problems during their time at Ayr. Burton-Gyles would have given Mr. Jordan a rather cryptic view of the circumstances and no doubt pushed for faster deliveries of the new units to bring them up to operational readiness.

The first week of July was seemingly taken up answering distress calls to search for ditched aircraft until the first of the new Mk III training Mosquitos were finally delivered on the 8th July. These were dual control models set up for training purposes and replaced an earlier model that was found to be unserviceable following delivery from No. 96 Squadron. The following day, W/C Burton-Gyles with S/L Frank Davison as his co.-pilot air tested the new aircraft. F/L Jimmy Gunn, arguably the best of the Beaufighter pilots, was airborne at the same time in his Beaufighter and carried out mock air attacks on the Mosquito. He reported it much faster and more manoeuvrable than his aircraft, in particular finding that he was unable to turn inside the Mosquito, a key factor in dominance during a "dogfight".

There was a setback with the deaths on 13th July of F/O Edgar C. Watt, RNZAF from Gore, NZ and his crewman, P/O. Adkins RAF, although this accident occurred in a Beaufighter, this crew were listed as a potential crew combination with the new Mosquito. The pair were killed in fading light just on dusk after Edgar Watt lost control attempting a high-speed steep turn to port over the airfield at an altitude of just 1000 metres. Their aircraft plunged into the ground near Ayr and burst into flames. At that height, there was no margin for error and no altitude available to make a recovery. Both were killed instantly. F/O Watt had seven hundred hours of flying time with Beaufighters so it was not an accident brought about by inexperience and was thought at the time to be an equipment failure of some kind. Watt had earlier successes with the so called *"Ranger"* operations over Belgium and Holland, operations that required pilots with incredible skill to make low level attacks on railway and road traffic over unknown territory at night. Both Watt and Adkins were buried in the Ayr Cemetery in Ayrshire, Scotland on the morning of 17th July with full military honours. The Father of F/O Adkins was able to attend his son's funeral.

One of Edgar Watt's earlier crewmen, F/Sgt. Edgar (Ron) Rayner RAF was particularly saddened by the death of Edgar Watt. Ron Rayner flew many missions with the New Zealander but Ron's career as a navigator was ended when he suffered a serious bout of pleurisy brought about with night flying in cold and wet conditions during the squadron's time at Ayr. His illness was serious enough for him to be hospitalised for many months and eventually forced him to be discharged from flying duties. His grandson, Steve Whiteley recalls Rayner expressing his sadness but saying that he had enjoyed his time with 488 Squadron. Rayner attributed Edgar Watt's earlier successes to his *"headstrong and gutsy"* nature. He had a very determined attitude which sometimes could be a huge advantage when faced with adversity and felt that he (Rayner), being somewhat older than his pilot had a steadying influence over him during their time together.

Edgar Watts and Ron Rayner had in fact carried out one of the squadron's first operational interceptions when they were directed from Ayr by Control to intercept German aircraft bombing Newcastle. Despite getting close to the scene of the action their radio unfortunately packed up at a key moment and they were forced to return to base without making any contact with the enemy.

New crews arriving at the squadron on 20th July included New Zealander F/L Ron Watts of Auckland to be partnered by F/O Roger Folley from Rochester in Kent, Peter Hall from Gisborne NZ and his

F/L Ron Watts (Judy Anderson)

crewman Dick Marriott from London, and a second tour of duty for a returning F/L Edward "Cecil" Ball RNZAF, although born in Kinsdale, Ireland, and his crewman F/O William "Jock" Kemp RAF, from Aberdeen in Scotland.

For Ron Watts, it was to be the start of a long and illustrious time with the squadron. In fact, he was to have almost unbroken service until the end of the war, a period of commitment not rivalled by any other of the longer serving squadron members.

Further discussions were held on the squadron's manning and re-equipment issues when the Air Officer Commanding No. 13 Group visited the base on 27th July. The squadron hierarchy were still far from happy with the progress and setting up of 488 to become fully operational. They were constantly struggling with a lack of componentry and the ground crew would have been really stretched trying to carry out just basic maintenance let alone trying to prepare their aircraft for the coming battle. The aircraft they had available to them at the time were at the end of their serviceable life so the situation must have been thoroughly frustrating with them knowing that new aircraft were not that far away.

On the first day of August a signal was sent from Headquarters No.13 Group that 488 Squadron was to put itself in readiness to move to a new base at R.A.F. Drem. The following day, orders were received to be prepared for just 24 hours notice and literally on the next day, the 3rd of August, the squadron made the move across country to their new base in the county of East – Lothian. It was a bit of a rush after all those months of no activity but they responded well to the new challenge.

Some of the New Zealand members of 488 Squadron shown at Ayr during the visit of the New Zealand High Commissioner in London, Mr.W.J. Jordan 27th September 1942
Back Row: *Manifold, Hillier, McWha, George, Gager, Pearson, Mullholland, Jeffreys, Barker, Brown, Gray, Gibbs, Vasta, Smith, Turner (all ground crew)*
Second Row: *Affleck, Longhorn, Kemp, Spence, Gordon, Jeffs, Vaughan, Anderson, Taylor, Smith,*
Wilson, McQueen, Bricker, Bradley, Ball, Spedding, Grant
Front Row: *Peacocke, Westcott, Skinner, Trousdale, Jordan, Rabone, Gard'ner, McKinnon, McChesney,*
Seated behind front row: *Reed, Browne, Cutfield, Davison, Evans*

F/L. Athol McKinnon RNZAF    F/O Raleigh Peacocke RNZAF
(Dave Homewood)

98

Above: Beaufighters over the coast during a daytime patrol. Below: 488 Squadron ground crew with a Beaufighter at Ayr 1942 / 1943 (Alastair Gager)

Above left: P/O Rupert O'Gara RNZAF (Peter O'Gara). Right: W/C John Nesbitt-Dufort DSO, 488 Squadron's second Commanding Officer 14th February 1943 to 30th May 1943. Below left: Train Busters – P/O. Graeme Reed RNZAF and his crewman F/Sgt. Ralph Bricker RAF (Leslie Hunt). Right: Wng.Comm. P. R. Burton-Gyles DSO. DFC & bar, 488 Squadron's third Commanding Officer 22nd May 1943 to 3rd September 1943

Above: The Mk.11F Beaufighter. Below: In readiness for another night's operations (from Beaufighter Squadrons by Simon Parry)

Above: Mosquito NF Mk XIII showing 488 Squadron codes. This aircraft, of Jamie Jameson and Norman Crookes, is an interesting comparison with the Beaufighter profile shown on the previous page. Below: Factory construction of Mosquito fuselage frame halves made from wood, being fitted out before assembly (from "De Havilland Mosquito" by Stuart Howe)

Above: Exterior plywood shell of fuselage half being worked on (from "De Havilland Mosquito" by Stuart Howe). Below: The early model Mosquito NF 11 used by 488 Squadron. (Wigram Museum Archives – Jameson Collection)

103

Above: Mosquito NF XIII Night Fighter. Below: Armourers shown loading ammunition and cleaning the Mosquito lower gun ports prior to an operational flight (AM photo)

104

Above: This is a photograph of a later model Mosquito (Mk.35 Version) but gives some idea of the cramped conditions in the cockpit – the Crewman's seat is set back and just out of sight on the right-hand side (From Defence until Dawn). Below: The massive fire power of the Mosquito is apparent in the test firing of the four Browning machine guns and four Hispano cannon (from 'Combat legend de Havilland Mosquito by Robert Jackson')

Above left: F/Sgt. Edgar (Ron) Rayner (Steve Whiteley) Right: F/O Edgar Watt RNZAF 404434. Below: Charles E Brown's classic study of a Mosquito, over Hatfield in 1944 (from Mosquito Fighter Bomber Units 1942-45).

Chapter Three

Drem – East Lothian, Scotland
3rd August 1943 to 3rd September 1943

After having suffered a period of relative inactivity while based at Ayr in the west of Scotland, the Squadron was relocated at very short notice from that coast over to the eastern side where there was some expectation that armed with new aircraft they could expect a bit more of the action. The squadron could be excused for thinking that the war would be over before they in fact saw any action. They were to be somewhat disappointed for a little while yet. Their stay would turn out to be a short one and it was to be the 8th of August before the first of the fully operational Mosquitos were delivered. A further three Mk.III's were delivered on 11th August followed by another four on 15th August.

Drem is located close to the Scottish coast on the Firth of Forth, thirty kilometres to the east of Edinburgh. The airbase had been constructed in 1916. It was a grass strip and on the outbreak of the Second World War was set up for the defence of the Firth and of Edinburgh city. The first ever attack by the Luftwafe over Britain was made by Ju 88's when on 16th October 1939 they attacked British warships anchored in the Firth of Forth.

The Squadron was still under the command of W/C Burton-Gyles, DSO, DFC and Bar. Burton-Gyles had been selected to command the squadron despite having had no experience on night fighters. His selection by Fighter Command Headquarters had come as somewhat of a shock to him but he had been selected to try and rebuild the morale of the squadron following large periods of inactivity by the majority of the squadron while based at Ayr. Burton-Gyles proved to be the tonic that the squadron needed. He was a born leader. He led from the front having a bit of the cavalier in him. The squadron had had success on ranger patrols over enemy territory but those left at Heathfield close to Ayr in

Scotland had in the previous twelve months not seen a single enemy aircraft.

Burton-Gyles was a very much 'hands on' leader and was very keen to build up his own personal experience on the new aircraft. He had asked for an experienced navigator to be assigned to him and was joined by S/L Lewis Brandon DSO, DFC and Bar. Brandon was also appointed the squadron Navigator Leader. Brandon, quite candidly in his memoirs was "upset" at his posting to 488 and decided to *"give up worrying"* about it and get on with the job. His posting was made on the basis of results he obtained by attending a ten-day navigator leaders course at Ford air-base in Essex. He commented that on his arrival at Drem he found a *"shambles"*.

Brandon's first meeting with his new C.O. was eventful as when Brandon first introduced himself he was asked to wait as Burton-Gyles was about to severely reprimand a sergeant pilot who had the day before, accidentally retracted his undercarriage while taxying and badly damaged his Beaufighter. A little later on in the day and only hours after the sergeant's reprimand, Burton-Gyles ended up making the same mistake and placed his own Beaufighter on its belly much to the chagrin and amusement it must be said of the squadron ground-crew.[18]

Brandon had come from an interesting background having worked in the film industry as a "stand-in" for the stars of several movies popular at that time – in fact he was cast as a Gestapo Officer when his call up papers arrived for him to join the RAF. He had noted on his arrival that the squadron demographics showed that most of the pilots were New Zealanders, but the navigators were almost exclusively from the RAF and English born. I suspect this would have given him a reasonable comfort level given his very English background.

Brandon being a bit of a story teller reported being highly amused to find one of the squadron's navigators that was supposed to be in his group, F/L Terry Clark, whom he had not yet met, was in hospital suffering from a fractured skull. What amused him was not the extent of Clark's injury but the nature of it. He had suffered his injury by falling backwards off a bar stool during a night of revelry. Clark, on returning to the squadron had recounted his experiences at the hospital. He told them his injury healed reasonably quickly but the medical staff had kept

---

[18] *Notes from reminiscences of S/L Lewis Brandon, DSO, DFC & Bar published in Aeroplane Monthly, July 1988 edition*

him in the ward a lot longer than necessary, suspecting that the injury was self inflicted to avoid military service. He had been very open and honest about the cause of the injury but there must have been some disbelief among the medical staff.

His Majesty King George VI and Queen Elizabeth had visited the Hospital when Clark had returned for further tests and the Royal couple had moved quietly down the ward speaking with each patient in turn, no doubt asking them how they had suffered their injury. Most would have reported trauma associated with bailing out of stricken aircraft or being wounded in combat or while performing some valiant deed. Brandon would have to remain disappointed as despite much prompting, Clark never let on what he had told the Royal visitor. Clark did say in a wartime autobiography authored by Steve Darlow, "Five of the Few" that the Queen commented on the "lovely" Hospital Gardens and Clark had heartily agreed with her but felt embarrassed as he had never seen the gardens. I did correspond with Terry Clark and asked the same question but Terry, with I am sure a twinkle in his eye referred me to Steve Darlow's book for my answer.

The Mk VIII AI. radar systems installed in the new Mosquitos were from the latest technology developed at the time and S/L Lewis Brandon although new to the squadron was the only member of 488 squadron familiar with the new system. The course that Brandon had attended at Ford air-base prior to his transfer to 488 was obviously set up for him to impart his knowledge on the new system. He was able to set up training systems and by the end of August the situation had improved remarkably. Just as Brandon felt he had achieved a huge improvement in the squadron's operational ability with the new equipment and built good rapport with his Commanding Officer, Air Operations saw fit to relieve Burton-Gyles of his command and give him a new posting away from the squadron. He was posted to No. 23 Squadron in Malta and sadly killed on air operations just a few months later on 10th December. A further blow to the operational development of the squadron occurred when the Special Signals Officer who had worked closely with the AI. Training system was repatriated to New Zealand and further, the squadron was advised that they were to be eventually transferred to Bradwell Bay Air Base in Essex and placed on a fully operational footing. Things were happening real fast and there was some apprehension at the time that despite great progress with the squadron's welfare and expertise, operational readiness was still some way off.

On the morning of the 15th August, P/O. Neil Knox, with his crewman P/O. Terry Ryan were doing low level circuits around the Drem Base when they noticed petrol streaming past the fuselage. Further inspection revealed the caps on two fuel tanks missing obviously not replaced during re-fuelling earlier in the day. With some very careful and nerve-wracking flying they managed to land their brand-new Mosquito without the aircraft turning into a fireball. Knox commented later that any changes in direction had to be gradual and at slow speed to keep the steaming fuel away from the open exhaust pipes of their aircraft. Luck was on their side as the open exhaust pipes were a clear and present danger!

The short time at Drem was spent with fairly intensive training. The changeover from Beaufighters to Mosquitos was still underway with the new aircraft slowly taking over from the old. Knox and Ryan were in a bit of bother again just two days later when they gave themselves a terrible fright during a training exercise. Whilst the Mosquito was a twin engined aircraft it was quite capable of flying on a single engine which was invaluable if you suffered from engine failure. There was however a different set of skills required to attain proficiency and much practice was required to ensure survival in the case of failure. The secret of flying on one engine in any twin engined aircraft is the ability to feather i.e. to turn the blade edges of the stationary propeller into the wind so that they remain stationary and do not cause drag on the performance of the aircraft. In this instance, Knox lost control of the engine speed and could not unfeather the propeller. The Mosquito lost height rapidly down to around 400 feet. They were over the sea at the time and barely made it back to base with their aircraft losing altitude as they struggled homeward desperately trying to remain airborne.

The squadron spent some time running regular patrols down the east coast to Aberdeen and Peterhead and some of these resulted in some very successful rescues of pilots from downed aircraft in the sea. On one special occasion on 30th August they located a small fleet of Danish fishing boats that had escaped from German occupied Denmark and were struggling to reach the coast of Britain. They were being hunted by the Luftwaffe but were found by a patrol of eight squadron aircraft some two hundred kilometres off the coast and herded to safety in the vilest of weather conditions into the safety of Scottish ports.

The last day of the month proved disastrous for the crew of HK182 when P/O. Gordon, with P/O. Rawlings on board, stalled in a turn and dived into the ground SSE of East Fortune, killing both crew members. The Mosquito reportedly got caught in the slipstream of a Beaufighter operating out of East Berwick Aerodrome while almost at stall speed and the resulting lack of air pressure caused the wing to flip over. The Mosquito was at a very low altitude at the time and recovery from that height was just not possible. The body of P/O. Gordon was sent home to Northern Ireland for a private funeral and that of P/O. Rawlings, to Edinburgh for cremation at the request of his family back in New Zealand.

Above: S/L Lewis Brandon D.S.O., D.F.C. & Bar. Below: Photo of air-crew billets at Drem in East Lothian in Scotland, the home of the Horlicks family of hot drinks fame (both photos from Defence until Dawn).

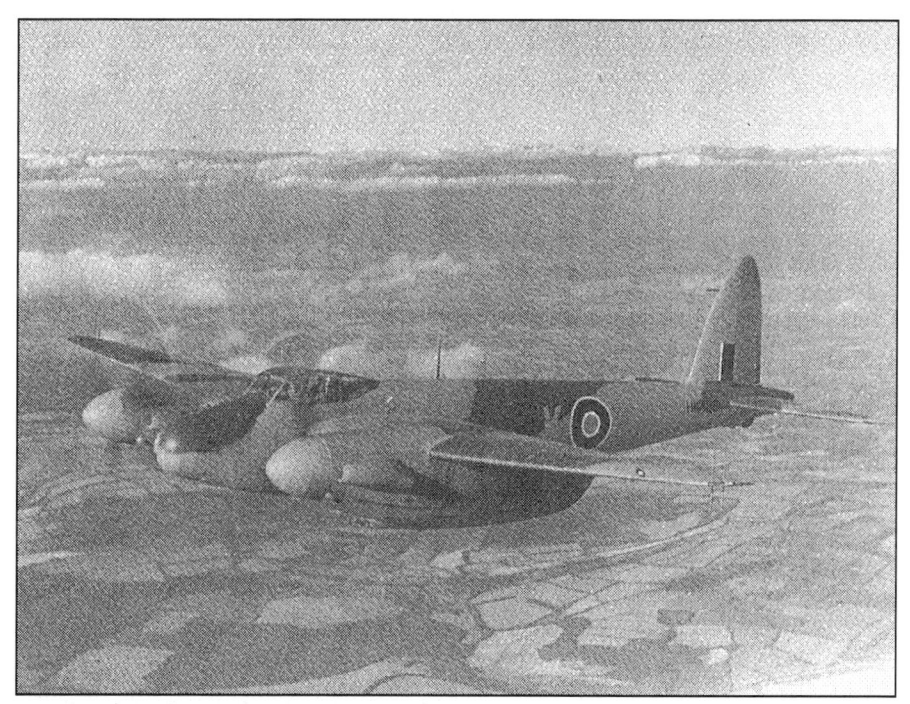

Above: Mosquito N.F. Mk. III allocated to 488 Squadron at Drem Air Base in Scotland (de Havilland). Below: The all-important afternoon system test of equipment and use of the AI set – aiming to get slightly under and astern of the target - in this case a fellow squadron Mosquito (Reg Mitchell)

Chapter Four

BRADWELL BAY - ESSEX, ENGLAND
3rd SEPTEMBER 1943 TO 6TH MAY 1944

On September 3rd 1943 the squadron began their move to Bradwell Bay in Essex in the South of England and came under the control of No. 11 Group of Fighter Command. This was a move the squadron had long been waiting on as they rightly felt that this would be the area that all the action would be taking place. They were not to be disappointed. The main party arrived at 22.55 hours on 4th September 1943 and the first defensive patrols were flown on the following day. The Station Commander at Bradwell Bay was another New Zealander, Wing Commander "Digger" Aitken, a man who welcomed the 488 personnel and was hugely supportive of the squadron during their stay there.

"Digger" Aitkin, who was to be awarded an O.B.E and the A.F.C. by the end of the war, had received a short-term commission in the RAF in 1935 and on the outbreak of war had sought and received a transfer to the RNZAF. His early wartime work was training Fleet Air Arm pilots mainly in catapult work off the decks of the earlier aircraft carriers. He had narrowly escaped death when he was forced to ditch his Hawker Osprey after engine failure, close to aircraft carrier HMS *Ark Royal*. He was saved by being picked up some thirty minutes later by a following vessel despite being without a life jacket.

Aitken was the prime mover for using seaplanes to patrol off the coast on readiness to pick up downed airmen over the channel. Much of this work of waiting and watching had the seaplane landing and floating in the calmer waters. On many occasions the crews found themselves floating close by a Luftwaffe Heinkel 59 seaplane obviously intent on carrying out the same work. There was some nervousness about the situation from both crews but eventually each *"tactfully refrained from attacking the other, much – it may be admitted, to the relief of the Allied crew as the German Heinkel was much more heavily armed".* Aitken reported a mutual liaison was established between the two crews and when required each of the aircraft would lift off to pick up surviving airmen as they were notified by their respective Controllers. [19] Downed Luftwaffe pilots were treated humanely the same as their British counterparts when they were pulled from the water.

Aitken carried out much experimental work in tactics that helped the Allies pioneering work on defensive tactics over the channel and initiated the earlier intruder patrols so that they became regular features of Allied defences. He was just twenty-nine when he arrived to take control of RAF Bradwell base.

RAF Bradwell Bay was located on the south side of the Blackwater estuary opposite Mersea Island overlooking the North Sea and surrounded by marshy coastal inlets. Visibility was always a problem on this base and was compounded by particularly bad wintry conditions that had met the squadron's arrival. Coastal fog was a nightmare for returning pilots and the airfield was set up with a fog dispersal system known as FIDO (Fog Investigation Disposal Operation). The system was simplicity in itself with steel pipes running down both sides of the main runway with vents cut in at regular intervals. Kerosene was pumped down the pipes and ignited. Reg Mitchell commented tongue in cheek that *"given the Mosquitos wooden frame it was paramount that the pilot did not get too close to Fido"*

During the move to Bradwell Bay, Ron Watts recounted an episode that started out being a bit of fun but could have turned out a lot more serious than he could have thought at the time. A number of aircraft were left behind at RAF Drem to be brought down later. One of the aircraft still in Drem was a Miles Magister, a very small single engined aircraft that the squadron had used as a run-around. They were an open cockpit two-seater training aircraft. Ron volunteered to go up and bring the Magister back for a bit of fun. He ran into bad weather just after he left Drem and was forced to follow the coastline down keeping the aircraft just above sea level and just below cloud level which was a tricky operation at the best of times. Unfortunately, the Magister developed oil pressure problems and he was forced to head inland to local airbases for a top up several times during the flight. When he eventually reached Bradwell Bay with some relief he was not in a very

---

[19] *The information on Wing Commander Aitken was sourced from "New Zealanders in the Air War" written by Alan W. Mitchell and published in 1945.*

good frame of mind. He made a normal approach as if he was flying a Mosquito and once over the boundary fence dropped it down and stopped it. As he said *"I looked a complete idiot"* as the runway stretched away from him for a further 2000 yards. He actually pondered on whether he should take off again to reach 488's dispersal area unseen away in the distance. He said at the time he felt a complete fool as he set off chugging down the length of the runway hoping nobody was going to notice him.

There were a number of personnel changes at this time that had started with their commanding officer, W/C Burton-Gyles being replaced by W/C Peter Hamley AFC who had little experience with night fighting but quickly settled into his work. He was very much a "team" commander and brought his own Navigator P/O. Andrew Broodbank so that he became part of the team rather than a stand-alone commander. The departure of Burton-Gyles was a little difficult for the remaining squadron members to understand as the squadron under his command had seemingly lifted itself out of the doldrums and Burton-Gyles had overseen a complete culture change that had everyone keen to play their part in the coming conflict.

The ground-crews had a particularly difficult job with the move to Bradwell due to the logistics of transporting tonnes of equipment and the added pressure of working with totally new aircraft and the need to come up to speed and get the squadron operational as soon as possible. It was a real learning curve for these men as systems needed developing for the first time and they were always conscious of the fact that they were going to be the innovators and the first in the field. The ground-crew, known officially as 6488 Echelon, were led by Engineering Officer, F/O Richard Norman newly posted to the squadron. Norman was to be known as 'Monty' and he had a support team of F/Sgt. Aviss, Sgt. "Pat" Palmer, Sgt. Bill Howarth and a very skilled group of ground-crew who collectively solved many of the teething problems associated with the new equipment and saved countless hours for the squadrons that followed when their turn came to get new aircraft and radar systems. The squadron echelon worked closely with the De Havilland factory technicians giving them constant feedback during the set-up process, something that has not been widely acknowledged publically.

S/L Lewis Brandon commented that the Bradwell Bay move put them straight onto the firing line and the training, particularly for the aircrew had to be very intensive if they were to be an effective defensive unit as soon as possible. Fortunately, they had a quiet couple of weeks where practice was the order of the day.

The squadron was to share the base and its facilities with 605 Squadron, a Mosquito Intruder squadron. They were a collection of vastly experienced air-crew who had fought against the Luftwaffe night fighters over enemy territory and there was much collusion and note taking as the 488 crew drew on the experiences of their fellow squadron. Again, there was a measure of coincidence with the link as the original 488 squadron pilots that were still operational in the Netherlands East Indies in 1942 following the fall of Singapore had combined forces with 242 Squadron. Both squadrons were combined into one and reformed as 605 Squadron for the month or two that it took until the Japanese forced the surrender of the islands of Sumatra and Java.

The two dogs shown in the group photograph taken at Bradwell Bay were adopted as the squadron mascots during their stay. 'Bruce', a very large Great Dane had a prodigious appetite but fortunately for the small dog, he was never considered in the meal category. 'Bruce' was looked after by the squadron Adjutant F/L Westcott MBE who had been a pilot in the First World War as well as having had much experience in different theatres of this war prior to his posting to 488. The aircrew officers contributed a monthly levy to keep 'Bruce' in food. Unfortunately, he was unable to travel with the squadron and when 488 eventually moved to the Continent 'Bruce' was retired to a local Radar Ground Control station.

The smaller dog, 'Becky' belonged to the Squadron CO, W/C Haine and Reg Mitchell tells of the time that he was being persistently annoyed by the little spaniel. He eventually hoofed the dog away with some considerable force just as a very surprised 'Dickie' Haine walked into the room. Haine clearly disapproved but without a word turned and left the room without Reg getting the time to explain his actions. Reg Mitchell had only that day made his application for an Officers Commission, something that needed the full approval of his CO. He remembers thinking that would be the end of his RNZAF career path! He did get that approval a little while later and to Haine's credit Reg Mitchell's indiscretion apparently had no effect on his air force future.

The night of the 15th September 1943 proved to be a significant night in the history of the squadron when the first airborne *"kill"* was recorded.

(1) *15/09/1943 – 21.38 hrs – Ex Bradwell Bay – Gunn and Affleck – He111 – Nth of Foreness*

It came about almost by chance when 'B' Flight had two aircraft out practicing with the local ground control stations when enemy bomber aircraft appeared. Four more of the squadron Mosquitos took to the air around 9:30pm and a *"dogfight"* took place over the base, clearly seen and heard by those waiting on the ground. The ground-crew were fascinated to hear over their RT set [20], the ground controller of the Foreness Radar Station, directing the Mosquito of F/L Jimmy Gunn (HK209) towards the position of one of the enemy bombers that appeared to be laying mines in the Thames estuary. Gunn had left his RT on open channel. They heard a shout from Jimmy that he had a visual sighting of a "Heinkel" and his Scottish crewman, F/O Jock Affleck RAF from Roslin, Midlothian, confirmed that that he had a fix on his AI system. At that point there was no further RT contact but cannon fire could be clearly heard from the ground and an aircraft was seen in the distance going down in flames. The staff of the ground control station at Foreness went outside in time to see and hear a large explosion.

There was much jubilation but as time went by concern was raised due to fact that there had been no further contact with Gunn's aircraft. An ominous silence reigned and there was no sound of the twin Merlins returning to base. The awful reality of the time hit those waiting back at Bradwell Bay. Calls were made to ground control and checks made with the local coastguard and it was eventually established that two aircraft were seen to have gone down in flames into the sea. Wreckage from both aircraft were later found on the beach. It was confirmed later that both a Mosquito and a Heinkel HE 111 had crashed in flames in close proximity to one another.

It would appear that Jimmy had possibly fallen foul of the Heinkel's rear gunner as he pressed home his attack. His body was recovered after being washed ashore at Margate on 23rd September. Sadly, Jimmy Gunn's new bride ended up attending her newly wedded husband's funeral and his interment at Margate Cemetery in Kent where he was

---

[20] RT – Radio telephone communication directly between aircraft and ground receiving station

buried with full military honours on 25th September 1943. They had been married barely four months.

The official conclusion cited on the Intelligence and Combat Report was that F/L Gunn *"gun fired at or rammed the bandit and in doing so exploded the mine or bombs carried by the bandit, the resultant explosion destroying both aircraft"*.

The death of F/L Jimmy Gunn and his crewman F/O Jock Affleck was a huge loss so early in 488 Squadron's operations. The loss was softened a little by F/L Ron Watts (HK204) from Auckland and his crewman, F/O Roger Folley, returning from the same sortie, having downed a Dornier 217 bomber.

> **(2)** *15/09/1943 – Ex Bradwell Bay – Watts and Folley – Do 217 – Thames Estuary*

The Watts / Folley crew had been directed by the same ground controller and Ron Watts established contact with the Dornier at a very low altitude, just seventy metres above the wave tops. After a long chase with the enemy aircraft trying low level evasive tactics Ron locked on and set the Dornier's starboard engine on fire with just a four second burst. He continually lost contact with the Dornier, in each case asking Foreness Control for directions. Control repeatedly advised him to break off from trying to maintain contact due to the very low altitude of the target but Watts persevered. HK204 made radar contact again with their target and as they circled for another attack the still burning Dornier went down into the sea.

Sqd Ldr. Lewis Brandon was with the squadron when all the drama around the loss of Jimmy Gunn and Jock Affleck was happening and he remembers the night well. He recalled the elation from the ground crew at the time and the aircrew room buzzing with excitement with the five other crews having returned, discarding their flying kit as they discussed the events that had just unfolded above them. It was Brandon that had to call for silence in the crowded room so that the C.O. could break the news that Gunn and Affleck would not be coming back. It was a savage reality check for those young men who had been starved of action for all those long months and now that the waiting was over, disaster prevailed. It took a long time for the sad events of that night to wash over them.

F/L Ron Watts had joined the squadron earlier while they were based at Drem in time to be part of the conversion from Beaufighter to

Mosquito. He had arrived with considerable experience training pilots yet he was not long out of flying school himself. Ron Watts in a very short time rose through the ranks to be Commanding Officer of 488 Squadron but that was to be in the future. He had come from a farming background in New Zealand and joined the RNZAF, leaving his civilian job of shearing sheep. Ron epitomised for me an example of what constituted the backbone of the New Zealand people in human terms. He demonstrated independence, strength of purpose, courage and conviction, qualities that many men drawn from New Zealand rural life brought to the world. His was not of an academic background but he certainly earned the respect of those around him.

Ron Watts linked up with Roger Folley, an ex professor from Rochester in Kent who became his crewman for the duration of the war. Ron, in fact roomed with Jimmy Gunn and both were on duty the night that Jimmy was to die. Ron had a problem with his aircraft which delayed his takeoff and by the time he had got his aircraft airborne Jimmy Gunn was already reporting by radio that he had contact with an enemy aircraft. Ron Watts and Roger Folley were also directed by the same Foreness Control to apprehend enemy aircraft that were laying mines in the Thames estuary. Ron remembers flying very low that night, just seventy metres above the surface and more dramatically having to make a steep banking 180 degree turn at that altitude in the dark, usually not recommended but necessary to carry out the manoeuvre to put him behind his target, a Dornier 217. After a short chase, he was able to destroy the Dornier still at very low altitude, so low in fact he had to attack from above and from behind his target, which was not a good technique given the upper rear defences of the Dornier 217. Ron remembered the Dornier flying very low and seemingly landing on the water and skipping across the surface, burning fiercely. This aircraft, a Dornier 217M-1 of 9/KG2 was piloted by Oberfeldwebel Erich Mosler[21].

The Mosquito crew were by this time out of radio contact with their controller, probably due to the low altitude they were at so they climbed up to a safer altitude and headed back to Bradwell Bay where they learnt of the tragic death of a friend and Ron's roommate.

Jimmy Gunn's body was recovered from the sea several weeks later reportedly with a row of bullet holes down one side despite the findings

---

[21] *Information supplied by Stephen Darlow in his publication "Victory Fighters"*

of the official report. His end would have been very quick. The airfield local to where he was found organised his funeral and several of the 488 aircrew flew down for the service. It was a particularly sad time for Ron Watts who attended, but the day was lightened somewhat by a bizarre incident when one of the firing party in the second row at the graveside pre-empted the second volley of shots by accidentally discharging his rifle as he lifted it up to the firing position and blew the hat off the serviceman in the front row. Fortunately, they were firing blanks but the poor man pulled his head into the large collar of his greatcoat turtle-wise trying desperately to maintain some semblance of dignity while those about him were in a state of collapse with suppressed laughter. Ron thought it was a ridiculous situation all around and although he organised many funerals later not once was a firing party used again. [22] Jimmy Gunn was buried in the Margate Cemetery.

Later in September the squadron had the crew of F/L Bill Cook RNZAF of New Plymouth and F/O Jack Warner RAF of West Hartlepool join them. Bill Cook had, on an earlier posting with another squadron, famously destroyed a low flying German "sneak raider" by harassing him and causing the raider to crash into a gasometer at high speed near Bognor while trying to get out of range of Cook's guns. The German pilot must have been looking over his shoulder at the time of impact as one would have thought that a gasometer would make a fairly obvious profile on the landscape! Bill Cook was reported to have been highly amused at the outcome of the sortie. He commented it was a great way to save on ammunition. This situation was even more unique in that Cook was flying a Beaufighter at the time, an aircraft not known for its manoeuvrability and the incident happened during daylight hours! The legend surrounding this Cook / Warner crew was further enhanced when both safely bailed out of a Beaufighter at night, something that not many had achieved successfully. This was no mean feat given the design of the access into and more importantly egress out of the aircraft. Graham White in his classic work *"Night Fighter over Germany"* best describes the situation:

> *The pilot enters under the belly of the aircraft via a metal hatch bearing a short ladder, which gave access to a well*

---

[22] *From interview with Ron Watts with Dave Homewood and published on Dave's website.*

behind the pilot's seat. However, there was no room to pass around the seat to enable him to sit in it, so he had to operate a side lever that collapsed the back and arms, so allowing him to clamber over into position, complete with parachute and dinghy. Then he relocked the seat and prepared to fly. The hatch was closed from the outside by the ground-crew and formed part of the floor behind him. At the other end of the aircraft, hidden from sight behind armour-plated doors, the navigator struggled through a similar hatch opening of his own. That was the easy bit! Getting out again in anything like a hurry was a much more athletic feat. First, the pilot opened the outside escape hatch by remote control, leaving a gaping hole in the floor behind his seat; he then released his safety straps and collapsed his seat once more by its unlocking lever. Meanwhile set in the cabin roof over his head were two long steel tubes. The pilot had to reach back as far as he could above his head, grasp the tubes, and haul himself, parachute pack, and dinghy, backwards until he dangled over the dark hole in the floor below. He then dropped down through the still airspace created by the open hatch flap into fresh air. Always assuming, of course, that that down was still down and hadn't suddenly changed to being up, a not unknown event in flying.

On his way out the pilot had to dodge the navigators open hatch at the rear as the navigator always beat the pilot into fresh air as he only had to open his hatch and step out onto the square yard of nothing that appeared in the floor – no hanging about on metal bars for him. And if you managed to avoid the open back hatch there was always the tail-wheel to clobber you.

A somewhat light-hearted account but it does explain why there was a satisfactory outcome for both Cook and Warner when they bailed out of their Beaufighter and survived the experience. The chances of parachuting to safety from such a confined situation were not great.

On 23rd September, F/Sgt. Vlotman and Sgt. Wood made an emergency landing at R.A.F. Gravesend in Beaufighter X8027 not altogether successfully it was reported. They were uninjured but the

Beaufighter suffered enough damage to cause much muttering among the ground-crew that had to recover the aircraft and made it serviceable again.

On the 28th September 1943, F/O Leslie Hunt arrived to replace F/O M.E. Davies as the squadron Intelligence Officer. Leslie Hunt later authored the book *"Defence until Dawn"* published in February 1949, a firsthand account of 488 Squadron during its UK sojourn and a classic in its time. This book was the only book published that specifically relates the activities of 488 Squadron. Hunt carried many fond memories of his time with 488 Squadron and treasured his connection with New Zealanders generally.

Another important posting to the squadron at that time was a searchlight liaison officer, Lt. Henry Burr from 56 Brigade of the British Army. Lt. Burr was to prove an important link between the aircrews and the searchlight system and his input greatly improved the co-operation needed between these units to defend the region. He was also reported as being a great man to have at a party and he was friend to everyone in the squadron.

Just a few days later the squadron was visited by the New Zealand High Commissioner, Mr. W.T. Jordan who no doubt was very keen to see what difference his representations to Winston Churchill on the squadron's behalf back in May 1943 had made. He would I am sure have been very pleased. This was a squadron despite early losses of crews, on the move and now well into the operational defence of their allocated sector.

The Luftwaffe intensified their night attacks over South East England with operations over twenty-one nights in October 1943. London was hit with over three hundred sorties against the city with the heaviest raid being the night of 6th October. These attacks saw the Luftwaffe using their latest fighter – bomber, the Junkers JU 188.

P/O. Neil Knox and crewman, P/O. Buck Ryan (HK234) severely damaged a Dornier 217 over Canterbury the same night but could only claim it as a *Damaged*. The Dornier had luck on its side as Knox hit it many times as it twisted and turned trying to escape before disappearing into the dark mist of the night. Knox got a fleeting glimpse of his target silhouetted against the moon and this was enough for him to launch his attack. The Kiwi pair gave up the chase when they found that their gun sight had collapsed completely. They were confident that the Dornier had no chance of escaping their onslaught and were hopeful that their claim would soon be converted to a *"Destroyed"* but this was not to be.

The 9th October 1943 saw tragedy again striking 488 with the very experienced pair of F/L Cecil Ball, RNZAF and F/O Jock Kemp, flying HK 204, crashing into trees while returning from an operation, close to the end of the runway at Tolleshunt Knight near Tiptree, north west of Bradwell. They had flown into extensive mist and fog on their approach to Bradwell Bay and had difficulty finding the base despite searchlights being deployed to assist them. There was some irony in that they had both only recently returned for a second tour of duty with 488 and were probably at that time the most experienced team the squadron had.

Ron Watts spoke of the night that Ball and Kemp died. They had taken off earlier than Watts on patrol and were returning to base as he took off on his flight. Ron recalled that immediately after lift-off he found he was in thick cloud which had rapidly descended to almost ground level. He called flying control and told them to close the airfield and divert all air traffic away as he considered anyone trying to land would be in danger with the ground conditions which were rapidly deteriorating. His call to Control was followed by the other aircraft responding saying *"Don't listen to him, it is perfectly all right"*. Ron called control to get them to get the responding crew to check their altimeter as he felt the crew of the other aircraft had misread the dial and thought they were at 1000 feet when they were in all probability only at 100 feet. This proved to be the case as Ball and Kemp ploughed into the ground in the middle of this conversation. Ron, felt they had concentrated on the runway flight path lights rather than relying on what their instruments were telling them. A simple error with disastrous and tragic results.

The Squadron Operations Record Book records the fact that two American *"Negro"* soldiers were badly injured by being struck by the aircraft or by flying debris, one of whom subsequently died.

Both the 488 airmen were buried at Maldon Cemetery in Essex on 13th October with full military honours. The wives and relatives of both men attended the funeral. There was some comment at the time that Ces Ball remarkably was still undecorated despite flying fifty-seven operational sorties and had over a thousand hours of flying time in his logbook.

A further crew were lost in an accident a few days later on 16th October when their aircraft HK 235 disappeared into the Blackwater

River estuary after one of their engines cut out and they lost height while in the circuit for a final landing approach. Being so close to home compounded the tragedy even more. They were P/O. D.N. Green RAF, and his Navigator F/Sgt. R.A. Creek RAF. The body of F/Sgt. Creek was never found. The funeral for P/O. D.N. Green was held on 22nd October and he was interred in the Boston Cemetery in Lincolnshire. The impact of these continuing accidental deaths must have been particularly hard on the young men of the squadron. The fact that the deaths had occurred in flying accidents rather than in fighting situations must have been hard to take at the time.

On the 25th October 1943, a young man by the name of John Hall was promoted to the rank of Flight Lieutenant and at almost the same time received notice that he was to be posted to Bradwell Bay to join the New Zealanders of 488 Squadron. Hall was serving with No. 85 RAF Squadron at the time and was in the final stages of a gunnery course at the Central Gunnery School at Sutton Bridge in Lincolnshire. There he had come under the tutelage of a gunnery expert named Antony Fisher and it was this training that produced one of the most successful and accurate night fighting pilots of the Second World War. Hall in fact despite being under training himself showed enough aptitude to become the deputy trainer to Antony Fisher, looking after the practical airborne work.

The "new" concept was simple. The training was based on the ability to draw the target, that is, to anticipate the speed and direction of the target and provide deflection gunfire that in essence lays a stream of molten lead in the path of the target that effectively arrives at same position in the sky as the target. The best example is clay pigeon shooting with shotguns. Despite the simplicity of the method it was not widely taught but those that mastered the technique proved to be successful on most occasions they came across *'trade'* in their particular patch in the sky. It is well to remember that these sorties were carried out in the darkness of the night sky so a separate set of skills needed to be utilised to have a successful outcome. Johnny Hall developed a skill that under the circumstances was incredible. Given that these situations happened at night it is difficult to comprehend how it was possible to lay gunfire in the path of an aircraft moving at speed and in an uncertain direction!

It was apparent from Hall's own account [23] that he sought the posting to 488 Squadron and had organised to be rejoined with John (Jock) Cairns who he had served with in No.85 Squadron earlier in the year flying Beaufighters. They were to begin a lasting and successful partnership in the night skies over Britain and Europe. It was a relationship and friendship that was to last all their lives. It was obvious that their mutual respect for one another, they described it as their *"fussiness"* set a new standard for the squadron. They insisted on doing extensive airborne testing of their aircraft systems in the daylight hours before each and every operational night flight. Hall did not have an immediate start at 488, being posted on to an engine course and then subsequently enjoying a period of leave before returning to the squadron for operational work on 30th November 1943. The engine course was at Derby at the Rolls Royce factory and John felt it important to be completely up to date and have extensive knowledge of the Rolls Royce Merlin engines that his Mosquito was fitted with. This knowledge seeking of their equipment was borne out when Jock Cairns commented much later that they never had a single occurrence of engine failure during their time together. John Hall clearly had a complete understanding of the limits to which he could load the Merlins.

"Jock" Cairns, his crewman, was an interesting character who had considerable experience with the AI Radar system and also had the advantage of having flown with a number of very experienced pilots since his early days in the RAF. He like John Hall was delighted with their posting to 488 Squadron. He commented *"One could not wish to serve with a more congenial, loyal and tough bunch than Kiwis. We were warmly accepted and swiftly adapted to the relaxed 'no worries, mate' style of the doughty colonials"*[24] Cairns noted in his memoirs that he was pleased to be flying in the Mk.X11 Mosquito and commented on how much he enjoyed it when the cannons were firing, the wooden floor of the cockpit vibrating below their feet and the cordite fumes wafting into the cockpit. This together with the clatter of the gunfire really got his adrenalin pumping he claimed.

It was common practice for the armourers to tape over the gun ports before every flight so that moisture was kept at bay. Cairns noted that

---

[23] *From John Hall: A Memoir written by his sister Alison Fenton and published by the Charlebury Press in 2005.*

[24] *From "Owls and Fools Fly at Night" by John (Jock) Cairns*

the ground crews almost invariably first checked to see if the tape was shredded when the aircraft returned from a sortie before carrying out any of their allocated tasks. Shredded tape meant the guns had been fired and the possibility of success was eagerly anticipated by them.

On the last day of October, the squadron was joined by six naval airmen from the Fleet Air Arm who were to be trained on the Mosquito night-fighter aircraft during a stay lasting three months. A large contingent of trainee pilots had also arrived during October and all these extra inexperienced personnel must have impacted on the squadron's normal operational activities. The Naval group, all Lieutenants consisted of three pilots and three observers and brought a new dimension to the squadron having only had experience on aircraft carrier mounted biplanes. They fitted in well particularly with the social side of station life, all important during the days and nights of constant stress and strain.

One of the naval group, was Lt. Murray Richardson from Wellington. He had left New Zealand in 1941 to train in the UK as an Observer in the Fleet Air Arm. He served on the HMS Victorious, an aircraft carrier flying torpedo bombers and then two-seater fighter aircraft. They were deployed on the Arctic convoys to Russia, to the Mediterranean during the relief of Malta and then took part in the landings on the Algiers coast.

Murray Richardson found himself and his navigation skills almost redundant when the Navy in its wisdom decided to replace their two-seater aircraft with single-seater marine Spitfires. The Navy was keen on the development of night fighters but a serious delay in the delivery of the new single seaters and the difficulties of redesigning the aircraft to take the new AI radar units meant a number of pilots and observers being redundant. Officially this was the reason that the Royal Navy sent thirty of their carrier-based air-crews on to the RAF for night fighter training. Unofficially the theory was advanced that the surplus crews had heard that the replacement aircraft were to be the Fairy Barracuda torpedo bombers so they all promptly volunteered to be posted. These aircraft were having serious safety problems and had a growing reputation as killers of pilots during conversion training.

I had tracked down Murray, now living in Wellington in New Zealand and he was happy to recall his time with 488 although his stay was relatively short, being around three months. The Admiralty heard sometime during their posting that 488 Squadron was listed to travel to Europe and decided to transfer the naval group over to a Canadian squadron, No. 410 in order to let them carry on with their training locally rather than being taken away to Europe. As it turned out the Canadians travelled across the channel before 488 Squadron anyway.

Murray Richardson and his group had ended up like the proverbial travelling circus after leaving HMS Victorous. First port of call for Murray was being sent to a Radar course in early October at RAF Twin Woods near Bedford. After two weeks, he was posted to 264 Squadron at RAF Fairwood Common in Glamorgan without his pilot Lt. Bill Bale before linking up with Bale again at 488 Squadron in November 1943. In early January 1944, he was posted on to 85 Squadron at West Malling but was returned to 488 the following day. Then, to cap it all off Murray ended up in hospital with German measles and Scarlet Fever on the 5th February 1944, not surprising given the stress of all the comings and goings! On leaving Hospital on 8th March he ended up with 410 Squadron for operational flying.

Richardson recalls the situation when he was able to confirm at least one of Jamie Jameson's "kills" when on a flight with 410 Squadron. He and his pilot Lt. Bale, were forced to return to base when their AI unit packed up and started to smoke. As they made their way homeward they saw two German aircraft being shot down close to their flight path and observed them crashing into the ground. Cross checking showed at least one of these being one of the four aircraft that Jamie Jameson famously shot down that night.

Lt. Murray Richardson was finally recalled by the Navy on 11th of November 1944 with just the one notable scare during his time away when Lt. Bill Bale collapsed unconscious at the controls of their Mosquito leaving Murray pilotless at night for some time until he was able to revive his pilot. Bale was subsequently grounded and Richardson found himself crewing for a new pilot for the rest of his land-based flying.

One of the newer trainee crews to arrive from flying training courses on 12th October 1943 was F/O Harold Longley with his crewman, F/O Malcolm Graham on their first Operational posting. Harold Longley was to stay until being posted on to No. 3 Squadron RAF in January 1945. He had no success in the air during his time with 488 but he must have had a great learning curve as within weeks of his leaving he had built up a good score of "kills" that eventually led to him reaching "Ace" status and being decorated with the D.F.C. He had progressed to single engined Typhoon fighter-bombers and later

Tempests and carried our daytime intruder missions and ground attacks deep into German territory. His skill at low level attacks earned him a reputation second to none. He destroyed many enemy aircraft on the ground and shared significant successes with attacks with his squadron on the railway networks well back behind enemy lines.

Another new member for the squadron was F/Sgt. William Breithaupt who was a Canadian pilot who joined the squadron on 3rd November 1943. 488 Squadron was his first operational posting. His stay was relatively brief, being posted on to 409 Squadron then to 239 Squadron where he was killed during a shootout with a Me 110. He was escorting bombers at the time when attacked from the rear by the Me 110, who overshot the Mosquito during his attack and allowed Breithaupt to turn the tables on him. Both aircraft crashed as a result of the engagement and the Mosquito crew both died although the Luftwaffe crew survived. He was just 24 years old and was awarded a posthumous DFC for his exploits.

The 5th of November 1943 saw the Bradwell Station Commander, W/C Aitken, presenting each of the squadron members with a medal to commemorate service to the Allied war effort between 1939 and 1943. Despite the pomp and ceremony attached to the presentation there was a feeling among squadron members later, that the value of the medals was diminished when they found out that all serving members of the allied forces also received the same medal. There was further disappointment when they realised that the staging of the medal ceremony meant they would be missing out on their annual fireworks celebrations! The cynicism carried on for some time after as there were several recorded instances of the medal being known as the *"Naafi Gong"* ie. able to be purchased in the local services confectionery shop for a few pence.

The Luftwaffe had put further pressure on the British defences with the introduction of the new and very fast Me 410 and the equally formidable Fw 190. The new Mosquito NF X111 however was up to the task and F/O Graeme Reed RNZAF and his crewman, F/O Ralph Bricker RAF, the squadron's train busting experts, flying Mosquito HK367 were the first night-fighting NF XIII crew to down one of the super fast Me 410A's when they sent their target spinning into the sea off Clacton-on-Sea just before mid night on the night of 8th November. Reed and Bricker were on a routine patrol when 'Trimley' Control vectored them onto a 'bandit' at 17,000 ft.

> **(3)** *8/11/1943 – 23:00 hrs – Ex Bradwell Bay – Reed and Bricker – Me 410 – Nth of Manston*

The Me 410 had a very distinct and bright exhaust pattern and when approached from the rear could be relatively easily recognised by the four evenly spaced blue coloured glowing exhausts. The Me 410 in this case for some inexplicable reason carried on with a straight and level flight path for some time after Reed's initial burst which had been aimed right up those exhaust pipes. The second burst however caused the aircraft to roll over on its side and dive vertically down. Ralph Bricker watched it disappear below them and saw the port wing collapse and buckle under the doomed aircraft. There was a lot of conjecture from the pair as to just what was the reason for the Me 410 seemingly not noticing bursts of cannon fire going up its exhaust system. The only explanation would have been the pilot and / or his crew being hit with the first burst and therefore unable to take evasive action.

The Messerschmitt 410 known as the Hornisse ("Hornet") was a high speed heavy fighter and was capable of handling a very big bomb load comparative to its size. It was initially developed to improve on its badly flawed predecessor the Me 210. It had a top speed of 390mph (625 kph) and as well as a big payload could carry two 110lb bombs attached under each wing. It was a fairly decent adversary for the Mosquito.

This particular victory by the "A" Flight crew fanned the competitive flames of rivalry between the two flights and gave them encouragement to try and haul back the small lead that "B" Flight had established with earlier "Kills". Immediately after Reed and Bricker finished their first tour with 488 and were posted on to their rest period.

The rest of November 1943 was a relatively quiet month with defensive patrols flown every night until the night of 25th November when F/O Peter Hall, and P/O. Dick Marriott flying Mosquito HK288 shot down another Me 410 off the French coast at Calais at 3:15 am on the morning of the 26th.

> **(4)** *26/11/1943 – 03:15 hrs – Ex Bradwell Bay – Hall and Marriott – Me 410 – Calais*

They had chased their target in a high-speed descent down over the south of England, following those "electric blue" exhausts and out across the English Channel. When closing in on the enemy aircraft, 'Trimley Control' ordered Hall to return but he was determined not to let this one, his first "kill" to escape and pressed home his attack. The rear gunner of the Messerschmitt returned fire at the Mosquito but was firing high and to the port side of Hall's aircraft. Hall very reluctantly had to break off the action under pressure from Control without seeing what he thought had to be the inevitable ending for his target. He was sure that he had hit the pilot of the Me 410 with his first burst. Control was obviously concerned about the chance of Hall losing his aircraft over or close to enemy territory with the still top-secret AI unit on board. Hall however had taken the risk and his perseverance was later rewarded when German radio mentioned that one of its aircraft had not returned that night and this was subsequently confirmed by other sources. Hall and Marriott were credited with its destruction later on the 3rd December 1943. He had only used ten rounds from each of his cannon.

The night's action was to be the forerunner for a very successful run for Peter Hall and Dick Marriott. Leslie Hunt commented that in a conversation with Peter he had told Hunt that he *"just wanted to do well because it will please my Father so much"*. In fact, the two Halls, Peter and later Johnny would turn out be the most successful pilots in 488 Squadron. They were in opposing flights and the competition between them was keen. Later when their ranks coincided there was often confusion over them by squadron members and they were eventually to be known as Hall A and Hall B. Both were gunnery experts and were vital to the training of crews in the noble art of air combat. As successful as they were they were quite unalike, Peter Hall being the shy studious type and John the more extroverted. They were both an important part of 488 operations with their skill and dedication.

The same night was however tragically marred with the loss off the North Foreland in the North Sea of S/L Dudley Hobbis RAF and his crewman, P/O. Oliver Hills RAFVR. Hobbis flying HK 423 reported to Control that his port side engine had suddenly burst into flame and that he had ordered Oliver Hills to bail out. It was obvious to Control that Hills had left the aircraft as the engine noise from the open escape hatch had masked any further voice messages from Hobbis and nothing further was found until the body of Oliver Hills was washed ashore some months later. Hills was buried in the Epsom Cemetery in Surrey with full military honours. Hills had been a Solicitor for four years in

Malaya prior to joining the RAF Volunteer Reserve in 1941. He was 32 years old.

Dudley Hobbis from all accounts tried to bring his aircraft back and the last message received from the aircraft was him indicating that he was going to bail out. The loss of Hobbis was particularly tragic as this was to be his last operational sortie and he had in fact told his regular navigator, Terry Clark earlier that day that he would need to find himself another pilot for that night. Clark has pondered for many years just why Dudley Hobbis decided to not fly with him as his crewman that day given that this was to be their last operational flight before a compulsory stand down rest period. Dudley Hobbis was never seen again and his name is recorded among the *"Missing believed Killed"* on the Runnymede Memorial

The loss of Dudley Hobbis, the "A" Flight leader and the departure of S/L Frank Davison to a posting on a non-operational unit left both "A" and "B" Flights leaderless. Ron Watts was promoted, much to his surprise to Squadron Leader to replace Dudley Hobbis and took over "A" Flight, continuing his rapid rise in the squadron ranks.

There was a very recent poignant moment when a then 90years old Terry Clark was interviewed at a thanksgiving function held at York Minster to mark Battle of Britain Sunday and the 70th Anniversary of the start of the Second World War. Clark talked of his late friend Dudley Hobbis;

> *"Today at the service I closed my eyes during the Last Post and I was back in the crew room. It was a time to remember colleagues who were there one minute and gone the next, never to be seen again. I particularly thought of my pilot friend Dudley Hobbis. I was with him for three years and to me he was more like family than friend. When he was lost, I missed him greatly, I still do".*

Dudley Hobbis and Terry Clark had a long and lasting friendship since being partnered with one another from early days with 219 Squadron back in 1940. Clark spoke of the wonderful sense of humour and endless capacity for practical jokes that Hobbis was capable of. Clark had served as a crewman for Hobbis almost continuously since that time. Just prior to their sojourn with 488 an incident occurred that sort of summed up Dudley Hobbis and ended breaking up the partnership for several weeks. They were returning to Hunsdon back in August 1942 when Hobbis decided to "beat up" the house of a friend close to the base. After several very low passes Clark noticed some vegetation on the leading edge of the wing on his side of the aircraft. He told Hobbis to look along the starboard wing. Impaled on the leading edge was a selection of tree branches. Hobbis was not impressed and the air was blue with bad language from him for the rest of the flight home. He knew he was going to be in serious trouble. Sometime after they had left the aircraft at dispersal after landing, Hobbis was ordered to report to the Station Commander. When Clark met Hobbis later he had been reduced to the rank of Flight Lieutenant and taken off operational flying. They had a further separation a little later when Clark suffered the head injury recounted earlier that so amused Lewis Brandon. Seemingly they were a pairing that had their share of "activities" in addition to their operational work.

Two days later the squadron had instant value added when S/L Nigel Bunting arrived with his crewman, F/L Phil Reed. They were a vastly experienced pair and had transferred over from Hunsdon where they had been serving with No. 85 Squadron RAF. Nigel Bunting took over as the new Commander of "B" Flight. Bunting was a very popular character, described as a *"quiet young chap, lightish red hair, an excellent and reliable pilot"*. Reed had been senior navigation leader at 85 Squadron and was described as *"sharp featured, quick witted and a remarkably fast thinker"*. These attributes undoubtedly helped him become half of a very successful duo in terms of numbers of "kills" recorded while on posting with 488 Squadron. Both arrived with four "kills" to their credit and had already been decorated for their efforts.

There was no further action in the air until the night of the 19th December when P/O. Douglas Robinson and his new crewman, F/O Terry Clark, flying Mosquito HK457 shot down another of the fabled Me 410's from Luftwaffe 14/KG2 following a high-speed chase and probably the highest altitude combat that the squadron had recorded.

(5) *20/12/1943 – 02:49 hrs - Ex Bradwell Bay – Robinson and Clark – Me 410 – Rye, Sussex*

They had picked up their target with the help of one of the ground-based search light units. Speeds of in excess of 480 kilometres per hour were reported during this chase. Their quarry tried to out climb them but was picked up and held by searchlight beams. A frantic chase ensued with the Me 410 alternately climbing and diving but Robinson doggedly stuck with his target and despite coming under heavy cannon fire from the rear gunner finally despatched the enemy aircraft where it crashed near Rye in Sussex.

The action was made doubly difficult due to the altitude, in excess of 25,000 feet at times and the visual difficulty caused by the vapour trails being left in the darkness by the fleeing bomber. Reading of the official Combat Report shows excellent and intelligent use of the Allied Search Light batteries where Robinson was able to skirt around the "coned" aircraft and snipe away until he was eventually able to destroy it despite the attention of the Me 410's rear gunner. This particular "Bandit" did not give up without a fight though as they covered a fair bit of the sky before their victim succumbed from the relentless attack from the Robinson and Clark Mosquito. The Pilot desperately tried to save himself by crash landing his aircraft but was killed in the attempt.

On 22nd December 1943 F/Sgt. Reg Mitchell joined 488 Squadron at Bradwell Bay. His experience was typical of the many young New Zealanders posted to the squadron. He had come through the trainee pilot scheme in Canada, followed by induction courses in the UK. These by any standard were brief and basic and many course members struggled with the conversion to unfamiliar aircraft. It seemed too many to be literally the survival of the fittest. Those not up to scratch were taken off flying courses and dispersed into navigation or gunnery courses. Reg Mitchell remembers Bradwell Bay being an exciting place with its size and its tremendous variety of aircraft. It was the largest and nearest operational airfield to the Continent and used for refuelling of bomber aircraft and for an emergency field as the bombers returned, many badly damaged from their sorties over Europe. The number of bombers that crash landed on their return was nothing short of spectacular.

Reg was able to catch up with a good number of his old mates from training school. He remembers well his introduction to the Mosquito. He was taken up by the "B' Flight leader, S/L Nigel Bunting for an hour's induction and demonstration and at the end of this was sent back up on his own, that is *'solo'*. This was total immersion at its best and there was never any thought given to a gradual learning process. Reg enjoyed the Mosquito and thought it a great aircraft to fly. He was at first paired up with Arthur Church as his crewman, but mysteriously

Arthur was taken off the squadron and he ended up having Ron Ballard as his navigator for the rest of his time with 488.

Reg Mitchell and Ron Ballard flew operationally in Mosquito MT 463 ME-Y until an engine failure while landing on 25th November 1944 caused them to crash and write off their aircraft, fortunately without serious injury to either of them. A replacement aircraft was needed to get them operational again. A good number of the photographs in this book are from the camera of Reg Mitchell – A very ordinary "Box Brownie", and these produced an enduring record of his time at Bradwell Bay and later on the Continent.

Reg Mitchell spoke of his good friend Wally Green. Wally was from all accounts a bit of a character. He was never an operational pilot but instead flew an Oxford, the squadron hack, a twin engined aircraft usually used for training or for transportation. It was this latter use that Wally had made a bit of a name for himself. He generally flew between bases but mostly back and forth from the Continent to England. Wally was a bit of a trader. He always had deals going, either with squadron members or with the local populace. He would fly off-duty squadron members back to the UK for a couple of days' break. They inevitably would be squeezed into the cabin of the Oxford sharing the journey with cases of wine, flowers, food or other specialities from the continent destined for his buyers in England. He was a born trader and could get his hands on anything, all at a price of course. It was rumoured he returned to New Zealand a wealthy man. He would have been I imagine like a ray of sunshine, bringing little luxuries to men struggling without the normal good things in life and his activities must have been great for the morale of those so far from home and living in the direst of circumstances.

Christmas 1943 was celebrated with all ranks, ground and aircrews combining for an ongoing celebration of a festive spirit that can only enjoyed by young men perhaps knowing that this may be their last. Those thoughts tend to foster a determination to make the most of the situation to enjoy the present, not to dwell on the past and forget about the future. There were wild and raucous times. According to Leslie Hunt the air-crews excelled by organising "flight parties" for the ground-crews and the opportunity was taken to mix and mingle with squadron personnel that you had never met on a one to one basis due to the operational requirements of forty-eight hours on followed by forty-eight hours off. This meant of course that you could go for months on end without meeting up with any personnel from the other flight.

Comments were made many times of the egalitarian nature of the New Zealand squadrons overriding the stiffness and protocol normally observed with other squadrons in the RAF and this informal contact between ranks was a feature of 488 Squadron and actively encouraged by each of the various Commanding Officers.

It was noted by Leslie Hunt that *"many of the airmen were blessed with good voices while others performed brilliantly on the piano or other musical instruments"*. Many of the events leading up to the Christmas party were held in the nearby village of Tillingham at a venue called "The Swan". The Christmas party was no exception and following an excellent dinner and a camp show, a dance was held for all ranks and invited guests. The venue's food was supplemented by food and supplies saved from food parcels from New Zealand and these extra delicacies were enjoyed by everyone used to the limitations imposed by wartime rationing of food.

The BBC had requested a representative from the squadron to take part in a Christmas broadcast to families at home and Graeme Reed was chosen. Leslie Hunt remembers having to rise very early on a cold December morning and having to walk some distance with other squadron members to the Officers Mess as they were the only ones with a radio and listen to the Christmas messages being broadcast. He remembers the feeling at that time of being humbled by the warmth of the "Kiwi" welcome and their ready acceptance of all the non-New Zealanders to share in the celebrations with them.

The Squadron's Christmas and New Year celebrations were however marred tragically with the loss of another crew. F/Sgt. Ernie Behrent and his crewman Flt. Sgt Noel Breward flying Mosquito HK375 on a Ground Control exercise had engine trouble during a flight on 30th December and the subsequent fire caused a total failure of the aircraft in flight and both were killed when they crashed into the sea thirteen kilometres south east of Bradwell Bay. They were in the last stages of their operational training and had been looking forward to being part of 488 Squadron's operational crews. Their bodies were never recovered.

The year of 1943 finished with Wng.Comm Peter Hamley receiving notice of his promotion to Group Captain and a posting to a new command. He had enjoyed his stay with 488 Squadron and it was reported that he initially declined his promotion in order to stay with the squadron but the powers to be decided otherwise. Leslie Hunt wrote of Peter Hamley's fondness for his New Zealand squadron and that he had kept in very regular touch over the following month's right up until the final disbandment of the squadron in 1945.

With the departure of Peter Hamley to his new posting his original crewman, F/O Andrew Broodbank continued crewing for F/O Jack H. Scott in January of 1944 until his eventual posting to No.1 Radar School.

W/C R.C. "Dickie" Haine took over command of 488 Squadron on the 2nd January 1944, taking over from Peter Hamley. Haine flew down from Charter Hall in a Mk VI Beaufighter. After a couple of days' orientation Haine flew Peter Hamley in a squadron Mosquito back to his new posting at Ouston air base. Haine's inexperience of the Bradwell Bay area almost proved very costly on his return flight. He left Ouston late in the afternoon on what he described as *"a pleasant evening of a sunny day"*. He was surprised when Bradwell Control called him to say that thick 'smog' was moving in and visibility was very limited. He was at this stage only about ten minutes away and found on his arrival that the smog was now down to ground level with a top at around three hundred metres. He approached upwind but found he was looking directly into the setting sun. He said that at this point he *"made one of the worst decisions in the whole of my flying career"* He spoke to Bradwell Control and despite them offering him several alternate airfields close by, he made the decision to make an approach downwind from the opposite direction with a tail wind. This was not a wise decision as he was to find out. He found the visibility better and determined not to be denied a landing at his new base told control to talk him down. After a trial run he was successfully directed down until the runway became visible and he then took over setting his Mosquito down perfectly but realised to his horror that he had touched down more than halfway down the runway. He knew ahead of him was the beacon hut and the airfield seawall and that he had no way of pulling up in time. In a split second, he decided to release the manual over-ride and retracted the undercarriage to collapse his aircraft onto its belly. He slithered to a screeching, sliding halt just short of the seawall. It was a serious misjudgement which haunted him for the rest of his career.

Not a good start to his new command but the response from his New Zealand air-crew which he initially dreaded started out as he said with *"mild sympathy"* but quickly changed to good natured ribbing. In his words:

> *"I did not enjoy relating this incident, and I was pretty upset by it, but the reaction of my New Zealand aircrew, which I had dreaded, was much better than I deserved. Firstly, they were mildly sympathetic, and then they kept ribbing me about it; this treatment I applauded and it endeared them to me, for it lightened the load of my shame"*

Haine was a colourful character, English born, enlisting as a direct entrant Sergeant Pilot in 1935 and leaving the R.A.F. as a Group Captain in 1970 after a long and distinguished career. He was well regarded by his squadron but reading his account of his time with 488 Squadron showed a man who enjoyed the social side of air force life and he seemed to spend a great deal of time away from his base with his social contacts. He described himself as *'impatient and impulsive'* and found it difficult to settle down happily in his role in air force life but was always eager and anxious to make a success of the tasks he was given. He formed up with his new crewman, Pete Bowman and they together involved themselves in a fair share of operational flying.

Haine spoke of his frustration whilst acknowledging the skills of his AI operator that they were unable to themselves score a kill or even a near miss during the many hours spent in the air in their early days at Bradwell Bay. He did point out rather tongue in cheek, that he had twenty-eight operational crews in the squadron and what enemy *'trade'* came their way had to be shared among them! During his tenure, the squadron tally rose significantly and morale was probably at its peak among the squadron members.

Bradwell Bay, due to its proximity on the coast had more than its share of badly damaged bombers struggling back from missions over Europe desperately seeking refuge on a landing ground after crossing the channel. Many were B-17 bombers from the US air force. They were very vulnerable as there were very few fighter aircraft that had the necessary range to escort them to and from their targets and their losses were very high. Often the Mosquitos of 488 Squadron were called upon to escort or guide these badly damaged aircraft into Bradwell and the rescue squad members often had to face the dreadful sight of some of these aircraft sitting damaged on the tarmac with badly injured crewmen onboard and blood dripping onto the ground under the aircraft.

There was a successful start to the New Year on the 2nd January 1944 with the crew of F/O Douglas Bergemann and F/O Ken Bishop flying Mosquito HK461 destroying a ME 410, twenty-five kilometres south of Dover. This was the fourth of the ME 410's to be destroyed by the squadron and this one did not come easy for the crew.

(6) *02/01/1944 – 23:59 hrs – Ex Bradwell Bay – Bergemann and Bishop – Me 410 – Sth of Dover*

The Luftwaffe had started their New Year bombing campaign with sustained after dark attacks by Me 410's from KG2 Gruppe and Fw 190's from SKG10 Gruppe in a renewed campaign to bomb at low level and high speed over Kent, Sussex, Surrey and London. The first bombing force of twenty aircraft, were in action on the night of 2nd January with little success for the enemy. Six of the Luftwaffe aircraft were known to have been destroyed and several of the others would have struggled to return to base.

Bergemann had an earlier target put on to him by Control but despite following directions for some time without making AI contact he was called off and redirected to a new target. The second bogey was identified as a Me 410 and he laid into the enemy aircraft with three sustained bursts from his cannon as the Messerschmitt tried somewhat gentle weaving manoeuvres to escape his tormentor. Several times there were near collisions, and when the target finally blew apart HK461 was close enough, just thirty metres, to be hit from flying debris on his port side, causing Bergemann to make a sharp turn to avoid colliding with his victim. The Me 410 was last seen in a vertical dive with pieces of burning wreckage flying off it as it disappeared from sight. It came from Luftwaffe 16/KG2 based in France.

After making a steep climb back to an operational height Bergemann was forced to feather his starboard engine as the temperature went off the clock. He had to make an emergency one engine landing on one of the coastal airfields at Manston on the Kent coast but later stated that the engine fault was not due to damage from his encounter with the Me 410. The crew on board the Me 410, code number U5+AJ, Fw Friedrich Hess and Uffz Maximilian von Poblotzki were reported missing after

Doug Bergemann's strike at midnight and were presumed killed when their aircraft went into the sea off the coast at Dover.

Doug Bergemann was trained as part of the Commonwealth Training Scheme in Canada. After the War, he moved on to civil aviation and was killed in mysterious circumstances while flying a Constellation airliner from Lisbon in Portugal to the States. The aircraft simply disappeared after running into a violent thunderstorm off the Portuguese coast and all on board were presumed to be lost.[25]

The squadron received a visit from the Air Officer Commanding, Air Defence of Great Britain, Air Marshall Sir R.M. Hill, K.C.B., M.C., A.F.C. The reason for the illustrious gentleman's visit was the squadron's success in shooting down four of the fabled Luftwaffe ME 410's. He was greatly excited and very pleased according to the squadron Diarist. These were the latest of the German night fighter / bombers and were thought to be invincible by the Germans so the psychological effect on the public of both protagonists was important.

The Luftwaffe launched 'Operation Steinbock' on the night of 21st January 1944, known to the British as the 'Baby Blitz' and this was to be the largest airborne attack on British defences since Birmingham was attacked in June 1942. The Luftwaffe had been taking a punishing from concerted airfield bombing by the Allies and they formulated a plan that saw their bomber units shifting from airfields and constantly on the move to avoid destruction while still on the ground. This nomadic existence created havoc for the German ground-crews as they had no idea whose aircraft they would be servicing on a daily basis and they would have lost that closeness and connection with their own crews. It must have been a logistical nightmare.

The Luftwaffe had over four hundred bombers at their disposal for the "Steinbock" campaign. The squadrons consisted of the lightweight but speedy Me 410's and Fw 190's with Ju 188 and Do 217 medium bombers. The only heavy weight bombers available were the very unreliable He 177 "Greif" bombers. They were powered by coupled, inverted V-12 Daimler-Benz DB610 engines geared to each four bladed propeller units. They suffered from transmission and cooling problems.

The Luftwaffe had long conceded that the massed bombing raids being carried out by the Allies were logistically beyond them at this stage of the war. New tactics were organised to try and counter the climbing

---

[25] Information on Douglas Bergemann, from "Aircrew of Northland" by Ted Edwards

success rates of the sixteen Beaufighter and Mosquito night-fighter squadrons now defending the southern areas of England. The new tactic saw individual "Gruppes" taking off on bombing missions in small groups over a ten-hour period with the idea of putting pressure on anti-aircraft and civil defence systems over longer periods around the selected target areas.

The "Steinbock" attacking forces had been distributed around fourteen different airfields in a rough arc spanning Belgium, Holland and Northern France. This allowed different Gruppes to hop from airfield to airfield before the final order was to given to take off for targets in England. This rapid deployment of men and machines caused no end of problems as maintenance issues could not be handled and in one instance only one aircraft out of twenty that should have been available actually took off as orders were received to make the first attack on the Waterloo area in Central London. The first attack eventually took place with around 250 aircraft as dark kicked in around 7:30pm on the night of 21st January 1944.

The first stage of "Steinbock" was an absolute disaster for the Luftwaffe. The lumbering He 177's who were prone to engine problems; literally fell out of the skies, some before they had even reached the channel. In the end, only fifteen bombers were reported as reaching the target over London as the anti-aircraft defences and the night-fighter squadrons got in among the lighter bombers well before they reached their targets. 488 Squadron were on patrol the same night waiting for them.

The all British crew, of F/L Johnny Hall and F/O Jock Cairns, flying Mosquito HK 380 scored the first double for the squadron on that night.

(7) *21/01/1944 – Unknown Hrs – Ex Bradwell - Hall and Cairns – Do 217 – Sth of Dungeness*

(8) *21/01/1944 – Unknown Hrs – Ex Bradwell - Hall and Cairns – Ju88 – Sellindge, Kent*

The start of the "Steinbock" campaign was also the start of a very successful period for the squadron. Johnny Hall and Jock Cairns downed a Dornier 217 and a little later a Junkers Ju 88 over the channel. They had been on a searchlight exercise and lost radio communication with Control. They decided to *'freelance'* for a while before returning to base and were fortunate enough to pick up the distinctive tail end of the Dornier in the light of a searchlight beam. They closed in, following the enemy aircraft on their AI unit and crossing the channel heading towards France, scored a good hit from a short burst of cannon fire and sent the Dornier spinning into the sea 13 miles south of Dungeness. At one stage Hall was just a hundred metres from his target trying to seek final confirmation that the aircraft was the enemy. Two of the German crew bailed out and survived the attack.

This particular aircraft was recorded as being U5+IH from I/KG2 Gruppe which had earlier taken off from Eindhoven at 8:15pm. The Do 217 was piloted by Lt. Anders and had just unloaded his bomb load of AB 1000 incendiaries. Following Hall's first strike Anders ordered his crew to bale out. Uffz Erich Kliene was listed as missing with Anders but Uffz Willi Engelhardt and Uffz Wilhelm Kuhne survived uninjured to be picked up by launch and taken to Dover to be prisoners of war.

Hall and Cairns second success followed a little later as they crossed back over the coast on their return from their earlier success. They spotted a Ju 88 caught in the cone of several searchlights over Horton Priory in Sellindge, Kent. Anti aircraft fire from the ground caused the enemy aircraft to make a sudden turn right across the gun sight of HK 380 / ME-Y and Hall gave him a burst which straightened him up and a later second burst did the job, sending the Ju 88 into the ground at 9:50pm.

This particular aircraft was recorded as being a Ju 88 A-14 serial number B3+AP of 6/KG 54. The Ju 88 was flown by Oberleutnant Karl Egon Hellwig, with crew members, Uffz. Hans Jehle, Fw. Roland Kuhnert and Uffz. Walter Flossmann. The Ju 88 had left from Laon/Athies base around 8:30pm to attack London with 27 aircraft of 11/KG54. The first burst from Johnny Hall caught Hellwig completely by surprise as he tried to escape the searchlight beams that had him exposed for all the world to see. Hall's first strike set the port engine on fire. Hellwig was at the time at 4000 mtrs. and immediately jettisoned his two AB wing mounted incendiary bombs. He activated fire extinguishers in the port engine bay and put the Ju 88 in a steep dive which took his aircraft down to around 2500 metres. Hellwig ordered his crew to bale out. Unteroffizier Flossman chose to exit from the upper hatch while Jehle and Kuhnert used the under-belly hatch. Hellwig was not to survive being found dead in the wreckage but his crew survived to become prisoners of war.

The news service was on the job really early with the second 'kill' for the night being made in the early hours of the Saturday morning and just hours later revealed on the 7:00 am BBC news bulletin. The authorities were very keen to bring the British public good news and seized upon their success. Their enthusiasm was commendable but some restraint was also required due to the top-secret nature of the squadrons work at that time.

Leslie Hunt in his book *"Defence until Dawn"* recounts the follow up to the success of the Hall / Cairns crew. It was the first "double" for the squadron and they were both photographed for the Sunday papers on 23rd January 1944, with smiles on their faces and the caption *"The smile on the face of the Flying Tigers"*. They took a bit of leg pulling over that. That night in the Mess they were both served plates of raw meat and it took a long while for the leg-pulling to fade away. Both Hall and Cairns were mortified to see the heading in the Sunday newspaper that morning and knew that it was going to take some living down.

A week later Hall was interviewed on the BBC after the BBC Nine o'clock news and the squadron joined in the jubilation for what was to be a very successful period in the operational life of the squadron.

The John Hall BBC interview on the night of 24th February 1944 put a typical night's work of a defending aircrew in perspective. As with the newspaper interview there was great care taken to ensure the Hall and Cairns were never identified by squadron number and it was interesting to see Cairns described as an 'Observer' rather than the 'Radar' operator that he actually was. The text of Halls interview repeated here described a typical sortie for a night-fighter:

> *"You're patrolling over a dark countryside, not a light to be seen, and suddenly you get a warning: 'We may have something for you.' If you've had a lot of nights with nothing much to do, you are rather pleased.*
>
> *What happens next may be rather astonishing – one minute it's completely dead and black; the next minute there's all this activity. Searchlights spring up all over the ground. You see the flashes of the anti-aircraft bursts – pinpoints of yellow flashes. And then the flashes of the incendiaries, scattered prickles of light and among them perhaps the raiders flares. They look like yellow single headlamps and on the ground the*

big white short flashes of high explosive, and perhaps if the raiders have been lucky, well – maybe a fire. [26]

The air suddenly comes to life in the cockpit too. Where it's all been silent, suddenly the radio telephone is full of excited conversations circulating around the calm voice of the Controller on the ground. Some of these exclamations from the air are rather unclerical in character.

At this moment, there is any amount of business in the sky. Packets of rockets arrive. They twinkle and they are red coloured; they're indescribably vicious looking. You get the idea that there are rapid pinpoints of red all over the sky at once, and if you happen by mistake to have got a bit too near their particular piece of sky, you get rocked about too roughly for comfort.

The searchlights which had been hunting around have settled into a cone and you make towards it to see what they've got. And round the cone there may be little prickles of anti-aircraft bursts. On one of London's recent raids it was an eerie effect. There was a good deal of cloud about, and it was a very dark night with no horizon, and the searchlights were making a silvery cold blur in the cloud, rather as though the cloud was glowing. My observer said: 'I think I can see something there.' And a few seconds later we saw a small speck twisting and turning in the cone. As we closed the range, the anti-aircraft gunners made way for us and by this time we could recognise it for a Junkers 88. He caught fire and we saw the white flash as he hit the ground behind some trees.

When the searchlights have picked up an enemy raider and he is moving fast through the sky, each group holds him until he's out of their range and others constantly pick him up and follow him. And so the effect you see is though the cone itself was moving through the darkness, travelling over the ground with this small speck in the apex. The second enemy raider we met on that night was caught like that and the searchlights followed him out to sea. He was heading for home. And we followed the searchlights. When he'd passed over the coast

---

[26] Verbatim dialogue from speech given to BBC Radio on the evening of 14th February 1944 by John Hall being broadcast throughout networks worldwide.

the searchlights could follow him no longer. And at first, we could not make out what he was. There was as a matter of fact a furious argument in the cockpit. But very soon we came close enough to see six small pin points of light which are characteristic of the exhaust flames of the Dornier 217.

On a very dark night when there are no searchlights, the exhaust flames are sometimes the first things you can see: sometimes they're yellow, sometimes they're red, and some of them are even electric blue. They look like round plates of colour. This particular night we followed the Dornier and opened fire at a hundred yards, aiming between the two rows of exhausts, and he went down into the sea.

You can tell when your cannon shells are hitting the thing because they make bright white flashes and we can see them strike the fuselage.

Those exhaust flashes may be all you can actually see at first, but as you get closer the aircraft begins to have a shape. The vague blur assumes a sharper and sharper shape, until you get so close that you can pick out details. In bright moonlight, you may be able to see a silhouette moving against a white cloud. But that doesn't seem to happen very often. As a rule, you have to use all your wits and all your eyesight to make sure that you are finding and identifying your target. There's no such thing as a carrot- eyed or cat-eyed vision that will enable you to spot your target ten miles away.

The above dialogue was a verbatim account of an interview that John Hall gave to the BBC. The last comment he made must have caused some consternation with the authorities when they were desperately trying to hide the fact that it was advances in Radar technology that were giving Allied night-fighters a huge advantage at the time while spreading propaganda stories of our pilots being fed vitamins and organic compounds to enhance their night vision.

F/L Lewis Brandon, the squadron navigation leader left for a new posting on 23rd January 1944. He had ended up enjoying his time with 488 and like many of the RAF air-crew spoke fondly of the regular food parcels that arrived from New Zealand. He was charmed by the sharing of these goodies by the Kiwi's and was staggered by the range of food that appeared at the night flying suppers served in the Dispersal huts before each night's operations. He commented that:

> *"488 (New Zealand) Squadron were to make quite a name for themselves later (after I had left), for they became part of the Allied Expeditionary Air Force and operated with great success. in spite of the fact that they had no opportunity to fly against the enemy until their move to Bradwell in September 1943, by the time the squadron was disbanded in April 1945 they had destroyed no fewer than 67 enemy aircraft with three probables and eleven damaged. During this time, they lost only four crews in action and eleven in flying accidents – a very creditable record indeed and I am proud to have served with them as Navigator Leader even if only for a comparatively short time. They were a great bunch of fellows".*[27]

As seemed to be the terrible pattern in those days, tragedy seemed to follow success soon after, with the deaths of one of the 'B' Flight crews, F/Sgt. Keith "Snowy" Watson and his crewman, F/Sgt. Ernest Edwards, ironically on searchlight exercises as were Hall and Cairns, but with a very different outcome. Flying HK 363, they were blinded by the searchlights they were working with and were both killed when they lost control and crashed close to Bradwell Bay on the 3rd February. They had earned high praise from the US Army Air force and Allied command for successfully guiding a badly damaged American Super Fortress back to the safety of Bradwell Bay just a few nights before. Both were buried in the New Zealand Cemetery at Brookwood with full military honours. The aircrew photograph on page 97 with them first and second in the back row was taken just hours before they died.

The following night, F/Sgt. Christiaan Vlotman, and his crewman Sgt. John Wood shot down the first of their tally of four kills flying Mosquito HK 367. They destroyed a Dornier 217 sixty kilometres east of Foulness Point. It took some perseverance on Vlotman's part as despite obvious strikes all over the German aircraft it refused to go down. When it finally went into a spin he followed it down firing just to make sure of the kill. His first strike was made from just 300 metres

---

[27] *Notes from "Night Flyer" by Lewis Brandon DSO, DFC & Bar*

dead astern but his port inner 20mm machingun stopped, fouled by loose rounds. No one appeared to escape the blazing Dornier as it went down into the North Sea.

(9) *04/02/1944 – unknown – Ex Bradwell - Vlotman and Wood – Dornier 217 – E of Foulness Pt*

Chris Vlotman, known as the *"Flying Dutchman"*, had an interesting background. He had left his native Holland to work in England before the war. At the age of seventeen, after attending an agricultural college in Holland for two years, he borrowed 100 guilders from his uncle to pay for his passage on a coal boat travelling from Holland to Hull in the north east of England. It turns out he was the only paying passenger on board. On reaching Hull he asked a policeman how to get to Hitchin in Hertfordshire where he had arranged to work in a local rose nursery. He travelled by train still on his own in a strange land with presumably limited English as a language. He worked for the company for some time and met and eventually married the English daughter of his employer. [28]

He was at the onset of hostilities still working in England and travelled back to Holland and joined the Netherlands Army (The Irene Brigade). He was sent back to England to serve in a transport battalion driving trucks, motorbikes and Bren gun carriers. There was some theory that the Dutch authorities had sent Chris back to England as part of a scheme they had in place to purge their army units of possible German collaborators. He was in the end snapped up by the air force who were keen to involve personnel of their allies in aircrew positions and given air crew training.

Chris became a flying instructor immediately after the war at RAF Croydon, training aircrew on Netherlands Air Force Dakota transport aircraft. His first flight under this scheme was on 31st July 1945. He stayed at Croydon until he joined up with the civilian Dutch airline KLM on 10th March 1946. He had a long and illustrious career with the airlines, including spells with Atlantis and Martonair. He did at one stage go back to his old pre-war job growing roses commercially but problems with managers and irrigation for his crops saw him passing it up for a well-earned retirement. At the end of the war he had run up a

---

[28] *Chris Vlotman's background notes courtesy of his daughter, Mrs Ann MacPherson*

total of 1,542 operational hours with the RAF and a staggering 24,479 hours during his civilian airlines career. The British authorities had been keen to publicise Chris Vlotman's successes with 488 Squadron but some caution was taken when it was found that he still had close family members living in German occupied Holland. Even the author of an account of Vlotman's successes published in 1945 was unable to name him, just referring to him as "the Dutchman". Following Vlotman and Woods first "Kill" on 5th February a Dutch Journalist, by the name of Kiek visited the squadron and interviewed Chis Vlotman on behalf of the Free Dutch Newspaper. He also arranged for Vlotman to be interviewed on the Radio Orange program.

Chris Vlotman's crewman, John Wood was the youngest aircrew member on the squadron at the age of eighteen. Johnny Wood by contrast to Chris was quiet and reserved, slightly built but had a tenacious quality, complimenting Vlotman's flying ability with his Radar skills.

There was a sad irony that during the research stage for this book I was able to link up Ann MacPherson, Chris's daughter with Piers Wood, Johnny Wood's son only to find that Chris and Johnny had lived for some time after the war within two miles of one another without making contact. At the end of hostilities both men had gone their separate ways and never made contact again. Johnny Woods passed away in 1997 aged 74. Chris sadly passed away on 14th October 2011 during the research stages of this book. He was 96 years old.

John Woods was demobbed from the RAF at the end of the war and took on a civilian job working for the Westminster Bank. He had difficulty in settling into civilian life and in 1947 rejoined the RAF and within twelve months received his Officer's Commission. He was posted to RAF Wunsdorf and served three years working as an aircraft controller guiding aircraft during the Berlin Airlift that were ferrying supplies as part of an international effort to alleviate starvation in and around the German capital. It would not have been difficult for him to slide into this role given the expertise he showed guiding Chris Vlotman into position during their wartime years together.

He married in 1950 and started work in important positions of RAF Intelligence at Nuneham Park in Oxfordshire and for a time was seconded to the USAF in a posting to Korea. He was further posted to Germany and was posted as Commanding Officer of Photographic Intelligence to RAF Bassingbourne and then on to RAF Episkopi in

Cyprus. He retired from the RAF with the rank of Squadron Leader in 1976 at the age of fifty-three. John never really recovered from the effects of his wartime experiences, the stress of which finally saw him pass away with major health problems at the age of seventy-four. [29]

The 22nd February saw F/O Rick Riwai and his crewman, F/Sgt. Ian Clark in HK 367 taking off on a before dawn *'scramble'* [30] call from Control (their second sortie for the night) but at a crucial moment lose control and crash into the steel anti-invasion defences on the edge of the airfield with both being killed. It had been very busy in the early hours of the morning with attacking Luftwaffe raiders arriving overhead after the normal night patrols had completed their work and returned for the night. The crews had just returned after a long tiring series of night patrols but bravely answered the call to get airborne once again. The Luftwaffe attacks had increased in intensity by this time, so much so that often crews were asked to double their shift time. Six hours on call was often the case and it was this situation that prevailed at the time Riwai and Clark were lost.

Despite the proximity of a minefield around the area of the crash site it was reported that many of the ground-crew rescuers risked their lives in trying to get aid to the stricken crew. Rick Riwai in particular was very well regarded by the squadron, bringing a unique style with his Maori background to those around him. He was a dab hand with the guitar and a talented musician with a ready smile and an infectious humour. He had in fact composed a *Haka* (Maori war dance) dedicated to the squadron and there had been many hilarious moments with him teaching the non-New Zealand aircrew the movements and intricacies of the Haka.

Riwai and his crewman Ian Clark had only joined the squadron in early December. Leslie Hunt spoke fondly of him on his arrival. Hunt was fascinated by Riwai's good humour and it was probably his Maori background that Hunt was intrigued with. Hunt had written in his book *"Defence until Dawn"* the words of the Riwai *"Haka"* phonetically and it looks hilarious to any New Zealander familiar with the Maori language. They were both to be buried in the Brookwood Military Cemetery close to the village of Pirbright in Surrey.

---

[29] *John Wood's background notes courtesy of his son, Piers Wood*
[30] *"Scramble" – A quick call to get airborne and get into position to defend against or apprehend approaching enemy aircraft.*

It was almost a "double" for F/L Peter Hall and F/O Dick Marriott flying Mosquito HK 228 on the night of 24th February, when they attacked a Dornier 217. They had been sent by Control into another sector and had permission to *"Freelance"*. They worked with the searchlight batteries which was common practice for the area. The patrolling aircraft skirted around the darkened perimeter of the searchlight area hoping for a sighting. Once an aircraft was targeted all the adjoining searchlight batteries tried to *"cone"* the target which left it mercilessly exposed to either anti aircraft fire or the attention of a patrolling night-fighter. There was some risk from "friendly" fire for the defending aircraft but advance warning would normally be given to the batteries that an allied aircraft was in the vicinity and care was taken to avoid the chance of shooting down one of their own. Once trapped by the searchlight cone in this manner it was difficult for the targeted aircraft to escape the beams of light despite desperate and high-speed manoeuvres.

One Mosquito pilot described being trapped, on this occasion by German searchlights and trying to outrun the light beams before the anti-aircraft batteries locked onto his aircraft. Despite a high-speed run away from his tormentors he was well and truly locked in and blinded by the dazzling lights which left him mercilessly exposed for all to see. Ahead of him was a towering cloud also lit up by searchlights; blue in colour but for the moment his only means of escape. He was fascinated to see the tiny silhouette of his own Mosquito which, as he watched it, grew larger and larger and developed wings and drop tanks, a tail fin and cockpit. Then all of a sudden, he whacked into the cloud through the middle of it and away to the obscurity of the cloud cover, thankfully leaving the searchlights behind. [31]

Many of the crewmen spoke of the effect that being trapped by searchlights had on them. Their pilots were obviously busy manoeuvring to remove themselves from the grip of the lights. In some cases, it was a sudden high-speed dive to break out of the blinding light, sometimes a dive of around 10,000 feet was needed under full power to make it difficult for the anti-aircraft gunners to pick off the targeted aircraft. While all this was happening the poor navigator usually found

---

[31] *Comment from Plt.Off. Chris Harrison, an Australian pilot with Night Intruder Squadron 515 based at Little Snoring in the UK. Extract from "The Men who flew the Mosquito" by Martin W. Bowman published by Pen & Sword Aviation.*

himself crouching down in the cockpit as if to escape this intrusion into his personal space. It mattered not that the searchlights emanated from British or German lights, the end result would be the same if the gunners being presented with a well-lit target were up to the mark. Ron Watts commented that when another aircraft was "coned" by the searchlights they were literally like a moth, looking tiny and far away but when the searchlights were on your own aircraft you felt as "big as a bus" and totally exposed and vulnerable.

It was just this scenario that presented itself to the crew of Mosquito HK 288 except it was an enemy aircraft this time. Hall and Marriott took the opportunity, with the Dornier trapped in the searchlight beams and with their first pass riddled the fuselage and the port side engine. Smoke poured from the Dornier but when HK 228 came in for a second run the Dornier had disappeared and was not sighted again. There was much disappointment but Hall and Marriott were granted a *"Probable"*. HK 228 resumed its perimeter patrol and the crew were rewarded with the sight again of a He177 "Greif" Bomber caught in the lights. Peter Hall came in from dead astern and hit the German bomber with three short bursts and had the satisfaction of seeing it breaking up as it went into a steep dive into the ground near Wadhurst.

(10) 24/02/1944 - *Unknown - Ex Bradwell - Hall and Marriott — Ju 188 – East of Wadhurst*

The He 177 was from A3 /KG Groupe and was one of eight of the Groupe shot that night over that sector. [32]

On 10th March F/Sgt. Anderson, a trainee pilot crashed and was killed flying Mosquito HK 461. He was on his second only solo flight at Bradwell and swung on landing, hitting a hedge attempting an overshoot and lost control desperately trying to get his aircraft airborne under full power. He never got the chance to fly operationally against the enemy. [33] The official report on the accident was critical of the circumstances of his death as he had only had experience with Beaufighters and had only just arrived from his Operational training unit three days before his tragic flight.

---

[32] *Martin Bowman notes that this aircraft was recorded as a He 177 "Greif" bomber but 488 Squadron lists this as a Do 217. Peter Hall was not too sure with his identification in his Combat Report.*
[33] *Details from the De Havilland Official accident register*

S/L Nigel Bunting and crewman F/L Phil Reed flying Mosquito MM 476 picked up their first success with 488 Squadron on the night of 14th March after sighting one of the newer Ju 188's caught in a searchlight beam near Great Leighs in Essex.

(11) *Leigh*	*14/03/1944 –Unknown time - Ex Bradwell – Bunting and Reed – Ju188 E – Great*

These aircraft were faster and better armed than the older version the Ju 88. They were only 500 metres away from their target which was laying 'window' at the time when they got visual confirmation from dead astern. By the time, they set up for an attack they had closed to less than 200 metres and it only took a short burst to send what would have been a very surprised Ju 188 crew to their destruction into the fields of White House Farm, Great Leighs, near Chelmsford.

The demise of this particular aircraft, U5+BM, a Ju 188E-1 of Luftwaffe unit 4 Staffel / Kampfgeschwader 6 was well documented with the crew members and their aircraft being photographed just before they left on what would turn out to be their last ever bombing run. None of the five on board survived. The aircraft was piloted by Leutnant Horst Becker and his crew were Unteroffizier's G. Bartolain, A. Lange, G. Goecking and Oberfeldwebel H. Litschke. All five are still buried in the German section of Cannock Chase cemetery in Staffordshire. [34]

Bunting had a huge amount of experience with many types of aircraft including a brief sojourn on a specially adapted Mosquito, one of three designed to counter a series of very high-altitude bombing raids by German bombers. Bunting reached 44,600 feet on one occasion which is a height rarely reached even by today's aircraft. The experiment was short lived however as the Germans did not persevere with the high-altitude program.

The funeral of F/Sgt. Anderson was held on the 15th March and he was buried with full military honours at Brookwood Cemetery. On the 19th March, F/O Douglas Robinson thought he was about to join F/Sgt. Anderson when local Allied anti-aircraft gunners opened fire on him whilst he was on the tail of an enemy aircraft. He was forced to break off his attack due to the *"unwelcome interference"* of the gunners when

---

[34] *Information on the Ju 188E-1 shot down over Great Leighs was obtained from Martin W. Bowman in his book "The Men who flew the Mosquito" published by Pen & Sword Books.*

he was close enough to bring the enemy aircraft down. He was reported as being very unhappy at his treatment.

P/O. Terry Clark left the squadron on the day of Anderson's funeral for a six-month break from operational flying. He comments in his memoir that the impact of the death of his long-standing pilot friend, Dudley Hobbis had a greater effect on him than he first realised [35] He readily acknowledged the great support he got from F/O Douglas Robinson, whom he partnered following the death of Dudley Hobbis but he never ever got over the loss.

The Germans had resumed bombing over the UK with renewed intensity with a new campaign they called *"Steinbock"*, the so called *"Baby Blitz"*. The first of four hundred and forty-seven bombing attacks over London had started earlier in the year on 22nd January 1944 with some success for 488 although the squadron was not actively involved until the night of the 21st March.

A large German bomber force of over ninety-five aircraft attacked London on the night of 21st March being plotted coming in from the Dutch coast. One of the main targets for this raid was the Marconi works at Chelmsford. Five of those aircraft were brought down over land by 488 Squadron in one of their more successful nights. The Luftwaffe, as a reprisal for the RAF's earlier attack on the Philip's Eindhoven factories in Holland had decided to wipe out the Chelmsford factories of Marconi. Marconi were major producers of radio and Radar components vital to the Allied war effort. Part of the Luftwaffe planning for this raid was the construction of a scale model of the Chelmsford plant which was found by an RAF officer on a Luftwaffe air base after the end of the war and returned and presented to Marconi to be placed in the factory showroom in Chelmsford. [36]

This was a well-planned raid but the German "pathfinder" section of the attacking force ran into 488 Squadron and their comrades from 410 Squadron on patrol over the area. F/Sgt. Chris Vlotman and Sgt. Johnny Wood flying Mosquito HK 365 destroyed the two-leading aircraft, the first a Ju 188, 3E+GS of 8 Staffel KG6 flown by Oberleutnant H. Diblik. Two of the crew were killed but one baled out and was captured on the ground. The second aircraft dealt to by Vlotman and Wood was a Ju 88 of 11 / KG54 Gruppe.

---

[35] *Comments from "Five of the Few" authored by Steve Darlow.*
[36] *Sourced from the Marconi staff magazine.*

| **(12)** | 22/03/1944 – 00:24 hrs – Ex Bradwell Bay – Vlotman and Wood – Ju 88 – English Channel |

| **(13)** | 22/03/1944 – 00:55 hrs – Ex Bradwell Bay – Vlotman and Wood – Ju 88 – English Channel |

One of these two aircraft was the pathfinder leader of the bombing raid. This was a very significant blow by Vlotman and Woods as it completely negated the intent of the Luftwaffe attack and so saved many lives of the Marconi workers.

This feat and the resulting publicity started a special relationship between Marconi and 488 Squadron and this was emphasised a great deal by one of the Marconi workers writing to Chris Vlotman some twenty years after the war and thanking him and Johnny Woods for saving his life and that of many of his workmates. What better tribute could you get from those whose lives the night fighter squadrons were delegated to defend.

The text unabridged as written:

21/01/1964

Dear Captain Vlotman,

Please forgive me for what may be a trouble to you, but I have just seen in my RAF Association Journal "Airmail", that you may have saved my life or even worse. My wife and son Christopher also say thanks to you and John Wood.

I and three more RAF chaps had the job of patrolling Marconi works for a long time, and I must have been on duty that night. Two of the four chaps lost their lives later. I do not know what happened to the other one but we had some rough times there.

I read the account of the battle you had with the Dornier. My wife loves her garden and says she thinks the tulips in Holland are a rare sight, we have seen them on TV. Christopher likes the windmills, wish (es) he had one at the top of our small garden, just about cover it I think. We have a Festival here at a park in Birmingham, we go every year, all Dutch clogs, small windmills etc, its grand. It gives no details of your civy life in the story, not that you would want it I bet. Anyway, Sir my family send there best wishes to your

family. If you ever see your old pal John Wood thank him from us. Sorry about the writing. Just bent a rib at work. You may not like me writing you, but I often wondered what went on that night at Marconi.
    God Bless. Look after yourself   C. Turner

The attack was not without considerable risk to the lives of the 488 crew, as wreckage from the second of the doomed aircraft struck HK 365, damaging one engine and forced Vlotman to land his aircraft on one engine. He ended up with pieces of fuselage and perspex imbedded in his port side radiator. That outcome was not surprising as Vlotman reported that he was within fifty metres of his target when he opened fire. He had problems due to the slow airspeed of the Ju 88 and it must have taken some skills to maintain contact when travelling at well under the stalling speed of a Mosquito. The radar work of Johnny Wood must have been exceptional as both enemy aircraft were dropping copious amounts of "Window" so the visuals obtained on the AI set would have taken a fair amount of sorting out given the bad signals resulting from the interference usually caused by the "Window".

S/L Nigel Bunting with crewman F/L Phil Reed in Mosquito MM 476 destroyed two further bombers just twenty minutes later, a Ju 88 which crashed into a field at Blacklands Hall north of Cavendish, and a Ju 188 which went down on Butler's Farm, Rochford in Essex both in the early hours of the morning of the 22nd March.

(14) *22/03/1944 – 00:41 hrs – Ex Bradwell Bay - Bunting and Reed Ju 88 – Nth of Cavendish*

The second Junkers brought down by Nigel Bunting was one of the new Ju 188E-1 bombers, 3E+BK from 2. /KG6 Staffel. Only one of the crew of Buntings second victim survived, Uffz. E. Kosch baled out but Lt. G. Lahl, the pilot and Uffz. J. Fromm, Obergefr. E. Schiml and Uffz. R. Budrat were all killed.

(15) *22/03/1944 – 01:06 – Ex Bradwell - Bunting and Reed – Ju 188 – Butlers Farm, Rochford*

The first of the two despatched by S/L Nigel Bunting with F/L Phil Reed as his crewman, a Junkers Ju 88A-4 from 9/KG30 flown from

Varelbusch by Oberfeldwebel Nickolaus Mayer, was picked out by searchlights and despite some desperate manoeuvring and dumping of lots of *window*, Bunting hit it with two bursts of 20mm cannon fire [37]. The Ju 88 rolled over into an inverted dive and exploded on impact just to the north of Cavendish at 12:45 am. An RAF intelligence team inspected the site and reported that the engine and fuselage were buried in a crater over four metres deep. The pilot, Obfw. Mayer and radio operator Obfw Szyska did not survive. Szyska's parachute did not open. Fw. Maser the observer and Fw. Elmshorst, a crewman, both bailed out safely and were captured. Karl-Heinz Elmhorst remembered baling out well before impact as he had time to take his pistol from its holster and strip it before throwing the parts all over so that it could not be used against him when he faced inevitable capture.

Chelmsford locals reported that the body of one of the crew was found lying in a field at the junction of Flax Lane and Hobbs Lane. He was buried in Chelmsford churchyard and his body taken back to Germany after the war. A piece of the wing section was found in a meadow on Claypits Farm in Foxearth over five kilometres away. One of the German aircrew that did survive was literally blown out of his aircraft and captured by the Southminster police. The writer of the Marconi article helped to hold him as 488 Squadron's doctor at the time, F/O Rowbotham, stitched a gash in his face where the jagged fuselage had caught him as the bomber disintegrated in mid-air. Bunting and Reed resumed patrolling after this success and twenty-five minutes later scored their other kill, the Ju 188 over southern Essex as recounted earlier.

This second aircraft, the Ju 188E piloted by Leutnant G. Lahl caused Bunting a bit more bother. He was closing on it at high speed when they were coned by searchlights. They managed to radio Control and got the light doused but Lahl and his crew has obviously spotted them. The Junkers began very violent evasive action at quite a low speed, so much so that Bunting almost undershot him. The enemy aircraft made a hard port turn but the mosquito managed to stay inside his turn then Lahl made a sudden climbing turn to starboard and Reed lost him on his AI set. They picked the Junkers up again on their scope and followed them through a series of high speed twists and turns until Bunting was able to get in close behind him. He pumped a series of short bursts into the Ju

---

[37] *The account of the Cavendish crash was supplied by Jeff Carless of the East Anglican Aircraft Research Group*

188E until it suddenly dived and went into the ground with a large explosion near Butlers Farm in Essex. Surprisingly one of the Junkers crew survived by baling out during the dogfight but the rest of the crew died on impact.

There was a sequel to these events when an aviation historical society was informed in 1990 by a local farmer that after he attained ownership of the farm that he was told that there was a buried German bomber in one of his fields. Excavations were subsequently made and some artefacts were found including a Ju 88's engine, a main wheel tyre and some smaller personal items, including a shaving kit and a lens from a small Kodak camera.

F/L Johnny Hall with F/O Jock Cairns in HK 380 completed the successful night by bringing down another Ju 88 onto the American Airfield at Earls Colne in Essex, the fifth success for the night for the squadron.

(16) *22/03/1944 - 22:45 to 01:48 hrs – Ex Bradwell – Hall and Cairns – Ju88 – Earls Colne, Essex*

The Ju88A-14 of 8/KG6 had earlier taken of from Melsbroek in Belgium. The Americans were reported as being not too pleased as the stricken Ju 88 dropped among some parked Mitchell bombers exploding its 500kg bomb. The 323rd Bomb Group of the US 9th Air Force lost three of their B-26 Marauder Bombers. The combat was watched with interest by F/O Harold Longley and F/O Moore who were on patrol in the area at the time and their eye witness accounts helped with confirmation of the "kill"

The successes of the night of the 21st March and the early morning hours of the 22nd put 488 Squadron right up there with the best in the defence of Britain. Eleven of the Luftwaffe attacking force did not return and five of these were victims of the 488 Squadron defence. They and their fellow Mosquito nightfighter squadrons had caused that much devastation among the Luftwaffe over the past few weeks that they were forced to rethink their night time bombing raids due to the losses of the cream of their fliers.

The next morning the squadron was visited by the top brass including the Air Officer Commanding, Air Defence of Great Britain, Air Marshall Sir Roderic Hill and the A.O.C. of No.85 Group, Air Vice Marshall Cole-Hamilton. The latter stayed on to discuss the proposed involvement of 488 Squadron in the planned invasion of Europe. There was tremendous publicity following the day's events with Press photographers taking the opportunity of capturing the crash scene at Cavendish with some of the participants and Air Marshall Sir Roderic Hill. Chris Vlotman unfortunately was unable to share in some of the public celebrations due to the restriction on his identity being known because of the potential risk to his family who were still living behind enemy lines in Holland. Johnny Wood was photographed without his pilot being present.

The terrible pattern of success followed closely by tragedy for the squadron struck again on 24th March when the two Wilson's, both New Zealanders, F/O Chris Wilson and his crewman, F/O "Kiwi" Wilson flying in HK 222 were lost. Their aircraft disappeared into the English Channel just after they had reported an interception and neither they nor their aircraft were ever seen again.

The squadron was joined by two American night fighter crews for a short stay of around ten days. The opportunity was taken to introduce them to the Kiwi way of doing things so it must have been somewhat of a jolt to their systems. The nearest American night-fighter squadrons were equipped with P41 Black Widow night fighters, one of which later figured in a nasty incident with one of our aircraft piloted by the squadron C.O. Wng.Comm Dickie Haine.

On the 30th March 1944, the squadron had a visit from the New Zealand Deputy Prime Minister, Mr. Walter Nash together with the Air Officer Commanding Royal New Zealand Air Force, Air Vice Marshall Isitt.

There were significant changes to the squadron living arrangements on the 8th of April when the personnel were moved from their accommodation into tents. Jock Cairns had found the entire process very amusing. He and all his fellow officers had earlier been issued with "Officers camp rolls" which contained a complete ensemble of canvas goods – a portable camp bed, bucket, wash bowl, bath and chair. These were all canvas with, as he put it, *"complicated metal and timber frames"*. The bed was rolled up after inserting all the bits and pieces in it and tied together with a leather strap and handle. It weighed a ton he said. Cairns claims he was told that the gear was designed for the Boer War and had never been updated! He said he was not surprised.

The equipment issue had earlier caused much hilarity among the crew members but the laughing soon stopped when a huge tented camp was erected not far from their existing quarters and it became obvious to them that they were about to be moved into less salubrious accommodation. In fact, there already had been subtle changes to the squadron procedures which seemed to have been brought about by those in command, to create a culture within the squadron to prepare the men for a degree of independence from the squadron collective. This was part of the planning for the squadron shift to the Frontline in Europe although that was to be many weeks away. There was obviously recognition that being operational close to the scene of the ground fighting meant individual aircraft being scattered defensively over a wider area and consequently losing the support from those around them.

There was an attempt to foster independence by having the crew, both air-crew and ground-crew formed as combined teams or operational units. For the first time, ever, air-crew carried out refuelling, re-arming and maintenance under the supervision of the ground-crew. They shared in basic defence work on the ground, handling small arms and generally sought to create small independent units based around each individual aircraft. The program was greeted by much hilarity initially but a new respect from one to the other was developed and made 488 Squadron a very close-knit team. The weather unfortunately was not great and the accommodation proved to be grossly inadequate due to the incessant rain and the tented site eventually became sodden with a sea of mud.

They were sharing tents; three to a tent and all the eating and cooking was done in large marquees. Baths were allowed only once a week and 'Jock' Cairns was highly amused with all the officers having to carry revolvers in holsters at all times.

The early morning hours of 19th April proved to be a busy one with successful interventions and an amusing interlude. F/L Johnny Hall and F/O Jock Cairns had a further success with MM 551 by shooting down a Ju 88.

(17) *19/04/1944 – 01:11 hrs – Ex Bradwell Bay – Hall and Cairns – Ju 88 – Off Belgium Coast*

The Controller at Trimley Heath put them onto a stream of raiders heading towards London intent on bombing. They intercepted one of a bunch of aircraft flying well below them. When Hall made his attack at high speed the Ju 88 immediately turned around doing a *"runner"* and headed back over the channel towards the Belgium coast jinking from side to side with MM 551 hot on its tail. Hall closed in to 250 metres and gave it a three second burst from his cannon which turned the enemy aircraft on to its starboard side and it dived into the sea with flaming pieces of the fuselage flying off it. A Canadian pilot from 410 Squadron was able to confirm the destruction.

W/O Rod Bourke and F/O Irwin Skudder on the same patrol had their first kill by destroying another Ju 88 from the same Luftwafe attacking group. They only expended twenty shells from each cannon in what was a textbook from behind attack.

(18) *19/04/1944 – 01:48 hrs – Ex Bradwell – Bourke and Skudder – Ju 88 – SE of Trimley Heath*

They followed this up with two further chases that night without success. They had a couple of firsts being the first New Zealand NCO pilot to shoot down an enemy aircraft and also the first all New Zealand crew to taste success.

Irwin Skudder was a Northland boy, joining the RNZAF in July 1942 and 488 Squadron was his first operational posting. Skudder was awarded a "Mention in Despatches" earned for his good work with 488.

The visibility issue at Bradwell Bay was never more apparent when the patrols returning from the night's operations were followed in by what was thought to one of the squadron's returning aircraft. However, this turned out to be a damaged German Ju 88 bomber which crash landed on the Bradwell Bay runway with the crew bizarrely claiming they thought they were over Holland. The account of this incident makes hilarious reading.

488 Squadron's Commanding Officer at that time, W/C Dickie Haine had just landed from a patrol and was concerned to see an aircraft he thought was one of his returning Mosquitos slithering down the flare path on its belly behind him. He leapt into a jeep and travelled at high speed towards the now stationary aircraft. His concern changed to surprise when the figures that emerged from the fog shrouded aircraft were found to be German. An ambulance arrived right behind him and the Wing Commander bundled the German airmen into the back along with his crewman, Pete Bowman and told the driver to take them to the station guardroom. He remembers suddenly being concerned for the

well being of Pete Bowman after the ambulance had departed but fortunately no harm came to him.

The four-man German crew led by Unteroffizier H. Brandt from 3/KG54 explained later that their compass and port engine had been knocked out by flak over London and the partially lit airfield at Bradwell Bay was the first airfield they had come across after ninety minutes of flying, and thinking they were over Holland made the decision to force land. They were apparently as surprised as the personnel at Bradwell at the outcome of their arrival. There was some scepticism though among the Bradwell crew as the war effort was not going so well for Germany at the time and this was possibly a way out for a bunch of disillusioned aviators. The arrest of the crew was made on the spot by W/C Haine but that was the only credit he got. His claim for one Ju 88 – *Captured* was not allowed by Air Operations in his personal tally! [38]

Two aircraft of "A" Flight carried out an unusual task on 22nd April when they were sent to provide "top" cover for a Walrus air-sea rescue flying boat that had picked up large numbers of American bombers aircrew who had ditched their aircraft off the coast. The Walrus was completely overloaded and as such unable to get airborne safely. The pilot wisely decided to taxi his aircraft into the nearest coastal port rather than take the risk of trying to get airborne in an overloaded condition.

On 3rd May an advance ground-crew party from 488 Squadron left Bradwell Bay lead by F/Sgt. Abrahams for their new base at RAF Zeals in Wiltshire, followed the next day by "B" Flight aircrew. The road party convoy totalled some fifty-eight vehicles which gives some idea of the logistics of transferring a squadron and its equipment to a new site. It proceeded not without incident when one of the vehicles overturned just outside Salisbury and put three of its occupants in hospital albeit with minor injuries.

On the 5th May "A" Flight were sent on to RAF Colerne after W/C Haine had flown down to Zeals with Pete Bowman and found the facilities there unfinished and not yet ready for them. "B" Flight were redirected over to Colerne in the evening with "A" Flight returning to stay on at Bradwell Bay. The convoy of vehicles remained at Zeals overnight and moved on to Colerne the next morning. A tented camp

---

[38] This Bradwell Bay Ju 88 account is from *Mosquito Aces of World War 2* by Andrew Thomas and also the personal memoirs of "Dickie" Haine.

had been set up for them on the eastern side of Colerne airfield. Fortunately, their tented stay was not too long and when the facilities improved they joined the rest of the squadron at Zeals on 11th May.

In the early hours of the morning of 6th May 1944, W/O Reg Mitchell with his crewman, Ron Ballard were sent from their temporary base at Colerne on a special mission codenamed *GCI Longload* accompanied by F/L *"Jamie"* Jameson. The two were briefed to fly their Mosquitos from Cherbourg to Dieppe over northern France at varying heights and speeds so that seaborne ground control radar interception stations could be set up to provide early warning of any enemy aircraft approaching the English coast. This information would have been vital for Air Operations to pre-empt any chance that the German Luftwaffe might sight the concentrations of troops and equipment being assembled on the coast for the planned invasion of Europe.

Above: Flying Officers, Ken Bishop, Douglas Bergemann and Harold Longley on the runway at Bradwell Bay with the "Fido" fog dispersal system burning alongside the runway in the background. (Reg Mitchell) Below: Two of the key men of the 6488 Echelon ground crew servicing unit, F/L "Monty" Norman on the left with Sgt. Bill Howarth (Ron Watts)

Above left: W/C Peter Hoare Hamley AFC. 488 Squadron's fourth Commanding Officer 3rd September 1943 to 31st December 1943. Right: 'Bruce' the larger of the two Squadron mascots pictured with F/L Neil Knox RNZAF & F/L Keith Fleming RNZAF (Reg Mitchell). Below: W/O Dick. Addison DFC, DFM and F/L Bill Cook (from Defence until Dawn)

488 Squadron aircrew at Bradwell Bay January 1944 (From the Reg Mitchell collection)

Back Row: *Edwards, Watson, Prescott, Marshall, Mitchell, Church, Hunt, Bale, Richardson, Pickthall, Linstead, Hardern, Concannon, Patrick, Green, Sommerville, Rowbotham*
Second Row: *Procter, Clarke, Clark, Broodbank, Bishop, Moore, Earl, Folley, Davies, Bowman, Reed, Crookes, Ryan, Skudder, Nagle, Warner, Riley*
Front Row: *Hughs, Riwai, Robinson, Scott, Bergemann, Westcott, Watts, Haine, Bunting, Jameson, Knox, Wilson, Fleming, McCabe,*
In Front: *Bruce and Becky*

A Heinkel HE 111, the type of Luftwaffe bomber that Jimmy Gunn and Jock Affleck destroyed but lost their lives in doing so.

165

Above: A daytime view of what most attacking night fighter pilots would see moments before firing into the target – in this case a Dornier 217 Bomber, the same type of aircraft downed by Ron Watts and Roger Folley. Below: The Ju 188 – Not the most glamorous of aircraft but much faster and more heavily armed than its predecessor, the Ju 88 fighter bomber.

A somewhat faded but unique photograph, showing a photograph of Jimmy Gunn on the left, together with Ron Watts shortly before the events of 15th September 1943. The photo was taken by a member of the 488 Squadron ground-crew during a lightning storm over Bradwell Bay. The shutter was left open and the exposure was lit by a burst of lightning. (Ron Watts photo) Below left: F/O Leslie Hunt 488 Squadron Intelligence Officer 28/12/1943 to 10/05/1944, and author of 'Defence until Dawn' (from Defence until Dawn). Right: F/O Jock Kemp and F/L Cecil Ball (from Defence until Dawn).

Above: A Mosquito N.F. Mk. 30 ready for flight with ground-crew pulling on toggles to remove the wheel chocks. Note the extended nose cone enclosing the AI Radar unit. (Philip Birtles). Below: Aerial view of the base at Bradwell Bay with the Blackwater Estuary top left-hand corner (from Defence until Dawn).

F/L N.M. (Knocker) Knox RNZAF & F/L T.P. (Buck) Ryan RNZAF (Reg Mitchell).

F/O James Affleck on the right standing alongside his pilot F/L Jimmy Gunn in this group photograph. (ex Mike McBey from Adam Forrest).

F/L Harold Watson Longley DFC RNZAF (Dharan & Brett Longley).

F/O Terry Clark DFM at 90 years of age at a memorial service at York Minster (Matt Clark).

Above: A Me 410A fighter bomber, whose speed and manoeuvrability was sometimes more than a match for a pursuing Mosquito. Below: Fw Friedrich Hess (left), the pilot of U5+AJ, a Me 410 bomber which failed to return after being shot down by F/L Douglas Bergemann (right) and Ken Bishop on the night of 2nd January 1944 (photo of F/L Bergemann c/o Ted Edwards).

488 SQUADRON.   INTELLIGENCE FORM "F" AND   SECRET
                PERSONAL COMBAT REPORT.

From:- R.A.F. Station, Bradwell Bay.   Serial 488/7

To:-   A.D.G.B.(2), H.Q. 11 Group (2), North Weald, Trimley, Sandwich.

STATISTICAL.

DATE.   (A) 20th December, 1943.
UNIT.   (B) 488 (N.Z.) SQUADRON.
TYPE AND MARK OF OUR AIRCRAFT.   (C) MOSQUITO XIII. AI Mk VIII.
TIME ATTACK WAS DELIVERED.   (D) 0240 hrs 20/12/43.
PLACE OF ATTACK.   (E) Near RYE, Sussex.
WEATHER.   (F) Good. Half Moon. Excellent Vis.
OUR CASUALTIES. AIRCRAFT.   (G) NIL.
OUR CASUALTIES. PERSONNEL.   (H) NIL.
ENEMY CASUALTIES IN AIR COMBAT.   (J) One ME 410 DESTROYED.
ENEMY CASUALTIES GROUND OR SEA TARGET. (K) NIL.

PILOT.   P/O D.N.ROBINSON. (NZ)   NAV/R. P/O W.T.L. CLARK RPM.

One Mosquito XIII, AI Mk VIII, airborne 0005 hours landed Bradwell Bay 0310 patrolling under Trimley Heath G.C.I. control was warned of possible activity and ordered to climb to 15,000 feet, being taken over by Sandwich G.C.I. (Controller F/Lt KIRBY). Pilot was given several vectors but was unable to make contact with a bandit so was then given vectors on to another e/a, climbing to 21,000 feet. A contact was obtained at twelve o'clock, range 2 miles with the e/a well above so Pilot climbed to 25,000 feet and obtained a visual on an ME 410, 2000 feet ahead and slightly below. Speed of e/a approx 300 mph.
Pilot closed to 250 yards and opened fire with a 2/3 second burst but owing to vapour trails no strikes were seen. The e/a took violent evasive action, climbing and diving in tight turns but the searchlights illuminated and held the e/a and our Pilot plainly saw the black crosses on the wings. A second attack was made from 150 yards closing to 100 yards, several short bursts during which strikes were seen on the port engine and fuselage a red glow appearing from the engine. Inaccurate tracer from the barbettes was passing above our aircraft and Pilot made his third attack from 100 yards with a 2 second burst and pieces flew off the e/a which then did steep port turn and dived towards the ground. The visual was temporarily lost but the aircraft was soon to hit the ground and explode shortly afterwards.
Pilot states that prior to first attack he was above and starboard of e/a and to escape illumination and possible sighting by e/a he did very steep turn to port, thus bringing himself just above and slightly to port of the ME 410 which was well held by searchlights from the port beam and he feels his first attack was made before the e/a knew our fighter was in the vicinity.

AMMUNITION. 174 rounds each Cannon SAI/HE equal. No stoppages.
CINE GUN.   (i) Yes. (ii) 0-15 degrees. (iii) One Ring (iv) 300 mph.

Pilot Officer.   Flying Officer,
"A" Flight,   Intelligence Officer,
488(N.Z.)Squadron.   No 488 (N.Z.)Squadron.
R.A.F. STATION.   R.A.F. STATION.
BRADWELL BAY.   BRADWELL BAY.

Original copy of Combat Report of the Robinson / Clark action in the early morning hours of 20th December 1943 (Terry Clark).

Reg Mitchell on right with fellow pilot and good mate Joe Buddle (Reg Mitchell).

Reg Mitchell and the inimitable Wally Green (Reg Mitchell).

R.A.F. STATION, BRADWELL BAY, AIRMEN'S MESS.

The Commanding Officer and Officers wish you all A Happy Christmas.

Christmas 1943.

MENU.

Tomato Soup

Roast Turkey
Stuffing, Sausage,
Bread Sauce

Brussels Sprouts
Potatoes, Roast and Creamed

Christmas Pudding
Rum Sauce
Mince Pies

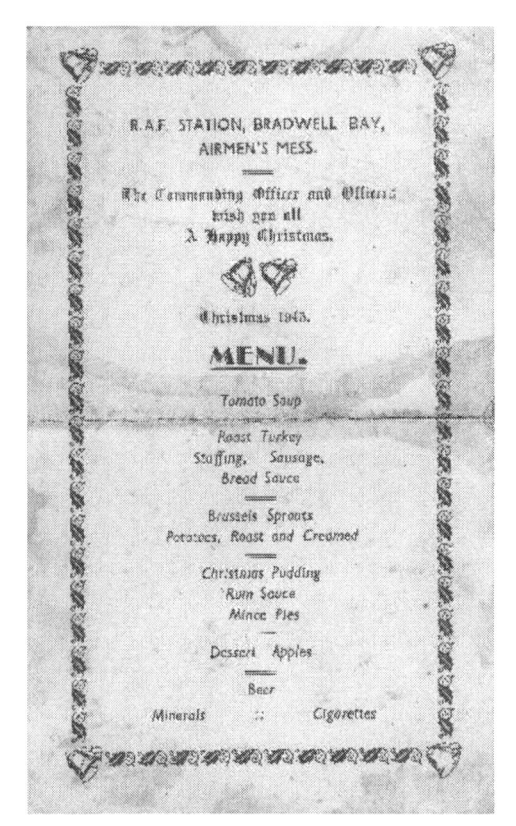

Dessert Apples

Beer

Minerals :: Cigarettes

Christmas Day 1943 at Bradwell Bay. It was autographed on the back by R. Gager, J.G. Knott, L. Whittikar, H. Seaward, G.S. Barker, W. Hawke, C.J. Vaughan, and Smithy J.C (Alastair Gager)

F/O Richard (Rick) Tohunga Riwai, RNZAF. He was killed aged 25 on 21/02/1944 (from Defence until Dawn).

F/O Irwin Skudder RNZAF (Ted Edwards).

W/C R.C. "Dickie" Haine DFC 488 Squadron's fifth Commanding Officer, 2nd January 1944 to 30th October 1944.

F/O Andrew J. Broodbank (Navigator) known as "Broody" An interesting photograph that gives some idea of the equipment worn by aircrew on operational flights (Adam Forrest).

Flt. Sgt. William Breithaupt DFC RCAF

F/O Jack Scott RNZAF who teamed up with F/O Andrew Broodbank when Broody's regular pilot, the squadron C.O. W/C Peter Hamley was posted on to a new command. (Adam Forrest).

Above: Three Mosquito FB VIs in formation photographed on 29th February 1944 (from Mosquito Aces of World War 2). Below: One of the 488 Squadron Mosquitos warming up at Bradwell Bay (Ron Watts).

The five-member crew of a Ju 188 Luftwaffe bomber prepare for a bombing raid over London as part of Operation "Steinbock"

The Ju 188E-1 shot down by Bunting and Reed over Great Leighs at White House Farm near Chelmsford in Essex (Air Crew Remembrance Society Web Site).

Another view of a Ju 188 – Note the distinctive long tapering wings which assisted the Allied pilots with identification of the type (Reg Mitchell).

The Heinkel "Greif" 177 heavy bomber that struggled to even stay in the air during the attacks on London.

The workhorse of the Luftwaffe - the Junkers Ju 88 fighter bomber.

Above: The Ju 88 crew of B3+AP shot down by John Hall and Jock Cairns pictured just before take-off on their last mission. They are from left, Jehle, Kuhnert, Hellwig & Flossmann. Below: A newspaper article commemorates the pair's success (from John Hall: A Memoir, by Alison Fenton).

Above: F/L Peter Hall, F/O John Bolingbroke (Head of Squadron Radar Unit) and F/O Dick Marriott (Ron Watts). Below: F/L T.P. (Buck) Ryan DFC RNZAF & Frank Wynn RNZAF (Reg Mitchell).

F/Sgt. Christiaan Vlotman on left with his crewman, Sgt. John Wood all smiles after their fourth success (Piers Wood).

Telling it how it was "A" Flight Commander, S/L Johnny Gard'ner on far right (New Zealand Fighter Pilots Museum).

Above: The original Marconi letter sent to Chris Vlotman in 1966 (Mrs. Ann MacPherson). Below: Photograph taken in 1970 showing Chris Vlotman DFC & Netherlands War Cross, on left inspecting the Luftwaffe model of the Marconi Factory, with Mrs. Vlotman and Leslie Hunt, 488 Squadron's wartime Intelligence Officer, together with the Managing Director of Marconi and the editor of the Marconi Staff Magazine (Marconi).

Mosquito HK137 ME-0 of 488 Squadron (Piers Wood).

Some disconsolate American officers inspecting damage from a Ju 88 brought down onto their base by Hall and Cairns (from "Owls and Fools Fly at Night" by Jock Cairns)

Above: The crew of the ill-fated Ju 88 downed by Bunting and Reed shown standing in front of their aircraft prior to the air raid that was to be their last. From left, Elmhorst (Gunner), Mayer (Pilot), Szyska (Wireless Operator), Maser (Observer). Below: S/L Nigel Bunting points to the impact crater made by the Ju 88 that he and F/L Phil Reed destroyed over Cavendish - F/L Phil Reed behind him, F/L John Hall, then Air Marshall Sir Roderick Hill with hands on hips, Wng.Comm Dickie Haine to the right of Hill, then Sgt. Johnny Wood, Chris Vlotman's crewman. (Piers Wood).

Happy Campers! - They certainly don't look like they are enjoying the experience (or should that be experiment?) Below: The tented site at Bradwell Bay (both Reg Mitchell).

HK 228 ME-C, normally the aircraft of Peter Hall and Dick Marriott, is hooked up with accumulator trolley and ready to go (Reg Mitchell).

F/L Johnny Hall and his crewman, F/O Jock Cairns, one of 488 Squadron's most successful crews.

The Supermarine Walrus Mk 1 that saw service during WW2 saving many lives after Allied airmen had ditched in the channel and the North Sea (Image from "Mission4today.com" Web Site)

ME Y, the Mosquito of Reg Mitchell and Ron Ballard, being set up for a cannon alignment test which involved zeroing in all eight cannons at a point 250 metres from the aircraft nose (Reg Mitchell).

The Ju 88 bomber that arrived unexpectedly at Bradwell Bay (Reg Mitchell).

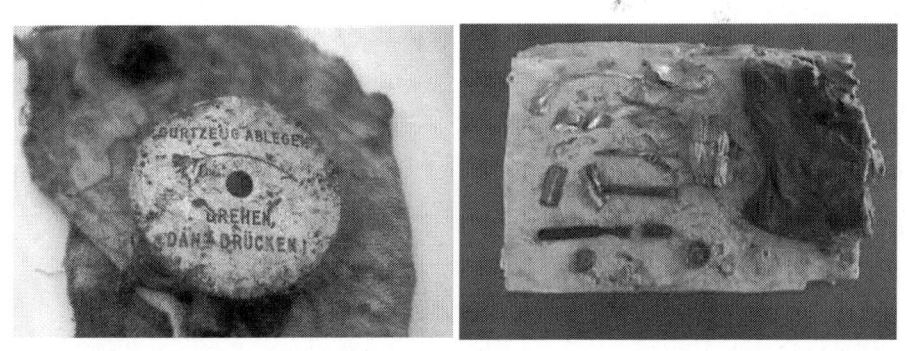

Items recently recovered from the Cavendish crash site – a seat harness buckle and one of the crews shaving kits (From Cavendish Web Site)

Chapter Five

ZEALS - WILTSHIRE, ENGLAND

12TH MAY 1944 TO 29th JULY 1944

By 11th May 488 Squadron were operational, and night flying started from Zeals. The squadron had moved to Zeals, Wiltshire to prepare for D-Day operations. Zeals was a relatively new airfield on the southern edge of the county of Wiltshire just thirty-two kilometres from the ancient site of Stonehenge. The airfield was established by Fighter Command when the Allies went on the offensive and needed forward airfields closer to the south coast of England to attack strategic targets in France. The airfields position meant that fighter aircraft could operate both offensively and defensively without fuel and servicing limitations imposed by leaving from airfields further back from the coast. Reg Mitchell [39] remembers Zeals being *"like a big farm"* due to it being fully grassed with no hard-surfaced runways. The airfield was just to the north of Zeals and was formed with a fully grassed centre with an asphalt perimeter track where the dispersal areas were positioned.

F/O Andrew Broodbank (Broody) also commented on the shortcomings of Zeals. He said that *"one of the worst features was a roadway that ran across the "main runway (which was simply a path outlined in the grass by runway lighting) and tended to break up with aircraft crossing it and throw pieces up at the tail of the aircraft. It was necessary to climb fairly hard to clear a ridge, which was succeeded by a valley notorious for down draughts, before another and higher ridge*

---

[39] *From the memoirs of W/O. Reg Mitchell, later Pilot Officer and written by his son, W.J. (John) Mitchell*

had to be cleared".[40] Not an ideal situation to be faced when trying to get away in good order in the night time hours.

Servicing facilities and admin buildings were dispersed around the countryside near the village. The airfield itself was opened operationally in May 1942 and used variously by fighter squadrons and the American 9th Air force until handed back to RAF Fighter Command on 20th April 1944.

From this airfield 488 Squadron teamed up with a Canadian squadron No. 410 RCAF and flew night patrols in defensive protection for the southern and western districts where the invasion forces for the D-day operations were forming and training. There was a bit of a respite in activities until the night of 14th May when Reg Mitchell and his crewman Ron Ballard (ME-Y) picked up a sighting on their radar and closed to confirm the identity of what turned out to be a Ju 88. Reg opened fire and scored several hits but frustratingly they lost their target before they could finish it off. Almost immediately searchlights fixed onto another target and they quickly zeroed in but just as they lined up to give the second Ju 88 a burst, the target exploded literally in their faces. In the flash of the explosion Reg noticed another Mosquito right on their port wingtip and reluctantly had to confirm a *"destroyed"* and admit to being gazumped by his fellow 488 pilot, F/O Ray Jeffs, with his crewman, Ted Spedding in HK 381 ME-W.

(19) *15/05/1944 – 01:56 hrs – Ex Zeals – Jeffs and Spedding – Ju 88 – NNW of Zeals, UK*

One of the German aircrew was seen to bail out and fortuitously appeared to escape the conflagration. This was an interesting situation as it was the first time on night fighting operations that two aircraft were reported attacking an enemy target simultaneously. Reg still to this day chuckles about it and we can only guess at what would have been the continuing dialogue between the two pilots for many days after. Ray Jeffs Combat Report of the action indicates that he was the "poacher" in this situation as he was being directed at the time to potential trade in another area but came across this bandit caught by searchlights so took the opportunity presented to him at the expense of Reg Mitchell's tally for the night.

---

[40] *From the personal notes of Flg Off. Andrew Broodbank supplied by his grandson, Adam Forrest*

After the successful destruction of the Ju 88 which was from 2/KG6, Jeffs and Spedding were sent by Control into an area over Yeovilton and less than fifteen minutes later came across a Dornier 217 illuminated by searchlights. With the help of his crewman Ted Spedding, contact was maintained until they had closed to within three hundred metres and got a positive identification. Jeffs gave a three second burst and saw strikes on the port wing and engine. The Dornier immediately went into violent evasive action and went into a vertical dive with smoke pouring from the port engine and disappeared from sight under the Mosquito. The doomed aircraft was seen by Jimmy Concannon as he alighted from his Mosquito after landing at Zeals Airfield and he reported seeing it in a vertical dive with smoke pouring from its port engine and held in the beam of a searchlight until it struck the ground to the southwest of Zeals.

There was some uncertainty expressed by Jeffs in his Combat Report as he claimed the Dornier as a *"Probable"* rather than destroyed. Ray Jeffs seemingly had a habit of under reporting as he made a later claim for another *"Damaged"* when partnering Norman Crookes which was proved to be a *"Destroyed"* by a researcher in the late 1990's. In this case, following considerable research it is highly likely that Jeffs had a fair claim to the Dornier being a *"Destroyed"* also.

From Luftwaffe records backed up by local records it would appear that the Dornier had left from its base in France as part of the second wave of bombers heading for their target at Filton Airfield near Bristol. The lead aircraft was one of four that night that were close to their target when attacked by Mosquito Night-fighters. This aircraft, Do 217 K-1, Wk.nr 4410 was flown by Lnt. Johannes Domschke with Uffz. Emil Chmielewski, Uffz. Waldemar Jungke and Uffz. Otto Schott as crewmen. They were carrying four 500lb bombs. The attack from the Mosquito Night-fighter ripped into the fuselage of the Dornier and the crew tried desperately to jettison the bombs. Domschke was hit and died at the controls. The rest of the crew baled out as ordered and spent the rest of the war as prisoners. The Dornier came down at Camel Cross Café, West Camel near Yeovilton in Somerset. The timing of the attack and the linkage with documents from that era almost certainly show Ray Jeffs and Ted Spedding flying HK 381 to have justification for claiming their victim as destroyed. However, the claim was never ratified by Air Operations so that's how it must remain.

It was a busy night for 488 following on from Ray Jeffs success. Johnny Hall and Jock Cairns had a rare *"freelance"* success when they chanced upon a Ju 188 and flew right up underneath it to finally make identification, dropped back to a safe distance and gave it a burst. There was an immediate explosion and they saw the wing mounted bombs in the light of the inferno. It dived straight into the ground and exploded.

> **(20)** *15/05/1944 – Unknown time - Ex Zeals – Hall and Cairns – Ju 188 – Henstock, Somerset, UK*

The German aircraft had dived into the grounds of Inwood House, Temple Combe, near Henstock in Somerset where Cairns wife and young child were living which caused him momentary concern. It was as he said *"a little too close to home"*. There was a sequel to this when information was passed on to the squadron from the Interrogation Officer at Middle Wallop Air Base that two of the crew managed to parachute out after Halls first burst and were taken prisoner. They said that they never saw the Mosquito and thought that they had been attacked from above. The Radio Operator was killed instantly by being shot through the head. They said they were carrying two 2000-pound bombs. The two that survived were Ltn. Gerhard Wentze (F) and Uffz. Karl Fritsch (Kb). Uffz. Hilmar Korf (Bf), Uffz. Karl Hoyer (Bs) and Gefr. Gerhard Buttner (Bs) were all killed.

On the 20th May the new squadron crest was presented to W/C Haine by the Air Officer Commanding 85 Group, Air Vice Marshall Cole-Hamilton. The crest had a somewhat faltering start when its original design was rejected by the Royal College of Heralds. The design incorporated the figure of a Morepork at rest holding in its claws a dead rat with the motto inscribed as *"Ka Ngarue Ratau"*, Maori for *"We shake em"*. The Inspector of badges was not at all happy with the rat figuring prominently on the design so the Crest was only approved with the rat removed. The Morepork, a native owl of New Zealand was certainly appropriate given the squadron's nocturnal activities. A special parade was set up for the presentation following approval of the crest by His Majesty the King.

The author was very privileged to attend a presentation of a squadron crest to the Officers Mess at RNZAF Base Whenuapai shortly before the research was started on this book. The presentation on this occasion was made by Reg Mitchell who spoke of the squadron's history to the assembled officers and related some of his personal experiences during his time with the squadron during the war years.

Even more recently Reg Mitchell and Ray Gager presented copies of the 488 Squadron crests to the Commanding Officer, Group Captain Darryn Webb of the new 488 Wing based at Ohakea Airfield in the central area of the North Island of New Zealand. It was the occasion of the Wing's inaugural parade held on the 8th of December 2010.

On 25th May both F/L Johnny Hall and F/O Jock Cairns were awarded the DFC. F/L Phil Reed and S/L Nigel Bunting were to receive bars to their DFC's, all for their work with 488 Squadron.

On the night of the 29th May there occurred an incident that more than anything brought home the fragility of the nature of the business that 488 Squadron were involved in. The correct identification of any other aircraft encountered during the hours of darkness was vital, and the process was fraught with danger to the defenders. This process involved constant stress as in most cases identification of either friend or foe could only be made by getting close to the target aircraft for visual identification and both "friend" or "foe" were more than capable of shooting first and asking questions later. These crews always lived with the possibility that the aircraft shooting at them could have been a fellow allied aircraft so any aggression on the part of the target did not necessarily mean that they were in fact the enemy. In most cases, they got it right but in this particular incident things went terribly wrong for the 488 crew. It would appear that the victim of an attack by one of the 488 Squadron Mosquitos was a RAF Wellington bomber. What made this incident particularly tragic was the same Mosquito almost certainly went on to shoot down a second Allied bomber that same night, also a Wellington bomber with loss of life although some crew members did survive. This information was first aired publically by English author Andrew Long in his book *"The Faithful Few"* published in 2007 but my research found that he had earlier initiated discussion in August 2006 on an internet forum. It was suggested from other sources that anti-aircraft fire was responsible for the losses but the subsequent court of inquiry found otherwise.

We know that the problem of mis-identification was an ongoing problem despite the electronic identification systems used on most Allied aircraft and the required application of very strict identification procedures, but accidents did happen. It is hard to imagine the despair that this crew must have felt when the realisation of what they had done was revealed to them. They would have been rejoicing at the time at their apparent success but the subsequent ratification process would have confirmed the disastrous consequences of their night's work. It was common knowledge among the night fighter crews that any target aircraft not using their IFF transmitter or Resins (rear facing identification lights) were fair game but anecdotal information from ex 488 Squadron members and any review of official combat reports indicates that all crews without exception, constantly put themselves in great danger by seeking clear visual verification of a potential target above any other method. This entailed moving in close, in some cases alongside or under these intruders to confirm identification. The two-downed aircraft were Wellington bombers, one being flown by a Canadian crew and both crashed with loss of life in the Gillingham area of Dorset, south west of Zeals.

What is known from Air Ministry files is that S/L Nigel Bunting was sent to the Court of Inquiry at RAF Ossington the following day to carry out a "watching brief" on proceedings on behalf of 488 Squadron and that the 488-pilot involved was found to be guilty of "faulty recognition". The Court went on to further state that there were mitigating circumstances for the pilot in that there was no expectation for the 488 crew that Allied bombers would be returning through their designated patrol area. The Court also stated if they had been expected they would possibly have been recognised. The Court went on to say that as both bombers were engaged by searchlights for a considerable period of time it was conceivable that this could give the impression that they were enemy aircraft. It acknowledged also that the 488-pilot stated that he received no response to his IFF interrogation to both aircraft. The Court acknowledged that the Mosquito pilot was very remorseful and did not recommend disciplinary action. The family of one of the deceased Canadian pilots after the war seemed more concerned that the actual details of his death were not given to them but were in the end accepting of the fact that accidents such as these were inevitable given the nature of the work.

It is not my intention to name the 488-crew involved despite the event being part of the history of the squadron. A lot of time has passed since the event and the crew involved remained with the squadron and carried on with their brave work in the night skies over Britain and Europe. It was clear from my research into this incident that it was not an uncommon problem. "Friendly fire" incidents were common place although most seemed to be between ground anti-aircraft defences and aircraft overhead. A good number of ground-based systems were radar directed automatically so any aircraft within range became fair game as the automated guns had no way of differentiating between enemy and friendly targets. Royal Navy ships were particularly singled out for "shoot first, ask questions later" behaviour and were avoided at any cost by our air-crews.

In fact, I received further news of an incident just as this book was going to publication that another 488 crew had been involved in an incident that had serious implications and resulted in the shooting down of another squadron's Beaufighter quite early in the operational time of 488 Squadron. Strangely this incident was not mentioned in the operational diary of the squadron but was highlighted by a correspondent from the reading of the logbook he had obtained of a squadron member. The squadron member was a relative of my informant and it took some courage for this to be revealed.

He carefully considered the impact on his family as he knew of the trauma and anguish expressed by the 488 crew at the time and the ongoing stigma that would have remained with them for the rest of their lives. These as with the earlier crew discussed were very brave young men who continued with unblemished records for the duration of the war. The pilot of the target aircraft managed to bail out but the crewman died in the resulting crash.

The contact was initially picked up on a free-lance patrol. Initial contact was visual but no resins (coded rear facing lights) or IFF responses were forthcoming. The Mosquito crew established contact with Ground Control who considered the target hostile. The visual was considered at length by both crew members in adverse moonlight conditions and it was decided that the target was a Ju 88. They commenced their attack with burst of cannon fire, hitting the port engine and fuselage. The target burst into flame and exploded on contact with the ground.

It is not clear at which point the 488 crew were made aware of their "mistake" but the effect on them both would have been hard to comprehend. The Beaufighter was from a fellow squadron that 488 would work with over their time ahead during the course of the War. A Court of Enquiry launched following the tragedy absolved the 488 crew of any blame but the crew's logbook recorded the Court *"deprecated the lack of Interrogator check"*. The official statement from the Accident Record Card (Air Ministry Form) states that the Court:

"Considers pilot wrongly recognised target and opened fire. NB no IFF seen through IFF on Stud 3. Recognition attempted when A/C flying into moon, windscreen misted. Ground reported A/C hostile. Bullseye (Allied practice bombing raid) with enemy aircraft at same time. Recommend closer GI co-operation. SD158 (Routeing, recognition and identification of aircraft) to be modified. Air Officer Commanding: Pilot's error of judgement not careless. Several (possibly general) rules re opening fire stressed "

My informant commented that he knew his relative who was the crewman on the Mosquito carried a lot of guilt about this incident for the rest of his life, but in his eyes, he understood the reason for this but would have liked to say to him: *"You did your duty and acted properly with the information you had available to you at the time. I understand how this incident came about, and in my eyes, you are no less of the great man that I remember you to be".*

It is clear from my research that *"Friendly Fire"* was not uncommon and has continued on since those early years until the present day. F/L Lewis Brandon had earlier recounted an incident in his memoirs "Night Fighter" written after the War. One of the crews from his squadron at the time, No. 157, returned from a night patrol claiming to have shot down a Ju 88. The rest of the squadron personnel were excited about their success as they were a relatively new crew. Their excitement was somewhat tempered by the fact that one of 157 Squadron's Mosquitos had failed to return. After several days, the squadron received word that the crew of the missing Mosquito had reported in safe and sound after successfully bailing out over Holland. On their return to the squadron some time later it was clear that by comparing notes on times, position, altitude and method of attack, the claimant crew had successfully shot down one of their own squadron aircraft. Brandon noted quite cryptically that the claim for one Ju 88 was quickly withdrawn and the liquor account for the claimants was in the "red" for a very long time.

Ron Watts also had a "friendly fire" incident that was close to disaster for him and his crewman Roger Folley. He arrived back at base with the nose cap from an anti-aircraft shell imbedded under the wing of his aircraft. The cap was embedded in the metal strap carrying the fuel tanks and just an inch either side would have proved disastrous for the crew.

The irony for him was the writing on the fuse cap. It was in English and they were patrolling over the American Sector at the time.

The squadron enjoyed a very close relationship with No. 410 Squadron RCAF which had a large Canadian complement and nowhere was there found any suggestion that the incident over the Wellington bombers caused any friction between them. In fact, there was a fierce rivalry between the two to bring down the most German aircraft and the socialising and partying between the two in stand down times was raucous and loud.

There was very little action in the lead up to D-Day scheduled for 6th June but this was due to the huge defensive effort put up by Air Operations to give the maximum protection to the troops and equipment being assembled on the ground. German aircraft rarely risked crossing the channel so the chance of intercepting enemy aircraft at night was minimal and resulted in very boring non-event patrols. The weather also played its part and seemed to worsen as the date for the invasion of Europe got closer.

The Germans had clearly anticipated invasion and the Luftwaffe tried to step up efforts to disrupt the build up but the Mosquito night fighter squadrons were shifted to bases closer to the south coast of England to provide cover for the invasion forces assembling there and this proved a stunning success. 488 Squadron at this time was under the control of the 2nd TAF number 85 Night fighter Group and they were part of the group known as No. 147 Wing, combined with 604 Squadron, designated to move onto the continent in the wake of the invasion and set up air cover and support for the invading land forces.

On the 4th of June 1944, W/C Haine was summoned to the airfield at Middle Wallop to pick up top secret orders that were to be kept sealed up until authorisation was given for them to be opened. The next day he attended a briefing at the headquarters of No.10 Group followed by a trip to Tangmere where it was announced that the Allied invasion of Europe would take place the very next day. It was clearly spelt out what part each squadron was to play over the beachhead in protection of the invading ground troops.

From the squadron aircrews' point of view, they had little knowledge of what was about to happen over the days ahead. The "D Day" planning had proceeded ahead in deep secret and Andrew Broodbank recalls sitting in their dispersal hut on the evening of 5th June with his pilot F/O Jack Scott and the other duty crews awaiting their call for the night's operations for what they thought would just be a normal night's operation. The first inkling they had that something was up was the arrival of the squadron C.O. W/C. Dickie Haine. He entered the hut closely followed by armed members of the Military Police who proceeded to shut and fasten all the doors and windows and took up position outside.

Broodbank commented in his journal that the crew were a *"trifle inebriated"* at that time as they had attended a lunch earlier in the day put on by the squadron to welcome some New Zealand guests that included Mrs. Fraser, the wife of the New Zealand Prime Minister, Miss Jordan, the daughter of Bill Jordan the New Zealand High Commisioner to Britain and Air Commodore Olsen, the Air Officer Commanding the RNZAF in England. It would have been therefore somewhat of a shock to hear the news that followed from W/C Dickie Haine.

Haine told them that the long-awaited invasion of Europe was to happen that very night. The squadron had been instructed to get two crews in the air to fly a patrol line from the south coast of England to a point close to the tip of the Cherbourg Peninsula in France. The patrols were to maintain radio silence but keep a Radar watch. The patrols would be monitored by a G.C.I. station well to the west and this station would break silence only if a significant attack were to develop and the patrolling aircraft had not spotted it.

Jack Scott and Andrew Broodbank took off from Zeals at 2:30am on June 6th in MM 588 code named ME-E. This was their normal aircraft and had just been returned from Exeter earlier that day after getting a new starboard engine fitted. Scott was from all accounts ecstatic as he had a reputation among the 488 aircrew for taking every opportunity he could to get in the air and amongst the enemy. Broodbank had earlier discussed the criteria for selection for these flights where a strict "pecking" order was established with these duty crews waiting their allocated turn to get airborne. He was somewhat surprised to find his crew selected as the second crew ahead of those who would normally take the first slots. It wasn't until some years later that he realised that the two 488 Squadron aircraft were effectively patrolling the western boundaries of the invasion fleet below them.

Their contribution to the invasion of Europe in the end turned out to be a bit of a fizzer as three and a half hours of steady patrolling yielded nothing from the darkness below and around them. Unlike Reg Mitchell and Ron Ballard who took a later patrol, they only glimpsed activity on the sea 15,000 feet below at the very end of their patrol when daylight was slowly arriving. The pre-dawn light did allow them to see ships below who appeared to be going in circles each time they made a pass overhead and they were amused to think that the poor beggars below assumed they were enemy aircraft and were taking evasive action.

When Scott and Broodbank left their patrol area to return to base they had been in the air for around three hours. They became quite excited when in the restricted light, they encountered what seemed to be a solid carpet of gliders and airborne tugs heading south. They had a problem in that they needed to get below them to reach base without getting involved with their tow ropes or creating problems for the glider pilots with the Mosquito slipstream. [41]

The actual day dawned fine but the weather gradually packed up as time progressed. 488 Squadron was part of a four-night fighter squadron force that kept aircraft in the air constantly from dusk till dawn under very strict ground control conditions. These were monitored from the south coast of England but one control station was part of the main sea going fleet along with the invading forces. W/C Haine was loud in his praise of the squadron members involved and he himself was fully operational being in the air on patrol nearly every night.

Getting radar control stations set up on the ground and close to the Frontline became a priority and the rapid advance of the Allied armies made the task very difficult. Haine flew with ground radar operators close to the Frontline to check out possible sites.

When D-Day finally came, it provided for Reg Mitchell probably the most thrilling event of his long flying career. He was patrolling the Normandy coast in the early hours of 6th June 1944 and *"I had the privilege of what could only be described as the most amazing sight ever witnessed. From our patrol height of 15,000 to 20,000 feet, in the dark with dawn about to break the whole area below was illuminated with gunfire and lit up the sea below. When dawn broke, we could see shipping of all kinds spread over the channel. From a grandstand seat, we had witnessed the opening barrages of the D-Day landings on the Normandy beaches".*

Both Johnny Hall and Jock Cairns were scheduled to take off at 3:00am that morning but they did not have the best of starts. Late in the afternoon of the 5th June they were handed two pails of paint and brushes

---

[41] *Reminiscences from Flg.Off. Andrew Broodbank courtesy of his grandson, Adam Forrest.*

and instructed to paint white stripes on the wings and fuselage of their Mosquito MM 551. Jock Cairns remembered it was raining at the time and commented it was *"damned hard work"*. He said that by the time they had cleaned themselves up and found something to eat it was too late to go to bed. Cairns said they were really fed up at the time as this was work usually done by ground crew and *"that this wouldn't have happened in a RAF squadron, but the New Zealanders were a tough lot, and they didn't differentiate so much between officers and men"*. He did note however that the ground crew were going to be kept at full stretch and needed all the rest they could get. The "invasion stripes" painted on all the allied aircraft operating in the area were essential for indication to the ground-based gunners that these were "friendly" aircraft and not to be shot at although as it later turned out they were no protection at all at night.

As with Reg Mitchell, the Hall / Cairns crew also were spellbound by the spectacle that unfolded below them as the light improved in the early dawn hours as they witnessed the greatest armada of ships that the world had ever seen heading towards the coast of France. There was a so-called safety zone designated for the Allied aircraft to patrol over but the Royal Navy clearly misunderstood as they tried their hardest to shoot down their own aircraft that were endeavouring to protect them from German night bomber attacks. In any event 488 squadron had little to do as the Luftwaffe simply stayed away, effectively fooled by the Allied tactics and it was not until much later on the morning of the 6th June that the Germans belatedly realised that what they were witnessing was just a bit more than an Allied diversionary attack.

The Allied aircraft came under the control of mobile GCI stations in the nights following the invasion. The Luftwaffe eventually filled the skies with large numbers of aircraft in a futile attempt to stop the invasion. 488 Squadron were tasked with protecting the large flights of gliders and tugs that were carrying airborne troops over the beach heads and onto the flat land behind.

The Mosquito patrols were forced to be more mindful of "friendly fire" as the days progressed as excited and apprehensive gunners on the ground were shooting at anything moving in the night sky. W/O Patrick and F/Sgt. Concannon took a burst into their port engine and had to struggle back to Zeals on one engine with a very meritorious piece of flying. P/O. Chris Vlotman and F/Sgt. Johnny Wood likewise were lucky to reach base intact after suffering Flak damage to the tailplane of HK515.

At 4:25am on the morning of 13th June, S/L Nigel Bunting shot down a JU 88 over Caen / Bayeux. This was the first German aircraft shot down over the Continent by 488 Squadron. His crewman, F/L Phil Reed used the new Ross night binoculars for the first time and this enhanced visibility helped his pilot track the enemy aircraft after the MkV111 AI unit had allowed them to make the initial engagement. These glasses rapidly became mandatory equipment on all Nightfighters and were an incredible help with the often fraught with danger identification process while on patrol in the night skies over Europe.

The Night Glasses were not new to the Allies as they had been developed for night use during the First World War but were only introduced for aircraft use once the night fighter squadrons were set up in 1942. They had the ability to allow identification over a long distance in conditions of very low light levels and became a welcome addition to the arsenal of a night fighter crew.

It was close to dawn and the early morning light gave good assistance in the identification process. The Ju 88 was perfectly silhouetted against the dawn sky between Caen and St Lo.

(21) *13/06/1944 – 04:25 hrs – Ex Zeals – Bunting and Reed – Ju 88 – Caen/Bayoux, France*

Earlier in the night Control had put Bunting and Reed on to two "bogeys" which in the end turned out to be firstly a Mosquito and then a Mitchell bomber which was a perfect example of the frailty of the systems that identified the aircraft as enemy. Their successful contact identification was helped by Bunting placing his target aircraft perfectly as it carried out evasive manoeuvres and when sure of the identification of his target, finishing it off. They overshot several times during the action but each time Phil Reed managed to guide his pilot back on to the tail end of the target. They could clearly see the external mounted bombs under each wing. It was not an easy process as the Ju 88 evaded them a half dozen times with violent manoeuvres before Bunting and Reed were able to spring the final trap.

Peter Hall and Dick Marriott flying ME-D had a lucky escape on the next night, having to fly back to Zeals on one engine after debris from a Ju 88 they had bowled over damaged their aircraft extensively. Their victim went down over St. Lo following a series of attacks by Hall. After each strike, he lost visual contact but Dick Marriott was able to keep Hall in contact with constant and clever monitoring of their AI unit.

(22) *15/06/1944 – 02:25 hrs – Ex Zeals – Hall and Marriott – Ju 88 – SW of St. Lo, France*

Nigel Bunting and Phil Reed (ME-V) had an almost identical mishap in the early morning hours of the 17th June when they brought down one of the newer Fw 190's over St. Lo. They used only seventeen shots from each of their four cannons in a one second burst but suffered engine damage from their exploding target. This success was particularly merited as the Fw 190 was the fastest fighter available to the Luftwaffe and was the first single engined fighter shot down by 488 Squadron.

(23) *17/06/1944 – 04:23 hrs – Ex Zeals - Bunting and Reed – Fw 190 – St. Lo, France*

This Fw 190 gave the Bunting / Reed crew a bit of a run around as the aircraft was faster and more manouevrable than any of the enemy aircraft they had countered to date. The Luftwaffe would have been very surprised to lose one of these new aircraft in these circumstances. The damage inflicted on the two 488 Mosquitos gave some idea of the closeness of the conflict needed to achieve success during these encounters. Both aircraft suffered damage on their starboard sides and both were forced to feather their starboard engines and fly home on one engine.

F/L Peter Hall and Dick Marriott added to their collection on the 17th June with a Ju 88 that literally blew to pieces in the air over the coast of France when hit by a very short burst from the cannons of their Mosquito ME-E. The Junkers hit the ground at very shallow attitude spreading flaming debris in a long line over the countryside.

(24) *18/06/1944 – 02:30 hrs – Ex Zeals – Hall and Marriott – Ju 88 – St. Lo, France*

There was further success for the squadron in the early morning hours of the 18th June when F/O Douglas Robinson and F/O "Cherub" Keeping, his crewman, during a routine patrol over the beaches happened upon an Fw 190 preparing to bomb our troops below. The Fw 190 must have been unsighted as he flew directly at our crew. Robinson manoeuvred into an attack position after identification and his first burst removed the bomb from its mounting. A second attack was a complete miss in the darkness but Robinson picked up his target again on a third approach catching the enemy aircraft at very close range, so close in fact that Robinson had to literally heave his Mosquito up and over the resulting explosion and badly scorched the underside of his aircraft.

> *(25)* 18/06/1944 – 04:21 hrs – Ex Zeals – Robinson and Keeping – Fw 190 – *Quinville, France*

The destruction of the Luftwaffe Fw 190's continued on the following early morning just before dawn when P/O. Chris Vlotman and his crewman, F/Sgt. Johnny Wood flying MM515, caught their target over Falaise and sent it spinning into the ground.

> *(26)* 20/06/1944 – 02:20 hrs - Ex Zeals – Vlotman and Wood – Fw 190 – *Sth of Falaise, France*

They had been circling around in a holding pattern whilst Control were trying to get another aircraft to deal with a 'bandit' in their patrol area. Vlotman was understandably getting annoyed with being on hold and talked control into letting him have a turn. No sooner had the first Mosquito been called off, the "bandit" made a run for it and Vlotman gladly took advantage and destroyed it as it fortuitously crossed his path.

P/O. Stan McCabe and W/O Terry Riley gained their first *"kill"* just after midnight on 22nd June when they made sure of the destruction of their target with three attacks of sustained cannon fire to send their victim crashing onto the beaches below.

> *(27)* 23/06/1944 – 00.12hrs - Ex Zeals - McCabe and Riley - Ju 188 - *East of Bayeux*

McCabe made the comment in his Combat Report that at one point he decided that the Ju 188 was not burning enough so he made sure of its destruction with a third and sustained burst of fire. He reported that the Junkers put up a fight by returning fire right up to the time it blew apart. McCabe was below his target and the burning aircraft diving steeply to port passed very close to the Mosquito spraying tracer all around them fortunately without effect. Stan McCabe enjoyed this success which was the first of his two "kills" with the squadron.

This same night F/Sgt. Howard Scott RNZAF and his usual crewman F/O Colin Duncan RNZAF were returning by car from Maiden Bradley when they were involved in a nasty accident. Their passenger, P/O. Alan Thompson RNZAF was hospitalised as a result of the accident but Duncan and Scott were not badly hurt. Just three weeks later the pair were to be involved in a much more serious accident and were both killed when their aircraft plunged into the forest at Holmesley South.

F/L Norman Crookes DFC and Bar, DFC (US) from Derbyshire, UK recalled joining 488 squadron at Bradwell Bay with his pilot, F/L George *'Jamie'* Jameson DSO, DFC from Christchurch, New Zealand in late January 1944   Both were very experienced airmen and had already been decorated for their exploits in previous squadrons. Both had been teaching their respective trades in O.T.U. units with night fighter crews after earlier extensive combat roles in Beaufighters. Jameson recording three kills while with 125 Squadron. The pair had travelled north to the Shetland Islands to run intercept patrols against Luftwaffe bombers that were harassing shipping in the North Sea. On one patrol an engine failed on their Beaufighter and Jameson brought the aircraft back on one engine 240 kms back across the North Sea to land safely at Peterhead.

They had a quiet start with 488 Squadron having not recorded any success until the night of $24^{th}/25^{th}$ June when they were to add to the mounting 488 Squadron tally for the month of June 1944.

They were patrolling over Normandy and shot down a Messerschmitt 410

(28) *25/06/1944 - 04:07 hrs – Ex Zeals – Jameson and Crookes – Me 410 – SW of Bayeux, France*

There was considerable confusion over the identity of this aircraft for some time before confirmed identification was made. The target was picked up by control well above Jamesons patrolling height and he was forced to apply full power for some time in order to get close enough to get the target identified. As they approached the target from the rear, the aircraft, which turned out to be a Me 410 fired off several small white flares. Norman Crookes thought it was another squadron Mosquito and despite him using their Ross night glasses they had difficulty identifying "friend or foe". No IFF signal was showing so Jameson closed to within 300 metres before he was certain about its identity. He drifted back after spotting the tell-tale wing tanks of a Me 410 and fired several bursts into the fuselage. The Me 410 continued in level flight for a little while before diving down out of control and exploded on the ground. Ray Jeffs who was in close proximity was able to confirm their target being destroyed.

The pair followed on this initial success by downing a Junkers Ju 88 three nights later on 29th June.

(29) *29/06/1944 – 00:40 hrs – Ex Zeals – Jameson and Crookes – Ju 88 – NE of Caen, France*

Jameson had spotted bursts of anti-aircraft fire off the coast close to some shipping and went *"freelance"* to check it out. Norman Crookes picked up the *"bogey"* on his AI unit and as it was for the earlier success identification became a problem. They got to within 75 metres before they were able to confirm a "bogey". At 75mtrs they were obviously spotted as the target slowed right up to stalling speed and then pulled the nose up to a complete stall. The German pilot dropped the nose down to offset the stall and passed right across Jameson's gun sight as he was close to overshooting. Jameson sent the Ju 88 down vertically in flames with only fifteen rounds from each cannon.

The shipping had been under attack at the time by the Ju 88. Just to show their appreciation the ships then directed their anti-aircraft fire on to the Mosquito putting at least one piece of shrapnel through the tailfin of the Jameson and Crooke Mosquito. The so called "friendly fire" incidents by this time had almost reached epidemic proportions when S/L Watts also returned a little later from a routine patrol with flak damage. It was starting to get a bit tiresome!

The first day of July 1944 saw some of the squadron on the move again, shifting from the static station at Zeals to tented accommodation at Colerne airfield known as No. 149 airfield.

The weather continued to play its part as little flying was carried out during the first week of July and sort of set the scene for the rest of the month. Any operational patrols that were carried out inevitably ended up with aircraft being forced to land on bases away from Colerne as the local weather situation was that bad with reduced visibility being a big problem for the returning crews.

On the 14th July, S/L Bunting, F/L Reed, Flt/Lt. Hall and F/O Cairns flew to RAF Hertford Bridge to be invested with medals and honours presented by His Majesty, the King in person.

On 15th July Mosquito MM 551 while descending in cloud, flew into the forest north east of Holmesley South in Zeals killing both Flt. Sgt Howard Scott and F/O Colin Duncan. Both were New Zealanders. There is very little detail available of the tragedy. Despite extensive research no more information has been found.

On the evening of 16th July, the Zeals Air base organised a social function in the Airfield main mess for both 488 and 410 Squadrons and airfield staff. It was noted as being a particularly successful event and presumably at the end the 488 boys would have trudged back to their tented accommodation. The squadron Diarist noted that they were visited by F/L Leslie Hunt who was at the time serving with another squadron but had become a regular visitor back to his old squadron.

P/O. McCabe got into a little strife the following night when forced to land once again at another base due to bad weather over Colerne. He got his aircraft hooked up on the barbed wire perimeter fencing at RAF Hurn causing some damage to the aircraft and some embarrassment to himself in the process.

F/Sgt. Scott and F/O Duncan were interred at the RAF Cemetery Broodwood on the 19th July. F/O Skudder and W/O. MacKay represented the squadron at the funeral.

The continuing saga of mishaps on airfields other than their own continued on 25th July when F/Sgt. Reg Mitchell, as he was ranked then, on a daylight landing at RAF Southrop, undershot the runway and left his tail wheel in the boundary hedge when attempting to land. When he finally touched down the aircraft swung badly off course and collected a sodium marker doing further damage. Reg Mitchell remembers being undone by the tail wheel striking a metal rail running along the top of a fence buried in the confines of the hedge. His ground-crew would not have been impressed!

July had been a relatively quiet month for the squadron but the end of the month saw a big increase in enemy activity in their area, right in the middle of the squadrons move to Colerne Airfield. The squadron at this time was under the temporary command of S/L Nigel Bunting with the squadron C.O. Wng Comm. Dickie Haine away on leave. Early on the morning of 28th July the first convoy of men and equipment left from Zeals to travel to Colerne. "B" Flight left shortly after, flying their aircraft over with "A" Flight following that afternoon. The main body of ground-crew arrived late afternoon and soon a tented city appeared in their designated area of Colerne Air Base. Once again, they were under canvas. "A" Flight were on call and operational that same night which considering the disruption caused by the movement of men, aircraft and equipment said something for the discipline and dedication of the individual squadron members.

They were back in action again when Peter Hall and Dick Marriott struck the double by shooting down two Ju 88's over Lessay in the late evening hours of 28th July, both within seven minutes of one another.

(30) *28/07/1944 – 22:52 – Ex Colerne – Hall and Marriott – Ju 88 – NW of Vire, France*

(31) *28/07/1944 – 22.59 – Ex Colerne – Hall and Marriott – Ju 88 – SE of Lessay, France*

It was to be a night of feverish activity. The patrol area was outside of a designated "gun area' which had to be avoided by allied defending aircraft as batteries of anti-aircraft guns were registered to specific heights and coverage and any aircraft straying into this area was considered fair game by the gunners below. It probably should be noted here that the high explosive anti-aircraft shells were set with pressure swiches which were programmed to activate at set heights. When registered correctly the guns could saturate the sky in clusters of exploding anti-aircraft shells at different levels. Their strike rate was very high and these were areas that needed to be avoided at any cost.

Hall and Marriott found a night sky full of *"window"* dropped by the Luftwaffe in huge quantities. This swamped the ground radar systems which was of course the intention of the attacking bombers. Their first strike of the night was reasonably simple, being picked up by Marriott on his AI set after being warned by control that there were enemy aircraft in the area. The second target took a bit more effort to dispose of. After the initial strike the target dived steeply away with Hall right on his tail. After some twisting and turning the Ju 88 levelled off and reduced speed dramatically, so much so that Hall overshot and ended alongside his target. The black crosses and swastika markings were clearly visible in the light of the by now burning aircraft. While they were lining up for another burst, a large dark object flashed past just below them buffeting their airstream, reminding them no doubt of the perils of flying into busy areas at night. Peter Hall got into a good attack position, close enough to get his windscreen coated with German oil, and after having given it a sustained burst the Ju 88 eventually rolled over on its side and dived vertically into the ground.

Control was having considerable difficulty in identifying who was who at the time due to the amount of "window" being dropped. They directed Hall and Marriott towards an aircraft that Control informed them was a bandit. The target was heavily engaged with searchlights and anti-aircraft fire. They moved in closer and identified it early thankfully, as a Lancaster bomber and left it alone. Just to show its gratitude the Lancaster turned towards them and fired a burst of tracer, fortunately somewhat inaccurately. Their final target for the night turned out to be an Allied Sterling bomber so they thought discretion was the better part of valour decided to head for home.

Peter Hall and Dick Marriott were both awarded DFC's after this encounter, with Peter being the first New Zealander to receive an award while flying with 488.

An hour or two after the time of Hall and Marriott's first success, F/O Douglas Robinson and F/L Terry Clark DFM were having a somewhat difficult time disposing of a Ju 188 due to very accurate fire from its rear gunner until Robinson got close in and destroyed the enemy aircraft. It hit the ground close to Mayenne with a horrendous explosion.

(32) *29/07/1944 – 01:18 - Ex Colerne – Robinson and Clark – Ju 188 – Nth of Mayenne, France*

F/L Clark had returned to 488 Squadron as a visitor from his Controllers work at North Weald. He was asked if he wanted to fill in for Douglas Robinson's regular crewman, F/O "Cherub" Keeping, who was away on sick leave. Clark had been away from active operational work for four and a half months so the outcome of the night was particularly meritorious. Clark had been very unsettled at North Weald and with his Senior Officer's permission had asked to return to Colerne and his old squadron for a couple of days. He thoroughly enjoyed the break and getting back into operational flying, although his enthusiasm was tempered somewhat due to him having just been married. After such an adventurous flight, reality kicked in and he very quickly came to terms with the fact that he was now a married man and had a new resolve to return to his bride in one piece without taking unnecessary risks. He left later that same day to return to his old unit and expected to get into a bit of trouble following his flight, but the news of his success with Douglas Robinson became known and his workmates at North Weald were quick to congratulate him. Although he had obtained permission from the C.O. to crew with Robinson, he was not classified as an "operational navigator" at the time.

Regular patrols continued over Normandy and in the early hours of 30th July over Caen, Jameson and Crookes flying ME-R bagged a Dornier 217, two Ju 88's, and a third Ju 88 as a possible but later confirmed destroyed.

(33) *30/07/1944 – 05:05 – Ex Colerne – Jameson and Crookes – Ju 88 – Sth of Caen, France*

(34) *30/07/1944 – 05:09 – Ex Colerne – Jameson and Crookes – Ju 88 - Sth of Caen, France*

(35) *30/07/1944 – 05:15 – Ex Colerne – Jameson and Crookes – Ju 88 – Sth of Lisieux, France*

(36) *30/07/1944 – 05:25 – Ex Colerne – Jameson and Crookes – Do 217 – Sth of Lisieux, France*

All this action occurred in less than a half hour of combat and resulted in 'Jamie' Jameson being awarded his D.S.O and Norman Crookes a second bar to his DFC. This action was one of the more incredible stories to come out of the Second World War. Never before, had so many enemy aircraft been destroyed on just the one patrol by any Allied night fighter. What was more remarkable about this feat was that Jameson had only fired ninety shells from each of his four cannons. Another fact that ensued from this patrol was the ground - crew reporting on their return that the aircraft's four fuel tanks were found to be empty. It sort of summed up the high degree of commitment by this crew and the self-imposed limits that gave them the successes that other crews struggled to achieve. The BBC news later that night reported the outcome of their success in the evening news bulletin without identifying the squadron.

It was however a mixed bag for 488 Squadron. The same night of the Jameson / Crookes successes the squadron tragically lost S/L Nigel Bunting and Ted Spedding flying MM 476 when they were hit by anti-aircraft fire near St. Remy, 33 km south west of Caen in France, just inland of the Normandy beaches. They were chasing a FW 190 at the time, very low to the ground when MM 476 was hit by anti-aircraft fire. Bunting reported over his radio that he had been hit and just fifteen seconds later an explosion was seen on the ground. Both Bunting and Spedding died instantly in the conflagration after ploughing into a field. Nigel Bunting was serving as "B" Flight Commander with the squadron. Both Bunting and Spedding were buried together in a joint grave in the St. Remy churchyard cemetery. With the demise of Nigel Bunting, S/L Ron Watts took over temporary command of 488 until the return of W/C "Dickie" Haine.

Reg Mitchell recalls the drama that occurred the following night, when on patrol over the same area, he and his crewman, Ron Ballard barely made it back to base after also being hit by anti aircraft fire. The deaths of the Bunting / Spedding crew were doubly tragic as it was later reported that the anti-aircraft fire originated from American guns.

The squadron C.O. "Dickie" Haine was away off duty from base when he received news of the disappearance of Nigel Bunting and Ted Spedding. He was particularly saddened at their deaths. Full of remorse for not being on base at the time he rushed back to Zeals. He was given permission to fly twice over the area where they disappeared looking for clues but was not to accept the nature of their deaths until long after he had left the squadron. He admitted at that time that he was spending too much time away from his men while off duty and resolved never to leave base again without good reason. There was further terrible irony with the deaths of the two men as Ted Spedding was not Bunting's regular crewman. Ted's pilot, Ray Jeffs was ill and unfit for flying and Phil Reed, Nigel's crewman, was away from base so Nigel asked Ted to stand in as his crewman with tragic consequences for him. Ray Jeffs would have been devastated to lose his regular crewman and good friend under circumstances like that.

The Jameson/Crookes effort in downing four enemy aircraft on the one patrol was well received by the squadron despite the sadness of the night's outcome and the success was extensively reported in the media at the time. It was considered the finest night fighter sortie of the Normandy campaign. Congratulations to the squadron came from many different sources including the Commander in Chief Air Defence and Commander in Chief of No. 10 Fighter Group.

Excerpts from the *Combat Report* submitted by Jameson and Crookes on their return to base printed as written makes interesting reading:

> Flt/Lt. Jameson reports: *I proceeded on the vector of 100 degrees at Angels 5 and the controller asked me to make my 'turkey gobble' and told me that he could not give me any assistance. I saw light anti-aircraft fire 2miles ahead and almost immediately, a contact was obtained, i.e. 0502 hours, range 2 miles, 10 o'clock. Height 5000 feet, head on. I obtained a visual on a Ju88 range 1 mile against the dawn, still approaching head on and at the same height. My navigator using Ross night glasses confirmed the identification. Meanwhile, I had turned hard to port after the enemy aircraft and followed it by means of A.I. as the enemy aircraft skimmed through the cloud tops. I closed in to 300 yards at full throttle as the enemy aircraft was doing 260 A.S.I. Meanwhile I saw a series of explosions on the ground caused, I believe, by the enemy aircraft dropping its bombs.*
>
> *Visual was regained in a clear spot (with no cloud) and I closed in and gave the enemy two short bursts from dead astern. Strikes were seen of the fuselage causing a fire in the fuselage and the port engine. The enemy aircraft went down through the clouds vertically and well alight, and about 20 seconds later, hit the ground with a terrific explosion. I reported the kill to TAILCOAT and gave him a fix. The enemy was destroyed 5 to 6 miles south of Caen at 0505 hours. When I was doing a port orbit over the scene of the kill, much WINDOW*[42] *was seen and a contact was almost immediately obtained, i.e. 0506 hours, range 2 miles, 11 o'clock, height 5000 feet. A visual was obtained very quickly on an enemy aircraft flying slightly above cloud. This aircraft was also skimming the cloud tops. I*

---

[42] **WINDOW** was composite metallic and paper strips dropped from aircraft in an attempt to confuse enemy radar.

gave chase at full throttle to overtake. His speed was approximately 280 A.S.I.

While giving chase, another Ju88 came up through the cloud, one mile range and flying in the same direction as the former aircraft. I closed in rapidly to 400 yards and confirmed the identity of the aircraft as that of Ju.88. The enemy appeared to see me and turned very hard port diving towards a thick cloud layer. I followed on the turn and closed in to 350-400 yards when I opened fire from dead astern. Strikes were observed which caused a large fire in the starboard engine. The enemy well alight disappeared vertically through cloud. At this moment, I saw two aircraft approaching me through cloud and as I was satisfied that the former combat had ended in a kill, and the Ju.88 would inevitably hit the ground, I did not follow but turned towards the two enemy aircraft whom I suspected to be customers. I closed in on both of them and I identified them as Mosquitoes. Sub/Lt. Richardson, a navigator of 410 Squadron (Jungle 33) confirms my first kill, having seen the E/A [43] well alight and hit the ground and he saw the second E/A well alight. I reported the second combat to TAILCOAT. The combat took place 5/6 miles south of Caen.

Although the pilot did not see the E/A actually hit the ground, and in consequence, only a probable was claimed, he is convinced that it was a kill and he is supported by an eye witness who saw large flames issuing there and the E/A going down. It is therefore respectfully requested that consideration should be given in stepping up this claim to destroyed. Almost immediately after identifying the Mosquitoes referred to above, I obtained a Freelance[44] visual on an aircraft 4,000 feet range, same height 5,000 feet, crossing starboard to port. I closed to 2000 dead

---

[43] **E/A** - Enemy aircraft
[44] **Freelance** - Flying your aircraft alone while not under control of Air Operations or your base.

astern and identified the aircraft as a Ju.88 which identity was confirmed by the navigator. When I was about 300 yards behind the E/A it dived steeply to port towards the cloud. I followed and gave two short bursts and I observed strikes from one of the bursts on the fuselage. The E/A took advantage of cloud cover and followed with use of A.I.[45] though it was taking violent evasive action and dropping large quantities of Window.

When we were almost at treetop height; visual was regained range 4,000 feet dead astern. The enemy had ceased evasive action. I closed to 250 yards dead astern and gave it a short burst from which strikes were observed. The E/A pulled up almost vertically and turned to port with debris falling and sparks issuing from it. The enemy stalled then nose dived into a four-acre field and exploded. The kill took place 5 miles south of Lisieux. I climbed to 3,000 feet called TAILCOAT, reported the kill and at my request, was given a north westerly vector back to the scene of the enemy activity.

I again saw A.A. fire ahead above cloud and I headed towards it and at 0522 hours' contact was obtained on two aircraft and much Window (a) at a range of 4 miles 10 o'clock (b) 2 miles 10 o'clock. I decided to intercept the nearer of the two and obtained a visual dead astern at a range of 4,000 feet on a Do.217. The E/A must have seen me for almost immediately it dived into cloud and took very intensive evasive action and threw out large quantities of Window for several minutes in cloud. I followed through cloud using A/I. And the E/A eventually straightened out at cloud base. Visual was regained at a range of 2,000 feet dead astern and below. I closed to 300 yards and fired a short burst. Strikes were seen on the fuselage which began to burn furiously. The E/A turned gently to starboard pulled his nose up and the dorsal gunner opened fire with

---

[45] **A.I.** - Aircraft Interception Radar unit usually mounted in the nose cone of the aircraft and operated by the navigator or crewman from a panel mounted screen in front of him.

a wild burst, which headed in the wrong direction. The E/A dived into the ground in flames and exploded.

Claim: 2 Ju.88s destroyed. 1 Ju.88 probably destroyed. 1 Do.217 destroyed. Cine camera gun used automatically. Ammunition P.I.89, P.O.90, S.I.94, S.O. 91

The 488 Squadron crest with the signed approval of the King appended (Reg Mitchell).

488 Squadron Mosquitos in formation (Reg Mitchell).

Above: The late Reg Mitchell presenting a copy of the old 488 Squadron Crest to Group Captain Darryn Webb O.C. of the new 488 Wing after the Inaugural Parade at Ohakea Air Base on 8th December 2010 (RNZAF Official Photo). Below: A quick de-brief against a dawn sky on their return from a "sortie" (from Defence until Dawn).

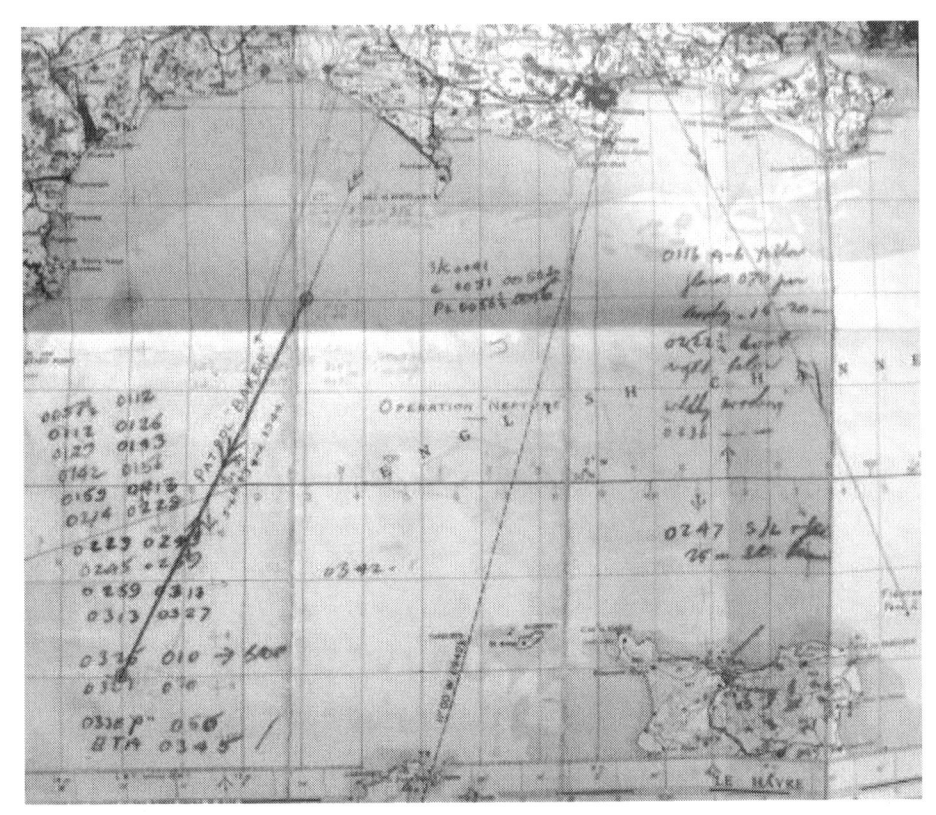

Copy of P/O. Broodbank's navigational map of operational flight on the morning of the D Day Landings on 6th June 1944 (Adam Forest).

6488 Echelon ground-crew refuelling a Mosquito ready for the coming night's operation (from Defence until Dawn)

Part of the invasion fleet with the Normandy beaches on the horizon (ex Reg Mitchell)

P/O. Reg Mitchell   RNZAF

F/O Douglas Robinson, RNZAF

Above: Typical Crew Room scene - cards again! F/O Jock Cairns is seated on right, F/L Chunky Stewart standing at right. (Ron Watts). Below left: Ross Night Glasses as used by Allied airmen during the Second World War. Below right: F/L Jamie Jameson DSO, DFC and Bar RNZAF, New Zealand's top night fighter ace of the Second World War.

Above and below; Fw 190 fighter aircraft of the Luftwaffe.

A Focke-Wulf FW 90 Fighter Bomber (Reg Mitchell).

Above left: F/L George Jameson D.S.O, D.F.C. RNZAF (James Jameson). Right: F/L Norman Crookes D.F.C. and two bars, D.F.C. (US) RAF (Norman Crookes).

Chapter Six

COLERNE - WILTSHIRE, ENGLAND
29TH JULY 1944 TO 9th OCTOBER 1944
No. 149 Airfield

The squadron transferred to Colerne, near Bristol during the daytime hours of 29th July 1944. Peter Hall and Dick Marriott flying MM498 almost opened the new month with a double in the early morning hours of the 2nd of August over St. Lo when they sent one Ju 88 crashing into the ground with a very short burst. The enemy aircraft at the time just happened to pass by accidentally as they were targeting another aircraft at a higher altitude that was taking rapid and strong evasive action for no apparent reason. This aircraft was seen to be doing complete vertical orbits as part of its tactics and while the bemused Mosquito crew were planning the best way to handle their approach a second aircraft hove into view, crossing their line of fire and ever the opportunist Hall quickly despatched it.

(37) *02/08/1944 – 01:01 hrs – Ex Colerne – Hall and Marriott – Ju 88 – St Lo, France*

The darkness of the early morning sky seemed to be busy with potential 'trade' as a third freelance target was soon encountered. The pilot of what turned out to be a Ju 88 took immediate evasive action and his tactics showed him to be very experienced. The Junkers immediately climbed at speed into the moon then suddenly dived steeply into the darkened sky. Hall and Marriott lost him after a long chase when he out turned them in a steep port turn and disappeared into the darkness. Hall, in his frustration fired a short burst at very long range but this put their AI unit out of action and they were forced to turn back and give up the chase.

F/L Allen Browne and W/O Tom Taylor flying HK532 had rejoined the squadron in July after a spell away instructing in an OTU unit. Later, on the same night of 2nd August on their first combat flight of the war they shot down a Dornier 217 which crashed onto the beach near Avranches.

> **(38)** *02/08/1944 – 23:05 hrs – Ex Colerne – Browne and Taylor – Do 217 – Avranches, France*

They had picked up their target after it crossed over in front of the moon. Browne managed to turn inside the Dornier's climbing turn at high speed as it tried to escape and clattered a good burst of cannon fire into its fuselage. He passed up and over it in very close proximity as it dived to its destruction. Some erratic return fire from the Dornier's dorsal gunner was experienced without any contact on the Mosquito. It must have been a close encounter as Browne reported the flaming target disappearing vertically under his wings.

The July successes continued in early August when another new all Kiwi crew had success over the beaches. W/O Tom MacKay with P/O. Thompson who by now had recovered from his car crash injuries, destroyed a Ju 188 as it made its bombing run over Avranches in early morning 3rd August.

> **(39)** *03/08/1944 – 00:52 hrs – Ex Colerne - MacKay and Thompson – Ju 188 – Avranches, France*

The enemy aircraft was a sitting duck really as its bombing approach was level and very slow. The enemy crew must have got a terrible fright when MacKay opened up on them. His approach from below and astern would have caught them by surprise and he was close enough to get his aircraft covered in oil from the stricken bomber.

Gordon Patrick and Jimmy Concannon flying HK532 also got their first "kill" the following night when they downed a Ju 88 over Avranches. They had earlier in their patrol witnessed a combat between a Mosquito and what they thought was a Ju 88 which would have been a unique experience due the solo nature of most of these night-fighter encounters. Most aircrew reported sensing rather than seeing aircraft in the darkness around them but very few sighted actual aircraft other than the glow from distant exhausts. Other than that sighting the Ju 88 was literally the first enemy aircraft they had encountered during their spell with 488 and they took the most of their chances, although the hit was with some finesse as Patrick only used up twenty rounds from each cannon to destroy the Junkers. Patrick complained

> **(40)** *03/08/1944 – 23:54 hrs – Ex Colerne – Patrick and Concannon – Ju 88 – Avranches, France*

of having been subjected to heavy Allied anti-aircraft fire during the whole of the chase which tended to create huge difficulties for any crew just trying to carry out their allocated work in the night sky.

Jamie Jameson was his normal frugal self a couple of hours later when he fired only fifteen shells from each cannon into a Ju 88 again caught by the light of the moon.

> **(41)** *04/08/1944 – 00:35 hrs – Ex Colerne – Jameson and Crookes – Ju 88 – Nth of St Lo, France*

Control put him on to a target that was climbing and they had a steep full power climb to get above the enemy aircraft. As they closed in they noticed it was dropping copious quantities of "window". The Ju 88 spotted them and did a hard turn to port but Jameson was ready for the move and gave him a burst. Strikes were seen around the cockpit area and the enemy aircraft went out of control into a port spin. As the doomed Junkers spun to the ground the port wing fell off leaving burning wreckage over a wide area. In a very short period of time, just several days, the squadron score had soared significantly and would continue for a few days yet.

One of newer crews serving with 488, F/O Andy Shaw and F/Sgt. Len Wyman (later Pilot Officer) flying MM 439, while on patrol in the early morning hours of 5th August, ran into two 'Bandits' in quick succession while trying to stop the Allied troops being bombed over St. Lo. Control warned them that 'trade' was approaching from the North West so the Mosquito crew lay in wait. Shaw stalked the first target, a Junkers Ju 188, and hit it while it was making a turn to port. The target pulled quickly around to starboard trying to shake off the Mosquito but when it turned back onto port it passed across Shaw's gun sights very, very close and caught a full salvo for its trouble.

(42) *05/08/1944 – 00:55 hrs – Ex Colerne – Shaw and Wyman – Ju 88 – NE of St Lo, France*

Len Wyman reckons they were as close as fifty metres apart. He remembers being very concerned at the time that they were going to collide and was convinced that the gunfire from their Mosquito thankfully blasted the enemy aircraft down and away from a collision course.

Shaw and Wyman watched their victim plough into the ground and then turned to try and pull in the second target, a Ju 88 which was in full flight away from them. They closed in but crossed through a firestorm of anti-aircraft fire directed at the Junkers and had to pull out of their attack or risk being shot down themselves. With his AI unit, unserviceable Shaw asked "Control" for directions and turned towards the area indicated to see another Ju 88 coming straight towards them. With Wyman keeping an eye on the target he managed a tight turn that put him back on the tail of the enemy but was forced to follow him back through the anti-aircraft firestorm he had just pulled away from. They also had to contend with return fire from the Junker's rear gunner. Shaw managed to get several hits on the target aircraft but due to the low altitude they were at and the total failure of his on-board radar he prudently gave it away and headed back to base.

Len Wyman remembers that early morning sortie happening in near daylight conditions with a full moon lighting up the early morning sky well before dawn. Although the pair of them were relatively new to 488 he had crewed with Andy Shaw for some time, teaming up when they were with No. 85 Night Fighter squadron. They had a full operational tour with 85 Squadron and at the end were posted separately as instructors on their repective trades. They then teamed up again on transfer to 488. They were a very experienced crew.

The Ju 88 that escaped put up a good fight with both aircraft twisting and turning trying to get the upper hand. Wyman commented to me that he thought the German pilot was a very skilful operator. He remembered thinking at the time that this episode was unusual in that they were actually dogfighting with the Ju 88 in near daylight conditions like a dayfighter, when they would normally be stalking their opponent in the dark of the night using their on-board AI radar system. Len also recalls them having used up all their ammunition in the exchange and that was the main reason for them having to break off the engagement.

W/C Dickie Haine with F/L Pete Bowman, his crewman, in HK 504 managed to get his first "Kill" on the same patrol.

> **(43)** *05/08/1944 – 01:05 hrs – Ex Colerne – Haine and Bowman – Ju 88 – ENE of Vire, France*

Ground Control put them on to an unidentified aircraft ahead of them. The aircraft was laying target indicator flares for what would have been following Luftwaffe bombers and was heavily engaged by Allied anti-aircraft fire at the time. Haine initially gave up the chase until clear of the exploding shells and when Bowman picked up a radar image he was able to put his pilot in perfect position for a visual contact. It was a Ju 88 and Haine was able to get within 300 metres before giving it a two second burst with his cannons which blew pieces off the enemy aircraft and started a fire in its port engine. They followed it down until it exploded into the ground east of Vire in Normandy. They returned to base highly elated at their first success coming after 112 operational patrols. They did in fact get on to the tail of another contact but had to abandon the chase when heavy flak from the Allied ships threatened to do serious damage to them. [46]

Peter Hall and Dick Marriott added to their already impressive record just after midnight on 6th August when they chanced upon a Dornier 217. They eventually got close enough in without being spotted to clearly see the black crosses and the distinctive tail fins. Hall was forced to keep his line but dropped back before giving it a couple of short bursts. Nothing much happened initially but all of a sudden, the Dornier exploded in mid air.

> **(44)** *05/08/1944 – 00:52 – Ex Colerne – Hall and Marriott – Do 217 – Rennes, France*

Hall and Marriott had a very frustrating time on this particular operation. They had earlier been directed by Control away from what was an obvious area of interest. When they arrived in their patrol area they saw flares and anti-aircraft fire towards the south east but Control

---

[46] *Extracts of incidents related by Group Captain Richard "Dickie" Haine OBE, DFC from his memoirs "From Fury to Phantom" published by Pen & Sword Aviation, 2005*

was adamant that they would be better employed away from what was increasingly obvious to those in the air that a raid was in progress to the south. They were reluctantly given permission to move towards the area and eventually were told that there were at least five enemy aircraft in the area. It turned out to be a bright moonlit night and they found themselves engaged in a chase over the bay where the famous monastery of Mont St. Michel was situated. They initially had some difficulty identifying the Dornier as the light was tricky despite the full moon. They had earlier been closing in on another target after a long chase but were called off at the last minute by Control.

After the destruction of the Dornier they were told to investigate a "bogey" travelling towards the south coast but after a long chase found they were latched on to an Allied Wellington bomber. They were then directed to another target much higher than them at the time. Another long climbing chase ensued with exactly the same result – a Wellington bomber. All the ducking and diving meant their fuel was getting dangerously low so they headed back to Colerne. Not a very productive night for a normally very keen crew.

It must have been the night for Dornier's as F/Sgt. MacLean and his crewman, F/O Brian Grant flying MM 502 had a crack at two of these Luftwaffe bombers despite this being their first encounter with enemy aircraft. The action took place over the coast west of Angers and resulted in them destroying one and making a damaged claim for the second after they lost track of it in a violent steep dive during which they knocked bits off it on the way down.

> **(45)** *06/08/1944 – 02:17 hrs – Ex Colerne – MacLean and Grant – Do 217, W of Angers, France*

Their night had started in a similar manner to Hall and Marriott as Control had initially directed them on to what turned out to be an Allied Stirling bomber.

Four nights after their initial success Allen Browne and Tom Taylor added to their score considerably when they destroyed a further three enemy aircraft, with two of them being destroyed without a shot being fired. In one of the more unique stories to come out of the war, two of the hapless Ju 88 aircraft were chased at high speed, at very low altitude and both crashed into the ground while trying to evade the attacking Mosquito.

(46) *07/08/1944 – 02:51hrs– Ex Colerne – Browne and Taylor – Ju 188 SW of Avranche, France*

(47) *07/08/1944 - 03:06 hrs - Ex Colerne - Browne and Taylor - Unknown – Rennes, France*

(48) *07/08/1944 – 03:31 hrs – Ex Colerne – Browne and Taylor – Unknown - Rennes, France*

The Browne / Taylor crew must have scared the living daylights out of them to get a result like that. Allen Browne's first victim was disposed of in the conventional manner with an attack from the rear and despite an overshoot Browne managed a hard turn to starboard and got back onto the tail of the Ju 188 again to finish it off. His second target was only identified as a "light". Browne was able to visually follow what he described as a large reddish amber light into a forty-five-degree steady dive. It was clearly an aircraft as Tom Taylor was able to track it on his AI unit. Browne was forced to pull out of the dive at the last minute but the object continued on and struck the ground. Browne and Taylor circled over the burning wreck trying to fix its position but eventually were called away by Control.

The third target for the night was approached at high speed by their Mosquito but as they closed in the enemy aircraft started a series of violent evasive manoeuvres. Browne momentarily lost contact but when he came across his target once more, the dorsal gunner fired a long burst of cannon fire which came close in above his starboard main-plane. He pulled away but when contact was established again they were faced with another wild erratic burst of gunfire. At this point the enemy aircraft half rolled to port and dived vertically down. Browne was forced to overshoot, being reluctant to follow his target at such a low altitude. This last evasive manoeuvre proved the undoing of their target as it also ploughed into the ground and burnt fiercely. Browne commented after that he had never seen such violent evasive action. The two aircraft downed without a shot being fired on them were never identified but were credited to the tally of Browne and Taylor. Allen Browne was awarded a DFC in September 1944 and was posted on to the Far East on October 1.

"Jamie" Jameson and Norman Crookes flew their last sortie together on the night of the 6th August. "Jamie" Jameson was to be unexpectedly recalled back to New Zealand due to the death of his father, and the loss of two of his brothers serving at that time in the services. The loss of his older brother John hit him particularly hard. He was very close to his brother. John Jameson, a 27-year-old Lance Corporal with the 26th Battalion of the New Zealand Division was killed on 28th April 1943 while in action in North Africa. He was already the holder of the Military Medal.

Jamie's combat report for their final combat makes good reading and gives you an insight into a young man with clearly developed flying skills and the courage that allowed him to get in close to his target and out-wit them with his quick reaction and skills:

> *"After several vectors my navigator fastened on to an aircraft crossing starboard to port and I opened up to full throttle to overtake the Hun who was doing about 280 m.p.h., obtaining a visual on a Junkers 88 flying directly towards the moon. The aircraft then started weaving violently and I closed to 200 yards and opened fire, seeing several strikes on the fuselage. The enemy aircraft dived steeply to port, jinking violently as I gave him three more short bursts, strikes being seen from at least one of these. He continued to dive very steeply and turned hard to port, disappearing under me. As I pulled up to avoid hitting the ground the visual was lost and we were unable to pick it up again as control could give no help. We returned to the Vire area picking up two friendly aircraft before free-lancing onto another bogey which proved to be a Junkers 88 with very bright exhausts, well above. The enemy aircraft seemed to know that we were in the vicinity as he began to take the usual evasive action, making things difficult for my navigator too. I closed to 200 yards' range and opened fire from which a few strikes were seen on the fuselage, at the same time we received some return fire in exchange but we were not hit. The enemy aircraft then did a half roll and I followed him down to 4000 feet and gave it another burst from astern and below. Strikes were seen on the cockpit and starboard wing root and debris fell*

away as the enemy aircraft dived fairly steeply at a low speed straight into the ground. As he was going down I closed fairly rapidly and flew alongside observing that the Hun was painted grey underneath. When he hit the ground, he exploded and burnt fiercely. I claim one Ju 88 destroyed and one damaged." [47]

> **(49)** 07/08/1944 - 00:15 hrs - Ex Colerne - Jameson and Crookes - Ju 88 - Avranches, France

Interestingly one of the two "friendlies" that Jameson and Crookes investigated over Vire was piloted by Sub.Lt. Murray Richardson who had earlier been with 488 Squadron with a Fleet Air Arm group but had been transferred to 410 Squadron. Richardson had witnessed both attacks by Jameson and was able to confirm one of these as a "kill". Murray told the author that he remembered that night in great detail. Their AI unit started smoking and eventually failed so they were heading back to base bitterly disappointed when they found themselves in the middle of the action. It has to be remembered that all this action occurred at night when even the hint of the moon's glow could sometimes keep both bombers and the defending night fighters either in cloud or still on the ground at their bases waiting for darker conditions to prevail. Having visual confirmation from the air was a real bonus and a great help with the Jameson and Crookes claim.

August was to be a good month for the squadron with this latest success taking the squadron tally to forty-nine and thirty-nine of those had been shot down since 488 Squadron joined 149 Wing of the Tactical Air Force Group. They were the newest squadron in the night-fighter group and led the "score" by a long margin with twenty successes in the last nine nights.

Despite his early return to New Zealand on 15th August 1944, George "Jamie" Jameson DSO, DFC was by war's end the most successful New Zealand night fighter pilot of the Second World War. He was just 22 years old. He destroyed eleven German aircraft with one probable and one damaged. His return to the family farm surely robbed the Allied war effort of an expert night fighter pilot. He would, I imagine have been reluctant to leave 488 Squadron but the emotional pull of returning

---

[47] This account is from *"Defence until Dawn"* by Leslie Hunt

to his family under such sad circumstances was completely understandable.

He died on 20th May 1998 in an accident on his farm at Nikiwai, North Canterbury, at age seventy-six while clearing scrub with his bulldozer. His son James, commented at the time of his wonderment *"at the irony of Bill being done in by his bloody bulldozer, but then how many 76-year-old men drive bulldozers these days?"* That in itself gives an idea of the determination of the man.

The man known as "Jamie" to his air force mates but "Bill" to his family and friends was described by Gerald Lascelles in an obituary in the Christchurch Press as a man who *"embodied the old virtues of loyalty, modesty and, above all, courage and, in these days when acknowledgement by the state has tended to become the plaything of politicians, it is well that lives such as his should remind us where true honour lies".* An indication of the special qualities of this man is reinforced by any lack of bitterness or attitudes of revenge exhibited by him in later life. He surely would have been entitled to some angst after losing both of his brothers in the course of seeking peace for the wider world or being forced to return to the family farm on the death of his father. This was a family who gave much more than most during those turbulent years.

Jameson had travelled to the northern hemisphere after enlisting at age 19 in the RNZAF and after training in the Commonwealth Air Training Scheme in Canada moved on to operational work in the UK where he was commissioned as a Pilot Officer in August of 1941. He quickly showed skills far beyond his years and his linking up with Norman Crookes unleashed on the Luftwafe a duo that enhanced the reputation of 488 Squadron with both the Allied High command and I am sure the Luftwaffe as well. It is now time that the general public knew of his exploits. On the 22nd of September, shortly after his return to the family farm at Rotheram in North Canterbury, F/L George Esmond Jameson was awarded the D.S.O. for meritorious services with 488 Squadron.

Jameson's navigator partner, Norman Crookes had developed a skill level with his AI radar work that more than complimented the flying and shooting skills of Jameson. Crookes went on after the war to have an illustrious teaching career retiring as Headmaster of William Rhodes School in 1981. His community service did not stop there as he continued with his work with the Air Training Corp started much earlier in his teaching career. He was in fact awarded the MBE in 1974 for the ATC work. He was involved also with Rotary service clubs and with the Barnardo's organisation.

An indication of the technical skill of this man was no better emphasised when, with the departure of Jamie Jameson, he partnered up with another New Zealand pilot, Ray Jeffs and carried on the same spectacular rate of successful interventions in the night sky over the UK and Europe. It was interesting that the last "kill" he had when paired with Ray Jeffs, a Ju 88 was not confirmed as destroyed until the 1990's when a researcher was able to provide sufficient evidence that unofficially converted their claim from "probable" to "destroyed".

Word was received from the authorities on 10th August that the body of P/O. Oliver Hills had been recovered from the coast at Sheerness. Hills had been reported missing during a mission way back on 25th November 1943 when he was forced to bail out of his aircraft piloted by S/L Dudley Hobbis when one of their engines caught fire during a mission out of Bradwell Bay. Hills was buried at Epsom with the squadron represented at his funeral by F/O Warner.

More awards came the squadron's way when P/O. Chris Vlotman was awarded a D.F.C and his crewman, Sgt. Johnny Wood a D.F.M, the only one awarded to 488 Squadron. There were further awards when the Netherlands Government recognised the crew for the work they were doing and Queen Wilhelmina of the Netherlands invested Chris Vlotman with the Dutch Flying Cross. Young Sgt. Johnny Woods was not forgotten, receiving the same medal and further being granted commissioned rank as a Pilot Officer. He was still not twenty years of age.

The fiftieth kill for 488 Squadron was recorded by F/L Johnny Hall on 15th August when with Jock Cairns they destroyed a Ju 88 after it had sprayed their aircraft with cannon fire fortunately without damage as it dived steeply to try and avoid an attack by the Mosquito crew.

---

(50) *15/08/1944 – 00:25 – Ex Colerne – Hall and Cairns – Ju 88 – Sth of Caen, France*

The Ju 88 was unsuccessful in his attempt to escape and Hall caught him with a short burst initially but finished him off with strikes down its fuselage causing it to turn on its back and spin into the ground. As it went down Hall commented to his crewman, Cairns, that there was a lot of flaming debris coming back. His demeanour changed somewhat when Cairns pointed out to him that the flaming bits coming back were cannon fire from the rear gunner. He later recounted that he was greatly amused as Hall carried out sudden and desperate manoeuvres to avoid being shot down by his target during its final moments. He had earlier put himself and his aircraft behind another Ju 188, all at high speed and had the Mosquito roaring along at maximum speed just to try and keep up with his target. He recalls firing three short bursts but they lost contact shortly after and the target was not seen again.

A "Fiftieth" victory party was held. A bounty of fifty pounds had been offered to the ground crew of the aircraft that achieved the fiftieth kill for the squadron and Hall and Cairns were pleased to be able to win it for their support crew and the pair of them no doubt played a big part in the celebrations.

Shortly after the 50th success party, John Hall, Jock Cairns, Ray Jeffs and two of the NCO Pilots, W/O Concannon and W/O Patrick flew in the squadron Oxford over into the Normandy area of France to visit some of the forward "Control" units they would soon be working when they eventually moved to France. They landed on an American base on the Cherbourg Peninsula but when they set off to leave for home the Oxford became very temperamental, so much so that they had to abandon any attempt to fly it home. They were now stranded in France. The only way back was by ship so the unfortunate crew were despatched to the nearest beach-head to await a ride back to England. Conditions were very primitive with the sounds of war all around them as they tried sleeping in small army tents among the sand dunes. Jock Cairns remembers attended a "bizarre" concert among the dunes while anti-aircraft guns blazed away during the show. Sleep was almost impossible that night as the racket did not diminish at all. Later the next day, they left the shores of France for England in an American tank landing craft accompanied by two military policemen and thirty odd deserters being sent home for punishment. They eventually arrived back at Colerne to rejoin the squadron.

The forward Control units that the crews had visited in Normandy would turn out to be vital for the night-fighter operations over Europe. They were still very experimental and were set up in all sorts of mobile situations. Armoured vehicles were used, trucks, railway wagons and some units were even sent in by gliders during the disastrous Arnhem landings. The night fighter squadrons of the Allied air command were rarely without GCI station control coverage anywhere in Europe. These portable stations moved with the Front line as the Allied armies slowly and inexorably took control and forced the German armies into retreat. These night-fighter units were still set up as defensive units and the troops on the ground and the navy off the coast benefitted greatly from these largely unseen and unknown nocturnal overhead protectors that only came out at night and with the dawning of the new day returned to base. Jimmy Rawnsley commented that the night–fighters became pawns being used by opposing Controllers as they sought to clear the night air of opposing aircraft.

P/O. Stan McCabe with his crewman, W/O Newman struggled back to a near emergency base in France with engine trouble after a confrontation with a Ju 88 south of Caen on 16th August. During the combat, he had to "feather" his starboard engine as the prop started to run out of control and threatened to self destruct.

(51) *16/08/1944 – Unknown - Ex Colerne – McCabe and Newman – Ju 88 – Caen, France*

He had hit his target long and hard with his first contact and had the satisfaction of seeing the Junkers plough into the ground and explode. McCabe reported his annoyance with the ground defences when despite having his navigation lights and his IFF identification radar on and flying at a low altitude looking for a safe landing, was plastered with intense and very accurate anti-aircraft fire from Allied guns. Even as he was about to land the Royal Artillery units positioned on the edge of the airfield near Caen opened up. The Mosquito crew fired off their "Verey" flare signal pistol and that seemed to stop them. When the Mosquito finally came to a stop some very agitated airmen came running up with flashing torches and shouted at them to stay in the aircraft. They had apparently ended up in the airfield mine field. They were forced to clamber out carefully and were guided back following the tyre marks from their aircraft. Stan later went over to the artillery units to give them a piece of his mind and found them shouting that they had nearly got a Jerry tonight and to his disgust found that they were all totally inebriated. No combat report was found for this action but HK 377 is credited with the 'kill' in the daily Operations Record Book.

While McCabe was struggling with his aircraft, and looking for an emergency base, F/L Bill Cook with F/O Don Proctor were over the mouth of the River Orne, where they latched on to a Ju 188 dropping parachutes. They closed in and hit the Junkers on the tailplane after a long chase. At a crucial moment, the gun sight collapsed and they lost sight of their target. Proctor managed to pick the enemy aircraft again on his AI unit but they were unable to get a visual so they could only claim a "Damaged".

Following the departure of "Jamie" Jameson back to New Zealand, Norman Crookes had teamed up with a new pilot, F/O Ray Jeffs, another New Zealand pilot, and on their first patrol together in MM 622, shot down a Dornier 217 over Rouen on the night of 18th August 1944.

> **(52)** *18/08/1944 – 23:43 hrs – Ex Colerne – Jeffs and Crookes – Do 217 – Sth of Rouen, France*

Following directions from Ground Control they were directed to investigate a "bogey" heading due east. They had followed it on a gently weaving course while it was dropping copious quantities of "window". They obtained a visual on a Dornier 217 from a hundred metres out and dropped behind ready to attack. The Dornier spotted its attacker and dived down to five hundred feet with Jeff's right on his tail. After several bursts of cannon fire from the Mosquito at a range of 400 feet a fire started internally and the Dornier turned gently to port and dived into the ground.

The attack they launched that night was particularly pleasing for Norman Crookes as it continued the successful results that he had achieved with Jamie Jameson. Crookes commented later that Ray Jeffs had got very excited at the time as this was the first actual encounter that he had with an enemy aircraft and he had opened fire from a great distance without initial success. Crookes managed to talk Jeffs in closer and success was to be theirs. He was very pleased that he was able to work well with Ray Jeffs and added that he was a very good pilot.

Two nights later over Caen, F/O Douglas Robinson, and W/O Addison teamed up and after a lead from Ground Control "Addie" worked magic with his AI and directed "Robbie" right onto the tail of their target. A good visual of a Ju 188 carrying bombs was silhouetted against a flare in the background and "Robbie" had no trouble firing several bursts to send the Junkers into the ground, bombs and all. He commented that the enemy aircraft must have been carrying incendiaries judging by the fire on the ground.

(53) *20/08/1944 – 23:55 hrs – Ex Colerne – Robinson and Addison – Ju 188 – E of Caen, France*

The same night W/O. Bourke, with F/O Skudder had four separate chases with each having to be abandoned frustratingly due to intense and very accurate anti-aircraft fire from Allied ground defences.

W/O. Dick Addison, DFC and DFM, known as "Addie" to all and sundry came to the squadron with an interesting background. He had joined the British army before the war but on the outbreak of war in 1939 decided he had a preference for the air force. He joined up and when his acceptance was confirmed he then advised the army of his decision. He actually won his DFM when still only a Lac (Leading Aircraftsman) and on one occasion was arrested by police in London. They thought it strange that such a low-ranking serviceman was wearing a ribbon for a Distinguished Flying Medal. In the early stages of the war the RAF recruited air gunners from the ranks and many of them were serving as aircrew gunners despite their non-commisioned status.

On 25th August 1944, news came in that Peter Hall and Dick Marriott had both received bars to their earlier won DFC's which they had received just three weeks earlier.

While on patrol the next night, Haine and Bowman had a call from their controller to say that they had a "friendly" aircraft on their tail that was showing "undue" interest in them and advised them to do a quick turnaround to shake him off. A friendly aircraft would normally not have been a cause for concern but identification was fraught with difficulty and a mistaken identity by either aircraft could prove fatal given the poor visibility in the air during the night time hours. Haine hauled his Mosquito round in a tight turn but as he straightened up was hit by a burst of cannon fire smacking into the fuselage behind the cockpit. He quickly outmanoeuvred and evaded his attacker and headed for Colerne not knowing what damage had been caused. They made it safely despite later finding 20mm cannon shells embedded in a dingy pack just behind their heads. They later found out their attacker was an American *Black Widow* night fighter from No. 422 U.S.A.F. Squadron. Despite later identifying their actual attacker, they never got an explanation or apology for the debacle. There was some satisfaction however for the pair as they had comprehensively outmanoeuvred their opponent and it was probably the reason they suffered little damage following the first strike on them.

This incident highlighted the problem of restricted radar coverage from the airborne units which had no coverage towards the rear of the aircraft. Very late in the war the Germans did develop rear facing defensive radar but the British at that stage had virtually nothing similar.

The Squadron Commander, W/C Dickie Haine flying ME-A and following instructions from Control claimed his final kill of the war on the night of 1st September when he spotted a silhouette of an aircraft overhead casting a moonlit reflection on the sea and travelling towards him. He hauled his Mosquito around in a tight turn, lifted the nose and despite an unserviceable gun sight fired off short bursts as he made the turn and scored hits on a Ju 188. Lots of debris flew off causing him to pull up to avoid damage and they temporarily lost sight of their target. Pete Bowman managed to gain contact again on his AI unit and Haine hit him again in the already burning starboard engine. That burst caused a further outbreak of fire and the Ju 188 dived vertically straight into the sea west off the French coast at Le Havre. Haine and Bowman were very pleased with the outcome.

(54) *01/09/1944 - 23:25 hrs – Ex Colerne – Haine and Bowman – Ju 188 – W of Le Havre, France*

The squadron was moved from their tented quarters on 3rd September to "Static" quarters in anticipation of a move to the Continent. Although there was general relief that they would at least be moving into billets with solid walls and a roof they were surprised that they were expected to still use camp kits and live under field conditions.

Their disappointment would however be tempered by the arrival that same afternoon of the first of their new Mk XXX Night Fighter Mosquitos. These were equipped with the new American developed Mk. X AI Radar system initially known as SCR 720. Ironically these were already fitted to the American Black Widow night fighters that very nearly caused Haine and Bowman some grief less than a week before. Detailed drawings and sketches of the SCR 720 system and its predecessor, the Mk VIII were scarce due to the secrecy limitations imposed at the time. The De Havilland identification numbers changed from the old HK prefix to the new MM series. The new radar units meant sudden and intensive training to become familiar with the new technology. It was clear that they were being prepared for operations deeper into Europe in the coming weeks. The training meant downtime from operational work but the break was very necessary. The characteristics of the new model Mosquito were radically different to the old Mk13's they had been using. The heavier armaments and the new Radar equipment in the nose changed the flying characteristics and Al Gabites recalls being very wary of the handling of his aircraft and found that his approach speed on landing had to be markedly increased.

The Mk.X AI Radar units were bulky and details shown of the new system show nothing sophisticated with the setup, miniaturisation was obviously unheard of at the time. The new system relied on the crewman using two screens in place of the single unit of the old Mk. VIII and most of the Radar operators of the time were unhappy with the change having just learned to master the old system.

These units were used in a multitude of aircraft well after the end of the war as the growing use of night-fighters and the concept of night fighting was accepted by many different countries when the secrecy surrounding the units was gradually lifted.

The crewman sat facing the AI screens as shown below. Some considerable skill was needed to track the target with the new system and many of the crew reported difficulty with the change to twin screens but once mastered there was a gradual acceptance that this was indeed a superior system that was more accurate although difficult to work with.

In an interesting development, the squadron records show the 6488 Servicing Echelon coming under the direct command of 488 Squadron at this time. These echelons had been set up as integral units with their own command structure and were generally placed on air bases to serve multiple squadron aircrews and aircraft. The logistics required to bring the echelon into and under the direct command of W/C Haine must have created huge problems with the sudden responsibility of an additional 304 personnel. The administration and responsibility for the extra bodies must had put considerable strain on what few Admin staff that Haine had available to him. The attachment was probably caused by 488 Squadron being readied for the move to the Continent and in effect taking their echelon with them rather than having to rely on probably already stretched maintenance services on the European aifields.

There was little or no operational flying during September 1944 owing to the training and the disruption caused by the ground-crews preparing for the squadron move to Europe. One of the squadron's new Mk. 30's, MT 456 was written off when it was hit by an out of control

Wellington bomber LP625 while parked in its dispersal area on the 18th September. The pilot of the Wellington had overshot his landing point and tried to take off again under full power. He landed on top of the Mosquito and bounced off and crashed into the "B" Flight Dispersal hut. Two of the crew of the Wellington were killed and two of the 6488 Echelon ground crew who were in the hut at the time were injured, fortunately not seriously. They were very lucky.

P/O. J.H. Moore made one of his numerous one engined landings when he was forced to feather the propeller on one of his engines when it failed while under power during take-off. He was forced to go around and make an unscheduled landing on one engine, again without damage to his aircraft or injury to his crewman or himself. Before the end of their tour of duty, his crewman, P/O. Alan Earl must have wondered what was in store for them every time they boosted full power during the many one engine take offs they were forced to make.

A successful take-off following a sudden loss of power in one engine was a particularly hazardous feat. The skill level of a pilot in this situation would have been severely tested. There would normally have been little warning as engine roughness or vibration would had given some warning to back off the throttle setting and abort the takeoff. Given that this event would occur under full power, probably while just airborne the risk of loss of control was enormous. Landing on one engine could at least be a controlled situation but losing power on takeoff and obtaining successful control again beggared belief.

By the end of September 488 Squadron had fifteen crews fully operational with the new aircraft and radar system and were classified operational ready and a new era in their wartime lives was about to start.

F/L Peter Hall, RNZAF   DFC and Bar,

The crew of W/O Jimmy Concannon and P/O. Gordon Patrick (Ron Watts)

Above: P/O. Len Wyman RAF in much happier times! (Chris Wyman). Below left: F/L Allen Browne DFC RNZAF. Below right: F/L George "Jamie" Esmond Jameson D.S.O, D.F.C.

Above left: Dick Marriott on left with Peter Hall (Reg Mitchell). Right: F/L Allen Browne DFC. on the left with his crewman W/O Tom Taylor.

A Dornier 217 Fighter Bomber of the Luftwaffe with that distinctive tailplane that helped the Allied crews considerably with identification.

Above: Norman Crookes and his wife Sheila shortly before he passed away at age 91 on 17th April 2012. Below left: F/L Owen (Stan) McCabe RNZAF (Ted Edwards). Below left: P/O. Jimmy Moore AFC, master of the one engined take-off and landing.

A photograph taken at Colerne and captioned on back "ground crew" but I suspect that the presence of John Hall (front row first from left with big smile) and Jock Cairns sitting third from left beside Monty Norman in the front row could indicate that this was the 50 th "Kill" get together and party for the "B" Flight ground crew (George Sutherland)

A good view of the characteristic extended "snout" enclosing the new Mk.X AI radar system. The parabolic dish that rotated continuously around its vertical and horizontal axis is the most visible part of the system. The radar dome "snout" was made from plexiglass and painted to match the camouflage colour of the aircraft. These units were used in a multitude of aircraft well after the end of the war as the growing use of night-fighters and the concept of night fighting was accepted by many different countries when the secrecy surrounding the units was gradually lifted. (Belgium Air force photograph).

W/O. Dick Addison and F/O Douglas Robinson standing in front of ME-H at Zeals. (Ron Watts)

The US Air Force P-61 Black Widow nightfighter – the same type that attacked Haine and Bowman on the night of 26th August 1944

Mosquito cockpit showing the Mk. VIII AI unit used extensively throughout 1943 and 1944 before being replaced by the later Mk.10 AI unit (Chris Poole).

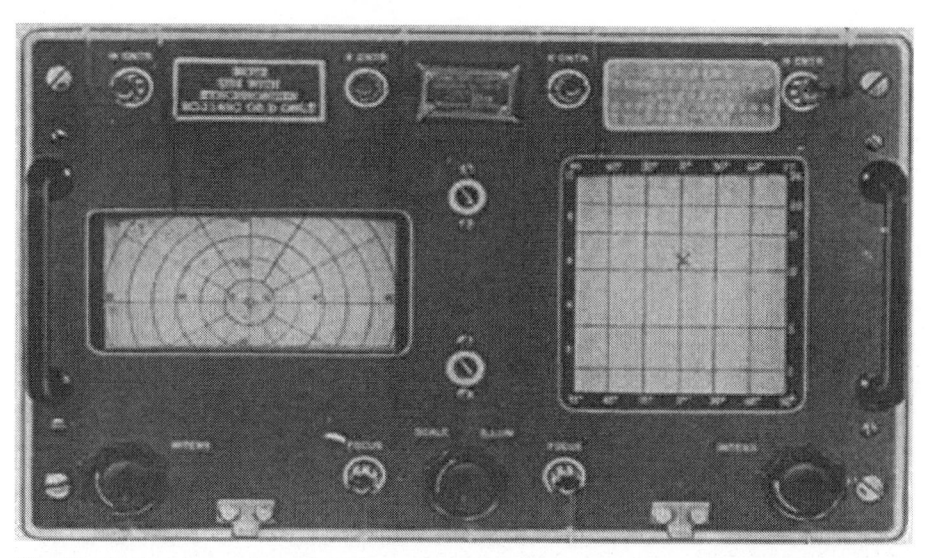

The Mk. X AI cockpit unit screen. The crewman sat facing these. Some considerable skill was needed to track the target with the new system and many of the crew reported difficulty with the change to twin screens but once mastered there was a gradual acceptance that this was indeed a superior system that was more accurate although difficult to work with.

Item	Description
	S.C.R. 720 items
SC	Scanner Unit
HF	High Frequency Unit
IO	Indicater observer's
SY	Synchroniser
CB1	Control Box
JB	Junction Box
HV	High Voltage rectifier
PU	Power Unit
RR	Regulated rectifier
M	Modulator
B	Blower
S	Suppressor type "P"
	S.C.R 729 Items
TR	
IU	
CB2	
A	
	S.C.R. Existing on A/C
AS	Aerial Starboard
AP	Aerial Port
CP	Control Panel
VR	Voltage regulator
R	Receiver R3078

The above componentry formed the basis of the Mk. X units and were distributed throughout the mainframe of the Mosquito as shown in the sketch below to try and trim out the aircraft.

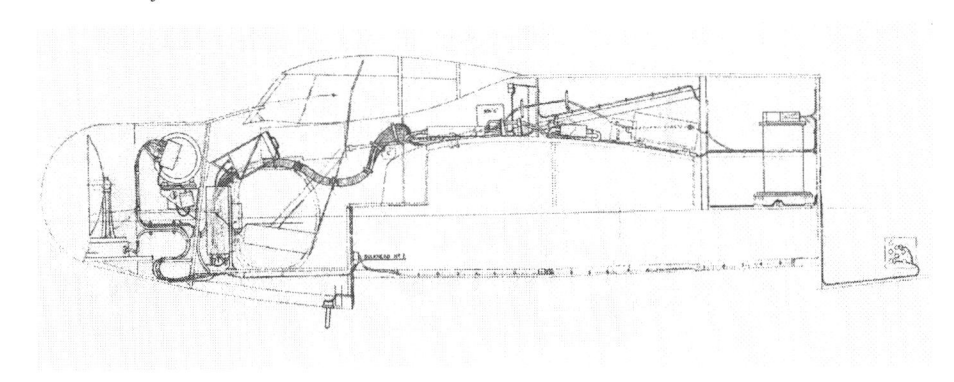

A pensive Ray Gager RNZAF pictured at Colerne. Ray was at the forefront in the ongoing development and servicing of the AI Radar units installed in both the Beaufighter and Mosquito aircraft used by 488 Squadron until the wars end in 1945. Ray was one of several New Zealand technicians serving with 6488 Echelon ground-crew as key members of the Radar systems Unit. (Alastair Gager).

Chapter Seven

HUNSDON - HERTFORDSHIRE, ENGLAND

9TH OCTOBER 1944 TO 15th NOVEMBER 1944

On the 9th October 1944, the squadron flew in formation from Colerne across to Hunsdon lead by their C.O. W/C Dickie Haine and almost immediately, started operational flying. It was clear that Hunsdon was only going to be a transitional base and the move was designed to prepare them for the move to the continent in less than six weeks' time. The squadron ground-crew in the meantime had a forward party already on the Continent with the bulk of the ground-crew packing up equipment back at Colerne in readiness for moving down to the coast and so on to France by ship. F/L "Monty" Norman took over command in the absence of W/C Haine

The accommodation at Hunsdon was not much better than that at Colerne being temporary at best, but the squadron was happy to be back flying operationally at last. Their last operational flight was back on the 14th September. At least four aircraft were in the air that night such was the keenness to get back in the fray. No contacts were made and the four aircraft had to be diverted to Manston airbase due to the weather packing up over Hunsdon.

On 19th October F/L Al Gabites experienced engine trouble during an afternoon test flight and overshot the runway while attempting a one engined landing and completely destroyed his aircraft.

The squadron was disappointed on the 22nd of October to hear that they would be losing the services at the end of the month, of their popular commanding officer, Wng.Com. Haine. Haine was to be posted to a staff position at 85 Group Headquarters and was to be replaced by the newly promoted W/C Ron Watts, the Flight Commander of "A" Flight and on him fell the responsibility for the re-organisation of 488 to prepare them for the move to the Continent. There was a considerable changeover of crews during this time with some of the old

488 crews returning for another tour of duty with the squadron. S/L Johnny Gard'ner returned to take over "A" Flight following Ron Watts' promotion to C.O.

Ron Watts came from a very humble background. He was born on 11th March 1916 in Auckland, New Zealand. After the end of the First World War the family moved onto a farming block to the west of Auckland City, later living in various parts of the Auckland area. He was brought up by his parents in a strictly Protestant home. Ron enjoyed the country life but the easy-going country life was tempered somewhat with the onset of the Depression which hit New Zealand hard. His first job out of school was farming and he eventually moved to the Waikato region, farmed for a while but ended up shearing sheep for a living.

In September 1939, the war clouds were heading his way and Ron decided that he would join the army. He missed the early intakes for the army to his frustration but took up the advice of the local recruiting officer and instead changed his mind and applied to join the air force. After early basic training he soon found himself on the Troopship "Aorangi" and heading northwards towards Canada for aircrew training under the Commonwealth Air Training Scheme. There he was to join the hundreds of other young men from New Zealand, Australia, Canada and South Africa.

The training in Canada was basic and fraught with danger as there were many accidents among the trainees. It was here that Ron spoke of his "Guardian Angel" first appearing, a reference that he was to mention many times over the coming months when he inexplicably got out of potentially life-threatening situations by the skin of his teeth seemingly by luck alone.

It was clear by this time by any reviewer that despite Ron attributing a lot of the near misses to luck alone, that he possessed skills and had an intellect and those qualities combined with his extremely high pass marks on all courses, that this was a man showing all the attributes of a leader at a very young age. Ron moved on to the UK and was transferred to a training unit as an instructor. He commented on the high casualty rate at the time of both trainees and instructors. He was promoted quickly to Pilot Officer then less than a year later to Flying Officer, something he attributed in his normal modest way to the high attrition rate of his fellow pilots at that time.

Ron Watts had joined 488 Squadron directly from his training squadron in July 1942. He brought with him Roger Folley who was to be his regular navigator for the rest of his time with 488 Squadron.

The ground crew Echelon known as 6488, left Colerne on the morning of the 24th by road to travel down to the coast to prepare for the Channel crossing. There had been considerable criticism of the lack of support and co-operation of the staff running Base Colerne and the parting remarks from the Station Commanding Officer reinforced just how unwelcome 488 Squadron had been during their brief stay there. 488 squadron's diarist commented that this was a unique experience for them as they had been most welcome and had the utmost co-operation from any other units they had associated with since the squadron's inception.

Jimmy Rawnsley commented in his book, "Night Fighter", of just this scenario when an earlier edict from Air Operations had set up almost "ethnic" based squadrons taking officers out of mixed race squadrons and forming "Dominionised" squadrons. The change in squadron demographics led to tensions based on ethnic lines where the earlier squadrons had in his opinion performed well, catering for a wide diversification of members which prevented the intense rivalry later experienced by rampant nationalism. Whilst we can never be sure that this was the reason for the enmity displayed by the resident station staff it was almost certain that the "Kiwi" characteristic would certainly have annoyed any hierarchy used to the stiffness, class distinction and formality of the old order.

The Squadron had a visit from Air Vice Marshall Saunders on 26th October to specifically thank 488 for the good work they had done under his command. As it was rare for the squadron to be shown any appreciation his visit was well received. He was relinquishing command of No. 11 Group and before he left he felt it was important to single our 488 for their efforts under very trying conditions. He had particular praise for the ground crew.

October 1944 closed out with no enemy aircraft shot down. The weather had been particularly bad and there was general disappointment that now they had the latest in updated machines and equipment the scoreboard had remained static.

The bad weather continued into November with many aircraft on completing their night patrols being diverted to other airfields due to the weather closing in over Hunsdon. These diversions were not good for the aircrew as they missed out on the comfort of their own beds and they could only get a short time to relax before getting airborne once more to return to their own base when the weather cleared to return their aircraft back for servicing and re-arming before the next night's sorties.

A strange incident occurred on 2nd November when W/O Fritchley with his crewman, F/Sgt. Ray on board damaged his aircraft during takeoff when one of his propeller tips struck the ground. He managed the takeoff safely but overshot on attempting to land on one engine and badly damaged his aircraft. It is difficult to imagine just what position the aircraft was in for this to happen. It would have to be one wing down and a rather savage "tail high" bounce to get the prop tips low enough for contact I would think. Although the aircraft was badly damaged both crewmen were unhurt.

The first and only "kill" in the month of November went to the crew of W/O Johnny Marshall and F/O Phil Prescott. They were put on to a target over Antwerp by Control on the 4th of November very early in the evening – just 7:00pm. The target was travelling head on towards them quite slowly estimated to be only 150mph. Marshall moved in very close and identified a bomb carrying Me 110. Marshall backed off to a safer distance but stalled his aircraft in the process. After recovering they established contact again and knocked the bomb off the port wing with a quick burst, following this up with a second burst and the Me 110 turned over into a dive from which it never recovered, hitting the ground east of Arnhem.

(55) *04/11/1944 – 18:58 hrs – Ex Hunsdon – Marshall and Prescott – Me 110 – Arnheim, France*

Marshall had joined the RNZAF relatively late in the war – in January 1942 and after the usual training courses in NZ and the UK was posted directly to 488 Squadron at Bradwell Bay. He was awarded a "Mentioned in Despatches" for meritorious service.

Two days after the Marshall and Prescott success on 7th November, F/O A.L. Shaw gave himself and his crewman a terrible fright and found himself the subject of a court of enquiry when his Mosquito MM814 collided with an accumulator trolley while taxying back to his dispersal after a night operation. The aircraft was badly damaged. The trolleys were mobile storage batteries and used to start the twin engines on each aircraft to save overloading or draining the aircraft's electrical systems.

The Squadron Diarist commented on the arrival of two further new crews and said that they already had three other crews not yet operational, all on the eve of travelling to the continent on a full war footing. He obviously had some concerns about this situation. The squadron had already been given orders to join 148 Wing based at Lille in northern France but these orders had been changed on 11th November following a visit by Wing Commander Watts to 149 Group Headquarters' where he was told that a change had been made and he was to set up his squadron at Amiens-Glisy under the control of 149 Wing. Some of the older squadron members were displeased about returning to this wing where they had some unhappy times previously. Reinforcement of the later decision was finally confirmed by Wing Com. Hayes, DFC who had earlier travelled back to Hunsdon for further discussion on the matter.

While the squadron were operating out of Hunsdon their repairs and maintenance had been done by 1018 Echelon with the 6488 Echelon, their normal maintenance unit in transit to France. For the first time ever, aircraft from the stand down flight had to be seconded to crews from the operational flight due to the maintenance of their own aircraft being sadly in arrears. It well indicated the high degree of efficiency that the 6488 Echelon under "Monty" Norman had operated on. As if to make up for the situation the 1018 Echelon organised a leaving party for 488 Squadron in a local pub and fortunately night flying was once again cancelled so both flights of the squadron were able and well pleased to attend.

On the 14th November, the date and timing of their leaving Hunsdon to the Continent was received from No.85 Group, under whose control the 149 Wing would come under. Arrangements were made for four Dakota transport aircraft to come from RAF Uxbridge to fly the radar equipment and remaining ground staff across to Amiens.

The ground crew party that had earlier left the squadron had been camped down on the coast with all the maintenance equipment for about six weeks and had finally left by ship for the Continent. They were to be at sea for another three weeks before landing on the coast of Belgium and then transporting all their equipment on to Amiens-Glisy in France. Quite while they were at sea for that length of time has never been explained but it was very likely that they were confined to ship while berthed in port somewhere I suspect.

There had been considerable drama on board the ship taking them across the channel. The ground crew echelon would have literally been like fish out of water. They were stuck in the middle of a convoy for some time but the feeling of safety engendered by being in the middle was tempered somewhat when the ship in front of them struck a mine with a tremendous explosion and sank rather quickly. One of the few survivors fished out of the water that day was F/O Rowbotham, the former Medical Officer of 488.

On the morning of 15th November, the remaining ground crew left back at Hunsdon were transported over the channel in Dakota transport aircraft to airfield B.48 at Amiens-Glisy.

Mosquito landing at Hunsdon (Ron Watts).

Above: S/L Johnny Gard'ner "A" Flight Commander, Capt. Henry Burr (Army Searchlight and Anti-Aircraft Co-ordinator,) F/L Johnny Bolingbroke (Radar and Electronics), with 'Monty', F/O Richard Norman, the Squadron Engineering Officer hatching some plot. (from Defence until Dawn). Below left: P/O. Allot Gabites RNZAF. Below right: W/C Ronald Graham Watts RNZAF, 488 Squadron's sixth and final Commanding Officer 30th October 1944 to 25th April 1945

Ron Watts and Roger Folley (Ron Watts).

A low flying 488 'Mossie', thought to be over Hunsden doing what was colloquially known as a beat-up! (Ron Watts photo)

One of the Mosquito Mk. XIIIs with "invasion" stripes plainly visible on final approach to land (from Mosquito, an illustrated history by Philip J Birtles).

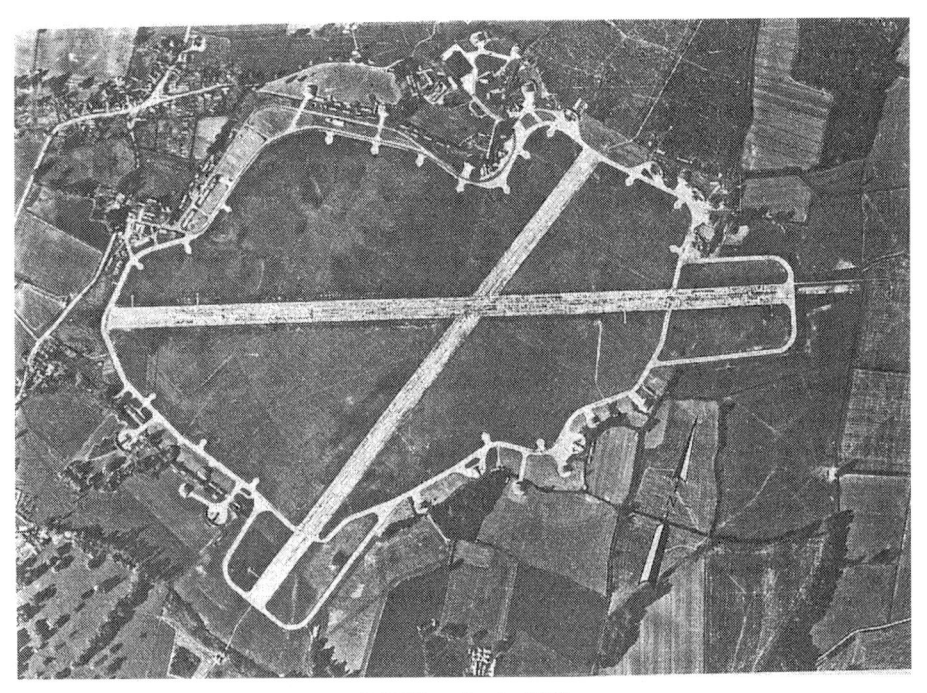

RAF Hunsdon in 1943

The 6488 Echelon Ground-Crew heading for the coast at Ostend (from Defence until Dawn).

Chapter Eight

AMIENS-GLISY B48 - FRANCE

15th NOVEMBER 1944 TO 4th APRIL 1945

488 Squadron joined two other squadrons at Amiens on 15th November 1944, No. 409 Squadron RCAF and No. 219 Squadron RAF, both also flying later model Mosquito Mk 30's with the Merlin 76 engines. Each squadron was instructed to provide its share of aircraft nightly and the evenings activities were pre- programmed to ensure full patrol coverage of their designated sectors. The coverage was to be from dusk to dawn. The squadron left behind Chris Vlotman and Johnny Wood when they made the move. They were posted to another squadron and were to be greatly missed.

The four Dakota's carrying equipment and ground crew landed around 1:30pm from Hunsdon followed by the first of the Mosquitos at 3:00pm. There was an expectation that 488 Squadron would be operational that very night and there was somewhat of a rush to get aircraft serviced in order to meet their commitment. Fortunately, as it turned out, bad weather once again caused a cancellation of the nights flying.

The officer's accommodation was a series of wooden huts in very poor condition and not the best place to bunk down given the appalling weather conditions they were experiencing at the time. Worse though for some of the aircrew was a rundown bomb-damaged chateau nearby. The NCO aircrew had much better sleeping quarters as they were housed in requisitioned houses although these were badly overcrowded. Of more concern was the washing and sanitary facilities which were primitive to say the least although the squadron Diarist commented that *"the poor facilities were more a subject of wit than worry"*. All those facilities were well away from the airbase itself some being several to travelling into town to use the Municipal Baths queuing as Johnny Hall commented with *"a mixed assortment of students, school girls, gendarmes, and army privates"*.

Both "A" and "B" Flights had tented sites on the base itself pending completion of new huts still some weeks away. F/L Johnny Hall, in correspondence to his family revealed the primitive nature of the accommodation, *"The stove in our hut still smokes, and there is a leak in the roof over my bed, but these are minor worries. Meanwhile we have evolved an ingenious means of heating shaving water. It consists of a tin filled with earth and petrol over which we poise our can in the best Boy Scout tradition"*.

Jock Cairns wrote of this time in his memoirs *"Owls and Fools Fly at Night"* One of his enduring memories is the day that W/C. Watts, the squadron C.O. and F/L Tom Mallon stood in deep discussion in front of one of the better huts that had been allocated to the squadron for use as their Dispersal hut. Cairns was amazed to see in a very short time a group of officers using poles and rollers moving the hut to a new and better position picked by Ron Watts. Cairns considered that the effort was somewhat aligned to the All Black rugby training methods, brute strength and a good dose of cunning.

The incessant mud was the biggest problem and proved a big challenge for the servicing echelon just to keep the aircraft from sinking into the soft ground. The difficulty of extracting a bogged in aircraft undercarriage was fraught with difficulty due to the slender nature of the undercarriage components and the high point loading and the potential to do serious damage was never far from the ground crew's minds. The mud and rain eventually changed to snow and ice which was little improvement on their current situation.

Many ingenious constructions arose around the base as materials were borrowed or stolen to build shelters or pathways to keep out the ground slush or the icy winds that swept the airfield. The large wooden building that contained the kitchen, dining room and bar was heated by a contraption put together by Monty Norman. It was simply a large oil drum fed by old engine oil which burned continuously. The Kiwi work ethic was put to a severe test while the camp was being set up but the squadron soon had accommodation that was a vast improvement on the other squadrons on the base.

The squadron C.O. Ron Watts recalled the bad weather and considered Amiens the coldest of any bases he had served on during the war. He slept for a time in a caravan with canvas sides which allowed snow to drift in overnight. He did have a kerosene heater but was fearful of having it burning away during the night because of the fumes. He commented on the conditions faced by the ground-crews having to work with tools out in the open and not having covered in workshops for protection from the elements. Even the parked aircraft needed constant heating. The engines were covered and had canvas tubes dropping down to ground level where kerosene heaters in the tubes on the ground fed hot air up the tubes to keep the engine oil and coolant from freezing.

It was during this period that W/C Ron Watts stood out for his leadership. His attitude towards his men created a great deal of respect for him and although 488 Squadron had been well served by its previous commanders, Ron Watts was very well spoken of by men of all ranks. It was he that organised transport to get his men down to the local town bath house at regular intervals when the ablution facilities on the base proved totally inadequate. They had been effectively destroyed by the retreating Luftwaffe. He was shocked to find that despite no bathing or showering facilities being available on the base he never once saw anyone from either of the other two squadrons on the base or even from the airfield headquarters down at the bath house.

Amiens had been a place where the New Zealand Division fought and won a decisive battle in 1918 although at great cost with dead and wounded. This author's grandfather was wounded there all those many years ago. The old trench systems and shell craters were still clearly visible from the air. For many of the New Zealanders in the squadron it was an emotional link with events that had occurred some twenty odd years and a generation before. The New Zealanders were to find considerable warmth and appreciation from the local population for the deeds carried out by an earlier generation of servicemen during the time of World War One. They had not forgotten.

Night flying was impossible for the first few nights and some semblance of normality returned when some sorties were flown for the first time on the night of the 19th November.

The squadron personnel set up a committee to organise sporting and recreational activities outside of working hours. The on again, off again nature of their operational rolls meant that at any one time at least half of the squadron were on stand down and these activities were considered important for morale and physical wellbeing. The squadron at that time had about 300 airmen – fitters, armourers, radio operators, radar operators and admin staff plus crews for at least 30 aircraft so organising any activity with that number of men under his command was a formidable task for Wng.Com. Ron Watts.

One of the recreational activities banned for the squadron in Amiens was areas where houses of ill-repute were established. A notice was posted informing the squadron members of places from which they should stay away. Len Wyman commented that the list was basically a list of bawdy houses and similar establishments of ill-repute. He noted that certain members thought the list was most informative and helpful though not necessarily in the manner intended by the person who posted the list.

Len Wyman went on to relate that one of the characters of the squadron was Johnny Mulgrew, a New Zealander although Irish by birth. He was known for carrying an American .45 revolver at all times as he maintained that the RAF issue .38 revolver *"did not have enough stopping power"*. One night Johnny headed off into the "Forbidden zone" area but not in search of anything more than more booze for the guys. Unfortunately, he lost his way and stumbled into a canal from which he could not extract himself. He had been there for some hours until his predicament was noticed by some French "ladies" who helped him out. They took him to their home where they gave him a hot bath. They also cleaned, dried and pressed his clothes. Finally, they gave him a slap-up meal before sending him on his way. He returned to the squadron much smarter in appearance than when he set out with a huge grin on his face but without the beer!

There were a couple of scary incidents on the 25th November when P/O. Jimmy Moore, and his crewman, P/O. Earl had engine trouble over one hundred kilometres from base and were forced to fly on one engine back to Amiens-Glisy and made a perfect landing despite the impediment. P/O. Reg. Mitchell with F/Sgt. Ron Ballard, his crewman, on board, were not so lucky when they were forced to return early from patrol and lost power on both engines literally as they crossed the boundary fence, slamming down hard and collapsing the undercarriage. Reg Mitchell was slightly hurt requiring stitches to a cut forehead but Ron Ballard was unhurt. Their aircraft MT463 (ME-Y) was badly damaged and written off as a result of the incident.

There was some excitement on 27th November when a tent containing electrical and instrumentation equipment caught fire and was razed to the ground. Some personal gear and the tent of course were lost but the equipment was fortunately saved. I do wonder if the culprit may have been one of the "shaving water" cans that Johnny Hall enthused about earlier.

The few flights that managed to get airborne during the month of November 1944 had little to report. Enemy activity was minimal to say the least with only six situations in the month when the aircraft encountered what could have been designated "enemy". The weather obviously had an impact on the Luftwaffe also. That *"kill"*, way back on the 5th of November being the only success for the month.

Al Gabites recalled that when he arrived at the base in mid November the mud was beginning to freeze and just a few weeks later the temperatures had dropped to well below zero. This temperature was a real hazard for aircraft as ice would form on wing surfaces very soon after takeoff and could affect the control of the aircraft. Each aircraft parked in dispersal had to be checked and if needed, be de-iced by ground crew regularly through day and night. The air-crews were accommodated in timber lined huts, most without glazing in the windows that had been systematically trashed by the retreating Germans. Most slept in full flying kit, including fleece lined flying boots despite having a plentiful supply of blankets. The air crew were full of admiration for the 488 ground-crew as they had to work out in the open in these conditions or if lucky under very make shift shelter or covers. Servicing was done around the clock, night or day and the men were very appreciative of the knitted woollen mittens and scarves that regularly arrived from New Zealand. [48]

The bad weather continued into early December and showed little signs of abating although the wet conditions were changing to icy periods again and the temperature fell even further as a result. F/L Bowman, the navigation leader applied for release from the service on compassionate grounds but following discussion with a visiting officer from Headquarters decided to continue with his valuable work. Bowman had been crewman to W/C Dickie Haine during his tenure with 488 and was very highly regarded as a skilful and very competent operator. He appears not to have been linked up with a new pilot after

---

[48] *From Allott Gabites, "Monkey's Birthday" – Recollections of a World War II Airman*

Haine was transferred to Headquarters so presumably he carried on with conversion training and navigation work with the new crews as they arrived at the squadron.

The 4th December was remembered for gale force winds that demolished several of the large marquees used for equipment storage and also for the visit of the New Zealand High Commissioner to London, Mr. W. Jordan. He brought with him several New Zealand public relations and welfare officers and they moved around the squadron personnel having discussions and much note taking was observed. Mr. Jordan had taken a big interest in the welfare of the squadron and was instrumental in organising linkage between New Zealand based welfare organisations and these contacts resulted in a steady supply of food and clothing "goodies" from home. These were well received by these young men so far from the comforts of home and were distributed widely and shared among the non-New Zealanders serving in the squadron. Jock Cairns, more than once in his memoirs, makes mention of the massive fruit cakes that arrived in a steady stream from New Zealand.

New orders were received from the Headquarters of No.85 Group on 6th December for patrol times following discussions of a more equitable share of the night flying program. Nine aircraft were to takeoff for patrol work at 1900 hrs, followed by two at 2300 hrs, two at 0400 hrs, one at 0530 hrs with one crew on standby. These requirements put a huge strain on the maintenance echelon but to their credit they never let the squadron down. This was the pattern to be followed on a nightly basis. Flight patrol times averaged two and a half to three hours maximum and crews were expected to be under direction of Control as long as there was *"trade"* about or until fuel or ammunition reached a critical point.

On the 9th December W/O Reg Mitchell and W/O Riley received word of their Officer Commissions, both to be Pilot Officers. There was a visit to the squadron from Squadron Leader Andrews of the Air Historical Section of the RNZAF HQ UK who wanted to ensure that all documents pertaining to the squadron's activities were archived to assist with the compilation of an official unit history for the future interest of squadron members and the public at large. It was seen to be particularly important to him as the top-secret nature of their work meant little information reaching the public at the time. The Squadron appointed one of its Admin officers to carry out the task in addition to his normal duties but it has to be reported that the system appears to have failed somewhat as the author of this narrative has been unable to track down the documentation as yet! It seemingly never saw the light of day.

Arrangements were being made to organise the Squadron Christmas party and one of the non-operational pilots was delegated to fly to the UK in the squadron Oxford to pick up beer and spirits for the event. A sum of fifty pounds was recorded by the squadron diarist as being put up from squadron funds for the purpose and fifty pound in those days was a goodly sum of money. He also noted that Squadron Leader Haine had paid a visit to the squadron on 12th December and remembering his penchant for socialising and partying he could have been forgiven for thinking that Haine was checking on party arrangements at his old squadron.

The 16th December saw good weather arrive at long last. Night flights resumed at full strength but no contact was made with the enemy. Extensive night flying tests had been made during the afternoon and the crews on call were desperate to get into some action. On the 20th December, some disturbing news was received that German troops wearing British officer's uniforms and driving British vehicles had infiltrated the airfields defences' intent on sabotage. Enemy paratroops were known to have been dropped less than a hundred kilometres away and it was thought that this is where the operations began. Additional guard patrols were set up around the squadron dispersal areas but the report does not make it clear how the infiltrators were known to be about.

The squadron put on a huge Christmas party for the orphaned children of Amiens. The local Mayor selected children who had lost one or both parents during the German occupation and these were selected from the neighbouring villages of Boves, Blangy-Tronville and Glisy. Over one hundred attended accompanied by parent helpers and local dignitaries. The ground-crew Echelon had produced handmade toys for the children. Father Christmas arrived by aircraft, being welcomed as described by Johnny Hall, by a string of rockets fired from the Control Tower. The kids were entertained with a Movie followed by a wonderful feed and piles of chocolates. Many of the squadron helped on the day and for most it would have brought to them thoughts of home, of loved ones and family life.

The good times and the Christmas cheer was soon to be severely tested as the German army, seemingly retreating at a considerable rate suddenly dug in and a new concerted campaign by the Allies was launched against them. Much of the German forces were now back in their own territory and supplies and logistical support were no longer a problem for them. Air support for the Allied armies became crucial, particularly at night as the Luftwaffe started a new campaign of attacking the Allied advance at night by bombing them as they advanced over the Ardennes.

The squadron was put on full readiness for the night of the 23rd December due to the full moon period, relatively clear weather with snow blanketing the land and a reported increase in aerial activity from the Luftwaffe. The following night the situation in the air changed remarkably after weeks of relative inactivity. It was if a button had been pushed when reports flooded in of enemy night fighters and bombers appearing all over the night sky.

Eleven Mosquitos from 488 Squadron "B" Flight were on patrol that night and it was not long before the first contact was made. In a very successful night four enemy aircraft were destroyed and one claimed as damaged. One of the more successful crews was F/O "Chunky" Stewart, and his crewman F/O Bill Brumby. This was only the fifth operational patrol by the pair and they bagged two on the same patrol. They were over Roermond, ten miles west of Maeseyck in the early evening when they noticed clusters of white flares in the distance. They sought permission from Control to investigate and Bill Brumby put his pilot onto the tail of what looked like a Ju 88. There was some uncertainty with its identification but "Chunky" got to within just thirty metres before they were positive they had an enemy aircraft in their sights. The aircraft was not taking much evasive action but at that close range it suddenly fired a red flare and, in its glow, they saw clearly the black crosses on the fuselage and wings. Chunky dropped back to two hundred metres to avoid collateral damage and fired a couple of short bursts. The port engine of the Ju 88 caught fire and it spun out in flames before hitting the ground near Maeseyck.

(56) *23/12/1944 – 19:56 hrs – Ex Amiens/ Glisy – Stewart and Brumby – Ju 88 – W of Maeseyck*

Shortly after this success they spotted more flares and again requested permission to investigate. This aircraft repeated the action of the earlier one and stupidly fired a red flare also which immediately gave the Mosquito instant recognition and they duly despatched their second victim in the same manner. When struck by the first burst in the fuselage fire broke out and the enemy aircraft did a diving turn to starboard. Chunky followed it down to three hundred metres and watched it hit the ground with a fearful explosion.

(57) *23/12/1944 – 20:40 hrs – Ex Amiens/Glisy – Stewart and Brumby – Ju 88 – W of Maeseyck*

Later the same night W/C. Ron Watts had been on patrol for some time over Nijmegen in the early evening when Control asked him and his crewman for the night, F/O Irwin Skudder, to investigate what was thought to be a *"Friendly"*. Skudder was sure it was a Ju 188 but Control were not convinced. Watts moved in close to try to confirm that it was a "bandit", in fact ending up flying right underneath the target, still without being spotted. All this time Watts was seeking confirmation that this was indeed an enemy aircraft. In the end, he was positive enough to withdraw to the rear and open fire from 250 metres behind. At this point the Junkers fired off a bunch of coloured flares which sort of confirmed its identity. A second burst of cannon fire from the Mosquito caused the enemy aircraft to turn hard to port and Watts gave him another burst that started a fire along the fuselage and sent the Junkers spinning into the ground. It was the C.O.'s second success.

(58) *23/12/1944 – 19:43 hrs – Ex Amiens/Glassy – Watts and Skudder – Ju 188 - Nijmegen*

F/L Ray Jeffs with F/L Norman Crookes had some disappointment when a Ju 88 that they had pursued all around the night sky over Malmedy gave them the slip and disappeared into the darkness after taking several good hits from the Mosquitos cannons. It was reported that a researcher established that this aircraft was in fact shot down and crashed. This information came to hand in the mid 1990's but no official confirmation has yet been sighted.

The final victory for the night came through the gun sight of Johnny Hall. Control had asked him to investigate a "bogey" and when the co-ordinates were reached his crewman, Jock Cairns took over and guided him on to the tail of an unknown aircraft. As Hall approached to try and identify his target which turned out to be a Me 410, the target did a hard turn to port and sprayed the Mosquito with cannon fire. Hall chased his quarry into hard turns port and starboard with the Me 410 twisting and turning trying to escape. Hall fired several bursts without effect. Hall in his Combat Report referred to the night's events as a "dogfight" with the enemy aircraft doing a series of suicidal dives followed closely by the pursuing Mosquito. At one stage the Me 410 almost struck the ground and while struggling to gain height Hall managed to hit the starboard engine and the Me 410 blew apart in mid-air.

(59) *23/12/1944 – 21:45 hrs –Ex Amiens/Glassy – Hall and Cairns – Me 410 - Malmedy*

This effort was to be the last for this very successful crew. Jock Cairns in particular was lavish with his praise of the New Zealanders in the squadron and they in turn were recognised for their expertise in the noble art of aerial warfare. In a little aside Cairns mentioned the incredible support that the women of New Zealand gave the squadron, particularly with food, specifically cakes. These he said, were shared among the squadron, something he had obviously not experienced before.

P/O. Tom Mallon and his crewman, F/Sgt. George Brock flying MM811 lost their quarry in the early morning hours of Christmas Day after an exchange of gunfire. Twice Mallon overshot his target through wrong calls from Control who put his target further away than its actual position. They were not seen by their target despite passing very close but on his third approach the Mosquito was spotted and the rear top gunner of what turned out to be a Ju 88 opened fire at very close range but his cannon fire was nowhere even near the approaching Mosquito. Mallon hit him as the Junkers peeled off to port but they lost contact at a very low altitude when their target disappeared visually in ground haze and the ground returns from their AI unit prevented them tracking it to its final destruction.

This brief flurry of activity and the successes that came from it were great morale boosters for the squadron following weeks of inactivity coupled with shocking weather conditions. The ground-crew and maintenance echelons would have been greatly heartened by developments and it proved to be a great start to the Christmas celebrations about to commence.

A congratulatory message was received from the Commander of 85 Group, Air Comm. Steele following their successes:

'Many congratulations on last night's very successful operations. A record number of sorties was flown since this Group has used only its own squadrons and score of nine destroyed is very satisfactory in the present difficult circumstances. I hope you will be able to keep this scale of effort and achievement during the current emergency' (signed) Steele

The Group score was nine destroyed shared between the three squadrons, four of which were from the guns of 488 Squadron. It was however business as usual even on Christmas Day with the day being designated a full working day. With the sudden flurry of enemy activity, the celebrations were almost forgotten as the crews worked on into the night. Those on stand-down attended church services and as was customary the airmen were served Christmas dinner by the off-duty Officers and NCO's. It was however a rushed affair compared with Christmas's past according to the reports.

The Allied offensive had started to gain some traction once more following the initial set-backs to the forces on the ground and the Second TAF forces of which 488 Squadron were an integral part over the Ardennes area slowly gained the initiative. The Germans however were far from finished yet.

F/L Hugh Webbe with his crewman, F/L Ian Watson DFC got caught in a situation on Boxing Day 26th December that every aviator fears when very soon after leaving base the weather closed in and left them virtually stranded in mid air over Ostend. Ever the opportunist Webbe picked up a target from Control and eventually came across a Ju 188. Interestingly instead of trying to out-run the Mosquito, the Junkers throttled right back, so much so that Webbe virtually flew alongside him and had an easy confirmation that this indeed was "enemy". The Junkers seemingly just spotting the Mosquito suddenly dived away in a series of spiral turns but Webbe managed to hit him many times during a rapid descent with pieces flying off his quarry at every turn. Unfortunately, the bad weather conditions prevailed and the Ju 188 was lost in the murk and not seen again. Webbe spent considerable time attempting to locate alternative airfields and with Mosquito MM 811's fuel almost gone the crew were forced to crash land on Melsbroek Airfield in Belgium in appalling weather conditions. Webbe overshot his landing in thick fog and had to raise his undercarriage to stop his aircraft safely. As a result, the Mosquito was damaged beyond repair and Webbe and Watson were stranded far from their home base. There was an interesting postscript to their story when Luftwaffe documents found recently, reported Webbe and Watson being shot down over Holsbeek in Belgium that night by a Ju 88G-6 of II. /NJG 2 Staffel. W/C Green of 219 Squadron was also recorded as being felled by the same Ju 88 but documentation of his squadron as well as that of 488 squadron rather dispels the claim and shows up the Luftwaffe claims as being an exaggeration and totally without foundation.

Sqd.Ldr Johnny Gard'ner with F/O Dickie Perfect as his crewman also ran into some bother that night taking strikes from flak in both engines forcing them to force land at Amiens badly damaging their aircraft but climbing out unscathed.

488 Squadron's airfield at Amiens-Glisy was visited by two German intruders late the same night, one of which crashed into the railway yards at Amiens, probably the victim of anti-aircraft fire from the railway defences. The airfield administration very quickly organised new defence procedures to cope with this situation in case of a repeat by further Luftwaffe intruder attacks.

In the early morning hours of 27th December five aircraft were flown to the American base B.58 to assist with air defences in the area and operate from that base. When they reached the base, the fog was down to ground level. Four of the aircraft managed to touch down safely but the fifth, MM 819 flown by W/O Fritchley with crewman F/Sgt. Ces Ray had to try the same trick as Webbe when he ran off the runway in thick fog at Florennes while returning from patrol. Fritchley was forced to raise the undercarriage and belly land the aircraft to prevent an overturn creating a fair amount of damage. The four remaining aircraft carried out patrol work from this base but F/L Johnny Hall with crewman F/L Jock Cairns flying MV 570, got themselves hopelessly lost in dreadful weather conditions and got very low on fuel when looking for an alternative base on which to land. Any base in their predicament would have done and by chance they spotted a flare being fired from what turned out to be an American Fighter base at Asch. Hall made a sudden dive towards the position of the flare between gaps in the clouds and hit the runway hard, skidding on the iced strip and collapsed an undercarriage doing considerable damage to their aircraft.

That flare was the only thing that saved them that night as they had no fuel left and visibility was zero in blizzard conditions. Baling out in those conditions was just not an option. Jock Cairns remembers clambering out of the grounded Mosquito very quickly as it came to a stop. They had an adventurous couple of days following their arrival on the American base. They were very impressed with the facilities the "Yanks" had and the treatment they received. Getting back to their squadron was somewhat of a problem and involved getting a lift to the local train station and catching a train to Brussels carrying their parachute packs and sundry gear over their shoulders. They were directed to a Brussels hotel that night and caught up with two other air crews who had arrived in similar circumstances. Two days later they were picked up and taken back to the squadron base at Amiens after having opened up their survival packs for cash to buy food and drinks. Cairns said later it was an eventful way to spend the days between Christmas and New Year and not one they ever hoped to repeat.

MV 567, flown by F/L "Chunky" Stewart, with F/O Bill Brumby struck problems also on the night of the 27th December, when after getting good visuals on two Ju88's, were struck by anti-aircraft fire and forced to make an emergency landing at Melsbroek. When they touched down on the runway their Mosquito MV 567 flipped over onto its back, fortunately without injury to the crew. This result indicated that they had possibly sustained damage to the flaps. The appalling weather played its part with a number of aircraft during these few days suffering damage, almost all during landings coming home from night patrol or forced to land on strange airfields due to damage, faulty engines or lack of fuel or visibility

The weather was that bad on the morning of the 28th December due to ice conditions that vehicles were unable to leave the base at Amiens-Glisy to pick up the stranded air-crews unable to fly back in because of damaged aircraft now scattered round various bases in the region. Only eight serviceable aircraft were left for their normal operational commitments but the crews were despite the number of accidents over the past few days still very keen to get back into the air.

The month of December rounded out with one more mishap with the trusty Oxford being flown by Tom MacKay going down on one wingtip when the port undercarriage failed to lock on arrival in the UK. Two of the crews left stranded on the base B58 finally returned to Amiens-Glisy.

Given that the Luftwaffe only had aircraft in 488's patrol area from 23rd December on, the squadron tally of four destroyed, one probable and two damaged claims was not a bad outcome. The bad weather caused flying cancellation on sixteen nights of the month. Both "A" and "B" Flights had by now moved out of tented accommodation into huts so the comfort level would have been raised considerably. Late in December the Luftwaffe were assembling huge numbers of aircraft and carried out an early morning attack on all the Allied airfields in Northern France and Belgium in the early hours of New Years day 1945. It was known to them as *'Bodenplatte'* (Baseplate). Over 1100 Luftwaffe fighters were involved. It was planned to be a master stroke for them as they descended en mass strafing and bombing the packed masses of Allied aircraft parked crammed on the ground. Over 260 aircraft, mainly fighter aircraft were destroyed at Maldegem airfield in Belgium alone but it was to be a last-ditch futile stand by the Luftwaffe as from that day on they became totally ineffective on attack and were increasingly withdrawn to defensive positions. The key element here was that the Allied aircraft damaged on the ground were relatively easy to replace but the crews for these aircraft remained complete something of which the German planners seemed to have overlooked. The Luftwaffe lost over 250 pilots that day, many of whom were shot down over their own territory by their own anti-aircraft fire due to the secrecy involved with the attack planning. It was a bit of a setback for the allies but the lost aircraft were to be quickly replaced and the Allied offensive soon gained sufficient momentum to increase the rate of progress of their attack across Europe and deep into Germany.

In these same early New Year morning hours, the Mosquito of F/L "Chunky" Stewart, and his crewman F/O Bill Brumby, were chasing one of the Luftwaffe fighter bombers returning to its base at Rheine. Stewart moved in far too close in all the excitement and ended up getting badly shot up by the German airfield defences. With his hydraulics shot away he scampered off back to the nearest Allied base at Brussels, arriving just before another wave of the attacking Luftwaffe fighter/bombers turned up. He managed to put his aircraft down on to the main runway but lost control when the undercarriage collapsed and swerved off course ending up under the huge wing of a parked American Flying Fortress bomber. They climbed out unhurt but were dismayed to soon find themselves in a maelstrom of strafing and bombing as waves of German Fw 190's attacked. When the invaders departed Stewart and Brumby found themselves surrounded by burning Allied aircraft but their Mosquito had somehow escaped the carnage. Gabites who arrived after the attack recalled that day on the Brussels airfield and hand drew a sketch of "Chunky's" aircraft lying under the wing of its protector.

Al Gabites in his memoirs published under the title of *'Monkey's Birthday'* spoke fondly of his good friend of the war years, "Chunky" Stewart. Chunky, born Kenneth William Stewart joined the RNZAF with Al Gabites and they shared many an experience as they progressed through their early training in New Zealand, Canada and later in the UK before their arrival together with Phil Bryers and Bill Brumby at 488 at Colerne. Stewart, with his crewman, Bill Brumby were shown on the squadron records as the "Last of the Aces" ending up with five destroyed and one damaged to their credit.

"Monty" Norman, the squadron's Engineering Officer was awarded the M.B.E. for his dedicated, skilful and hard work supervising the very many maintenance issues that crop up with aircraft operating in extreme weather and battle situations. On the other end of the scale W/O Fritchley was taken off flying duties according to the squadron diarist for *"due to lack of confidence in himself"*. This was the first recorded sign in the squadron operational notes of the stress levels that these young men found themselves under. The RAF at that stage had a cruel misconception of what is now known as post traumatic stress syndrome. Any aircrew member suffering with stress was officially designated *L.M.F.* Incredibly this designation appearing on Operational Records or on service files was known as "Lack of Moral Fibre".

The squadron Diarist noted that he hoped that W/O Fritchley would receive medical attention rather than the stigma of the L.M.F. tag on his files. It was to the squadron C.O. Ron Watts's credit that he bucked the usual convention and sent Fritchley away for medical treatment. Many of the aircrew interviewed spoke of what they called the "twitch", seeing it in others but more importantly recognising it in themselves as the constant stress they were under grew gradually and threatened to overwhelm them to the point of collapse. Moves were made to look carefully at the operational hours each individual was supposed to be carrying out. While Fritchley flew operationally on only six nights during December his last flight for the month resulted in a crash landing so it is not difficult to see why his "confidence" was somewhat shattered.

I thought that Jock Cairns summed things up nicely when he commented on the relationship between airmen in a squadron:

If it could be said that there is a quality engendered in war which ennobles man, it is to be found in that special relationship between men exposed to danger and the probability of violent death. Men always speak of it when recalling their experiences of war. They recoil from the love, and call it comradeship, but love it is, in the true biblical sense, and it grows from the recognition that in the others are reflected all the secret fears and vulnerability to which themselves are prey. It is from this shared compassion for the weakness in their comrades that each draws strength and the courage to continue when the spirit flags. It needed no expression, and hung tacitly between them. There was a convention to refer to the uglier face of the war only in the most oblique terms. Friends were never killed, they 'Got the Chop'; aircraft never crashed, they 'Pranged'. It would have been indelicate to admit to being scared, but perfectly permissible, indeed desirable, to be 'Twitched Up' on occasion.

Ron Watts had earlier spoken of the stress and the way it was handled by different personalities in different situations. He noted that alcohol played a significant part in that process and was an important ingredient in 'letting off steam'. He recalls being in the squadron crew room one day when news came in of a fatal crash. One of the pilots burst out with *"the bastard – that was my aircraft!"* That particular pilot was not an insensitive man at all and probably ended up being ashamed of his reaction. Ron himself noted that any time he landed after a flight, whether it was long and arduous or short and uneventful he always stopped and lit a cigarette. He assumed it calmed his nerves but commented that he was well accustomed to flying and was unaware of any tension at the time.

There was a tragic start to 1945 when W/O Neiderer and his navigator, F/O George Lawrence flying MM 815 were lost when they spun into the ground during a practice night interception on the 8th January. They were flying at around a height of 2000 metres at the time of the accident. They were both buried in Amiens Cemetery. The accident was noted as being a terrible shock to the squadron by the squadron Diarist. The explosion as the aircraft struck the ground was seen in the darkness by another squadron Mosquito that was airborne at the time but they were unable to pinpoint the position with any accuracy. Search parties were sent out but nothing more was found until late the next day. There was no evidence to indicate the cause of the crash as the aircraft had hit the ground with a terrible impact and fire had consumed most of the wreckage. Only six days earlier Neiderer had been promoted to Warrant Officer.

A search party led by W/C Ron Watts had found the wreckage of MM 815 near the village of Murlu and the badly mutilated bodies of the crew were found close to the scene of the crash. The two men were buried with full military honours on the 12th January, side by side in the small military cemetery called Asylum Dury and the entire crew of "A" Flight attended.

The Allied army ground offensive gained a new intensity in January and the Luftwaffe attacks at night closed down completely, so much so that 488 Squadron were sending aircraft over to Gilze-Rijen base in Holland each day for patrols that night and the aircraft came back to Amiens-Glisy in France at the end of each patrol. There was very little activity in January. The northern winter conditions were not good and I suspect the quietness was probably welcomed by a good number of the squadron personnel. You had to feel sorry for the ground crews as photographs taken at the time show ice and snow conditions that must have been unbearable for those forced to work with tools out in the open or under makeshift covers.

A heavier than usual snow and ice fall was recorded on 11th January and many complaints were recorded about the inadequacy of snow clearing equipment available for the squadron.

An investigation into the crash of Mosquito MM 811 on B58 flown by F/L Hugh Webbe on 26th/27th December was ordered rather belatedly by Operations on the 18th January. In a separate arrangement, F/O M.D. Graham, who had been taken off flying duties nearly twelve months before was posted to an Admin course at RAF Hereford to train him for work that he had been carrying out on an interim basis with the squadron since his earlier grounding. A small detachment of maintenance staff was sent to airfield B.77 at Gilze-Rijen on January 18th to set up a forward base so that 488 Squadron could operate from this satellite airfield closer to the frontline.

P/O. Johnny Hall and P/O. Jock Cairns were stood down from operational flying on 22nd January and despatched away from the squadron for a rest. They would have been sorely missed as their "kill" rate had been almost continuous since their joining the squadron. They were one of the hardest working and conscientious crews in the squadron. Hall had in fact spent some time in hospital two weeks before with what was designated as bronchitis but admitted later that he was badly run down and had teeth problems. Jock Cairns felt that the accident at the American Air base on 27th December had caused him more anxiety than he (Hall) cared to admit.

The Squadron C.O. W/C. Ron Watts was informed on 23rd January that he had been "Mentioned in Despatches" for his work with the squadron but it was the opinion of many that he should have received much more of a reward for his work with 488. Ron placed much emphasis on informality among the squadron personnel and carried on the reputation that 488 already had as a group of men that supported one another and all ranks were included in any activity going at the time. Regular parades were discontinued and officiousness was kept to a minimum. As Ron said *"You could be a bit scruffy and get away with it, it really did'nt matter, so long as you did your duty properly and made a good job of that".* He compared his squadron with that of a Canadian squadron on one of the bases they were at where there was a lot of bickering and abusive language between them. He thought it engendered a really unpleasant atmosphere and commented that 488 was never and would never be like that.

The next day after Ron Watts's award, it was reported that the squadron had received the sum of sixteen pounds from the De Havilland Aircraft Company for "Cheer". By today's standards it seemed a paltry sum but would probably have bought quite a few beers at that time. The squadron relationship with De Havilland was a special one with both air-crew and ground-crew working closely with the initial and later continuing development of the Mosquito as a fighting machine. As 488 Squadron were on several occasions the first recipients of the latest models of aircraft they were in a unique position of being if you like, 'guinea pigs", having to put up with the many teething problems that generally occur when changes are made with the release of new aircraft and systems. The squadron chief engineer, "Monty" Norman had worked closely with the De Havilland factory, particularly when the first operational model of the Mosquito was issued to 488 early in 1943. He was loud in his praise of the De Havilland engineers at the end of the war and in return would have greatly assisted the aircraft maker as modifications and updates were made as time went by.

F/Sgt. Stan McCabe was posted away from the squadron to a Communications squadron and soon after his departure he crashed during a delivery flight. He had been ordered to fly a Mosquito that was tour expired back to another base. He found the aircraft parked in long grass and was assured that it was airworthy. He very quickly found it had no brakes as he lined up for takeoff. Despite this McCabe applied full power and after a short run became airborne. As he levelled off into flight mode both engines failed. Although he managed to skilfully place his stricken Mosquito down between two houses he suffered bad burns to his face and upper torso while trying desperately to get out of the wreckage of his downed aircraft. Fortunately, Stan was flying solo at the time. He faced a long rehabilitation period with countless skin grafts. His treatment was carried out by the world-renowned New Zealand plastic surgeon, Sir Archibald McIndoe at the famous East Grimstead hospital burns unit. Thankfully he did recover well and returned to New Zealand to lead a normal and successful life as a Town Planner.

The month of January 1945 ended with no squadron "kills" being recorded and the lowest night flying hours in over a year of operational flying. The weather was appalling day after day. There seemed to be a "thaw" arriving on the last day of the month with a noticeable warming and thick fog present but the interminable weather carried on into the early days of February.

At long last there seemed to be some recognition from Air Operations that the stress factor in aircrews had been recognised with orders coming at the end of the month that unless the crews indicated their willingness to continue all crews reaching 200 hours of operational flying were to be stood down for rest and recreation away from the squadron. 200 hours was still a significant period of time given that the average flight operational time was around two and a half hours. Given the long hours of being on call but unable to get airborne until the weather cleared did not lower the stress level to any degree.

Two aircraft were sent over to Gilze-Rijen B77 in Holland on 1st February to begin night flying operations from this base. Although the aircraft were to return in the early morning hours back to Amiens this was an advance strategy ahead of the whole squadron being deployed, and continuing to move with the advance that the Allied armies were carrying out in their steady and resolute pursuit of the retreating German forces. S/L Davison the "B" Flight Commander was due for repatriation back to New Zealand due to the completion of his operational work but flew to RNZAF Headquarters in London to argue his case for staying on until his present tenure with 488 was completed.

Two further squadron Mosquitos were flown to Gilze-Rijen on 3rd February and in the evening the squadron hosted a number of French civilian guests in their newly acquired aircrew rest hotel in Amiens town. Wng Comm. Watts in the meantime was admitted to the Station Sick Quarters suffering from influenza. P/O. H.O. Watkins the squadrons' Intelligence Officer was posted to Headquarters of 85 Group for legal work after struggling with his duties in Intelligence for the squadron. F/L Leslie Hunt returned to his old squadron as his replacement and wrote at the time of how happy he was to be back among old friends.

Two Mosquitoes returned to Amiens after having to fly to Lille for a safe landing due to weather conditions following overnight patrol work. The same scenario was repeated the following night on the 6th February when three aircraft this time sought sanctuary away from their base. By the 10th February, operations had changed the night flying program to allow an earlier sunset take off time to be factored in. This extended the opportunity for night patrols to get into position early while some visuals were possible and to allow better visual sighting of Luftwaffe bombers heading homeward in the early evening from daylight bombing raids.

There was no escaping the beaurocracy involved in military affairs when W/O Green was reproved by the Base Commander for breaches of security regulations when a private letter he was sending home on 12th February was intercepted by security and the contents vetted. The next day saw the stupendous announcement that aircrew were to receive two extra eggs per week for their night flying suppers and the squadron Diarist noted that this would be really appreciated by the aircrews as the night flying suppers were not of a very good standard!

It was pleasing to see recorded the return of W/O Fritchley to the squadron on the 8th of February cleared to fly again although he was eventually posted on to a UK base away from operational flying.

The fog returned with a vengeance on 14th February and was to last well into the next week. On the 16th February, F/O J.K. Muldrew with his crewman, F/Sgt. R.G. Emerton were caught out trying to land in thick fog at Amiens and undershot the runway by 600 metres and hit an obstruction of some sort. Fortunately, and with a great deal of incredible skill, Muldrew recovered enough to get airborne again and flew his Mosquito MM 622 away to Lille and landed safely with the minimum of damage to his aircraft. 600 metres was a long way out from the start of the runway and the mind boggles as to what he might have hit. The obstruction may well have been a farm animal as when the fog did eventually clear nothing was found solid enough to cause any problem to a aircraft making a landing!

The weather finally cleared on 21st February and a night of some excitement ensued. W/O Rod Bourke started the ball rolling when his Mosquito MM 820, with his crewman, F/O Irwin Skudder sitting alongside him, swung hard to port on his takeoff run and had to be ground looped, collapsing the undercarriage. Bourke faced a severe reprimand for *"careless mishandling of his aircraft"*. Both crewmen fortunately were unhurt.

Later that same night Chunky Stewart and Bill Brumby were patrolling over Groenlo in Holland when they received a warning from Ground Control that they were being followed by a strange aircraft. Chunky took evasive action and very soon found himself trying every trick in the book to get into an attacking position behind his opponent. It was an unusual situation for a night fighter to be in as they were usually the ones attacking but clearly this one, which turned out to be a Ju 88 was the aggressor. Both would have been flying solely using their radar units as visibility was nil. Al Gabites described it as *"a duel to the death in complete darkness by two very well-matched opponents"*. Chunky managed after some time to get behind it, identified it as a Ju 88(G)-night fighter and managed to get it to fly through a heavy stream of cannon fire where it blew up in mid air. It was the crew's third victory while with 488 and probably the hardest fought dogfight they had been in.

(60) *21/02/1945 – 20:56 hrs – Ex Amiens/Glassy – Stewart and Brumby – Ju 88 – Groenlo, Holland*

This particular Ju 88 was in fact a specialist night fighter and the crew obviously trained well enough to give Stewart and Brumby a hard time.

The final week of February stuttered to an end with bad weather and a paucity of enemy contacts being the order of the day. The squadron dairy reported some innovative organising being carried out with junior aircrew being put in charge of the other ranks billets. It was also noted that there was an increase in the number of petty crimes being committed necessitating disciplinary action being taken, but gives an indication that the reason for this outbreak is not known. It may well have been boredom and the so-called petty crime being pranks rather than the implication that serious stuff was going down!

The 1st of March 1945 started with a bit of a bang for Johnny Hall and Jock Cairns. Back from a compulsory rest period and on patrol, they were shot up by British anti aircraft fire which must have given them a bit of a wakeup call. Fortunately, no damaged ensued. Hall must have been up to his old tricks of keeping down at a low level, something that he had perfected and contributed greatly to his successes in combat.

The RNZAF Rugby team played against a French team in Paris on 3rd March and lost 12 points to nil so the losses against French teams that have caused so much angst in New Zealand over recent years were happening in 1945. The Squadron C.O., W/C Ron Watts flew himself to Paris to give support to no avail. The New Zealand War correspondent, for the European theatre, Hon. Capt. Allan Mitchell visited the squadron on 5th March and had much discussion and carried out many interviews among the new crews serving with the squadron.

Ron Watts was a great supporter of the Rugby team and played a keen game himself from time to time. He commented several times about the fitness regimes that the various Base Commanders tried to instil in the squadron personnel. He said on more than one occasion that as far as he was concerned as long as his air-crew did their job then that was all that mattered.

W/C Ron Watts gave himself and his passenger, F/O Leigh, the squadron Adjutant, a bit of a scare on 6th March when they headed off in the squadron Oxford to Group Headquarters. The Oxford suffered engine failure on route and they were forced to make a one engined landing at Lille. There would have been a fair degree of skill required in this exercise as the Oxford was not noted for its single engined flying characteristics. There were further mechanical problems when the squadron Mosquitos were grounded when Group Headquarters asked for all aircraft to have the boost capsules examined for faults. The following day F/L Patrick with F/L Jeffs took one of the Group Engineering Staff to Ursel airbase in the UK to pick up a supply of Butterfly Boost capsules to replace the ones found faulty during the grounding inspection the day before.

P/O. Muldrew and W/O Emerton, less than a month after an earlier scare faced further problems not of their own making when a British Lancaster bomber mistook their Mosquito MM 818 for an enemy night fighter and riddled their port engine with cannon fire. Muldrew struggled on one engine to the nearest airfield, but overshot his approach and struck a lighting pole at the end of the runway. The damage was not significant and both were unhurt. These lighting poles figured time and again in accounts of aircraft striking them. Also known as "totem" poles they were not unlike the starting light systems used by modern day drag racers. They were situated just to one side of the starting position for take-off down the runway. They were remotely activated by the control tower and gave the green light to an aircraft waiting for an all clear to take-off. They were intended to simplify the signalling system for times of poor visibility giving the pilot an immediate and very nearby all clear, instead of him straining to look for the signal away in the darkness somewhere. Unfortunately, even a slightly off course approach by a landing aircraft, particularly on a grass strip often put this innovation at some risk.

March 1945 was a month again marred by bad weather and the deaths of P/O. Tom Mallon, and his crewman, P/O. George Brock flying MT 484 on 11th March. They were killed after a crash taking off on an operational flight from the squadron's advance base at Gilze-Rijen. There was a sequel and a possible link to their tragic accident when Al Gabites later recounted a series of bad experiences he and Phil Bryers had during takeoffs a short time before with this same aircraft. Gabites had at least two heart stopping moments when one of his twin engines either suddenly throttled back or another time raced away on full boost at a crucial time during takeoff. He explained that the Mosquito throttle controls were on the left-hand side of the control column and the undercarriage controls were on the right hand and opposite side. Once airborne and climbing under full power the pilot had to take his left hand off the throttles to hold the control column to use his right hand to raise the wheels and reduce drag on the climbing aircraft. Under normal circumstances the throttle controls could be left at their setting with the use of an adjustable friction nut but this nut on his Mosquito ME-K (MT 484) was faulty and allowed one of the throttles to move forward or back suddenly with potentially disastrous results for the aircraft.

On one occasion when this happened, ME-K flicked over into a half roll during takeoff and they denied themselves a place in European history by just missing Amiens Cathedral by a whisker. On a second occasion, they went out of control very shortly after takeoff and it was undoubtedly Al Gabites skill that got them out of trouble having to right the aircraft at a very low altitude. The ground crew tried unsuccessfully to fix the problem so after that Gabites usually got his crewman Phil Bryers to look after the undercarriage levers while he held the throttles with his left hand during takeoff. They got used to the situation and as nothing more could be done they thought no more about it. Gabites was posted away for a time to the Central Gunnery School in January and on his return to the squadron in early March he was told that his old aircraft ME-K had crashed into a barn on takeoff killing both its crew. He said he was too late to venture his opinion officially but he always had his own thoughts on the cause of the crash that killed both Mallon and Brock.

There was a further sequel to the Mallon / Brock tragedy when Len Wyman recently recounted a story connected with their deaths. In the crewroom that evening he joined Tommy Mallon for a card game called Crib. It was a favourite game of all the 488 crews and competition was fierce. The perfect hand in Crib is to have three "5's" and a "Jack", the next turned card must be the last "5" and it must be the same suit as the "Jack" in your hand. Len had only seen this hand once in all his eighty-nine years. This hand was worth the maximum score of 29 points. Tommy Mallon got this perfect score whilst they played cards immediately before that night's "sortie". Tommy was really pleased with himself and his good fortune. He talked about this being his lucky day as he and his crewman George Brock left the crewroom for their final sortie. They of course never returned. To this day, Len Wyman hopes he never sees or hears of someone he knows getting the perfect Crib hand.

The next day F/L Monty Norman drove to Gilze-Rijen to check out the fatal accident that killed Mallon and Brock. Their loss was a huge shock to the squadron. F/O Leigh the squadron Adjutant flew ahead to sort out funeral arrangements for the pair and to secure any personal effects from the crash scene. The Mallon family from New Plymouth in New Zealand had already faced a tragic loss with Tom's brother, P/O. John Charles Mallon, losing his life earlier in the war while serving with 53 Squadron in France on 8th October 1940.

The drama continued this day when F/O Jimmy Moore and navigator, F/O Alan Earl, on their last patrol together lost power in the port engine and while attempting a landing overshot the runway and hit a parked van 100 metres from the end of the strip.

The next couple of days were spent sorting out the Mallon / Brock tragedy. Both were buried in the Bergen-op-Zoom War Cemetery in Breda, Holland on 14th March and sadly transport difficulties on the day prevented any of the squadron members attending the funeral.

F/O Moore and F/O Earl, still suffering from the embarrassment of hitting the parked van were taken off operations just two days later and sent away for their scheduled rest period. Amazingly they had been forced to carry out nine single engined landings with only the last attempt causing damage to their aircraft. This was a fairly spectacular record and not equalled by any other pilot as most of them were done under very difficult circumstances. On the strength of that record, Jimmy Moore was to be recommended for the award of the Air Force Cross for distinguished flying.

There was however a very humorous incident reported by Leslie Hunt about the Jimmy Moore and Alan Earl crew. According to Hunt, when 488 were back at Bradwell Bay, Moore had brake trouble on landing and Hunt and others were in the dispersal area playing cards and generally filling in time when their peace was rudely disturbed when a section of the dispersal hut wall crashed in with bricks and glass flying and the nose of a mosquito pushed into the room with both Moore and Earl looking down on them with very surprised looks on their faces. Fortunately, no-one was hurt but the pair would have had some explaining to do relating to their unscheduled arrival.

The whole issue of single engined landings or engine failure on takeoff needed to be put into perspective as these were reasonably common occurrences and caused many accidents resulting in injury or death during the squadron's operational life. De Havilland, the aircraft's designer and constructor, recognised the problems early on in the war and issued 'Pilots Notes' recommending certain conditions that should be met to ensure the safety of the crews when landing or taking off with the Mosquito and suffering engine failure. De Havilland established a 'safe' take-off speed of 322 km/hr which was the minimum speed that would allow take-off on one engine, provided the propeller of the failed engine was instantly feathered (the blades turned edge on to the airflow to reduce drag), the radiator flap was closed, and the flaps were fully up. In other words, a very quick reaction was required from the pilot. Handling engine failure during flight and landing was fraught with difficulty. For landing, the pilot's handbook recommended a flight speed of between 257 km/hr and 275 km/hr for safe manoeuvring but leaving the lowering of the undercarriage as late as possible, but it needed to be locked down before the final straight approach. There was a reminder that lowering took thirty seconds, and a glide approach speed of 225 km/hr should be maintained and a warning that undercarriage and flaps down caused a high rate of descent and much more power would be needed to avoid an undershoot. When all this information was needed to put the aircraft down safely in normal daytime conditions, landing these aircraft on one engine and at night in adverse weather must have been a real test of the nerves. Jimmy Moore's effort with nine such landings certainly puts the awarding of his medal into perspective.

The air crew of "B" Flight organised a party for the ground crew on this day, the 15th March for their flight and it was recorded that *"eight barrels of English beer and an ample supply of New Zealand fruit cake and cigarettes were provided"* and a great time was had by all. The great day was marred by a particularly bad incident with F/L Al Gabites and his crewman, F/O Phil Bryers being misdirected in adverse weather conditions onto a "Q" site instead of landing at Amiens-Glisy. The result was quite spectacular with their aircraft MT 461 ending up badly damaged and nose down in a ditch with tail high in the air. The "Q" sites were set up near many airfields and were nothing more than false flight paths lit up with dummy landing lights across farm paddocks to divert attention away from the real airfield. Many were bombed by the Luftwaffe thinking they were real airfields but there were not many reports of aircraft trying to land on them! In Gabite's case he was struggling for height and position close to where Amiens should have been and mistakenly headed for the lights of the dummy runway. Poor Gabites had just returned from a seven-week course in the UK and the "Q" site had been set up in his absence. Rules were quickly formulated following the incident and training in the proper use of the diversionary airfield were given to those responsible for it.

On 19th March the Squadron's new Intelligence Officer arrived. He was F/O W.J.T. Hewitt. He had considerable experience particularly with night fighter squadrons. Two days later, F/O Keith Fleming, and F/O Ken Nagle MM 816 were flying out of Gilze-Rijen on patrol over the Ruhr on 21st March when Control directed them to check out what was thought to be a "friendly". Nagel identified the aircraft as a Me 110 through his Ross night glasses and Fleming closed in to about 150 metres before launching his assault. His initial strike resulted in an explosion that covered his aircraft in oil. The Me 110 slipped sideways still firing back at them and Fleming caught a glimpse through the only clear patch on his side window of the Messerschmitt [49]diving into the darkness. They claimed a "probable" but when Fleming and Nagle arrived back at base with their aircraft completely covered in oil, Air Operations upgraded it to a "destroyed" much to their excitement.

(61) *22/03/1945 – 05:22 hrs – Ex Amiens/Glassy – Fleming and Nagle – Me 110 – Dortmund*

On 22nd March the Air Officer Commanding No.85 group visited and spoke to all aircrews about the upcoming offensive against Germany and said that this was hoped to be the last big clash with the enemy. He emphasised the importance of the air defences in protection for the armies on the ground below and suggested that this would probably cause the Luftwaffe to come out in a desperate fight to avoid total annihilation. As a result of this visit an additional seven aircraft were put on readiness on 60 minutes' standby in support of the Allied 21st Army Group Frontline.

On the evening of 26th March F/L Johnny Hall destroyed a JU88 near Emmerich but very nearly destroyed his own aircraft in the process. His aircraft ME-P (NT 314) was struck by flying debris from his victim. He managed to steer his very badly damaged aircraft back to Gilze-Rijen in Holland with one engine feathered due to fire, where he thumped into the ground without wheels. Just as he touched down, both propellers disintegrated and literally fell off the aircraft. His aircraft caught fire and he and his crewman for the day, Tom Taylor scrambled out of the top hatch barely escaping with their lives. It must have been a real shock for Tom as he was standing in for a sick Jock Cairns who was John Hall's normal crewman.

(62) *26/03/1945 – 23:00 hrs – Ex Amiens/Glassy – Hall and Taylor – Ju 88 - Emmerich*

This same night, F/O "Chunky' Stewart and F/L Bill Brumby were having a real tussle with a Me 110 that Control had put them on to. The

---

[49] *The Me 110 was manufactured by Bayerische Flugzeugwerke and designated Bf110*

weather had really packed up by this time but they managed to out manoeuvre their target and sent it crashing out of the sky over Bocholt.

(63) 27/03/1945 – 00:05 hrs – Ex Amiens/Glassy – Stewart and Brumby – Me 110 - Bocholt

They had decided by this time to return to base because of the weather but Control had more *"Trade"* for them. They identified it as a Heinkel 111 and they started a long chase trying to bring down the elusive aircraft. They registered several strikes on their victim but the target turned into a tight starboard turn which had it heading directly back towards the Mosquito. Stewart managed to get several more strikes as the Heinkel headed towards them but it passed close by under them and disappeared into the darkness. Frustratingly Bill Brumby's AI unit had all but packed up so the target was lost. The weather by this time had closed in, so much so that they were forced to return to their old base at Bradwell Bay across the channel without the successful "double" they had hoped for.

By this time German resistance had ebbed and flowed with long periods with no contacts. Al Gabites recalled that at the time it was considered that the Allied strategic bombing was having great effect by destroying fuel stocks and synthetic fuel plants and this paucity of fuel was forcing the Luftwaffe to conserve fuel by cutting down regular bombing raids in favour of massed attacks at lesser intervals. 488 Squadron were being a little left behind as the squadron diary commented on the 29th March that there was little time for nightly active patrolling as the Front line was moving further away from the base with each day that passed.

The first day of April arrived with the news that F/O J.H. Moore was to be awarded the Air Force Cross for his flying expertise ably demonstrated by the nine one engined landings he made during his last tour with the squadron. On the 2nd April, the squadron was asked to prepare to move to Gilze-Rijen at short notice. It was taking two hours of flying time from Amiens to reach their operational patrol areas so the news was well received by the aircrew. The following day the advanced party left for Base B77 Gilze-Rijen, supposedly to set up facilities for the main body to follow but this was just wishful thinking for those planning the move. The advance party found nothing but confusion at the other end with the accommodation shambolic, the airfield badly damaged and unfit for operational use and the day fighter squadrons still operating from the airfield when they were supposed to have moved on.

On Wednesday 4th April, the rest of the squadron set out to move permanently across the border into Holland to their new base at Gilze-Rijen, the scene of Johnny Hall's earlier demise. They had flown operationally out of this base many times over the preceding months but had always returned to Amiens-Glisy at the end of their shift or for repairs and maintenance. This airfield gave them the opportunity to fly deeper into Germany than from their base in France. Al Gabites reported that facilities at Gilze-Rijen were very primitive and that refuelling of their aircraft had to be done using "jerry cans". He felt sorry for the poor ground crew who had to hoist the jerry cans one by one to fill the Mosquito wing tanks. Their new base was located halfway between Tilburg and Breda in North Brabant and their primary purpose was to be for the night defence of the port of Antwerp. The port was the staging point for the unloading of tonnes of stores and equipment destined for the allied armies as they surged through Europe. It was an area vital as an army on the move needed to keep moving with the assurance that they would not outstrip their supply line. The Germans knew this and increased their night bombing effort with a remorseless bombing campaign which included both V1 and V2 rockets being launched from just beyond the frontline.

Earlier that morning Dakota and Commando transport aircraft had landed at Amiens-Glisy and taxied over to 488 Squadron's dispersal area and parked ready to be loaded with the squadron equipment. A fleet of some fifteen trucks and vans had earlier formed a convoy and left at 6:00 am. with F/O Andrewes in charge. He lost one of his munitions trucks on the way, not through any enemy action but through one of his fellow travellers having decided to make a cup of tea using a small oil stove while mobile, a sudden lurch of the vehicle caused the oil stove to overturn and the following conflagration destroying the truck and its contents in a very sudden manner fortunately without casualties.

The aircrew of 488 took a last stroll from their Amiens Mess and sleeping quarters up at the old dilapidated Chateau Tronville on the banks of the Somme (formerly occupied by the Luftwaffe) and made their way down to the dispersal area which was nothing more than a collection of packing cases for buildings. [50]

Once the transport planes had left for Gilze-Rijen with their cargo onboard, "B "Flight aircrew took off at 0730 hrs being lead by S/L Frank Davison, the "B" Flight Commander with seven of the Mosquitos and headed in the direction of the Dutch border leaving behind "A" Flight to bring up the rear or so they thought. One of the pilots, (possibly P/O. Gordon Patrick) reported taking off with his just repaired aircraft MM818 that had not been air tested following some damage repairs for an earlier incident when P/O. Muldrew had struck one of the airfield lighting poles at the end of the runway. His aircraft had no radio or homing radar equipment fitted so they flew virtually "blind" relying on keeping the aircraft in front of them in sight. That situation was fine while they had good visibility but they very soon ran into cloud and his crewman P/O. Allan Ray had to keep in touch using their AI radar unit and following the leading aircraft by instructing his pilot accordingly. It was the ideal opportunity to make the best use of their AI unit. It must have been very accurate plotting as when they eventually came out of cloud, travelling at around 480 kph they were just 300 metres behind the aircraft they had followed on their AI screen.

Gilze-Rijen had a very high *"diver belt"* which was set at six thousand feet over the airfield. An aircraft approaching any lower than this would have presented themselves as a target to the radar controlled anti aircraft batteries which were unlikely to have discriminated between enemy or friendly aircraft given that they were only a few kilometres from the German Frontline. It meant a careful approach during daylight hours until directly over the airfield and entering a tight downward spiral to affect a safe approach to landing. Fortunately for them the sky above Gilze-Rijen was clear and they joined the crowded airspace and spiralled down until the airstrip appeared. It was obvious while on their final approach that the landing was going to be a rough one as the runway was in a state of complete devastation.

The runway at Gilze-Rijen had taken a fair plastering from the Allied bombers while in German hands and it was obvious that the Germans during their retreat had done their very best to make it even more

---

[50] *This account of the squadron leaving from Amiens-Glisy in France and moving on to the new base at Gilze-Rijen in Holland was sourced from an article written by an unnamed air-crew member (thought to be Plt.Off.G.S. Patrick) in the New Zealand Weekly News of Wednesday, January 1, 1947.*

unserviceable. It was constructed of brick with the shell or bomb craters patched and filled, but these had sunken over time and gave the impression and the feeling on landing of trying to negotiate a path through a turnip field. Landing successfully and safely was only half the battle as the aircraft then faced a three kilometre, very bumpy taxi through patchy forestation to their dispersal area.

Squadron line up on arrival at Amiens (Ron Watts).

Air-crew accommodation at Amiens-Glisy Base in France (Reg Mitchell).

The Officers Mess at Amiens – Glisy in France (Reg Mitchell).

Al Gabites and his crewman, Phil Bryers (Photo from "Monkey's Birthday").

A wonderful photograph of a Mosquito and its crew taken at night at Amiens-Glisy. Note the cover over the Perspex dome of the all-important nose mounted AI Radar unit (Ron Watts).

Ground crew servicing Mosquito at Amiens in more moderate weather conditions (Reg Mitchell).

Queuing for the "NAFFI" van at Amiens-Glisy, from left F/Sgt. Simcock, Cpl. Murray, Cpl. Hall, Cpl. Boumphrey, Cpl. Murphy, Cpl. Land, Cpl. Swan, Cpl. Haggerty, Sgt. McGuigan, Cpl. Squires, Lac. Folkard, Unknown, Lac. Roberts, Unknown (from Defence until Dawn).

The servicing goes on (Reg Mitchell).

'B' Flight ground-crew at Amiens.
Back row left to right: C. Sales, J. Pinnock, L. Coulson, J. Burns, G. Cain Middle row: S. Pike, T. Allen, 'Jumbo' Jackson, G. Merigan, Sgt. D. Howland, G. Holmes, G. Webb, 'Spud' Murphy, L. Whittaker Front row: D. Henning, Dixon, Crayton, Cpl. Swan, Sgt. Palmer, S.A. Boumphrey,

Some of the "B" Flight servicing crew in front of one of their charges MT467, ME-X usually the aircraft of W/O Tom MacKay while based at Amiens-Glisy in France (Reg Mitchell).

F/O Bill Brumby RNZAF and F/L "Chunky" Stewart RNZAF (Ron Watts).

488 Squadron Commisioned Officers at Amiens-Glisy – March 1945 Back Row : McLean, Moore, Watson, Marshall. Third Row : Ballard, Grant, MacKay, Thompson, Prescott, Herd, Watkins, Tuffil. Second Row : Bergemann, Bourke, Perfect, Taylor, Skudder, Emerton, Muldrew, Bishop, Wyman, Patrick, Concannon, Earl, Norton, Andrewes, Ray, Bolingbroke, unknown. Front Row : Mitchell, Crookes, Hickmore, Folley, Cook, Gard'ner, Watts, Davison, Leigh, Hall, Cairns, Jeffs.

"B" Flight Ground crew Christmas party at Amiens-Glisy December 1944 Reg Mitchell).

488 Squadron aircrew relaxing at Amiens-Glisy waiting for the photographer for the earlier formal photograph (Reg Mitchell).

Some of the damage inflicted by Luftwaffe bombers on New Years Day 1945 at Maldegem airfield in Belgium (Reg Mitchell).

As sketched by Allot Gabites at Brussels.

298

A squadron Mosquito taking off from Amiens-Glisy (Ron Watts).

Waiting for better weather at Amiens, clear but very cold (Ron Watts).

Landing at Amiens with work party in foreground (Ron Watts).

Aircraftsman Jeffs working on one of the Merlins (Allot Gabites).

F/O A.C. (Ces) Ray RNZAF and P/O. J.P. (John) Halligan RNZAF The long and the short of it! (Reg Mitchell).

Above left: A very young-looking P/O. John Hall DFC and Bar (Alison Fenton). Above right: Ron Watts as many remembered him, smiling, sleeves up and in charge! (Ron Watts).

ME- S heading out from Amiens-Glassy (Ron Watts).

"A" Flight Commander Johnny Gard'ner, Commanding Officer W/C Ron Watts and "B" Flight Commander S/L Frank Davison, photographed at Amiens Air base in France during 488 Squadron's operations over Europe (Reg Mitchell).

From left, R. Emerton, J. Mulgrew (without his .45 colt revolver), J. Gard'ner, Ron Watts, Frank Davison, Rod Bourke, Don Herd and Tony Thompson at Amiens 1944 (Reg Mitchell).

A group standing by the Amiens-Glisy Dispersal hut – from left: Dick Marriott, Douglas Robinson, Dick Addison, Peter Hall and Ron Watts (Ron Watts).

The Squadron Commanding Officer, W/C Ron Watts pictured with the Admin section under his command. (Ron Watts)

Above left: P/O. Tom Mallon RNZAF (Barrie Mallon). Above right: Ray Jeffs receiving a moustache trim from Phil Bryers (Allot Gabites). Below left: F/O Tom Taylor D.F.C. at Amiens-Glisy (Reg Mitchell). Below right: F/L Leslie Hunt on left with F/O Bill Hewitt his successor as 488 Squadron Intelligence Officer on 19th March 1945 (Reg Mitchell).

Allot Gabite's sketch of his own aircraft's demise after landing mistakenly on the "Q" Site (from Monkeys Birthday).

The Squadron airfield at Amiems-Glisy – on a good day but patches of ice remain in the background trapped in the numerous shell craters (Ron Watts).

John Hall's demise at Gilze-Rijen (C.H. Goss, from Mosquito Aces of World War 2)

Chapter Nine

GILZE-RIJEN - HOLLAND B.77

4TH APRIL 1945 to 26TH APRIL 1945
AIRFIELD B77

Gilze-Rijen Air Base, coded B77 was located in the Netherlands between the cities of Breda and Tilburg. The base was first built in 1910 so would have been one of the earliest air bases in Europe. The airfield, the second largest in Europe was taken and used by the Luftwaffe in 1940 and after that time was heavily bombed by allied forces until finally being taken over by the British following the invasion.

The German Army still occupied the territory north of the Meuse which was only ten kilometres from the airfield where the New Zealand squadron were to be based. The Germans had set up "Flying Bomb' sites which were aimed at the port of Antwerp where the Allied armies were landing equipment to support their push into Germany. Unfortunately, Gilze-Rijen was right under the flight path of these rockets that passed overhead at a very low altitude. There were several scary moments with one in particular going out of control and heading directly towards a group of 488 airmen. It missed them by just a few metres, landing behind their hut with a terrific blast which badly damaged the building.

Ray Jeffs and Norman Crookes also had a terrible scare when on a daylight flight from Amiens to Gilze-Rijen. They were skimming across cloud tops at around 5000 feet when they noticed the sinister shape of a V1 rocket approaching them on a collision course. In the very short time it took them to identify the object and well before they could react, the jet-propelled bomb passed at high speed behind them very close to their tail. It was a near thing. [51]

Gilze-Rijen had been badly bombed before the arrival of 488 Squadron. None of the original hangers or buildings were still standing. The squadron arrived in dribs and drabs throughout the day of 4th April 1945. The forward parties had established some makeshift wooden shacks for gear and equipment and there were aircraft parked up all over the area. There were literally hundreds of aircraft ranging from a Meteor jet engined fighter squadron, Tempests, Mustangs, Liberators, Mosquitos, a Polish squadron of Spitfires and even a humble high wing Auster or two. All around the clutter of serviceable aircraft were wrecks, victims of earlier conflicts, mostly German but also many Allied aircraft.

Equipment from the unloaded transport aircraft was stored away under make-shift shelters and the air-crew were transported through the village of Gilze-Rijen to their new accommodation. The village itself was neat and tidy and showed traces of new paintwork obviously done following liberation only a few short weeks before. The village church and the civic buildings had been badly damaged by bombing. Transport was not good though, as only one truck was allocated for the squadron to transport air-crew from billets to mess and to dispersal on the airfield so at any one time the truck was packed full of either returning or outgoing air-crew.

The squadron billets had originally been constructed by Dutch forced labour for the Luftwaffe and constructed in a manner which suggested that they had intended to be there for a long-term stay. They were laid out in a wooded area complete with a maze of paved brick roading. The buildings themselves were spread over the area and sturdily built using brickwork with high pitched roofs and side walls designed to absorb either bomb or shell blast. The description continued as *"tiled interiors, with large imitation antique candelabra, chromium bathroom fittings, central heating, beer parlours complete with painted scenic walls and mottos of Germanic exuberance and vision, huge log fireplaces in brick, cocktail bars, gymnasium with murals depicting larger than life perfections of Aryan blood, immense kitchens and beer cellars, now all strangely silent, empty and disused".*

---

[51] *Account from Victory Fighters – "The Veterans Story" by Stephen Darlow*

The lawns were well kept and the gardens all showed signs of spring. 488 Squadron was to have moved into one of these impressive buildings which the Polish squadron was vacating but the latter showed no sign of budging. Instead, to 488 Squadron's great disappointment they were allocated a couple of filthy derelict buildings. With the signs of elegance and privilege all around them they set up in their substandard accommodation with cold water supply only, a flooded bathroom area with blocked lavatories and were forced to sleep six to a room. Surprisingly they still felt they were better off than their accommodation in Amiens. When they turned in that night the concussion from the heavy guns at the Front rattled what was left of the glass in the windows of the buildings.

The shambles continued on the next day when "A" Flight aircraft and the ground crew that were supposed to be following the squadron up to Gilze-Rijen, ended up being diverted to Lille in France. The operational flying still needed to be continued so "B" Flight was under real pressure to continue without rest until "A" Flights arrival. There was much dissatisfaction throughout the squadron at the turn of events. They were however making the best of the situation and quickly settled in getting dispersal areas in action, when two days later they were told that they were to be shifted once again to make room for an American Mitchell bomber squadron.

The squadron was pushed away from relatively good facilities to an area across the other side of the airfield that had two dilapidated huts and a disused strip that was used as a taxi way. They were not a happy group of men. They soon settled into their work and managed to make the most of the situation they found themselves in.

Leslie Hunt at that time wrote of the spontaneous goodwill that quickly occurred between the local populace and the squadron members. These people had been hammered in the preceding months, with their homes and villages destroyed by both the German and Allied forces. Despite suffering great loss from Allied bombing particularly due to collateral damage from strikes on the air-base they were cheerful and pleased to have contact particularly with the New Zealanders. Hunt recalls chocolate and sweets being given in large quantities to the Dutch people and in return they offered to wash and care for clothes and uniforms. Those offers were thankfully received as many of the young men in the squadron had been struggling for months with their personal cleaning duties.

These humble villagers had risked their lives sheltering downed Allied airmen, having been under German occupation for nearly five years. Many of the villagers had been badly punished for this and their resilience and cheerfulness was a constant source of surprise.

The crew of F/O Bill "Chunky" Stewart and F/O Bill Brumby flying out of their new base made it a first for 488 at Gilze-Rijen just three days later by downing a ME 110 over Osnabruk on 7th April 1945. This success in rather unique circumstances made up for the one they lost in murky weather on the night that Johnny Hall had his "prang". They were patrolling over Osnabruck when Control gave them a *"bandit"* over the Ruhr valley. They got onto the tail of a ME 110 and chased it long and hard, twisting and turning with the German rear gunner opening fire on them several times as "Chunky" tried to get close enough to line him up for a burst. There was no anti-aircraft fire but as the chase continued the Mosquito crew noticed a small fire start in the tail of the Messerschmitt and it got larger until the aircraft suddenly dived into the ground and exploded. "Chunky" and Bill were credited with the kill but strangely they had not fired their guns. The inescapable conclusion was that the rear gunner had shot down his own aircraft!

(64) *07/04/1945 – 23:20 hrs - Ex Gilze/Rijen – Stewart and Brumby – unknown - Osnabruck*

Bill Brumby, the Radar operator, epitomised the staying power and determination of this crew. He had followed that twisting and turning ME 110 for over thirty-five minutes with his AI unit, with both men only getting momentary visual glances of their target until its rather dramatic end. To have it added to their "score" was due reward for their perseverance.

"Chunky" survived the war but only by a few short years. He and his crewman, Bill Brumby were both awarded Distinguished Flying Crosses but sadly they had both returned to New Zealand after the squadron disbanded and missed out on the presentation by the King at Buckingham Palace. Chunky Stewart had endeared himself to the 488 Squadron personnel with his wonderful command of the English language. His background in the legal profession would have helped. He had formidable debating skills and was often called on during Mess functions to propose toasts or reply to speeches given by others. He had an unsurpassed wit that had everyone rolling around in fits of laughter at his choice of expressions and he was never ever beaten in a verbal stoush.

The "A" Flight group finally arrived from Lille on the morning of the 8th April and made themselves as comfortable as possible given the conditions at the time.

On 10th April 1945 Reg Mitchell, by now commissioned with the rank of Pilot Officer and taking advantage of his leave period, had flown to the UK to marry his sweetheart Kit Adams in a ceremony at the village church in Ipplepen, near Newton Abbot in Devon. He was able to sneak in a week's "Honeymoon" before rejoining the squadron and continuing with the war. By this time the German war effort had all but collapsed and Reg reports flying with impunity over the Mohne, Sorpe and Eder dams of Dambusters fame, Cologne Cathedral, Krupps in Essen, up the Ruhr Valley to Aachen and back in broad daylight and without seeing any sign of enemy aircraft. Naturally the trusty box Brownie went along and Reg has the photographs to prove it.

The day that Reg Mitchell flew out back to the UK, F/O Craig with F/O Tauwhare were inbound after striking trouble during a training flight and had to make an emergency one engined landing right on dusk in limited visibility. Craig made it in safely which was particularly meritorious as this crew were new to the squadron and had very little experience with the Mosquito.

On 11th April 1945, 488 Squadron were given the news that they were probably going to be disbanded very soon. The morale of the squadron in the days following this announcement must have been very low. Conditions for the men were starting to improve, mostly from their own efforts and it was noted that the ground crew airmen that had been sleeping rough on the floor of their huts had managed to secure bunk beds which must have improved the comfort level somewhat. Just on a week later film crews arrived to spend time with the squadron ironically when most of the accommodation arrangements were settled and a modicum of comfort was in place. They were filming for a project entitled *"New Zealand was there"* presumably for taking back to New Zealand audiences. Somewhat ironic when 488 Squadron was to be disbanded before the war had actually finished!

F/L Jeffs and his crewman, F/L Crookes gave themselves a bit of a scare on 16th April, actually the day the film crew arrived when they ploughed into a bomb crater off the side of the runway when Ray Jeffs lost control after the port engine failed during an afternoon takeoff for a night flying test. The crew were slightly injured but the aircraft NT 272 was badly damaged and consequently written off. This was the fifth time they had suffered engine failure on takeoff and Norman Crookes commended Ray Jeffs for his flying skills. There was a similar accident on the 18th April when F/O McLean, and F/O Grant, also found themselves in a bomb crater albeit at a much slower pace. They were taxying at the time and seemingly wandered off the marked airstrip with disastrous results.

The official notification of disbandment was issued to the squadron on 20th April. It had been generally known for many days that this was going to happen but all the same the news was greeted with some dismay by most members of the squadron. They felt they had worked hard to develop great teamwork and took a lot of pride in their achievements and not unreasonably expected to be together at the end of the war. That end was now clearly in sight. The New Zealand members of the squadron took the attitude that if they were to be taken off active service they might as well go home. Talk of repatriation was rife and W/C. Watts flew to the UK to RNZAF Headquarters to discuss the situation. The war with Japan was still underway so many felt that the best option would be for them to be sent back to defend the shores of New Zealand from the Japanese intentions in the South Pacific.

F/O Craig and F/O Tauwhare flying MM 822 caught up with a Heinkel 111 on 21st April and on their very first operational flight caused some damage to the enemy aircraft but lost sight of it at the last moment so could only be credited with a "damaged". In the early morning hours of 22nd April, P/O. Gordon Patrick and W/O Jimmy Concannon flying MM 809 had an unusual "kill" when they came across a lumbering Junkers 52 transport aircraft. Patrick had a difficult job slowing up his Mosquito to get into position to shoot it down. With full flaps down and almost stalling he hit the Junkers in the fuselage causing the aircraft to disintegrate before hitting the ground near Rhinow

(65) *22/04/1945 – 05:30 hrs – Ex Gilze/Rijen – Patrick and Concannon – Ju 52 - Rhinow*

Two days later the "B" Flight Commander, S/L Frank Davison and his crewman F/L Dickie Hickmore got a repeat with a strike on another Junkers 52 transport.

(66) *24/04/1944 – 22:58 hrs – Ex Gilze/Rijen – Davidson and Hickmore – Ju 52 - Brandenburg*

Davison had three attempts to align his aircraft for a strike but the slow speed meant him overshooting and having to come around again for a further attempt. Finally, he was successful with the Mosquito in a stall situation when it struck the Junkers with just a fifteen-shell burst causing it to plunge into the ground.

The consensus at the time was that these aircraft were transporting high ranking military officers out of the battle areas to safety in neutral Sweden or one of the other Scandinavian countries. Both aircraft were heading out towards the coast which somewhat supported the theory. This possibility was confirmed after the war when the timing and positioning of these flights was investigated and linked with the German decision to evacuate officers away from the Frontline to avoid capture by the Allies. Interestingly the Junkers 52 Tri-Motors were ex Lufthansa Airline aircraft still fitted out as for civilian use. It was a good outcome for Davison as he had done two tours of duty with 488 Squadron without success and achieved this just one day before the squadron was officially disbanded.

The news that the squadron was to be disbanded was quite a shock at the time. It had been obvious that the war was clearly in its last days as enemy aircraft activity was almost nil. Most thought that the squadron would be re-established back in the UK before being disbanded but the date selected meant the end of an era for 488 Squadron as a fighting unit.

The Luftwaffe had withdrawn out of the area covered by 488 Squadron, leaving air bases largely intact. Oh, how things had changed. Leslie Hunt reported that it was now possible for the squadron aircraft to land on these bases with complete impunity and many of these flights were used as trophy hunts looking for souvenirs abandoned by their enemy. Gilze–Rijen soon became the repository for a bust of Hitler, a large painting of Herman Goering and from Wunstorf, a German aircraft tailplane. The squadron's successes were inscribed on this trophy and eventually presented to RNZAF Headquarters in London.

The official Disbandment notice was received from 85 Group Headquarters and took the following form:

Appendix "B" Form 540
April 1945. No.488 Squadron

From H.Q. 85 Group
To 488 (NZ) Squadron

O.970. 19th April Secret

488 RNZAF Squadron and 6488 Echelon are to be disbanded at Lille Vendeville B.51 W.E.F. 26th April 1945.

Squadron and Servicing Echelon are not, repeat, not to move from B77 until instructions are received from this H.Q. Detailed instructions for disbandment action will be issued as soon as possible. Meantime preliminary disbandment preparations are to be taken by Units concerned.[52]

The following day a letter arrived from the New Zealand High Commissioner in London, Mr. W.J. Jordan. Jordan had been an important ally of 488 squadron, particularly when they were struggling with bad equipment and very poor morale in those early days back in 1942. It was Jordan that linked the squadron up with patriotic groups back in New Zealand which resulted in a continuing stream of "goodies" arriving at regular intervals from home. His letter read as follows:

---

[52] *Taken from Squadron Archives*

> 415, Strand,
> London. WC. 2.
> New Zealand Government Offices
>
> 20th April 1945
>
> Wing Commander, R.G. Watts,
> 488 (NZ) Squadron
>
> My dear Wing Commander,
>
>   I am sitting here with our mutual friend, Wing Commander Robertson, and talking about your Squadron, which has done such a great job. We understand that you may be shortly 'rolled up', and I write to express to you and to all the members of the squadron the hearty appreciation and admiration of myself and of our Government and people for the great work you have done. You have brought credit not only to yourselves, but to the Dominion which you represent, and we are proud of you. I hope I shall have an opportunity of seeing you, perhaps before you leave the squadron.
>   With kindest good wishes, in which Wing Commander Robertson joins,
>
>   I am, Yours Sincerely,
>
>   W. J. Jordan

Just two hours later after the Davison / Hickmore strike, F/L Douglas Bergemann with F/O Ken Bishop picked up a Ju 88 on their AI unit while on patrol over Bremen. Bergemann closed to within 80 metres and opened up hitting the port engine. At that range and speed there was no room to manoeuvre and they were forced to overshoot and go around again. Unfortunately, they lost the target and could only claim a "damaged". The presence of another Mosquito on his "patch" did not help matters and the crew were sure that they would have located their stricken target again except for the radar contamination caused by the interloper.

A further message was transmitted to the squadron on 23rd April, this time from Air Headquarters in New Zealand and read as follows:

Appendix "H" Form 540
April 1945. No.488 (NZ) Sqd.

From A.H.Q. Wellington
To : R.N.Z.A.F. London.

890   APL 23

Please pass to Commanding Officer 488 Squadron from CAS (Chief of Air Staff). While we must all feel satisfaction that the general situation makes it possible to reduce front line strength I regret that it is 488 that is to be disbanded. Please congratulate all ranks on their fine effort and high reputation. The squadron has a record to be proud of first in the difficult days in Malaya and then in Europe. It is intended that the squadron identity should be perpetuated in R.N.Z.A.F. future organisation.

This latest homily from the RNZAF Headquarters in Wellington, New Zealand did nothing to dispel the huge disappointment and anger felt by particularly the New Zealand air-crews. They felt they were letting the side down and were annoyed that after all the hard work in establishing the squadron as a successful and motivated unit, they were going to be dispersed away from fellow squadron members they had fought and died with on the whim of office bound authorities on the other side of the world. It must have been heartbreaking. As it was, the intention to *"perpetuate"* the identity of 488 Squadron never happened for close on sixty-five years until the 8th of December 2010, when a new Wing, rather than a squadron was set up at Ohakea Airbase and designated No. 488. It was as Reg Mitchell said a long, long time to wait for some recognition.

F/L Bergemann, and his crewman, F/O Ken Bishop, were in with a chance for a victory on the second last day of 488's operations when their controller put them onto a target over Bremen. It was a moonlit night with clear skies. Bergemann manoeuvred into a good position at close range and hit his target from just 50 metres away with a short burst. The target made a turn to port which made Bergemann overshoot and when he came back on course what was indentified to be a Ju 88 had disappeared. They eventually made contact with what they thought was their victim again but this time they found a Mosquito in their sights. The disappointed pair had to settle for a "damaged' claim only.

There was a lot of pushing and shoving on the last day of operations for the squadron as all the crews were vying for the honour of success on the last patrol. "A" Flight had the honours for the last sortie. The last "kill" went to Johnny Marshall and Phil Prescott and without taking anything away from the deed; it was a bit of a soft target. Unfortunately for the German aircraft he had wandered into Marshall's sector and Control reported a slow-moving object to the Mosquito crew. It turned out to be a Focke Wulf 189, generally used as an observation aircraft. To the German pilots credit he did carry out a series of evasive measures albeit at slow speed and for a while Marshall was unable to slow down enough to register the target. When he finally got into position, flaps fully down and in a stall situation, it was all over in a flash with the FW 189 turning over on to its back and diving into the ground near Wittenburg.

(67) *25/04/1945 – 02:20 hrs – Ex Gilze/Rijen – Marshall and Prescott – Fe 189 – Wittenburg*

It was the sixty seventh and last official "kill" for 488 Squadron on operations that had started three long years ago. This patrol also resulted in the last German aircraft being shot down by a Mosquito night fighter in the Second World War. Although some weeks from the end of the war no more enemy aircraft were shot down by any of the squadrons of 149 Wing so nothing was in the end lost with 488's early departure from the operational scene.

Flt Lt. "Chunky" Stewart climbing through the entry hatch into the cockpit of his Mosquito (Allot Gabites).

Gilze-Rijen - General view of airfield - note belly landed Mosquito behind the Barber. (Noted on back of photo as from 410 Squadron) The portaloo structure in the background is just that – the one and only toilet facility for the entire use of all the "B" Flight personel. From left in foreground, Crayton, McIntyre, Webb and Allen (Alastair Gager).

A Junkers Ju 52 transport aircraft (Reg Mitchell).

All good mates - George Holmes, Ray Gager and Jock Crayton at Gilze – Rijen, March 1945 (Alastair Gager).

Fitters and Riggers of" B" Flight 6488 Echelon at Gilze –Rijen.. Ray Gager on left directly under spinner (Alastair Gager)

Another view of the squadron Dispersal Hut with from left Andrew Broodbank seated beside Douglas Robinson with Jack Scott standing at rear beside Ron Watts (Adam Forrest).

Chapter Ten

THE LAST FAREWELL

The 26th April 1945 dawned fine and calm. There was still disbelief among the Squadron members that 488 Squadron was to no more look for *"Trade"* in the night skies. There would have been some relief that for most their war would be over and thoughts of the sanctuary and warmth of home would be gaining some certainty in their minds. Many indeed would be repatriated home but some were to move on to other squadrons. Although the German war effort was in a state of collapse the war with Japan was still far from over so there was still work to do. It was clear that Germany was within days of surrender and there was just a little fear that some last-ditch action by the Luftwaffe might spoil the gathering mood of excitement and relief many felt as the last operational flights were made. For the first time the respective crews, both air and ground could be together and mix socially together. Operational work over the preceding three years had meant separation into "A" and "B" flights with one effectively in the air or on call for operational work while the other slept.

The following message was received from Headquarters 85 Group and no doubt passed on to the squadron members at some stage:

From: H.Q. 85 Group   261040B
To: 488 Squadron
Secret QQY BT

A 160 26 April   45 Secret

For Watts FR
OM Steele. On the disbandment of 488 Squadron I wish to express my appreciation of the excellent work the squadron has done in destroying 57 aircraft at night while in the Group. Unfortunately, 488 Squadron did not operate from bases on the Continent until November and long distances had to be covered from the UK before you reached your patrol lines yet a high standard of serviceability was maintained and whenever there were Huns about your score mounted. This reflected the greatest credit on the keenness and efficiency of both aircrews and ground crews. Your disbandment at the present time must be a bitter disappointment but you can be justly proud that the Hun has been thoroughly beaten at night and that 488 Squadron have played a leading part in that beating. Good luck to you all.

This was one day however when all of 488 Squadron gathered together, to have their official Disbandment Parade. The squadron was addressed by the Gilze-Rijen airfield Commander, Group Captain G.C. Moon AFC who read messages sent by RNZAF Headquarters in Wellington NZ, the New Zealand High Commissioner in London, Mr Jordan and the Air Officer Commanding No.85 Group. [53] Photographs were taken of various sections and Flights and then the squadron was dismissed.

No. 488 (New Zealand) Squadron of the Royal Air Force, for the second time in its illustrious history ceased to exist.

Wng Commander Ron Watts took the opportunity to speak to the assembled squadron giving the following address to his men; [54]

---

[53] *Copy of messages listed in Appendix*
[54] *Copy of speech notes – Ron Watts to disbandment parade.*

The disbandment of this squadron having now taken place, it seems a fitting time to review our efforts since forming on June 25th 1942, and list our successes and pay our last tribute to those that have fallen.

After a period of training the squadron carried out its first operational sorties in the form of night ranger (patrols) over France. These sorties resulted in attacks being made on many trains and sundry barges and motor transport etc, and even one bicycle and "crew". The squadron first met the Hun in the air shortly after moving to the south of England in September 1943, and from that date it might be considered fully operational. Since then a total of 81 enemy aircraft have been engaged in combat of which 67 were destroyed, 4 probably destroyed and 10 damaged. In addition to these we must not forget the 266 bogeys intercepted and positively identified as friendly; the very numerous aircraft contacted on which a completed interception was not necessary owing to early identification of their friendly character by means other than visual recognition; the assistance often rendered in the form of Air Sea Rescue operations; nor the occasions when our aircraft led crippled friendly aircraft to safety.

Of the enemy aircraft attacked 32 were Ju 88's, 15 Ju 188's, 12 Do 217's, 6 Me 410's, 9 Fw 190's, 9 Me 110's, 9 He 111's, 2 Ju 52's, 1 Fw 189 and 4 unidentified enemy aircraft.

Up to the end of March 1945, the squadron received the following awards, one D.S.O., one M.B.E., seven bars to the D.F.C., eight D.F. C's, one D.F.M., one A.F.C., three Mention in Despatches, and one Dutch Flying Cross. In addition to these, undoubtedly still further recognition will be granted for work accomplished in the last few weeks of the squadron's existence.

This record is indeed one of which we all may be proud and it does reflect the very greatest credit on all ranks who by their cheerful and willing co-operation have made it possible.

A record of this nature would be incomplete without mention of the 36 men who gave their lives in the performance of their duties, they were fine men and we all honour them for the supreme sacrifice they made.

In conclusion, may I express my personal thanks to all squadron members past and present who have helped to form this most creditable operational record.

I feel we may all hold our heads very high, secure in the knowledge that, when our services were required we were not found wanting and now that the Hun is well and truly beaten in the air, we may turn our efforts elsewhere with the knowledge that we have not failed in our duties but have left an impressive record of which we may indeed feel proud.

R.G. Watts,
Wing Commander, Commanding
No.488 (NZ) Squadron R.A.F

It was the perfect occasion for a big party and big it was. With the realisation that disbandment meant everyone going their separate ways the importance of the occasion was sheeted home to each and every man in the squadron. A large hall in Tilberg, the nearest town to Gilze-Rijen airbase was hired for the occasion and the dance and party went on until the wee small hours.

At the dawning of the new day the pack up and cleanup process began. Germany was to surrender officially on the 4th of May 1945 but there had been a lot of work to do to effect the squadrons disestablishment before that day. The ground crews worked long and hard to tidy up all the squadron's aircraft in readiness for the ATA pilots to arrive to ferry them back to bases and depots in the UK. All the squadron tools and equipment had to be collected up and boxed and packaged ready for the move back across the channel. There had always been considerable pride among the ground-crews in their work and in their servicing excellence. The proof of this was shown when they prepared their aircraft for handover. The Mosquitos were spruced up and cleaned and much to the amazement of the ATA pilots, many even had linoleum laid on the cockpit floors.

Less than a week later many of the squadron personnel had dispersed and left the base. Most of the Kiwi air-crew left for the UK on the morning of 2nd May 1945 just two days before the actual surrender. They were bussed through Brussels, Ghent, Bruges, to Blankenberge to wait on embarkation across the channel at Ostend. Norman Crookes remembers sitting in a Navy boat in Ostend Harbour when the news arrived that the war was over. He commented that he felt really down at the time as he always thought he would be flying home rather than travelling by sea. There was one consolation though as after the news broke the Navy opened the liquor store and he remembers very little of the rest of the trip home.

Those of the aircrew left behind transferred to No. 219 Squadron. This squadron was set up to provide assistance to the resistance movement in Northern Holland. The ground-crew 6488 Echelon in the meantime worked on.

W/C Ron Watts, now bereft of his squadron, was left behind as acting Airfield Commander then was promoted to Commanding Officer of 149 Wing based at Gilze-Rijen, after Group Captain Moon departed to take part in celebrations elsewhere. Ron, not particularly happy with this situation and unable to join in the widespread celebrations, was forced to stay behind at Gilze-Rijen alone. At a time when he surely deserved to be part of the celebrations he sat alone in the Officer's Mess, feeling quite despondent with the memories of all his friends that had died in the conflict and not even able to have a drink. He deserved a lot better. He had time on his hands, and with the few remaining sections on the base looking after themselves, he voluntarily set off on a mission to try and track down the burial sites of New Zealand aircrew that had died on the Continent. He was joined on his journey by Leslie Hunt. With the blessing of NZ Air Force Headquarters in London he travelled by any means available up to the Russian line on the Elbe River, to Aachen and as far as Luneberg in Germany. Unfortunately, he met with little success as the region was still in utter turmoil. It was as he said much too soon after the end of hostilities.

Ron Watts struck situations during his mission that appalled him. He recalled particularly the Russians being out of control at the Elbe River crossing and despite wanting to cross over to the Russian lines was warned by British troops in no uncertain terms that to do so would be a suicide mission as the Russian army was running amok, looting, raping and killing.

When he returned to his base at Gilze-Rijen, with nothing to do, he posted himself to the UK. He managed some sightseeing before travelling back to New Zealand in November 1945. The journey home by troopship was a torturous one, taking the best part of seven weeks. Like most returning servicemen, he found no hero's welcome on his return as he expected, and faced a long and miserable return to peacetime conditions. Ron considered however himself lucky after reflecting on the many near death situations he had been in during the war years.

When interviewed by Dave Homewood for his International website, Ron was asked what his most exciting sortie was. He recounted one of the most stressful sorties he experienced. In his own words:

> *"The most stressful was, one day; we used to be on duty by day as well. The flight that was flying at night flew two nights on, and the other flight was on standby during the day. The thing was, if you got any very, very bad weather, with low cloud and fog underneath it, the day boys couldn't*

intercept enemy aircraft so we still to have to stand by ready to take off under those circumstances".

"And when that happened, fog and low cloud, the enemy would put a radio beam across from France to London, with dots on one side, the dashes on the other and a steady beam in the middle. And the German fighter-bombers would fly along that, and when they got a cross beam from another part of France, they were over London and they'd drop (the bombs).

"And this one trip I had that will stay in my memory forever, it was a filthy, filthy day with very low cloud, at about 200 feet, and fog underneath it. And they insisted I take off. Really, it shouldn't have been, you shouldn't have been allowed to take off. It was virtually an instrument take off, which is not easy to do at any time."

"Anyway, I was fluttering around at about 150 feet, and I knew I couldn't get back in again, so I was stretching the endurance as best I could, flying very, very slowly and low revs, and all that sort of thing. And I was being directed from the ground where to fly. I was over the Thames Estuary, just going to and fro across to cut them off, you see. Nobody came by the way, I think they only put the beam on just to see if some idiot would get up and crash.

"But as we were going along, there was an object in the water on stilts. What they used to have, they had buoys moored in the Thames Estuary, so if any fighter pilot got shot down, he could paddle up to this buoy, and climb up the ladder, and get in to warmth and food and all that sort of thing. And they had a flag that they ran up the flag post if anybody was in residence. And I said to the navigator, "See if the flag's up". You see, I thought it was a buoy".

"No fear it was a fort! The royal navy had forts in the estuary, and they would fire at anything within range – no questions asked – with Bofors! And of course, I was sauntering along at about 170mph, which was at the point of stalling, at about 150 feet. And they opened fire on me, and the firing was beautiful. The line was perfect, it was right across my nose. Of course, if I turned away there would have been no deflection. They obviously thought I was doing 220mph or whatever and they had allowed that much deflection. And when I tried to climb into cloud cover, of course I was on the point of stalling, if I throttled too much I'd go much faster and fly into it (the firing line). It was a long, long while to get up into cloud, a long, long while".

"And the Bofors comes up. It looks like a dotted line as it comes up. And it seems to be very, very slow from the gun, and as it progresses it gets faster and faster, and when it gets in front of you, it shoots across at great speed. But I got up eventually, and everywhere else the cloud had been at about 200 feet, but here it was at about 1200 feet. So, I was staggering up on the point of stalling, and when I got in there, I had something to say to the ground control people for putting me over this thing and they apologised, and circled me around, and I was in cloud for a bit. Then they brought me down, and I was right over a Battleship! And they too would open fire on anybody within range! So, I said" Thank you very much, who's side are you on! "Oh, that was great!" he laughs.

"And then I had to go back, there was no raid, nobody came up, it was all a waste. I had to go back and for goodness how long did I have to wait till the fog would let me slip back in. So, that was really exciting, without enemy action, who needs the enemy?

There is a certain irony from Ron's account of that day's events. There was no way he and Roger Folley should have been airborne at all but it does give some indication of the desperateness of Air Operations knowing that weather conditions would keep defensive aircraft on the ground but the Luftwaffe could bomb London or the southern cities with impunity using their very simple targeting radar system. Is it not ironic the Ron considers this day his most stressful and yet faced greater danger from his own side that day without coming into contact with the enemy?

Ron Watts talked often in his memoirs of his "Guardian Angel" that he felt looked after him on many occasions. He spoke also of the many friendships he held over the years since 488 Squadron's sojourns in the UK and Europe.

Ron sadly passed away on 28th August 2009 aged 93 during the early research stage of this book.

The Germans surrendered on 4th May 1945 just four days later. It should have been a day of unbridled celebration but for the death of Sgt. Duggie Howland. He had been walking with two other squadron members on the footpath in Breda town just out of the base when a truck mounted the footpath and struck him down. He was killed instantly and probably never knew what had hit him. He was one of the senior NCO's on the squadron and had done more than his fair share over the preceding months to ensure that the aircraft in his care were prepared and ready for action. He had much experience, having served as an Air Gunner before the war and was "Mentioned in Despatches" for his exceptional work. He was buried in the military cemetery at Tilburg.[55]

Ron Watts and Leslie Hunt travelled out to the cemetery at Breda shortly before they left Holland to visit the graves of Duggie Howland and those of Tom Mallon and George Brock. They were checking to see if a cross had been erected on the grave of Duggie and that all the graves were being attended and looked after properly.

On a more personal note it is worth recording that there was considerable interaction between 488 personnel and the local populace with Leslie Hunt reporting that no less than nineteen members of the air-crew married either English or Scottish girls. One rather unique pairing was the wedding of Lac. George Sutherland to a Belgium girl, whom he had known since childhood in Poperinghe. George's Father had also married a Belgium girl after the First World War when working for the War Graves Commission hence the contact. The wedding of young George in 1945 was the event of the year in Poperinghe with the entire town reportedly attending. A wedding photograph taken at the time shows a large group of George's 488 ground-crew mates in attendance. George was posted to a local RAF unit at Courtrai when the squadron was disbanded and eventually ended up working for the Commonwealth War Graves Commission himself. At the time of the writing of this story George was still living in Poperinghe.

Two significant events in recent times have closed the final chapter in the history of 488 Squadron. The first and most significant was carried out on the 8th of December 2010. The date was ironic as it coincided with the anniversary of the Japanese attack on Pearl Harbour

---

[55] *This account sourced from "Defence until Dawn" by Leslie Hunt*

and the start of Japan's involvement in World War Two. More significantly for 488 Squadron it also coincided with the Japanese landings on the coast of Malaya, the repercussions of which impacted on the original "Far East" squadron in such a dramatic way. The 69th anniversary of this event saw New Zealand, at long last give due recognition to the squadron by re-forming a new "Wing" to be known as 488 at Ohakea Airbase in the central North Island of New Zealand.

The long-forgotten squadron and those brave men that had gone before were to be honoured by the New Zealand Government's approval in setting up a new "Wing". A parade was held and attended by some of the few surviving personnel of those two earlier squadrons. The parade was addressed by the then Chief of Air Force, Air Vice Marshall Graham Lintott, and in his speech, he paid tribute to the history of those that bravely defended the free world from the tyranny of the Axis powers all those years ago. I was honoured to be able to travel with the veterans and be part of the ceremony.

The consensus among those Veterans was that the recognition went a long way towards dispelling the perception that they were the "forgotten" squadron and that the rebirth of the new squadron identity would carry on the pride and honour that they felt at their brave efforts all those long years ago.

I am very proud to have been part of that.

The final parade (Ron Watts).

(New Zealand Fighter Pilots Museum)

Group.Captain. Moon, the Gilze-Rijen Base Commander, and the Commanding Officer of 488 Squadron, W/C Watts, take the final salute from the squadron, appropriately with one of the squadron Mosquitos in the background (Reg Mitchell).

Final Parade shot – this time taken from behind the Mosquito shown in background in previous photo (Ron Watts).

The late Wing Commander Ron Watts, C.O. of 488 Squadron. Photo taken in 2009 (Ross Vallely).

Pictured is Sgt. Duggie Howland, who was tragically killed in Breda, Holland just days after the squadron was disbanded. He was struck by an out of control truck which mounted the footpath when he was out walking with a group of 488 ground-crew (Ron Watts).

Some wit in the squadron came up with the idea of the grave site and memorial stone pictured and this was left behind when the last man left for home from Gilze-Rijen Air Base in Holland (Reg Mitchell)

Two mates from the opposite side of the world who served with 488 Squadron: left: LAC George Sutherland RAF, right: LAC "Pee Wee" Smith RNZAF.

This photograph of veterans was taken on 8th December 2010 prior to them being flown down to Ohakea to attend as guests of honour the Inaugural Parade of the new 488 Wing based at RNZAF Ohakea. From left: Reg Mitchell (488 UK), Bert Clayton (488 Far East), Ray Gager (488 UK), Ted West (488 Far East), Jim Cromie (488 Far East).

The reconstructed Mosquito takes to the air again on 29/09/2012 over Ardmore Airfield, Auckland New Zealand. Built by a New Zealand company AVSPECS Ltd.

The Aftermath

488 Squadron flew 2899 sorties, totalling 6689 hours, during which 67 enemy aircraft were confirmed destroyed, 4 probably destroyed, not able to be independently confirmed and 10 damaged. While employed on ranger patrols in 1943, crews also destroyed or damaged some 40 locomotives together with many individual road vehicles and sunk an unknown number of sea going vessels.

Wing Commander Dickie Haine tried in vain to claim a *"captured"* as a further category but was denied his claim by Air operations following the arrival at Bradwell of the Junkers 88 as described in Chapter Four.

On 23/24th December 1944, Ray Jeffs and Norman Crookes seriously damaged a Ju 88 over Malmedy but could only make a damaged claim at the time. A researcher found evidence in the 1990's that the Ju 88 did not return to base and the aircrew had bailed out and survived the crash. No official record exists of this event but it seems conclusive that Jeffs and Crookes had fair claim to the kill and their score should be upgraded to three victories and the squadron total to sixty-eight.

The tally sheets were a serious part of the war effort and there was great competition among the crews by all the squadrons to better rival flights even within their own squadron. It was a very healthy and rewarding scenario and in times of low activity in the air provided a stimulus to down as many of the enemy as possible. The competition between 488 Squadrons' "A" and "B" flights must have acted as a great incentive to try just that little bit more and produce good results for the sake of your flight, your squadron and the greater war effort.

It is hoped that this narrative has not been viewed as a scoresheet alone. I would hope that the efforts of those involved have been adequately described to accurately reflect their personal commitment to the cause. It was never my intention to compare these results with any of those of other squadrons that served in the conflict as circumstances varied greatly.

The word "Ace" appears in any narrative about the air war and this status was conferred on any air-crew downing five enemy aircraft. Each "kill" had to be verified by independent sightings and often these claims were subject to counter claims by ground based anti-aircraft units claiming that their fire power had been instrumental in downing the subject aircraft. Gun cameras were widely used and would usually confirm damage or destruction but identification of individual aircraft was difficult. Many of these claims and counter claims had to rely on a physical check on wreckage to ascertain which calibre of bullet had done the fatal damage. In some cases, claims were only to be settled when investigations were done into Luftwaffe records well after the war's end. A good many of course were shot down over the English Channel or the North Sea and those verifications were difficult, resulting in a number of claims being denied due to lack of confirmed independent sightings.

I thought it may be an interesting exercise to catalogue the official known claims as a mark of respect for the crews that gave their all in the defence of Britain. The source for all the listed claims were *"Intelligence and Combat Reports"* marked *"Secret"* and sourced from Government Archives in both the UK and here in New Zealand during the course of my research. Each report had been signed off by the squadron's Intelligence Officer and personally signed by each member of the crew. References were made in each report to supporting evidence from fellow pilots or ground based observations to confirm the result of each report.

The dates as shown on the "score" sheet is the start date for each night sortie but many would have been downed after mid night on the same sortie and so actually would have fallen on the next day's date.

SECRET.   SERIAL NO. 488/54.

FORM "F" - PERSONAL COMBAT REPORT.

From: 488 (N.Z.) Squadron of 85 Group, R.A.F. Station, Colerne.

To: H.Q. A.E.A.F.(2), H.Q. A.D.G.B.(2), H.Q. 85 Group (2),
      H.Q. 11 Group, H.Q. 25 Base Defence Wing.

STATISTICAL.
Date.   (A) 20/21st August 1944.
Unit   (B) 488 (N.Z.) Squadron.
Type and Mark of A/C.   (C) 1 Mosquito XIII Mark VI A.I.
Time attack was delivered   (D) 2355 hours.
Place of Attack   (E) 15 miles East of Caen.
Weather   (F) Hazy up to 5,000', Cloud 6/10
                                          7,000. Visibility poor.
Our Casualties A/C.   (G) Nil.
  "   "   Personnel.   (H) Nil.
Enemy Casualties in Air Combat.   (I) 1 JU.188 Destroyed.
  "   "   ground or sea target. (J) Nil.

PILOT: F/O. D. N. ROBINSON.   NAVIGATOR: W/O. N. ADDISON, D.F.C.,
                                                                    D.F.M.

I was airborne at Colerne at 2120 hours and reported to Pool 1, when I was handed over to Radox Control. I was then placed on a patrol line East to West just South of Caen. Eventually I was given various vectors to investigate a bogey but before contact was obtained I was called off and given vectors in a North-easterly direction to investigate second bogey. A contact was obtained on "window", range 2 miles. I followed and eventually a visual was obtained on an aircraft, range 800 feet, 7 o'clock, Angel 5,000, doing evasive action, issuing "window" continually and losing height. I followed, and the aircraft was silhouetted against a flare. I had no difficulty in identifying the aircraft as a JU.188 (which was confirmed by my navigator using night glasses) carrying bombs. The enemy aircraft, when I saw him, was turning to port and I followed. I had difficulty through bad visibility in retaining visual. However, I opened fire at a range of 250 yards, but no strikes were observed. I opened fire on three or four occasions and observed strikes on the port engine and later on the cockpit and fuselage. The enemy aircraft then banked steeply to starboard and went down vertically hitting the ground and exploding with the bombs in their racks which I believe were incendiaries. The place of destruction was 15 miles East of Caen.

I claim 1 JU.188 destroyed.

Cine Camera used automatically.

Ammo: P.O. 27.   P.I. 26.   S.I. 28.   S.O. 27.

PILOT .... F/O.

NAVIGATOR .... W/O.

Squadron Intelligence Officer .... P/O.

The above is a typical example of a "Combat report" filed with each claim. Each claim needed to be checked and confirmed from other sources before final confirmation of a "kill" was approved by Air Operations.

Squadron Combat Victories

The following are the lists of known enemy aircraft destroyed and confirmed. There was a great deal of competion from Army anti aircraft sites resulting in very slow confirmations coming through. Many were not settled until after the end of the War. Luftwaffe records were also good sources as time & place comparisons were made. Some downed aircraft went into the sea or waterways and were never seen again. The downed aircraft had to be sighted by an independent source to qualify as destroyed. This required either a clear sighting of the act of crashing or confirmation of debris found.

Confirmed Destroyed

No.	Crew	Target Aircraft	Date	Locality
1	F/L Jimmy Gunn / F/O Jock Affleck	Heinkel 111	15/09/1943	Forness UK
2	F/L Ron Watts / F/O Roger Folley	Dornier 217	15/09/1943	Forness UK
3	F/O Graeme Reed P/O Ralph Bricker	Me 410	08/11/1943	Manston UK
4	F/L Peter Hall / P/O Dick Marriott	Me 410	26/11/1943	Calais Fr
5	F/O Douglas Robinson / F/O Terry Clark	Me 410	19/12/1943	Rye UK
6	F/O Douglas Bergemann / F/O Ken Bishop	Me 410	20/01/1944	Dover UK
7	F/L Johnny Hall / F/O Jock Cairns	Dornier 217	21/01/1944	Lymph UK
8	F/L Johnny Hall / F/O Jock Cairns	Ju 88	21/01/1944	Kent UK
9	F/Sgt Chris Vlotman / Sgt Johnny Wood	Dornier 217	04/02/1944	Channel
10	F/L Peter Hall / P/O Dick Marriott	Ju188	24/02/1944	Wadhurst UK
11	S/L Nigel Bunting / F/L Phil Reed	Ju188	14/03/1944	Essex UK
12	F/Sgt Chris Vlotman / Sgt Johnny Wood	Ju88	21/03/1944	Channel
13	F/Sgt Chris Vlotman / Sgt Johnny Wood	Ju88	21/03/1944	Channel
14	S/L Nigel Bunting / F/L Phil Reed	Ju88	21/03/1944	Clare UK
15	S/L Nigel Bunting / F/L Phil Reed	Ju188	21/03/1944	Rochford UK
16	F/L Johnny Hall / F/O Jock Cairns	Ju88	21/03/1944	Earls Coln UK
17	F/L Johnny Hall / F/O Jock Cairns	Ju88	18/04/1944	Belgium Coast
18	W/O Rod Bourke / F/O Irwin Skudder	Ju88	18/04/1944	Belgium Coast
19	F/O Ray Jeffs / F/O Ted Spedding	Ju188	14/05/1944	Yeovil UK
20	F/L Johnny Hall / F/O Jock Cairns	Ju188	14/05/1944	Exeter UK
21	S/L Nigel Bunting / F/L Phil Reed	Ju88	1 2/06/1944	Caen Fr.
22	F/L Peter Hall / P/O Dick Marriott	Ju88	14/06/1944	St. Lo Fr.

23	S/L Nigel Bunting / F/L Phil Reed	Fw 190	16/06/1944	St. Lo Fr.
24	F/L Peter Hall / P/O Dick Marriott	Ju 88	17/06/1944	St.Lo Fr.
25	F/O Douglas Robinson / F/L Cherub Keeping	Fw 190	18/06/1944	Quineville Fr.
26	F/L Chris Vlotman / Sgt Johnny Wood	Fw 190	20/06/1944	Falaise Fr
27	P/O Stan McCabe / W/O Terry Riley	Ju 188	22/06/1944	Bayeux Fr.
28	F/L Jamie Jameson / F/O Norman Crookes	Me 410	25/06/1944	Bayeax Fr.
29	F/L Jamie Jameson / F/O Norman Crookes	Ju 88	28/06/1944	Caen Fr.
30	F/L Peter Hall / P/O Dick Marriott	Ju 88	28/07/1944	Lessay Fr.
31	F/L Peter Hall / P/O Dick Marriott	Ju 88	28/07/1944	Lessay Fr.
32	F/O Douglas Robinson / F/L Terry Clark	Ju 188	28/07/1944	Mayenne Fr.
33	F/L Jamie Jameson / F/O Norman Crookes	Ju 88	29/07/1944	Caen Fr.
34	F/L Jamie Jameson / F/O Norman Crookes	Ju 88	29/07/1944	Caen Fr.
35	F/L Jamie Jameson / F/O Norman Crookes	Ju 88	29/07/1944	Lisieux Fr
36	F/L Jamie Jameson / F/O Norman Crookes	Dornier 217	29/07/1944	Caen Fr.
37	F/L Peter Hall / P/O Dick Marriott	Ju 88	01/08/1944	St Lo. Fr.
38	F/L Allen Browne / P/O Thompson	Dornier 217	02/08/1944	Avranches Fr.
39	W.O. Tom McKay / P/O Thompson	Ju 188	03/08/1944	Avranches Fr.
40	F/O Gordon Patrick / P/O Jimmy Concannon	Ju 88	03/08/1944	Avranches Fr.
41	F/L Jamie Jameson / F/O Norman Crookes	Ju 88	04/08/1944	Airel Fr.
42	F/O Andy Shaw / F/O Len Wyman	Ju 188	04/08/1944	St Lo. Fr.
43	W/Com Dickie Haine / F/L Pete Bowman	Ju 88	04/08/1944	Vire Fr
44	F/L Peter Hall / P/O Dick Marriott	Dornier 217	05/08/1944	Not Recorded
45	F/Sgt MacLean / F/O/ Brian Grant	Dornier 217	05/08/1944	Angers Fr
46	F/L Allen Browne / F/L Tom Taylor	Ju 188	06/08/1944	Rennes Fr.
47	F/L Allen Browne / F/L Tom Taylor	Ju 188	06/08/1944	Rennes Fr.
48	F/L Allen Browne / F/L Tom Taylor	Ju 188	06/08/1944	Rennes Fr.
49	F/L Jamie Jameson / F/O Norman Crookes	Ju 88	06/08/1944	Avrances Fr.
50	F/L Johnny Hall / F/O Jock Cairns	Ju 88	15/08/1944	Caen Fr.
51	P/O Stan McCabe / W/O Newman	Ju 88	16/08/1944	Caen Fr.
52	F/O Ray Jeffs / F/O Norman Crookes	Dornier 217	18/08/1944	Rouen Fr.
53	F/O Douglas Robinson / W/O Addie Addison	Ju 188	20/08/1944	Caen Fr.
54	W/Com Dickie Haine / F/L Pete Bowman	Ju 188	01/09/1944	Le Havre Fr
55	W/O Johnny Marshall / F/O Phil Prescott	Me 110	04/11/1944	Antwerp Bel.
56	F/O Chunky Stewart / F/O Bill Brumby	Ju 88	23/12/1944	Maeseyck Bel
57	F/O Chunky Stewart / F/O Bill Brumby	Ju 88	23/12/1944	Maeseyck Bel
58	W/Com Ron Watts / F/O Skudder	Ju 188	23/12/1944	Nijmegen
59	F/L Johnny Hall / F/O Jock Cairns	Me 410	23/12/1944	Malmedy Bel

No.	Crew	Target Aircraft	Date	Locality
60	F/O Chunky Stewart / F/O Bill Brumby	Ju 88	21/02/1945	Groenlo Fr.
61	F/O Keith Fleming / F/O Ken Nagle	Me 110	22/03/1945	Dortmund
62	F/L Johnny Hall / P/O Tom Taylor	Ju 88	26/03/1945	Emmerich
63	F/O Chunky Stewart / F/O Bill Brumby	Me 110	26/03/1945	Holtern Bel
64	F/O Chunky Stewart / F/O Bill Brumby	Me 110	07/04/1945	Osnabruck Bel
65	P/O Gordon Patrick / W/O Jimmy Concannon	Ju 52	22/04/1945	Rhinow
66	S/Ldr Frank Davison / F/L Dicky Hickmore	Ju 52	24/04/1945	Brandenburg
67	F/O Johnny Marshall / F/O Phil Prescott	Fw 189	25/04/1945	Wittenburg

Probable

No.	Crew	Target Aircraft	Date	Locality
1	F/L Peter Hall / F/O Dick Marriott	Dornier 217	24/02/1944	Wadhurst
2	F/O Ray Jeffs / P/O Ted Spedding	Dornier 217	14/05/1944	Stourminster
3	F/L Hugh Webbe / F/L Ian Watson	Ju 188	26/12/1944	Not Recorded
4	F/O Chunky Stewart / F/O Bill Brumby	Me 110	26/03/1945	Bocholt

Damaged

No.	Crew	Target Aircraft	Date	Locality
1	P/O Neill Knox / P/O Buck Ryan	Dornier 217	06/10/1942	Canterbury UK
2	F/Sgt Reg Mitchell / Sgt Ron Ballard	Ju 88	14/05/1944	Ilchester UK
3	F/O Andy Shaw / F/O Len Wyman	Ju88	04/08/1944	St Lo France
4	F/Sgt MacLean / F/O Brian Grant	Dornier 217	05/08/1944	Angers France
5	F/Lt Jamie Jameson / F/O Norman Crookes	Ju 88	06/08/1944	Vire France
6	F/Lt Bill Cook / F/O Don Proctor	Ju 188	16/08/1944	Not Recorded
7	F/Lt Ray Jeffs / F/ Lt Norman Crookes	Ju 88	23/12/1944	Malmedy Bell
8	P/O Tom Mallon / Flt Sgt George Brock	Ju 188	24/12/1944	Not Recorded
9	F/O Craig / F/O Tauwhare	He 111	22/04/1945	Rhinow
10	F/Lt Douglas Bergemann / F/O Ken Bishop	Ju 88	24/04/1945	Bremen

The Men of 488 Squadron

The composition of the squadron was interesting in that it was designated a New Zealand squadron under the auspices of Royal Air Force command. At the end of March 1945, the squadron demographics were listed as follows

488 (NZ) Squadron
Aircrew Officers	13 RAF	35 RNZAF		
Aircrew Other Ranks	4 RAF	3 RNZAF		
Ground staff Officers	2 RAF			
Ground staff other Ranks	3 RAF			

6488 Servicing Echelon
Officers	2 RAF			
Flt/Sgts.	8 RAF			
Sgts	9 RAF	1 RNZAF		
Cpls	50 RAF		2 RCAF	
Acs	214 RAF	2 RNZAF	6 RCAF	

One of the more surprising things that stood out during the research stage of this narrative while looking through the personal data from the files of the individual squadron members was the relative inexperience of almost all those that formed the air crews. Very few were career servicemen including some of the more senior men. Fast promotion was common and many that joined the squadron as NCO's quickly rose through the ranks and in a very short space of time left with senior commissions. Most had only joined up for active service after the outbreak of hostilities.

The air-force in the UK and more so in New Zealand were relatively new organisations, in fact there were only 91 officers and 665 other ranks active air force personnel in the RNZAF at the outbreak of the Second World War.

The pre-war occupations of 488's air crew make interesting reading. "Chunky" Stewart joined up in May 1941 and was a Solicitor, Allen Browne joined in December 1940 – Factory Manager, Athol McKinnon, March 1940 – Clerk, Jimmy Gunn, August 1940 - Motor Mechanic,

Stan McCabe, January 1942 – Civil Servant, Jamie Jameson, January 1941 – Farmer, the last Commanding Officer, Ron Watts, Dec 1940 – Shearer. Not the occupations that you would ever associate with flying killing machines in situations of war. Their background and lack of military experience gives you a wonderful idea of the guts and determination to master the skills needed in such a short time to pilot aircraft around the night skies using what would have seemed very sophisticated systems for that time. Life after the war must have seemed very tame and the adjustment back to peacetime conditions and normality must have taken a very long time indeed.

One of the more interesting factors that emerged from the research into the story of 488 Squadron was the humanity demonstrated by many of the aircrew members. These guys were not natural born killers and their occupational backgrounds and home situation reflected this. Whilst they were driven to extraordinary lengths to destroy the "enemy" most reported waiting apprehensively for signs of survival from the stricken aircraft that they had just hunted down and shot from the skies. The feeling was entirely mutual as there are many reported instances of Luftwaffe aircrew expressing the same feelings, hoping and wishing for a parachute to open or if the aircraft hit the ground that somehow there would be survivors.

Sadly, many of the Allied flyers shot down over enemy lines were dealt to by either the local inhabitants or police or army units in the area. Many in fact were saved from lynch mobs by the intervention of local Luftwaffe personnel intervening and whipping them away to safety. There seems to have been a slow build up of mutual respect as the war progressed that surpassed any great feelings of animosity between the two air forces.

There were times of great trauma in the skies for the aircrews but there were many occasions when the war seemed a long way off - Al Gabites, in his memoirs talked of:

> *"Looking back on those night flights over Germany I can well remember occasions when we were hunched over the instruments and flying in thick cloud for most of the trip. But it was a marvellous sensation at times to break cloud and climb into the starlit atmosphere. The North Star which has been a sure guide to mariners over the centuries stood out as a beacon. When compass and gyro were set spinning by steep turns or other rapid*

manoeuvres the aircraft could be put back on course by reference to this friendly star. Moonrise could be spectacular but tended to sharpen one's concentration. Once we were treated to a dazzling display of static electricity. As we flew along the whole aircraft was wrapped in flickering streamers of blue light. The propellers were outlined in this weird glow and the static played over the windscreen like the jets in a gas oven".

This natural phenomenon was reported by many crews with varying opinions on its effect. Known as St Elmo's fire some crews were concerned that some spontaneous ignition of fuel or ammunition might occur and were greatly relieved when they pulled out of cloud and left the dancing lights behind. Gabites also reported of light effects in the darkness in another form, that directly relating to the reason why they were airborne in the first place:

On relatively clear nights the results of a raid on some German city could be seen on the horizon fifty miles away long after the bombers had left. Searchlights still wavered around looking for stragglers and here and there the odd flare burned fiercely for a while and then faded. As the armies below advanced star shells and pinpricks of gunfire marked the Front. In the latter stages one could watch the V2 rockets setting out from their launching pads, painfully slowly at first amidst a sheet of flame, and then accelerating on their way to London. And once, about three miles away, a highly visible German jet shot past shooting fire from its turbines……..

Epilogue

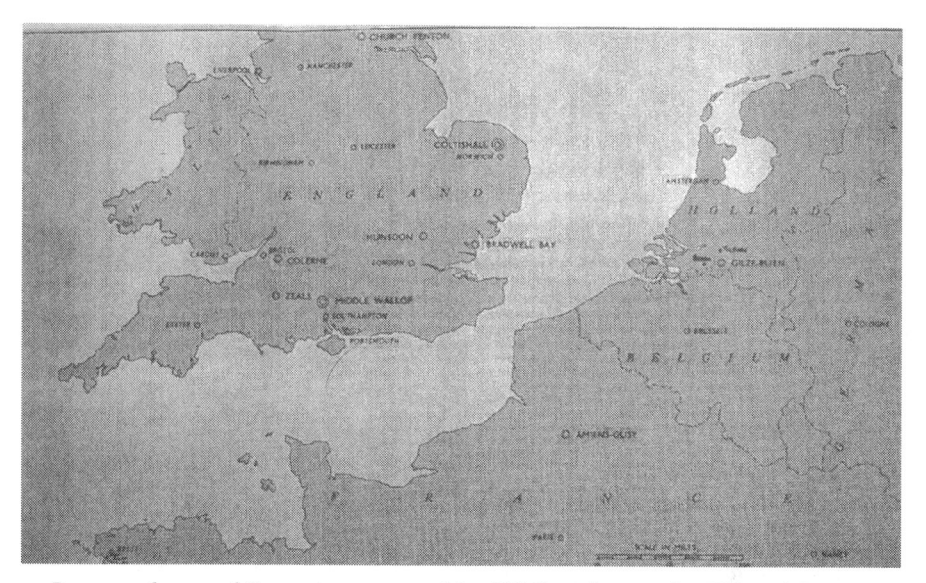

Bases and area of Operations covered by 488 Squadron in the UK and Europe.

3,687 RNZAF personnel were to lose their lives on active service during the Second World War. The following personnel from both the RNZAF and RAF gave their lives in the service of their country while serving with 488 Squadron between June 1942 and April 1945. Many more that had served with 488 Squadron on Operational work were to lose their lives on postings to other squadrons. Their deaths were no less felt as those that died serving with 488 Squadron as they had formed a unique bond during their time on active service. Those that survived the war years maintained regular contact with one another well into the post war years. A good number of the ex RAF crews travelled out to New Zealand to make contact again with their New Zealand colleagues.

Roll of Honour

Those who died while serving with 488(NZ) Squadron, Royal Air Force in defence of the free world 1942 – 1945.
They gave their lives so others might live.

Name	Rank	Force	Operating Base	Date Killed
McKinnon	F/L	RNZAF	Ayr, Scotland	06/12/1942
McChesney	F/L	RNZAF	Ayr, Scotland	06/12/1942
Peacocke	F/O	RNZAF	Ayr, Scotland	06/12/1942
Spence	P/O	RAF	Ayr, Scotland	06/12/1942
O'Gara	F/O	RNZAF	Ayr, Scotland	02/04/1943
Masters	Sgt	RAF	Ayr, Scotland	02/04/1943
Watt	P/O	RNZAF	Ayr, Scotland	13/07/1943
Adkins	P/O	RAF	Ayr, Scotland	13/07/1943
Gordon	P/O	RAF	Drem, Scotland	31/08/1943
Rawlings	P/O	RNZAF	Drem, Scotland	31/08/1943
Gunn	F/L	RNZAF	Bradwell, England	15/09/1943
Affleck	F/O	RAF	Bradwell, England	15/09/1943
Ball	F/L	RNZAF	Bradwell, England	09/10/1943
Kemp	F/O	RAF	Bradwell, England	09/10/1943
Green	P/O	RAFVR	Bradwell, England	16/10/1943
Creek	F/Sgt	RAFVR	Bradwell, England	16/10/1943
Hobbis	S/L	RAF	Bradwell, England	25/11/1943
Hills	P/O	RAF	Bradwell, England	25/11/1943
Behrent	F/Sgt	RNZAF	Bradwell, England	30/12/1943
Breward	F/Sgt	RNZAF	Bradwell, England	30/12/1943
Watson	F/Sgt	RNZAF	Bradwell, England	03/02/1944
Edwards	F/Sgt	RNZAF	Bradwell, England	03/02/1944
Riwai	F/O	RNZAF	Bradwell, England	21/02/1944
Clarke	F/Sgt	RNZAF	Bradwell, England	21/02/1944
Anderson	F/Sgt	RNZAF	Bradwell, England	11/03/1944
Wilson C.	F/O	RNZAF	Bradwell, England	25/03/1944
Wilson A.	F/O	RNZAF	Bradwell, England	25/03/1944
Scott	F/Sgt	RNZAF	Zeals, England	15/07/1944
Duncan	F/O	RNZAF	Zeals, England	15/07/1944
Bunting	S/L	RAF	Amiens/Glisy, France	30/07/1944
Spedding	F/O	RAF	Amiens/Glisy, France	30/07/1944
Niederer	W/O	RNZAF	Amiens/Glisy, France	08/01/1945
Lawrence	F/O	RNZAF	Amiens/Glisy, France	08/01/1945
Mallon	P/O	RNZAF	Rize/Gijen, Holland	12/03/1945
Brock	P/O	RNZAF	Rize/Gijen, Holland	12/03/1945
Howland	Sgt	RAF	Rize/Gijen, Holland	08/05/1945

The Memorial at Bradwell Bay for all the air-force personnel that died while serving at the air base. Seventeen were from 488 Squadron. Little else is left of the base.

R.A.F.
BRADWELL BAY
1942 – 1945

THIS MEMORIAL HAS BEEN
ERECTED IN MEMORY OF
THE 121 MEMBERS OF THE
ALLIED AIR FORCES WHO IN
ANSWER TO THE CALL OF DUTY
LEFT THIS AIRFIELD TO FLY
INTO THE BLUE FOREVER

Honours and Awards

THE SQUADRON LIST OF HONOURS AND AWARDS MADE TO PERSONNEL SERVING AT THAT TIME WITH 488 SQUADRON

Distinguished Service Order (All ranks shown as at time of award)
    F/L George Esmond Jameson D.F.C
Member of the Order of the British Empire
    F/L Richard Norman
Distinguished Flying Cross and Two Bars
    F/L Norman Crookes
Distinguished Flying Cross and Bar
    F/L John Hall
    F/L Jock Cairns
    F/L Peter Hall
    F/O Richard Marriott
Distinguished Flying Cross
    F/O Douglas Robinson
    F/O Chris Vlotman
    F/O Tom Taylor
    F/L Ken Stewart
    F/O Bill Brumby
    F/O Richard Perfect
    F/L Graeme Reed
    F/L Ralph Bricker
    S/L Allen Browne
Bar to Distinguished Flying Cross
    S/L Nigel Bunting D.F.C.
    F/L Philip Reed D.F.C.
Air Force Cross
    F/O James Moore
Distinguished Flying Medal
    F/Sgt. John Wood
Dutch Flying Cross (Vliegerkruis)
    F/O Chris Vlotman D.F.C.
    P/O. John Wood
American Distiguished Flying Cross
    F/L Norman Crookes D.F.C.
Mentions in Despatches
    W/C Ron Watts (twice)

F/O Jack Scott
Lac. Phillips
F/L Bill Cook
F/L Ray Jeffs
P/O. Gordon Patrick
P/O. Jimmy Concannon
S/L Johnny Gard'ner
S/L Frank Davison
F/O John Marshall
F/O Phil Prescott
F/O Cyril Hughes
F/O Ian Skudder
Sgt. Duggie Howland

Those Who Served

25ᵀᴴ JUNE 1942 TO 26ᵀᴴ APRIL 1945

SQUADRON AIRCREW

Personnel listed are those known to have served with 488 Squadron in the UK and Europe at some time after 488 was re-formed on 25th June 1942 and until the squadron was officially disbanded on 26th April 1945. Most aircrew listed were time and date scheduled and removed from operational flying following eighteen months of frontline service. They were then transferred into training positions at Operational Training Units and then either posted on to new squadrons or in many cases posted back to 488 Squadron for another tour of operational flying. As all aircraft flown by the squadron were two man crews these combinations were generally kept together where possible throughout the duration of the war. Each squadron member is listed here in alphabetical order rather than rank which somehow epitomises the egalitarian nature of the relationship between ranks for which 488 Squadron was well known. The dates shown in brackets are periods when they were known to be serving in 488 Squadron. A single date indicates that the length of service is unknown but is a recorded date when the individual was known to be with the squadron.

Surname	Rank	Forenames	A/F	Service no.	Trade	Dates of Service	Comments
Addison	W/O	William Nathan	RAF	622688	Nav	30/07/1944 to 25/04/1945	Awarded DFC, DFM
Adkins	P/O	Peter Ernest	RAF	123855	Nav	05/04/1943 to 13/07/1943	
Affleck	F/O	James	RAF	130906	Nav	29/08/1942	Killed Air Operations 15th September 1943 with Jimmy Gunn
Anderson	Flt.Sgt.	John	RNZAF	415234	Pilot	07/03/1944 to 11/03/1944	Killed after crashing at Bradwell Bay on first solo flight
Andrewes	F/O	Arthur Edmond	RNZAF	NZ1946	Nav	01/03/1945 to 25/04/1945	Ex Capt. NZ Army
Andrews	F/O	Arthur Charles	RAF	131662	Nav	25/06/1942 to 09/01/1943	
Arthur	F/O	Clifford C	RNZAF	424406	Pilot	11/05/1944 to 25/04/1945	
Austin	Sgt.	P.C	RAF		Pilot	05/11/1942	
Bale	Sub. Lt.	William	FAA		Pilot	23/10/1943 to 15/02/1944	Seconded from Royal Navy Fleet Air Arm
Ball	F/L	Edward Cecil	RNZAF	40749	Pilot	13/09/1942 to 21/01/1943 and 06/07/1943 to 10/10/1943	Killed on Air Operations 10th October 1943 with Jock Kemp
Ballard	P/O	Ronald	RAF	18731	Nav.	07/03/1944 to 25/04/1945	
Barnson	P/O	James Dudley	RAF	134040	Nav.	29/01/1943 to 16/04/1943	
Behrent	Flt / Sgt	Ernest Henry	RNZAF	416079	Pilot	16/06/1943 to 30/12/1943	Killed on air operations with Noel Breward
Bergemann	F/L	R.Douglas	RNZAF	412191	Pilot	29/01/1943 to 17/03/1944 and 26/10/1944 to 25/04/1945	
Bishop	F/O	Kenneth Richard	RAF	143214	Nav	01??/1943 to 17/03/1944 and 23/10/1944 to 25/04/1945	
Boulton	Sgt		RAF		Pilot	01/09/1942	
Bourke	P/O	Roderick F.D	RNZAF	413993	Pilot	22/12/1943 to 25/04/1945	

Name	Rank	First Names	Service	Number	Role	Dates	Notes
Bowman	F/L	Peter	RAF	116573	Nav	18/01/1944 to 19/01/1945	
Bradley	Sgt					01/09/1942	
Brandon	F/L	Lewis	RAF	116886	Nav	4/08/1943 to 23/01/1944	Awarded DSO, DFC & Bar
Breithaupt	P/O	William Ransom	RCAF	J17271	Pilot	5/11/1942 to 28/01/1943	Awarded DFC
Breward	Flt Sgt	Noel	RNZAF	421668	Nav	16/09/1943 to 30/12/1943	Killed on air operations with Ernie Behrent
Bricker	F/O	Ralph	RAF	146684	Nav	20/11/1942 to 10/12/1943	Awarded DFC
Brock	Flt/Sgt	George Herbert	RNZAF	429138	Nav	11/05/1944 to 11/03/1945	Killed on Air Operations with Tom Mallon
Broodbank	P/O	Andrew John	RAF	145037	Nav	3/09/1943 to 06/10/1944	
Broom	P/O	Philip William	RAF	50924	Nav	1/09/1942 to 13/03/1943	
Browne	S/Ld	Allen Edward	RNZAF	404986	Pilot	22/07/1944 to 14/10/1944	Destroyed three enemy aircraft without firing a shot !
Brumby	F/O	Harold Edward	RNZAF	421827	Nav	14/10/1944 to 25/04/1945	
Bryers	F/O	Philip R.P.	RNZAF	429938	Nav	14/10/1944 to 25/04/1945	
Buddle	P/O	Joe	RNZAF		Pilot	22/12/1943	
Bunting	S/Ldr	Edward Nigel	RAF	60523	Pilot	27/11/1943 to 29/07/1944	Killed on air operations with Ted Spedding
Burton-Gyles	W/Com	Peter Robert	RAF	40077	Pilot	22/05/1943 to 03 09 1943	Replaced Nesbit-Dufort as Commanding Officer
Bush	Sgt	D.M.	USAF		Pilot	1/09/1942 to 28/09/1942	
Cairns	F/L	John P.W.(Jock)	RAF	124540	Nav	16/11/1943 to 25/04/1945	Awarded DFC & Bar
Carcasson	F/L	George Vincent	RAF	115004	Nav	1/09/1944 to 14/02/1945	
Cheetham	Sgt	Ronald William	RAFVR	1473152	Nav	27/03/1943	
Church	F/S	Arthur James	RNZAF	427188	Nav	24/07/1944	
Clark	F/L	William T.M. (Terry)	RAF	126026	Nav	11/05/1943 to 31/08/1944	Awarded DFM & AE

355

Surname	Rank	First Name(s)	Force	Service #	Role	Dates	Notes
Clark	F/Sgt	Ian	RNZAF	425491	Nav	8/12/1943 to 21/02/1943	Killed during takeoff at Bradwell Bay with Rick Riwai
Collins	Sgt	C.W			Pilot		
Concannon	F/O	James Joseph	RAF	1506938	Nav	24/11/1942 to 21/08/1944 and 12/12/1944 to 25/04/1945	Awarded Mention in Despatches
Cook	F/L	William R.	RNZAF	411375	Pilot	1/10/1943 to 02/04/1945	Awarded Mention in Despatches
Cottrell	F/Sgt	Rex Frederick	RNZAF	416214	Nav	16/09/1943 to 31/01/1944	
Craig	F/O	William Albert	RNZAF	4210081	Pilot	25/04/1945 to 26/04/1945	
Creek	F/Sgt	Ronald Arthur	RAFVR	1254796	Nav	30/08/1943 to 16/10/1943	Killed on Air Operations with P/O Green
Crookes	F/L	Arthur Norman	RAF	135428	Nav	18/01/1944 to 25/04/1945	DFC & Bar (2) and MBE
Cutfield	F/L	Arthur Stapley	RNZAF	40719	Nav	18/08/1942 to 25/12/1943	
Davies	Sub/Lt	H.	RNFAA		Pilot	12/10/1943 to 15/12/1944	Seconded from Royal Navy Fleet Air Arm
Davison	S/Ldr	Frank W.	RNZAF	41885	Pilot	05/06/1942 to 19/01/1943 and 13/08/1944 to 25/04/1945	Awarded Mentioned in Despatches
De Renzy	F/Sgt	Thomas David	RNZAF	415751	Pilot	16/09/1943 to 31/01/1944	
Doherty	F/L	H.E.	RNZAF	40645	Pilot	10/11/1944	
Dosier	Sgt	J.	USAF		Nav	9/09/1942 to 28/09/1942	
Duncan	F/O	Colin Campbell	RNZAF	427193	Nav	7/02/1944 to 15/07/1944	Killed on air operations 15 July 1944
Earl	F/O	Allan C.	RNZAF	42101	Nav	16/09/1943 to 28/02/1944	
Edwards	F/Sgt	Ernest Frank	RNZAF	422378	Nav	12/10/1943 to 03/02/1944	Killed on air operations with Snowy Watson
Emerton	W/O	E.G.	RAF	1324264	Nav	7/03/1944 to 25/04/1945	
Evans	P/O	H.J.				23/02/1943	
Ferri	W/O	Raymond A.			Pilot	12/10/1943	

Fleming	F/L	Keith	RNZAF	413401	Pilot	14/12/1942 to 02/03/1944 and 13/10/1944 to 25/04/1945	
Follows	F/O	Noel Evans	RAF	187006	Nav	2/04/1944 to 25/04/1945	
Folley	F/L	Roger R.W.	RNZAF	88502	Nav	20/07/1943 to 25/04/1945	
Fox	F/L	J.D.			Pilot	10/02/1943 to 02/03/1943	
Fritchley	W/O	N.A.	RNZAF	421697	Pilot	11/04/1944 to 05/01/1945	
Gabites	F/L	Allot (Al)	RNZAF	413054	Pilot	21/09/1944 to 25/04/1945	
Gard'ner	S/Ldr	John, Rushton	RNZAF	23177	Pilot	14/08/1942 to 12/11/1942 and 31/10/1944 to 25/04/1945	Awarded Mention in Despatches
Gordon	P/O	Samuel John	RAF	155089	Nav	1/09/1942 to 31/08/1943	Killed in Training accident at Drem with P/O Rawlings
Graham	F/O	Malcom D.B.	RNZAF	422566	Nav	12/10/1943 to 18/01/1945	
Grant	F/O	Brian C.	RNZAF	429663	Nav	8/02/1944 to 25/04/1945	
Green	W/O	W.W. Wally	RNZAF	421044	Pilot	22/12/1943 to 25/04/1945	
Green	P/O	Dennis Norman	RAFVR	149208	Pilot	30/08/1943 to 16/10/1943	Killed on air operations with F/Sgt Creek
Gunn	F/L	James Athol	RNZAF	402866	Pilot	29/08/1943 to 15/09/1943	Killed Air Operations with Flg.Off. Jock Affleck
Haine	W/Com	Richard Cummins	RAF	43147	Pilot	2/01/1944 to 30/10/1944	Replaced Peter Hamley as squadron Commanding Officer. Awarded DFC
Halligan	P/O	John P.	RNZAF	424040	Pilot	5/08/1944 to 25/04/1945	
Hall	F/Lt	J.A.S. (Johnny)	RAF	107269	Pilot	16/11/1943 to 25/04/1945	Awarded DFC & Bar
Hall	F/Lt	Peter F.L.	RNZAF	413841	Pilot	20/07/1943 to 22/01/1945	
Hamley	W/Com	Peter Hoare	RAF	32010	Pilot	2/09/1943 to 31/12/1943	Commanding Officer replacing Wng. Comm. Burton-Gyles

Hardern	Lt.	Bruce (Bull)	FAA		Nav	12/10/1943 to 15/02/1944	Seconded from Royal Navy Fleet Air Arm
Harding	F/Lt	F.	RAF		Pilot	26/03/1944 to 27/10/1944	
Henderson	F/O	A.B.	RCAF		Nav	12/10/1943	
Head	F/Lt	Norman Sydney	RAF	66516	Pilot	13/07/1942 to 09/01/1943	
Heckels	Sgt.	J.			Nav	21/08/1943	
Herd	F/O	Don	RNZAF	427052	Nav	11/05/1944 to 25/04/1945	
Hickmore	F/Lt	Edward S. (Dicky)	RAF	109497	Nav	13/08/1944 to 25/4/1945	Awarded DFC
Hills	P/O	Oliver L.R.	RAFVR	161337	Nav	11/05/1943 to 25/11/1943	Killed on Air Operations with Dudley Hobbis
Hobbis	S/Ldr	Dudley, Ormston	RAF	42709	Pilot	11/05/1943 to 25/11/1943	Replaced Paul Rabone as Flight Commander. Killed on Air Operations with Oliver Hills
Hoile	Sgt	Reginald Thomas S.	RAF	1254287	Nav	01/09/1942	
Horspool	W/O	A.	RAF		Nav	1/04/1944 to 31/10/1944	
Hughes	W/O	Cyril, Patrick, Francis	RNZAF	414629	Pilot	16/05/1943 to 29/11/1944	Awarded Mention in Despatches
Irvine	P/O	Alexander	RAF	139513	Pilot	29/01/1943 16/04/1943	
Jacobs	F/L	Henry	RAF	78685	Nav	9/11/1942 to 04/08/1943	
Jameson	F/L	George Esmond (Jamie)	RNZAF	41479	Pilot	18/01/1944 to 15/08/1944	Awarded DSO & DFC
Jeffs	F/L	Raymond G. (Ray)	RNZAF	40645		1/09/1942 to 04/08/1943 and 13/03/1944 to 25/04/1945	Awarded Mention in Despatches
Keeping	F/O	Kenneth, C. (Cherub)	RAF	135154	Nav	17/02/1944 to 01//10/1944	
Knox	Sgt	Gordon					
Knox	F/Lt					17/12/1942 to 24/04/1944	

Surname	Rank	Given Names	Service	Number	Role	Dates	Notes
Kemp	F/Lt	William (Jock)	RAF	122557	Nav	21/08/1942 to 21/01/1943 and 06/07/1943 to 10/10/1943	Killed on Air Operations with Cecil Ball
Kennedy	Sgt.	V.A.	RAF		Nav	05/11/1942	
Lamond	Sub.Lt	L.	RNFAA			23/10/1943 to 26/10/1944	Seconded from Royal Navy Fleet Air arm (Navigator)
Lawrence	F/O	George Bruce	RNZAF	4211018	Nav	10/11/1944 to 08/01/1945	Killed on Air Operations with W/Off. Neiderer
Lewis	P/O	W.R.V.			Pilot	14/12/1942 to 10/03/1944	
Linstead	Sub Lt	E. S.			Pilot	12/10/1943 to 15/02/1944	Seconded from the Royal Navy Fleet Air Arm.
Longhorn	F/Sgt				Nav	1/09/1942 to 18/02/1943	
Longley	F/O	Harold Watson	RNZAF		Pilot	12/10/1943 to 20/08/1944	
McBride	F/L	Patrick Stewart	RNZAF	40980	pilot	14/09/1942 to 14/05/1943	
McCabe	F/L	Owen j. (Stan)	RNZAF	42242	Pilot	18/08/1943 to 21/02/1945	
McChesney	F/L	Robert Ian	RNZAF	40194		1/08/1942 to 05/12/1942	Killed with F/Lt McKinnon, air accident at Ayr, Scotland
McDonald	F/O	F.J.	RNZAF	4216517	Nav	22/03/1945 to 25/04/1945	
MacKay	F/O	Thomas.G.C. (Tom)	RNZAF	421074	Pilot	7/03/1944 to 25/04/1945	
McIntyre	S/Ldr	Athol Gordon	RNZAF	36257	Pilot	(16/11/1942)	Airfield Commander
McKinnon	F/Lt	Athol Charles	RNZAF	40722		1/08/1942 to 05/12/1942	Killed with F/Lt McChesney, air accident at Ayr, Scotland
McLean	F/O	Thomas Allan	RNZAF	422344		18/02/1944 to 25/04/1945	
McQueen	Sgt	J.S.			Pilot	1/09/1942 to 11/10/1942	
Mallon	P/O	Thomas A. (Tom)	RNZAF	415338	Pilot	11/05/1944 to 11/03/1945	Killed on Air Operations with George Brock
Mansill	F/O	N.M.W. (Bill)	RNZAF	4212686	Nav	10/11/1944 to 25/04/1945	

Name	Rank	Full Name	Force	Number	Role	Dates	Notes
Marriott	F/O	Richard D'Arcy (Dick)	RAF	141377	Nav	20/07/1943 to 22/01/1945	
Marshall	F/O	John William (Johnny)	RNZAF	42784	Pilot	28/02/1944 to 25/04/1945	Awarded Mention in Despatches
Martin	Sgt.	F.	USAF		Nav	9/09/1942 to 28/09/1942	
Masters	Sgt	Derek Gordon	RAF	143873	Nav	5/11/1942 to 02/04/1943	Killed Air Accident with P/O/ O'Gara
Mitchell	F/O	Reginald Walter	RNZAF	416812	Pilot	22/12/1943 to 25/04/1945	
Moore	F/O	James (Jimmy)	RNZAF	415351	Pilot	16/09/1943 to 28/07/1944	
Moores	F/O	G.W.	RAF	128682	Nav	14/02/1944 to 26/04/1944	
Morgan	F/O	A.			Nav	27/05/1943 to 28/11/1943	
Muldrew	F/O	J.K.	RNZAF	422086	Pilot	7/03/1944 to 25/04/1945	
Nagle	F/O	Kenneth L.	RAF	146343	Nav	14/12/1942 to 02/03/1944 and 15/10/1944 to 25/04/1944	
Neiderer	W/O	Rex Keith	RNZAF	426179	Pilot	10/11/1944 to 08/01/1945	(Killed on Air Operations with F/Off. Lawrence
Nesbitt-Dufort	S/L	John	RAF	29164	Pilot	9/11/1942 to 22/05/1943	Replaced Trousdale as Squadron OC 14th Feb 1943. Awarded DSO.
Newman	W/O	J.F.	RAF		Nav	2/01/1944 to 22/08/1944	
Norton	F/O	Raymond C. (Ray)	RNZAF	41649	Pilot	1/03/1945 to 25/04/1945	
O'Gara	P/O	Rupert Clarke	RNZAF	414327	Pilot	5/11/1942 to 02/04/1943	Killed Air Accident April 1943 with Sgt Masters
O'Neil-Dunne	F/Lt	Patrick C. (Paddy)	RAF	116609	Nav	25/01/1944 to 19/04/1944	
Patrick	P/O	Gordon Stewart	RNZAF	41501	Pilot	24/11/1942 to 21/08/1944 and 25/02/1945 to 25/04/1945	Awarded Mention in Despatches
Payne	Sgt	No Further data found					

Peacocke	F/O	Raleigh J.B.	RNZAF	403049	Pilot	1/09/1942 to 06/12/1942	Killed with P/O Spence in Air Accident
Pearson	F/O	J.M.	RNZAF	421651	Pilot	20/03/1945 to 25/04/1945	
Perfect	F/O	Richard (Dicky)	RAF	149495	Nav	31/10/1944 to 25/04/1945	
Pickthall	Sub/Lt	A.H.			Nav	12/10/1943 to 18/02/1945	Seconded from Royal Navy Fleet Air Arm
Pittwood	F/O	George Ernest	RAF	129725	Nav	29/01/1943 to 04/08/1943	
Prescott	F/O	Philip F.	RNZAF	424516		22/12/1943 to 25/04/1945	Awarded Mention in Despatches
Proctor	F/O	Luther D. (Don)	RAF	149326		13/11/1944	
Pryor	P/O	Clifford A. (Cliff)	RAF	133211	Nav	10/02/1943 to 02/03/1943	
Rabone	S/Ld	Paul Watling	RNZAF	2171	Pilot	22/08/1942 to 24/04/1943	
Ray	F/O	Allan (Ces)	RNZAF	421007	Nav	11/04/1944 to 25/04/1945	
Rawlings	Sgt	Leslie	RNZAF			5/11/1942 to 31/08/1943	Killed in training accident at Drem
Rayner	F/Sgt	Edgar R. (Ron)	RAF		Nav	1/09/1942 to 21/11/42	
Reed	F/O	Graeme Frederick	RNZAF	402215	Pilot	4/09/1942 to 10/01/1944	
Reed	F/L	Charles Phillip (Phil)	RAF	104432	Nav	27/11/1943 to 17/08/1944	
Richardson	Sub/Lt	R.M. (Murray)	RNFAA		Nav	26/10/1943 to 15/02/1944	Seconded from Fleet Air Arm
Riley	P/O	J.T. (Terry)	RAF	187896	Nav	29/01/1943 to 21/02/1945	
Riwai	F/O	Tohunga R. (Rick)	RNZAF	421764	Pilot	8/12/1943 to 21/02/1944	Killed during takeoff for sortie at Bradwell Bay with Ian Clark
Robins	P/O	E.P			Pilot	29/01/1943 to 08/08/1943	
Robinson	F/O	Douglas Neville	RNZAF	413481	Pilot	1/02/1942 to 05/09/1944 and 24/03/1945 to 25/04/1945	
Roe	Sgt	J.E.	RAF		Nav	05/11/1942	
Ruckldige	F/O	John Michael	RAF				
Ryan	F/L	Terance P. (Buck)	RAFVR	1323333	Nav	17/12/1942 to 24/04/1944	

Surname	Rank	Name	Air Force	Service No.	Role	Dates	Notes
Scott	F/Sgt	Howard George	RNZAF	424527	Pilot	7/02/1944 to 15/07/1944	Killed on air operations with F/O Duncan
Scott	F/O	John Hancock (Jack)		413896	Pilot	7/02/1944 to 19/09/1944	Awarded Mention in Despatches
Shaw	F/O	Andrew L. (Andy)	RNZAF			3/06/1944 to 04/02/1945	
Skudder	F/L	Irwin C.	RNZAF	412272	Nav	22/12/1943 to 25/04/1945	Awarded Mention in Despatches
Smith	S/Ldr	Irving Stanley (Ted)	RNZAF	423234	Nav	25/01/1944 to 29/04/1944	Awarded AFC
Snoddy	F/O	V.	USAF	43048	Pilot	5/11/1942 to 09/02/1943	
Sommerville	F/O	A.A Slim	RNZAF		Pilot	22/12/1943 to 13/04/1944	
Southall	P/O	B.			Nav	29/01/1943 to 28/03/1943	
Spedding	F/O	Ted	RAF	148334	Nav		Killed on Air Operations with Nigel Bunting 29th July 1944
Spence	P/O	Ian Philipson	RAF	131661	Nav	7/03/1944 to 29/07/1944	Killed in Air Accident with F/O Peacocke
Stewart	F/L	Kenneth W. (Chunky)	RNZAF	413145	Pilot	21/09/1944 to 25/04/1945	Awarded DFC
Sumner	F/L	F			Pilot	29/01/1943 to 23/03/1943	Awarded AFM
Tauwhare	F/O	A.L.	RNZAF	437353	Nav	22/03/1945 to 25/04/1945	
Taylor	F/O	Thomas F. (Tom)	RAF	188134	Nav	22/05/1944 to 25/04/1945	
Thompson	P/O	A.A.	RNZAF	42820	Nav	7/03/1944 to 25/04/1945	
Tozer	Sgt		USAF		Nav	16/11/1942	
Trousdale	W/Co	Richard Maclow	RAF	42163	Pilot	9/07/1942 to 15/02/1943	Squadrons First Commanding Officer
Tufill	W/O	E.S	RAF	1801319	Nav	15/08/1944 to 25/04/1945	
Turner	P/O	A.L.	RNZAF	405664		26/06/1942 to 27/08/1944	
Vlotman	F/O	Christiaan Johan (Chris)	RAF	174839	Pilot	2/11/1943 to 26/10/1944	Awarded DFC & Dutch DFC
Waller	W/O				Nav	16/11/1942	

Surname	Rank	Name	Service	Number	Role	Dates	Notes
Warner	F/O	L. W. Jack	RAF	146789	Nav	1/10/1943 to 26/08/1944	
Watson	F/L	L. I. (Ian)	RAF	128549	Nav	14/08/1944 to 25/04/1944	
Watson	F/Sgt	Keith James (Snowy)	RNZAF	421799	Pilot	12/10/1943 to 03/02/1944	Killed on Air Operations with Flt.Sgt Edwards
Watt	F/O	Edgar Coutts	RNZAF	404434	Pilot	1/09/1942 to 13/07/1943	Killed in training accident at Ayr Scotland with P.O.Adkins
Watts	W/Co	Ronald Graham(Ron)	RNZAF	404974	Pilot	20/07/1943 to 25/04/1945	Last Commanding Officer. Awarded Mention in Despatches
Watts	Sgt	S.J.	RAF		Nav	1/12/1942 to 29/10/1943	
Webbe	F/Lt	H.D.C. (Hugh)	RAF	121207	Pilot	26/03/1944 to 25/04/1945	
Whewell	W/O	J.	RAF		Nav	12/04/1944 to 22/09/1944	
Wilmoth	Sgt	R.S.			Nav	14/12/1942	
Wilson	F/O	Alan William (Kiwi)	RNZAF	416568	Nav	12/10/1943 to 25/03/1944	Killed on Air Operations with Flg.Off. Chris Wilson
Wilson	F/O	Chisholm M. (Chris)	RNZAF	421128	Pilot	12/10/1943 to 25/03/1944	Killed on Air Operations with Flg.Off. Kiwi Wilson
Wood	F/sgt	John Leslie (Johnny)	RAF	182378	Nav	2/11/1943 to 29/11/1944	Awarded DFM, DFC & Netherlands Cross
Worsley	Sgt					29/01/1944	
Wise	Sgt					29/01/1944	
Wyman	F/O	Leonard James (Len)	RAF	184799	Nav	3/06/1944 to 25/04/1945	
Wynn		Frank Desmond	RNZAF	404982			

363

SQUADRON GROUND-CREW

Personnel listed are those names that have appeared on official records and known to have served as ground-crew with 488 Squadron in the UK and Europe at some time after 488 was re-formed on 25th June 1942 and until the squadron was disbanded on 26th April 1945. Complete records of the Echelon seem to have been lost in the mists of time so an unknown quantity of those that served will not appear as they rightfully should.

The bulk of the ground crew maintenance men were formed in a separate autonomous ground crew unit known as 6488 Servicing Echelon and there was no formal connection with 488 Squadron until late in 1944 when the Echelon was officially linked with the squadron coming under the direct command of Wg.Com. Ron Watts. At one point, it was designated 6488 (New Zealand) Servicing Echelon (16th August – 9th October 1944) with headquarters being at RAF Thorney Island in Hampshire UK. These dates seem to coincide with the time that they were sent in advance of the squadron to set up a new base at Amiens-Glisy in France and appear to have been a temporary arrangement whilst they were in transit.

These servicing echelons were created to provide maintenance services for airfields rather than individual squadrons but 6488 is known to have worked specifically and exclusively for 488 Squadron during the course of its postings throughout the UK and Europe. This would tie in with them working with what was top secret radar equipment at the time.

The Echelon had a reputation second to none and when on a rare occasion that they were sent ahead of the squadron to France, the maintenance work was carried out by a different ground crew echelon and the standard and serviceability of the squadron's aircraft was substandard by comparison.

It was quoted on several occasions that although the echelon consisted predominantly of RAF serviceman, the camaraderie and morale of the men was greatly enhanced with the egalitarian nature of the squadron set-up. On social occasions and on times of relaxation, rank and nationality had no boundaries and officers and other ranks mixed freely unlike most RAF squadrons. The New Zealand influence was paramount and many of the RAF members were taken aback to find their "Kiwi" officer aircrew helping out with menial tasks normally carried out by humble aircraftsmen. The New Zealanders that served with the Echelon are highlighted in Blue.

Again, as with the air-crew listing each squadron member is listed here in alphabetical order. The listings show Surname, Rank, Initials or "Nickname", Service No., Service, Trade when documented and the date represents a known date that the individual was serving.

Name	Rank	Initials	Service No.	Force	Trade	Service Date
Abbot	LAC	S.G.	1102 992	RAF	M/Asst	24/10/1944
Addison	LAC	A.	1007849	RAF	M/Asst	24/10/1944
Allen	LAC	T.	1489651	RAF	F.M.E	24/10/1944
Allen		T.				
Amor	F/Lt				Engineering Officer	01/07/1942
Anderson	Cpl	R.A.	405632	RNZAF		Sep-42
Anstec	LAC	F.I.	1146724	RAF	Elect/1	01/09/1944
Arblaster	AC1	R.	1690547	RAF	ACH/GD	01/09/1944
Ashcroft	LAC	R.	1521405	RAF	R.T.O.	24/10/1944
Aspinall	LAC	F.	1489028	RAF	Arm	01/09/1944
Aviss	F/Sgt				Ground Crew Engineer	
Baker	LAC	G.R.	1544356	RAF	Arm	01/09/1944
Barker	LAC	C.S.	404654	RNZAF		Aug-42
Bartlett	AC1	J.A.	1261010	RAF	Carp/1	01/09/1944
Barton	Cpl	J.A.	1084755	RAF	F2E	24/10/1944
Basterra	LAC	F.				
Bell	LAC	W.	1698804	RAF	F2A	01/09/1944
Berendt	Cpl	J.A.	977318	RNZAF	F2	01/09/1944
Berry	F/O				Intelligence Officer	25/06/1942
Bevan	LAC		1079411	RAF	A/Asst	24/10/1944
Biglands	AC1	L.	2203378	RAF	F.M.E	24/10/1944
Bolingbroke	F/Lt				Head of Sqd Radar Unit	
Boumphrey	Cpl	S.A.	1205305	RAF	F2A	01/09/1944
Brown	LAC	A.J.	41451	RNZAF		Aug-42

Name	Rank	Initials	Number	Service	Role	Date
Brown	LAC	D.M.	1361098	RAF	F.M.E.	24/10/1944
Brown	LAC	H.L.	1720095	RAF	Carp/1	01/09/1944
Burns		J.				
Burr	Lt.	H.			Searchlight Liason Officer	13/03/1944
Cain	LAC	V.G.		RAF		24/10/1944
Caister	AC1	P.J.	1877104	RAF	Carp1	01/09/1944
Chantler	LAC	W.R.	1281909	RAF	M/Asst	20/10/1944
Charlton	LAC	E.	1379876	RAF	F.M.E.	24/10/1944
Chitty	Sgt	H.	1204358	RAF	F2A	01/09/1944
Cooke	LAC	A.	1155428	RAF	F1 Arm	24/10/1944
Cooper	LAC	H.G.	1648095	RAF	B&V1	01/09/1944
Coulson		L.				
Cowdell	LAC	S.E.V.	1539121	RAF	Arm	01/09/1944
Cowley	LAC	W.	1215626	RAF	Carp/1	01/09/1944
Crayton	LAC	J.M.	1573820	RAF	F.M.E.	24/10/1944
Cross	AC2	J.I.	3021236	RAF	A/asst	01/09/1944
Crossley	AC2	J.E.	1519134	RAF	Elec 1	01/09/1944
Crouch	LAC	S.G.	1383046	RAF	Arm	24/10/1944
Curtis	AC1	E.C.	1872113	RAF	in/Rep	24/10/1944
Dage	LAC	J.	2205475	RAF	F.M.A.	24/10/1944
Daley	AC2	D.N	2217295	RAF	F.M.E.	24/10/1944
Darwin	Sgt	J.	1133468	RAF	F2E	01/09/1944
Davies	F/O				(Intelligence Officer)	
Davies	2nd Lt.	E.H.		USAAC	Signals	27/11/1942
Davis	AC1	J.	1317005	RAF	R.T.O.	10/02/1943
Dixon	LAC	J.C.	1202367	RAF		24/10/1944
Dowdall	LAC	J.P.	1586212	RAF	Carp/1	01/09/1944

367

Draper	LAC	A.	1567957	RAF	F/Arm	24/10/1944
Drinkwater	LAC	A.D.	1142737	RAF	W/Mech	24/10/1944
Dunbar	Cpl	J.H.	1514418	RAF	Carp/1	01/09/1944
Dyson	Cpl	N.	1012863	RAF	F21	01/09/1944
Ellis		"Chota"				
Eastwood	Cpl	A.E.	538764	RAF	Elect/1	01/09/1944
Edgard	AC2	F.E.	1876763	RAF	F.M.A.	24/10/1944
Evans	F/O			RAF	Medical Officer	11/06/1942
Elliott	AC2		2265050	RAF		24/10/1944
Feakes	AC1	C.C.	1614481	RAF	Cook	24/10/1944
Fernandez	Cpl	P.A.	625731	RNZAF	in/Rep	24/10/1944
Finn	LAC	A.C.	2210617	RAF	Cook	01-Sep
Flook	Cpl	N.	575322	RAF	F2E	01/09/1944
Folkard	LAC	J.S.W.	1427993	RAF	Arm.	01/09/1943
Ford	LAC	W.G.	1552755	RAF	F2E	01/09/1944
Fordyce	Cpl	T.	1554969	RAF	Elect/1	01/09/1944
Foster	LAC	H.	1861346	RAF	DMT	01/09/1944
Fowers	LAC	W.	1495399	RAF	Arm	24/10/1944
Frame	LAC	T.M.	1001605	RAF	F2E	01/09/1944
Fromings	LAC	A.W.	1492949	RAF	Arm	01/09/1944
Gager	Cpl	R.C.	404657	RNZAF	RADAR	Sep-42
Gandy	LAC	C.N.	1878741	RAF	E/Asst	01/09/1944
Gardner	AC1	T.	1692061	RAF	Elect 2	01/09/1944
George	Cpl	C.D.	404658	RNZAF		Jul-42
Gibbs	LAC	E.G.	41735	RNZAF		Aug-42
Gilbert	AC1	P.A.	2217302	RAF	F.M.E.	24/10/1944
Girvan	LAC	D.M.	1698253	RAF	Elect/2	01/09/1944

Name	Rank	Initials	Service No	Service	Trade	Date
Gowers	LAC	W.	1495399	RAF	A/Asst	01/09/1944
Goodenough	Cpl F.		1113425	RAF	F2	01/09/1944
Gray	LAC	D.C.	401928	RNZAF		Jun-42
Greening	Cpl	A.	1016498	RAF	F2A	01/09/1944
Griffiths	Flt. Lt.	T.			Squadron Engineering Officer	15/04/1943
Hagger	Cpl	A.J.	626355	RAF	F2E	24/10/1944
Hall	Cpl	G.H.	1088024	RAF	F2A	01/09/1944
Haslam	Cpl	W.F.	553668	RNZAF	Elect/1	01/09/1944
Hardman	LAC	F.S.	1479655	RAF	In/Rep	24/10/1944
Harris	AC2	R.	1835510	RAF	Carp/1	01/09/1944
Hatt	Flt.Sgt	A.A.	505555	RAF	Fitt/1	01/09/1944
Haywood	AC2	W.J	1878596	RAF	A/asst	01/09/1944
Helms	Cpl	H.V.	968536	RAF	F2E	01/09/1944
Hearn	LAC	H.L.	1264961	RNZAF	Elect/2	01/09/1944
Henderson	LAC	H.P.	405640	RNZAF		Sep-42
Heglett	Cpl	W.B.	1189283	RAF	F2E	24/10/1944
Hemming	LAC	D.J.	1447991	RAF	F.M.A.	24/10/1944
Heselden	AC2	R.H.	1176490	RAF	In/Rep	24/10/1944
Hewell	LAC	G.H.	622149	RAF	F2E	24/10/1944
Hewitt	F/O	W.J.T.	161200	RAF	Intelligence	19/03/1945
Hill	LAC	W.	1465822	RAF	ACH/GD	01/09/1944
Hillier	LAC	M.J.	404661	RNZAF		Aug-42
Hinde	Cpl	J.C.	1024038	RAF	F2	01/09/1944
Hinton	LAC	R.G.	861768	RAF	F2A	0109/1944
Holmes		G.			Engine Fitter	
Houghton	AC2	A.E.	3002368	RAF		24/10/1944
Houghton	LAC	C.	1698489	RAF	DMT	24/10/1944

Howland	Sgt	G.	528418	RAF	F2E	01/09/1944
Howarth	Sgt	W.	1168605	RAF	F2E	24/10/1944
Howitt	LAC	A.E.	1634116	RAF	Cook	24/10/1944
Hudson	Sgt	G.	1066545	RAF	Arm	24/10/1944
Hughes	AC2	F.H.	2245049	RAF	M/assist	24/10/1944
Hughes	LAC	S.	515782	RAF	F2E	01/09/1944
Hunt	Flt. Lt.	L.		RAF	Intelligence	28/09/1943
Hunt	LAC	C.H.	1417041	RAF	Arm2	01/09/1944
Hurst	LAC	J.	1611305	RAF	DMT	01/09/1944
Jackson	AC1	L.R.	1723704	RAF	F.M.E.	24/10/1944
Jeffreys	LAC	A.	404702	RNZAF		Aug-42
Johnson	LAC	F.G.	1869696	RAF	F.M.A.	24/10/1944
Jones	AC1	A.J.	1437522	RAF	Carp/1	01/09/1944
Jones	LAC	J.G.	1619239	RAF	R.T.O.	24/10/1944
Kennedy	F/Lt.	E.J.		RAF	Adjutant	11/06/1944
Kidson	AC2	H.	3021277	RAF	A/Assist	01/09/1944
Kinsman	LAC	A.D.G.	1571353	RAF		01/09/1944
Kirby	LAC	F.	1657608	RAF	Clk/GD4	01/09/1944
Krelle	AC1	F.	1461405	RAF	Cook	01/09/1944
Land	Cpl	L.A.	907286	RAF	F2E	01/09/1944
Lane	LAC	E.	1543359	RAF	Arm	01/09/1944
Lang	Cpl	L.A.	907286	RAF	F2E	24/10/1944
Langley	Cpl	W.	1513628	RAF	W/Mech	24/10/1944
Large	LAC	H.	1085852	RAF	Arm 2	01/09/1944
Largo	Cpl	H.C.	530364	RAF	F2E	24/10/1944
Largo	LAC	J.	1321798	RAF	Arm	24/10/1944
Leigh	F/O	H.	51303	RAF	Adjutant	22/07/1944

Name	Rank	Initials	Service No	Trade	Force	Date
Light	Sgt	D.J.	566841	F2	RAF	01/09/1944
Little	LAC	R.B.	1574176	F2E	RAF	01/09/1944
Littler	AC2	B.W.	1755463	AC2	RAF	24/10/1944
Lyndsay	LAC	R.	1794526	Arm.	RAF	01/09/1944
MAC1AChlan	F/O	H.A.		Medical	RAF	05/01/1943
McBride	Cpl	D.S.	1275119	F2E	RAF	01/09/1944
McClymont	AC2	R.	1569302	Arm	RAF	01/09/1944
McGuire	AC2	B...	1563342	A/Asst	RAF	01/09/1944
McJannett	F/O	Mac		Radar Officer	RCAF	
McQuilton	LAC	M.J.	1566233	F.M.A.	RAF	24/101944
McWha	LAC	D	404178		RNZAF	Jun-42
Maguire	LAC	F.J	1448396	F.M.E.	RAF	24/10/1944
Mahood	LAC	W.W.	417741		RNZAF	Aug-42
Manifold	P/O	D.M.C.		Intelligence	RAF	Sep-42
Manderville	Cpl	W.H.	867810	Elect/2	RAF	01/09/1942
Matthews	LAC	C.	1138405	F/Arm	RAF	24/10/1944
May	AC2	C.	1642126	Arm/2	RAF	01/09/1944
Merigan	G.					
Miller	LAC	T.C.E.	1850568	Carp/1	RAF	01/09/1944
Mitchell	Cpl	E.J.	1559156	F2E	RAF	24/10/1944
Morris	LAC	J.S.	1508486	Arm	RAF	24/10/1944
Muholland	LAC	G.C.	41742		RNZAF	Aug-42
Murphy	Cpl	Spud	1205305	F2A	RAF	01/09/1944
Murray	Cpl	H.	1085852	Arm	RAF	012/09/1944
Naylor	LAC	C.	1512950	F.M.E.	RAF	24/10/1944
Norman	Fl/Lt	N.R.	48386	engineering	RAF	17/09/1943
Oakes	AC1	F.	1614481	cook	RAF	01/09/1944

Oliver	LAC	G.	1129404	RAF	E/asst	01/09/1944
Oliver	LAC	R.R.	1666708	RAF	Arm 2	01/09/1944
Palmer	Sgt	P.	568614	RAF	F2	01/09/1944
Paris	LAC	H.L.	1545641	RAF	Elect 2	24/10/1944
Pavitt	Cpl	J.A.	1192364	RAF	F2	01/09/1944
Pearson	LAC	K	404665	RNZAF		
Piercy	LAC	H.P.	404667	RNZAF		
Pinnock	LAC	J	1448206	RAF		
Plumbridge	F/Sgt	L.R.	553382	RAF	Elect 1	01/09/1944
Pollard	AC2	J.F.	1124084	RAF	Clk/GD4	01/09/1944
Poulton	LAC	W.C.	1666320	RAF	Dmt	01/09/1944
Pryke	LAC	V.G.	990830	RAF	Elect/2	01/09/1944
Reddaway	Cpl	F.G.	979335	RAF	ARC/GD	01/09/1944
Reilly	AC1	J.	1902383	RAF	M/assist	24/10/1944
Reynolds	Cpl	H.	540278	RAF	D.M.T.	01/09/1944
Roberts	LAC	J.S.	1489026	RAF	Arm	01/09/1944
Robertson	Cpl	I.F.	969663	RAF	F2A	01/09/1944
Rowbotham	F/O		Medical Officer			20/04/1944
Rucklidge	P/O		Signals Officer			22/08/1942
Rumbold	AC1	W.	1414026	RAF	MC	01/09/1942
Sackett	LAC	A.E.	1473029	RAF	Arm 2	01/09/1944
Sale	LAC	G.H.T.	1446486	RAF	F.M.E.	24/10/1944
Savell	LAC	B.	41743	RNZAF		
Seaward	LAC	H.M.	41453	RNZAF		
Seymour	Cpl	A.	576439	RAF	F2E	01/09/1944
Sharp	LAC	W.K.	1640446	RAF	In/Rep	24/10/1944
Shorrock	LAC	A.C.	2210617	RAF	carp/1	24/10/1944

Short	LAC	C.F.	1872559	RAF	F.M.E.	24/10/1944
Simcock	F/Sgt	RAF	524186	RAF	Disiplinarian	
Sinclair	AC1	W.J.N.	1571641	RAF	Arm	01/09/1944
Smith	LAC	I.G.	637684	RNZAF	F2E	24/10/1944
Smith	LAC	J.	1513443	RAF	Elec2	24/09/1944
Smith	LAC	R.N	1607699	RAF	F.M.E.	24/10/1944
Smith	Cpl	H.C.	404668	RNZAF		
Smith	LAC	H.R.	404669	RNZAF		
Spong	AC2	F.L.	1146724	RAF	Elect1	24/10/1944
Spong	LAC	R.S.	1612243	RAF	Elect1	24/10/1944
Springett	AC1	E.	1220968	RAF	W/Mech	24/10/1944
Starmer	LAC	A.J.	1577240	RAF	FME	24/10/1944
Steele	LAC	G.	1512412	RAF	Arm2	01/09/1944
Stewart	AC2	T..	3040505	RAF	A/asst	01/09/1944
Sunderland	LAC	C.M.	1020456	RAF	Arm2	24/10/1944
Sutherland	LAC	G.A.	1343975	RAF	F2A	01/09/1944
Tack	2nd Lt.			USA	Signals Co.	26/08/1942
Taylor	LAC	C.P.	1143030	RAF	F2E	24/10/1944
Taylor	P/O	T.M.	188134	RAF	Intelligence	10/02/1944
Thomas	LAC	T.J.	1416832	RAF	A/Assst	01/09/1944
Thomas	P.O.	D.A.		RAF	Tech RDF	04/05/1943
Thomas	LAC	H.J.	1630545	RAF	R.T.O.	24/10/1944
Tinsley	Fl.Sgt	T.	518816	RNZAF	Arm	24/10/1944
Tilling	F/O	S.	Adjutant	RAF		1904/1944
Tucker	2nd Lt.		USAAC Signals		R.D.F.	15/08/1942
Turton	AC1	R.	1543299	RAF	Arm	01/09/1944
Vann	LAC	C.J.	1506483	RAF	W/Mech	24/10/1944

					R/Mech	
Vasta	Cpl	A.I.	40565	RNZAF		25/04/1942
Vaughan	LAC	C.		RNZAF		
Venn	P/O	M.K.F.		RAF	Enginering	01/09/1944
Vickers	LAC	A.	1509545	RAF	F2A	24/10/1944
Warman	AC1	S	1868172	RAF	In/Rep	13/06/1944
Watkins	F/O	H.			Intelligence	24/10/1944
Webb	LAC	A.E.H.	1536123	RAF	F.M.E.	01/09/1944
Webber	LAC	E.J.	1196001	RAF	DMT	01/09/1944
Webster	Cpl	S.	1190102	RAF	F2E	06/06/1942
Westcott	F/O	G.			Adjutant	01/09/1944
White	AC1	A.R.	1720095	RAF	F2A	21/02/1943
White	P/O	J.M.			Signals Officer	24/10/1944
White	LAC	G.	1247306	RAF	R.T.O.	24/10/1944
Whittaker	LAC	L.F.N.	338359	RNZAF	F.M.E.	01/09/1944
Whittington	Cpl	P.E.	1288809	RAF	F2	01/09/1944
Wilcox	Cpl	K.G.	900833	RNZAF	F2A	01/09/1944
Williams	LAC	E.D.G.	1655891	RAF	DMT	01/09/1944
Williams	Cpl	L.T.	1401708	RAF	Carp/1	20/04/1944
Williamson	Flt.Lt.	J.P.			Medical Officer	01/09/1944
Wilson	LAC	G.J.	1615476	RAF	Elect 2	

The Pilot Speaks

Give to this Erk – not us – the word of praise
One of those sturdy types – the L.A.C.'s
Who laboured cheerfully whole nights and days
On jobs that would have daunted Hercules,
When hangers and machines were blown to bits,
In heat and freezing cold, blackout or light,
In dire fatigue, in hours of frightful blitz;
His life is dedicated to his kite;
There is no glamour in his dull D.I.'s,
No "gongs" for him but he is satisfied
To watch his "Mozzie" roar into the skies,
Or see it land safe home again with pride;
He serves and waits with British grit and skill,
And shares the honours of the chase and kill.

W.A.G. Kemp

488 Squadron Aircraft

The following are the lists of known aircraft sourced from both the Operations Record Book and the De Havilland Factory Register supplied to the Squadron from June 1942 through to April 1945. With the squadron operating two flights on alternate "shifts" no one crew had exclusive use of their "own" aircraft but generally shared with those on the other flight crew.

The aircraft used by 488 Squadron were prefixed ME followed by a specific alphabetical identification code for each aircraft. These codes were transferred on to replacement aircraft following being written off or the current aircraft being passed over to other squadrons.

The following schedule lists all the aircraft delivered to the squadron and all the known significant events that happened to each aircraft including tracking the movements when the aircraft finally ended up during or after the end of hostilities. [56] Any incidents or items of interest relating to a particular aircraft are recorded here also.

The squadron used 54 Bristol Beaufighters and 100 De Havilland Mosquito Night Fighters during their postings to various airfields throughout the UK and Europe. These aircraft were regularly replaced due to attrition rates or were updated as armanents and systems were modified.

---

[56] *Mosquito Information sourced from the official De Havilland Factory Register*

Beaufighter Log from Operational Record Book (ORB)

Model	Factory No.	Squadron Code	Date of Event	Event and Crew Details
	T3008			No further information found
BF IIF	T3009	ME-H	01/09/1942	First recorded flight in ORB - McQeen and Gordon
BFIIF	T3091		18/01/1943	First recorded flight in ORB - Roe and McBride
BFIIF	T3092		01/09/1942	First recorded flight in ORB - Boulton and Hoile
BFIIF	T3218		01/09/1942	First recorded flight in ORB - Rabone and Longhorn
BFIIF	T3220		02/09/1942	First recorded flight in ORB - Bush and Spedding. Flt/Sgt Bush had the dubious distinction of being the first 488 pilot to damage his aircraft. He was seconded from the U.S. Airforce.
BFIIF	T3230			No further information found.
BFIIF	T3281		21/11/1942	First recorded flight in ORB - Rabone and Longhorn
BFIIF	T3320		21/11/1942	First recorded flight in ORB - Watt and Raynor
BFIIF	T3373		01/09/1942	First recorded flight in ORB - Browne and Taylor
BFIIF	T3376		04/09/1942	First recorded flight in ORB - McQeen and Garden
BFIIF	T3379		01/09/1942	First recorded flight in Orb - Peacocke and Spence. This aircraft collided in mid-air with V8162 with the crews of both aircraft being killed. These were the first fatalities for the UK based Squadron.
BFIIF	T3410		01/09/1942	First recorded flight in ORB - Trousdale and Affleck
BFIIF	T3411		05/09/1942	First recorded flight in ORB - Kemp and Reed
Tiger Moth			01/09/1942	First recoded flight in ORB - Gunn and Broom
BFIIF	V8120		25/10/1942	First recorded flight in ORB- Boulton and Hoile

BFIIF	V8139	03/09/1942	First recorded flight in ORB - Jeffs and Bradley
BFIIF	V8143	03/09/1942	First recorded flight in ORB - Robinson and Watts
BFIIF	V8155	01/09/1942	First recorded flight in ORB - Browne and Taylor
BFIIF	V8160	02/09/1942	First recorded flight in ORB - Davison and Cutfield
BFIIF	V8162	01/09/1942	First recorded flight in ORB - Bush and Spedding
		05/12/1942	This aircraft collided in mid air with T3385 with the crews of both aircraft being killed. These were the first fatalities for 488 squadron. Both sets of of crewmen were from the RNZAF. McKinnon and McChesney.
BFIIF	V8163	03/09/1942	First recorded flight in ORB - McKinnon and McChesney
BFIIF	V8164	05/09/1942	First recorded flight in ORB - Watts and McWha
BFIIF	V8165	05/09/1942	First recorded flight in ORB - Davison and Cutfield
BFIIF	V8168		No further information found
BFIIF	V8169		No further information found
BFIIF	V8170	01/09/1942	First recorded flight in ORB - Head and Andrews
BFIIF	V8193	02/09/1942	First recorded flight in ORB - Jeffs and Bradley
BFIIF	V8199	05/09/1942	First recorded flight in ORB - Gunn and Gard'ner
BFIIF	V8210	01/09/1942	First recorded flight in ORB - Jeffs and Bradley
BFVI	V8221	18/05/1942	First recorded flight in ORB - McMillan and Bricker
		18/05/1942	First used on Ranger missions over France attacking railway rolling stock at night - McMillan and Bricker
BFVI	V8453	12/03/1943	First recorded flight in ORB - Gunn and Broom
		16/05/1943	Two trains attacked with one damaged during Ranger mission.
		17/05/1943	One train attacked during Ranger mission over France - Watt and Atkins.
BFVI	V8458	02/07/1943	First recorded flight in ORB - Browne and Taylor

BFV1	V8517		No further information found
BFV1	V8588	16/04/1943	First recorded flight in ORB - Davison and Cutfield
		16/04/1943	Attack rail yards and damaged one train on Ranger mission over North West France - Davison and Cutfield
		20/04/1943	Two beam attacks made on goods train - Davison and Cutfield
BFV1	V8590	02/03/1943	First recorded flight in ORB - Gunn and Broom
		17/06/1943	Attacked goods train at Gaces. Davison and Cutfield.
BFV1	V8676		No further information found
BFV1	E.L.154	25/03/1943	First recorded flight in Orb - Fleming and Nagle
		25/03/1943	Two trains attacked result unknown - Fleming and Nagle
		15/06/1943	Attacked one train at Guincamp and one in Caulnes - leaving both burning - heavy flak on return journey.
		17/06/1943	One train attacked at Courances - Browne and Taylor
		19/06/1943	One train attacked at Vendoma - Flemming and Nagle
		20/06/1943	Unable to find airfield in bad weather and crashed on landing Jeffs and Spedding.
BFV1	E.L.148	16/04/1943	First recorded flight in ORB - Reed and Bricker. Three trains attacked and stopped in North West France - Reed and Bricker
		18/04/1943	Further three trains attacked with two stopped in same area.
		19/04/1943	Further three trains attacked and stopped - Reed and Bricker
BFV1	X7884	12/08/1943	First recorded flight in ORB - Scott and Morgan
		14/08/1943	Checked out intruder - Robinson and Watts
BFV1	X7894		No further information found
		19/04/1943	One railway engine attacked and stopped - Bergemann and Bishop

BFV1		20/04/1943	Three trains, water tower and lorry attacked - Reed and Bricker
BFV1		15/05/1943	Attacked train - Reed and Bricker
BFV1		21/05/1943	One train damaged - Reed and Bricker
BFV1	X7952	21/05/1943	First recorded flight in ORB. Damaged four locomotives Watt and Adkins.
BFV1		13/07/1943	Watt and Adkins were both killed attempting a high speed low altitude turn over Ayr airfield.
BFV1	X7965	15/05/1943	First recorded flight in ORB - Reed and Bricker
BFV1		15/05/1943	Two railway engines attacked. One damaged - Davison and Cutfield
BFV1		17/05/1943	Two trains and two cars attacked - Davison and Cutfield
BFV1		18/05/1943	Two trains stopped and damaged - Davison and Cutfield
BFV1		19/05/1943	Three locomotives and one lorry damaged -Reed and Bricker
BFV1	X8027	03/07/1943	First recorded flight in ORB - Bergemann and Bishop
BFV1		23/09/1943	Vlotman and Wood crash landed at RAF Gravesend
BFV1	X8148	16/06/1943	First recorded flight in ORB with successful attack on a goods train in NW France - Jeffs and Spedding
BFV1	X8155		No further information found.
BFV1	X8210		No further information found.
BFV1	X8215	16/05/1943	First recorded flight in ORB with one locomotive and one lorry attacked and damaged - Reed and Bricker
BFV1	X8253	31/07/1943	First recorded flight in ORB - Patrick and Concannon
BFV1	X8263	02/04/1943	Aircraft crashed into high ground just after taking off from Ayr with both crewmen, P/O O'Gara and Sgt. Masters, being killed.
BFV1	X8490		No further information found

Mosquito Log from Operational Record Book (ORB)

Model	Factory No.	Squadron Code	Date of Event	Event and Crew Details
Mk XII	HK121		17/09/1943	First recorded flight in ORB - Browne and Taylor
Mk XII	HK132		17/09/1943	From 29 Squadron - passed on to 307 Squadron before being ditched into the North Sea on 12/07/1944
MkXII	HK134		15/09/1943	First recorded flight in ORB. Received from 256 Squadron before being passed on to 54 OTU - Knox and Ryan. SOC 23/04/1946
Mk XII	HK137		07/09/1943	First recorded flight in ORB - Bergemann and Bishop. From 256 Squadron - passed on to 406 Squadron. SOC 23/04/1945
Mk XII	HK182		31/08/1943	Stalled in turn and crashed at Drem killing P/O Gordon RAF and P/O Rawlings RNZAF
Mk XII	HK186		04/09/1943	First recorded flight in ORB - Hobbis and Hills. Passed on to 51 OTU SOC 23/10/1946
Mk XII	HK194		05/09/1944	First recorded flight in ORB - Patrick and Concannon
Mk XII	HK203		05/09/1943	First recorded flight in ORB - Browne and Taylor
Mk XII	HK204		15/09/1943	First recorded flight in ORB - Watts and Folley. After destroying a Dornier 217 over Forness HK204 flew into ground close to Bradwell Bay killing both F/Lt Ball RNZAF and F/O Kemp RAF

Mk XII	HK206		08/10/1943	First Recorded flight in ORB - Hobbis and Hills
Mk XII	HK209		15/09/1943	Destroyed Heinkel 111 over Forness UK but HK209 also destroyed in the exchange killing both Gunn and Afleck
Mk XII	HK222		24/03/1944	F/O Chris Wilson and F/O Kiwi Wilson disappeared over the English Channel and were never seen again. Both were from the RNZAF and had just reported an interception.
Mk XII	HK225		08/10/1943	First recorded flight in ORB - Hall and Marriott
MkXII	HK226		07/09/1943	First recorded flight in ORB - Gunn and Affleck
Mk XII	HK227	ME-E	30/08/1943	First recorded flight in ORB - Hobbis and Hills. Passed on to 51 OTU where it was written off 09/03/1945
Mk XII	HK228	ME-C	30/08/1943	First recorded flight in ORB - Browne and Taylor
			26/11/1943	Destroyed a Me 410 over Calais - Hall and Marriott
			24/02/1944	Destroyed a Ju88 over Wadhurst UK - Hall and Marriott. Passed on to 406 Squadron where it collided with a 307 Squadron Mosquito and was written off.
Mk XII	HK233		30/08/1943	First recorded flight in ORB - Reed and Bricker. Passed on to 307 Squadron then 54 OTU. SOC 26/6/1946
Mk XII	HK234		07/09/1943	First recorded flight in ORB - Knox and Ryan
			06/10/1943	P/O Knox and P/O Ryan, both RNZAF severely damaged a Dornier 217 over Canterbury UK - passed on to 307 and 264 Squadrons ending up at 51 OTU. SOC 1/08/1945
Mk XII	HK235		16/09/1943	First recorded flight in ORB - Davison and Cutfield
			16/10/1943	Engine failure and crash into Bradwell Bay Estuary killing both P/O Green and Flt Sgt Creek of RAFVR

Mk XII	**HK294**	28/11/1943	First Recorded flight in ORB - Moore and Earl
Mk XII	**HK299**	28/11/1943	First recorded flight in ORB - Browne and Taylor
Mk XII	**HK334**	13/12/1943	First recorded flight in ORB - Know and Ryan
Mk XII	**HK363**	04/11/1943	First recorded flight in ORB - Proctor and Hamley
		03/02/1944	Written off after training accident killing F/Sgt Edwards and F/Sgt Watson, both RNZAF.
Mk XIII	**HK365**	16/10/1943	First recorded flight in ORB - Hughs and Proctor
		21/03/1943	Destroyed a Ju 88 over channel UK - Vlotman and Wood
		21/03/1943	Destroyed a 2nd Ju88 but suffered damage as a result. Passed on to 409 and 85 Squadrons. DBR 01/01/1945
Mk XIII	**HK367**	09/10/1943	First recorded flight in ORB - Davison and Cutfield
		08/11/1943	Destroyed Me 410 over Manston UK - Reed and Bricker
		04/02/1944	Destroyed Dornier 217 over channel - Vlotman and Wood
		21/02/1944	Crashed on takeoff at Bradwell Bay killing F/O Riwai and Flt/Sgt Clarke, both RNZAF - Aircraft written off
Mk XIII	**HK368**	09/10/1943	First recorded flight in ORB - Hamley and Brandon
Mk XIII	**HK369**	07/11/1943	First recorded flight in ORB - Reed and Bricker
Mk XIII	**HK375**	29/10/1943	First recorded flight in ORB - Bergemann and Bishop
		30/12/1943	crashed into sea off Bradwell Bay killing Flt/Sgt Behrent and Flt/Sgt Breward both of tht RNZAF
Mk XIII	**HK377**	16/08/1944	Destroyed a Ju 88 over Caen, France - McCabe and Newman. Passed on to 151 then 604 squadrons. Flown into a house in bad weather in Northern France on 02/01/1945.

Mk XIII	**HK380**		21/01/1944	Destroyed a Dornier 217 over Lymph UK - Hall and Cairns. Also destroyed two Ju 88s, one over Kent and a second over Earls Colne, all on the same night. SOC 09/12/1946
Mk XIII	**HK381**	ME-W	15/11/1943	First recorded flight in ORB - Fleming and Nagle
			14/05/1944	Destroyed a Ju 188 over Yeovil, UK - Jeffs and Spedding This crew came across a Dornier 217 later in their flight and severely damaged it but only claimed a probable. Passed on to 264 and 409 Squadrons. SOC 25/10/1946
Mk XIII	**HK420**	ME-B	04/12/1943	First recorded flight in ORB - Bale and Richardson
			06/08/1944	Destroyed a Ju 188 over Rennes, France - Browne and Taylor, who also destroyed two unknowns over Rennes, France. The last two aircraft were forced down to low level and dived into the ground without a shot being fired.
Mk XIII	**HK423**		12/11/1943	First recorded flight in ORB - Trousdale and Crowther
			26/11/1943	S/Ldr Hobbis and P/O Hills both RAF abandoned burning aircraft over North Sea. Only the body of P/O Hills was recovered months later.
Mk XIII	**HK 427**	ME-L	30/08/1943	First Recorded flight in ORB - Robinson and Watts
Mk XIII	**HK457**		13/03/1943	First recorded flight in ORB - Mitchell and Church
			19/12/1943	Destroyed a Me 410 over Rye UK - Robinson and Clark
			19/03/1944	Aircraft struck by friendly fire and - Robinson and Keeping. Passed on to 604 Squadron. SOC 16/09/1946
Mk XIII	**HK461**		02/01/1944	Destroyed Me 410 over Dover UK - Bergemann and Bishop

Mk XIII			10/03/1944	Swung on landing, hit hedge on attempted overshoot at Bradwell Bay and killed F/Sgt Anderson on his first solo
	HK504	ME-M	25/01/1944	First recorded flight in ORB - Haine and Bowman
			04/08/1944	Destroyed a Ju 88 over Vire, France - Haine and Bowman Passed on to 29 Squadron. Missing believed crashed 06/10/1944
Mk XIII	**HK513**	ME-D	14/06/1944	Destroyed a Ju 88 over St. Lo, France - Hall and Marriott
			05/08/1944	Destroyed a Dornier 217 over Rennes - Hall and Marriott. Passed on to 307 then 29 Squadron
			03/02/1945	Overturned while landing at Hunsdon and written off
Mk XIII	**HK532**		23/04/1944	First recorded flight in ORB - Patrick and Concannon
			02/08/1944	Destroyed a Dornier 217 over Avranches - Browne and Taylor
			03/08/1944	Destroyed a Ju88 over Avranches - Patrick and Concannon. Passed on to 264 Squadron. SOC 06/07/1945
Mk XIII	**HK534**		01/03/1944	First recorded flight in ORB - Longley and Moore. Passed on to 264 Squadron. SOC 31/12/1946
Mk XIII	**MM439**		07/03/1944	First recorded flight in ORB - Scott and Broodbank
			18/06/1944	Destroyed an Fw 190 over Quineville, - Robinson and Keeping
			22/06/1944	Destroyed a Ju 188 over Bayeux Fr. - McCabe and Riley
			28/07/1944	Destroyed a Ju 188 over Mayenne Fr. Robinson and Clarke

			03/08/1944	Destroyed a Ju 188 over Avranches Fr. McKay and Thompson
			04/08/1944	Destroyed a Ju 188 over St.Lo. Fr. Shaw and Wyman
			20/08/1944	Destroyed a Ju 188 over Caen Fr. Robinson and Addison
Mk XIII	MM466			Passed on to Royal Navy
			01/03/1944	First recorded flight ORB - Knox and Ryan
			25/06/1944	Destroyed an ME 410 over Bayeux Fr - Jameson and Crookes
			28/06/1944	Destroyed a Ju 88 over Caen Fr. - Jameson and Crookes
			29/07/1944	Destroyed a Ju 88 over Caen Fr. - Jameson and Crookes
			29/07/1944	Destroyed a Ju 88 over Caen Fr. - Jameson and Crookes
			29/07/1944	Destroyed a Ju 88 over Lisieux Fr. - Jameson and Crookes
			29/07/1944	Destroyed a Dornier 217 over Caen Fr - Jameson and Crookes
			04/08/1944	Destroyed a Ju 88 over Airei, Fr. - Jameson and Crookes
			06/08/1944	Destroyed a Ju 88 over Avranches Fr. - Jameson and Crookes
			15/08/1944	Destroyed a Ju 88 over Caen Fr. - Jameson and Crookes
MkXIII	MM467			No Data available
Mk XIII	MM476	ME-V	01/03/1944	First recorded flight in ORB - Bunting and Reed
			14/03/1944	Destroyed a Ju 188 over Essex UK - Bunting and Reed
			21/03/1944	Destroyed a Ju 88 over Clare UK - Bunting and Reed
			21/03/1944	Destroyed a Ju 188 over Rochford UK - Bunting and Reed

Mk XIII			12/06/1944	Destroyed a Ju 88 over Caen Fr. - Bunting and Reed
			12/06/1944	Destroyed an Fw 190 over St.Lo Fr. - Bunting and Reed. This was the first single seater Luftwaffe fighter shot down by 488 Squadron.
			30/07/1944	This aircraft was shot down by friendly fire while chasing an Fw 190 over Lisieux. Both S/Ldr Bunting and his crewman, F/O Spedding, were killed.
Mk XIII	MM498	ME-S	25/04/1944	First recorded flight in ORB - Hughs and Proctor
			01/08/1944	Destroyed a Ju 88 over St Lo. France - Hall and Marriott. Passed on to 29, 409, 604 and 26 Squadrons. SOC 26/10/1945
Mk XIII	MM502		01/05/1944	First recorded flight in ORB - Scott and Duncan
			05/08/1944	Destroyed a Do 217 over Angers, France - McLean and Grant
			14/08/1945	Passed on to 29, 409, and 264 Squadrons. Written off after being driven into back of truck
Mk XIII	MM504		13/06/1944	First recorded flight in ORB - Haine and Bowman
			25/08/1944	Attacked by American Black Widow fighter. Passed on to 409 Squadron. SOC 02/09/1946
Mk XIII	MM513	ME-D	25/04/1944	First recorded flight in ORB - MacLean and Grant
			18/04/1944	Destroyed a Ju88 over Channel, UK - Bourke and Skudder
			28/07/1944	Destroyed a Ju88 over Lessay, France - Hall and Marriott
			same night	Destroyed a Ju88 over Lessay, France - Hall and Marriott. Passed on to 29, 409 and 264 Squadrons. SOC 22/08/1945
Mk XIII	MM515	ME-Z	20/04/1944	First recorded flight in ORB - McLean and Grant

Mk XIII			20/06/1944	Destroyed a Fw190 over Falaise - Vlotman and Wood. Passed to 264 Squadron where badly damaged and written off after undercarriage collapsed on takeoff in Lille.
Mk XIII	MM519	ME-F	05/03/1944	First recorded flight in ORB - Patrick and Concannon. Passed on to 29 Squadron where it went missing over Lippstadt on 02/12/1944
Mk XIII	MM551		01/03/1944	First recorded flight in ORB - Vlotman and Wood
			18/04/1944	Destroyed a Ju 88 over Belgium Coast - Hall and Cairns
			14/05/1944	Destroyed a Ju188 over Exeter, UK - Hall and Cairns
			15/07/1944	MM551 crashed into forest near Holmsley killing F/sgt Scott and F/O Duncan, both RNZAF
Mk XIII	MM556	ME-B	21/04/1944	First recorded flight in ORB - Marshall and Prescott. SOC 02/09/1945
Mk XIII	MM558	ME-E	18/04/1944	First recorded flight in ORB - Knox and Ryan
			17/07/1944	Destroyed a JU 88 over St Lo. France - Hall and Marriott. to 29 Squadron and written off after runway overshoot
Mk XIII	MM566	ME-A	01/08/1944	First recorded flight in orb - Bowman and Green
			01/09/1944	Destroyed a Ju1188 over Le Havre, - Haine and Bowman. Passed on to 604, 410 and back to 604 Squadron. SOC 07/08/1946
Mk XIII	MM588		06/06/1944	First recorded flight in ORB - Scott and Broodbank
			16/08/1944	Damaged a Ju 88 - Cook and Proctor. Passed on to 409 Squadron and written off after collision with another Mosquito
Mk XIII	MM622		10/06/1944	First recorded flight in ORB - Arthur and Herd

Mk 30			18/08/1944	Destroyed a Dornier 217 over Rouen - Jeffs and Crookes. passed on to 264 and 409 Squadrons.
			09/11/1944	Damaged by Flak
Mk 30	MM809	ME-H	11/10/1944	First recorded flight in ORB - Cook and Carcasson
			22/04/1944	Destroyed a Ju 52 over Rhinow - Patrick and Concannon. passed on to 54 OTU. Destroyed in crash 09/11/1946
Mk 30	MM811		11/10/1944	First recorded flight in ORB - Webbe and Watson
			24/12/1944	Damaged a Ju 188 - Mallon and Brock.
			26/122/1944	Probably destroyed a Ju 188 but wrote off their aircraft in the process after crash landing at Melsbroek with no fuel left and in heavy fog conditions - Webbe and Watson
Mk 30	MM813		29/10/1944	First recorded flight in ORB - Arthur and Earl. Passed on to 219 and 141 Squadrons. SOC 08/11/1949
Mk 30	MM814		16/10/1944	First recorded flight in ORB - Hall and Cairns
			04/11/1944	Collided with ground accumulator trolley - Shaw and Wyman. Passed on to 151 Squadron and lost wing while recovering from a steep dive over Essex
Mk 30	MM815		19/10/1944	First recorded flight in ORB - Mallon and Brock
			08/01/1945	Spun into ground during night training killing both W/O Niederer and F/O Lawrence
Mk 30	MM816		17/10/1944	First recorded flight in ORB - Davison and Hickmore
			22/03/1945	Destroyed an Me110 over Dortmund - Fleming and Nagle. Passed on to 51 OTU and then on to a French civil operator on 26/06/1947

Mk 30	MM817	ME-M	27/10/1944	First recorded flight in ORB - Muldrew and Emerton. Passed on to 54 OTU. SOC 11/08/1948	
Mk 30	MM818		11/10/1944	First recorded flight in ORB - Mudrew and Emerton. SOC 05/02/1948	
Mk 30	MM819		29/10/1944	First recorded flight in ORB - Fritchley and Ray	
			27/10/1944	Ran off runway in fog and badly damaged - Fritchley and Ray	
Mk 30	MM820		18/10/1944	First recorded flight in ORB - McCabe and Riley	
			04/11/1944	Destroyed a Me 110 over Antwerp - Marshall and Presscott	
			21/02/1945	Swung on takeoff and badly damaged at Amiens - Glisy	
Mk 30	MM822		05/11/1944	First recorded flight in ORB - Arthur and Herd	
			23/12/1944	Destroyed a Ju 88 over Maeseyck - Stewart and Brumby. Passed on to 51 then 54 OTU. SOC 11/03/1948	
Mk 30	MT454		27/10/1944	First recorded flight in ORB - Watts and Folley	
Mk 30	MT456		10/09/1944	First recorded flight in ORB - Cook and Carcasson	
			18/09/1944	Hit by out-of-control Lancaster Bomber LP625 while in dispersal area at Colerne and was written off.	
Mk 30	MT457	ME-S	13/10/1944	First recorded flight in ORB - Fritchley and Ray. SOC 08/07/1944	
Mk 30	MT458		01/11/1944	First recorded flight in ORB Hall and Cairns	
			23/12/1944	Destroyed an Me410 over Malmedy - Hall and Cairns. SOC 07/09/1954	
Mk 30	MT459		03/02/1945	First recorded flight in ORB. Webbe and Watson. Passed on to 54 OTU. SOC 08/07/1948	

Mk 30	MT461		16/10/1944	Bourke and Skudder. Passed on to Armee de L'Air
Mk 30	MT463		17/10/1944	First recorded flight in ORB - Mitchell and Ballard
			25/11/1944	Bounced on landing at Amiens and tore off undercarriage. Aircraft written off.
Mk 30	MT467	ME-X	16/10/1944	McKay and Thompson. Passed on to 51 OTU. SOC 20/01/1945
Mk 30	MT 468		16/10/1944	First recorded flight in ORB - Marshall and Prescott
Mk 30	MT 469		11/10/1944	Passed on to AODU/ Med and was lost on 19/03/1944
Mk 30			14/10/1944	First recorded flight in ORB - Hall and Marriott. SOC 31/07/1946
Mk 30	MT 477		13/10/1944	First recorded flight in ORB - Mitchell and Ballard. Passed on to 54 OTU. SOC 10/09/1946
Mk 30	MT484	ME-K	01/11/1944	First recorded flight in ORB - Watts and Folley
			11/03/1945	Both P/O Mallon and P/O Brock were killed when ME-K swung badly on takeoff and crashed
Mk 30	MV538		02/11/1944	First recorded flight in ORB - Fritchley and Ray. Passed on to Armee De L'Air 31/12/1947
Mk 30	MV567		12/12/1944	First recorded flight in ORB - Davison and Hickmore
			27/12/1944	Hit by flak and overturned on landing at Melsbroek in Belgium - Stewart and Brumby
Mk 30	MV568		24/11/1944	first recorded flight in ORB - Gard'ner and Perfect
				Passed on to Armee de L'Air 04/09/1947
Mk 30	MV 570		02/11/1944	First Recorded flight in ORB - Hall and Cairns

Mark	Serial	Code	Date	Notes
Mk 30			28/12/1944	Skidded and collapsed undercarriage at Asch - Hall and Cairns
Mk 30	NT 260	ME-K	01/03/1944	First recorded flight in ORB - Gard'ner and Perfect. Passed on to 54 OTU. SOC 11/03/1948
Mk 30	NT 263		12/12/1944	First recorded flight in ORB - Watts and Folley
			21/02/1945	Destroyed a Ju88 over Groenlo - Stewart and Brumby
			26/03/1945	Destroyed a Me 110 over Holtem - Stewart and Brumby
			07/04/1945	Destroyed a Me 110 over Osnabruck - Stewart and Brumby
			05/02/1946	Passed on to 51 and 54 OTU Written off after belly landing
Mk 30	NT 268		09/04/1945	First recorded flight in ORB - Watts and Folley. Passed on to 307 Squadron. SS 08/07/1948
Mk 30	NT 272		27/02/1944	First recorded flight in ORB - Gard'ner and Perfect
			16/04/1945	Engine failure at Gilze-Rijen and written off after hitting bomb crater - Jeffs and Crookes.
Mk 30	NT 308		21/02/1945	First recorded flight in ORB - Jeffs and Crookes
			25/04/1945	Destroyed Fe 189 over Wittenburg - Marshall and Prescott. Passed on to 54 OTU. SS 08/07/1948
Mk 30	NT314		22/02/1945	First recorded flight in ORB - Hall and Cairns
Mk 30	NT327		22/02/1945	First recorded flight in ORB - Davison and Hickmore. Passed on to 51 and 54 OTU. SOC 07/07/1947
Mk 30	NT350		20/02/1945	First recorded Flight in ORB Gard'ner and Perfect. Passed on to 51 and 54 OTU. SOC 07/07/1947

Mk 30	NT350	26/03/1947	Destroyed a Ju88 over Emmerich but forced to crash land on ruway at Gilze-Rijen where aircraft burnt out - Hall and Taylor
Mk 30	NT372 ME-B	14/03/1945	Jeffs and Crookes. Passed on to Armee de L'Air 13/09/1950
Mk 30	NT450	04/03/1945	Moore and Earl. Passed on to 125, 264 and 505 Squadrons. SS 29/10/1953
Mk 30	NZ511	21/03/1945	Bourke and Skudder. Passed on to 54 OTU. SOC 11/11/47
Mk 30	NZ512	24/04/1945	Destroyed a Ju 52 over Brandenburg - Davison and Hickmore. Passed on to 54 OTU. SOC 13/05/1947
Mk 30	NT517	29/03/1945	First recorded flight in ORB - Davison and Hickmore. Passed on to 51 and 54 OTU. SOC 08/07/1948
Mk 30	NT532	23/03/1945	First Recorded flight in ORB - Patrick and Ray.
Mk 30	NT588		Passed on to 54 OTU. SOC 08/03/1943
Mk 30	LR 562		Passed on to 51 and 54 OTU - Destroyed
Mk 30			Passed on to 51 OTU. Damaged in accident 28/10/1944 SOC 28/12/1944

BIBLIOGRAPHY:

New Zealand Electronic Text Centre - Internet

'Night fighting with the New Zealanders' - personal account written by Mr. Norman Crookes for 'The Peoples War Site', a BBC internet archive

Birtles, Philip J. *Mosquito – The Illustrated History*, Sutton publishing Limited Gloustershire England

Bowman, Martin W. *The Men Who Flew the Mosquito,* Pen and Sword Aviation, 2003

Bowman, Martin, *Mosquito Bomber/Fighter Bomber Units 1942-45* Osprey Publishing 1997

Brandon, Lewis, DSO, DFC and Bar, *'Night Flyer'*, Crecy Publishing Ltd, 1999

Cairns, John DFC, *'Owls and Fools Fly at Night'*, Kingsland Publications 2003

Charlwood, Don, 'No *Moon Tonight'* Crecy Publishing Limited 2000

Clostermann, Pierre, *'The Big Show'*, Cassell 2004

Darlow, Stephen, Victory *Fighters: The Veterans' Story*, Grub Street Publishing, London 2005

Darlow, Stephen, *Five of the Few*, Grub Street Publishing, London 2008

Edwards, Ted, *"Aircrew of Northland"* Northland Branch of RNZAF Association

Enright, Michael, *Flyers Far Away*, Longueville Books, 2009

Fenton, Alison: *'John Hall: A Memoir',* The Charlebury Press, 2005

Gabites, Allott, 'Monkey's *Birthday* - Recollections of a World War Two airman Self published 1998

Green, William, 'Famous Fighters'   McDonald and Co. 1957

Haine, Grp.Capt. 'Dicky', *'From Fury to Phantom'* An RAF Pilot's Story 1936-1970, Pen and Sword Aviation, Great Britain 2005

Hancock, Kenneth R. *"New Zealand at War",* A.H and A.W. Reed 1946

Harris, Stephen 'Under *a Bombers Moon'* Exisle Publishing 2009

Howe, Stuart, *De Havilland Mosquito*, Crecy Publishing, 2006

Hunt, Flight-Lieutenant Leslie, *'Defence until Dawn'*, Washburn and Sons Ltd, 1949

Jackson, Robert: *'Combat Legend de Havilland Mosquito'* Airlife Publishing 2003

Kemp, W.A.G. *"Men like These'* Chapman and Hall, London 1946

Lambert, Max: *'Day after Day'* New Zealanders in Fighter Command Harper Collins, 2011-12-12

Lambert, Max: *'Night after Night* 'New Zealanders in Bomber Command Harper Collins, 2007

Lewis, Bruce 'Aircrew' Cassell, London 2000

Long, Andrew: *'The Faithful Few'* Victory Books International 2007

McIntosh, Dave: *'Terror in the Starboard Seat"* PaperJacks Ltd. 1981

Mitchell, Alan W., *New Zealanders in the Air War*, George Harrap and Co. Ltd, London 1945

Nesbitt-Dufort, John, *'Black Lysander'* Whydown Sussex 1973

Overy, Richard, **'Bomber Command 1939 – 45** HarperCollins 1997

Parry, Simon: *'Beaufighter Squadrons'* Red Kite 2002

Pearce R.T.: *'Operation Wasservogel'* Sheila Hamblin Pearce 1997

Price, Alfred: *'Battle of Britain – The Hardest Day'* Arms and Armour Press London 1979

Rawnsley C.F. and Robert Wright, *"Night Fighter",* Crecy Publishing Ltd Manchester, England 1998

Sawyer, Group Captain Tom: *'Only Owls and Bloody Fools Fly at Night'* Goodall Publications Ltd 1982

Shacklady, Edward, *'De Havilland Mosquito'*, Cerberus Publishing, 2005xz

Shores, Christopher and Thomas, Chris, '2nd *Tactical Airforce'* Vol. One, Classic Publications, Surrey, UK 2004

Thomas, Andrew: *'Mosquito Aces of World War 2'* Osprey Publishing 2005

Thomas, Andrew: *'Beaufighter Aces of World War 2'* Osprey Publishing 2000

Veitch, Michael, *'Fly'*, Penguin 2008

White, Graham, *'Night Fighter over Germany'* Pen and Sword Aviation, 2006

Wilson, Kevin, *'Bomber Boys*, The RAF offensive of 1943, Weidenfeld and Nicolson, 2005

Wilson, Kevin, *'Men of Air'*, the Doomed Youth of Bomber Command, Weidenfeld and Nicholson, 2007

Confidential Memo dated 21/05/08 from Air Commodore Neville sourced from RNZAF Museum Archives 85/410.14

Tribute to F/O Reg. Mitchell – written by his son, John Mitchell, unpublished

Watts, Ron: *Memoirs* - unpublished

MAGAZINE ARTICLES

Moving Day for 488 Squadron, Author Anonymous, from the Weekly News of 1st January 1947

New Zealand Fighters from Air Pictorial, Leslie Hunt. March 1963

Aeroplane Monthly, Lewis Brandon, **July** 1988.

ARCHIVAL INFORMATION

Official De Havilland Mosquito Accident Register

Appendix 'E' File 540 dated 24th December 1944
Congratulatory message from 85 Group O.C. AVM Steele

Appendix 'B' File 540 dated 19th April 1945
488 Squadron Disbandment Notice from Headquarters 85 Group

Appendix "H" Form 540 dated 23rd April 1945
Message Re Disbandment for Air Headquarters Wellington NZ

Appendix "J" Form 540 dated 26th April 1945
Message from A.V.M. Steele to W/C Watts

Appendix "I" Form 540 dated 20th April 1945

Message from W.J. Jordan, NZ High Commissioner in London to W/C Watts

Appendix "K" Form 540 dated 26th April 1945
Squadron Order of the Day O.C. 488 squadron Wng.Comm R.C. Watts

Document titled "Publicity Papers" No. 488 (NZ) Squadron AHB /M5
Ex Archives New Zealand (Archives Ref: AIR 171/8)

Operations Record Book for months of October 1944 to April 1945
Ex Archives New Zealand (Archives Ref: AIR 171/1)

Operations Record Book   UK

Combat Reports September 1943 – April 1945
Ex Archives New Zealand (Archives Ref: AIR)

Combat Reports June 1944 – April 1945
Ex Archives New Zealand (Archives Ref: AIR 171/6)

REPORTS

The Mosquito 50 years on - A Report on the 50th Anniversary Symposium held at British Aerospace Hatfield 24th November 1990. Published by GMS Enterprises

Squadron Memorabilia and Items of Interest

Identity Card issued to Reg Mitchell

A remarkable memento – A copy of the rear side of the photograph shown on page 190 signed on the back by a good number of the Aircrew. The presence of Bill Hewitt's autograph dates it from 19th March 1945, his joining date as Intelligence Officer of 488 Squadron. (Len and Chris Wyman)

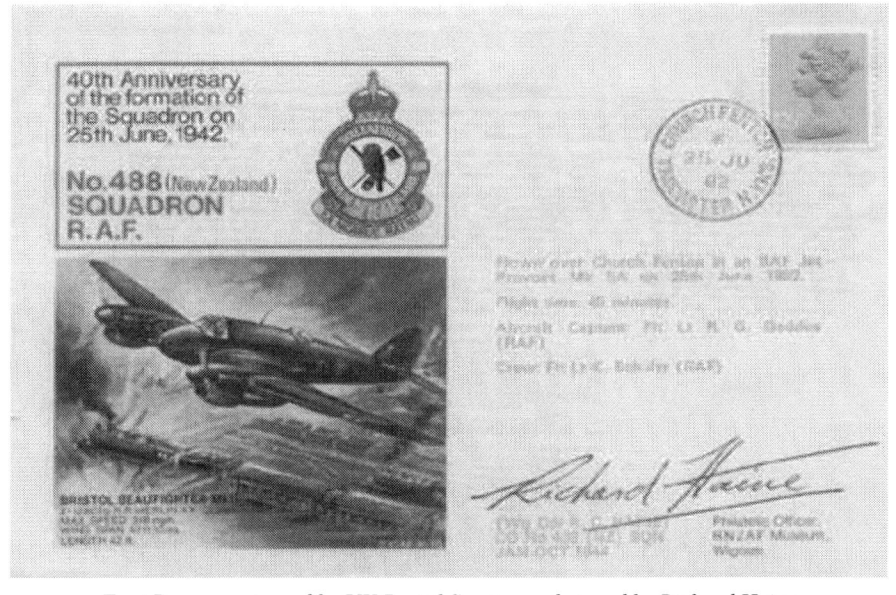

First Day cover issued by UK Postal Service and signed by Richard Haine

Diploma sent to Reg Mitchell by a grateful French Government in recognition of his service in France during WW2

Year of the Veteran
Honouring Those Who Have Served

Certificate of Appreciation

The Government and people of New Zealand express their thanks to

Reginald Walter Mitchell

for the service given to New Zealand during

World War Two

Rt Hon Helen Clark
Prime Minister

Hon Rick Barker
Minister of Veterans' Affairs

Belated recognition by the Government of New Zealand (From the Reg Mitchell Collection)

Copy of Citation signed by King George VI of England for the Distinguished Service Order awarded to George "Jamie" Jameson for bravery while serving with 488 Squadron (Air Force Museum of New Zealand Archives)

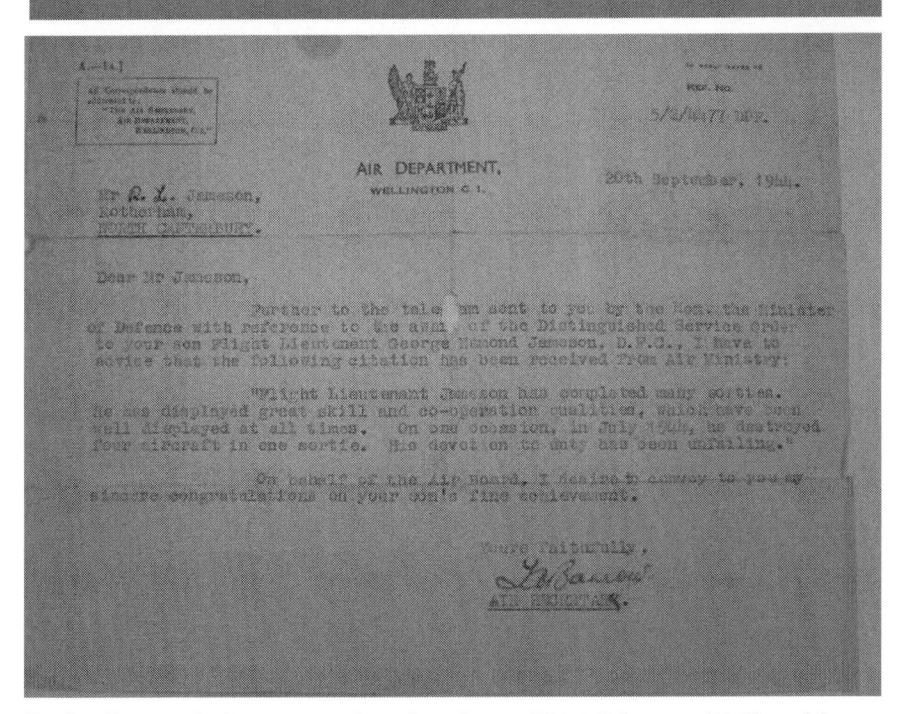

Further Citations for bravery awards made to George "Jamie" Jameson (Air Force Museum of New Zealand Archives)

Pilots Notes for the Beaufighter from the Jameson Collection (Air Force Museum of New Zealand Archives)

Copies of hand-written orders for an exercise carried out over London on 21/04/1944 (Adam Forrest)

Left: F/O James Affleck RAF (Navigator) (Adam Forrest ex Mike McBey). Right: F/L George Vincent Carcasson (Adam Forrest Ex Seb Carcasson)

About the Author

The Author, Graham Clayton pictured at the 2008 book signing of his earlier work, *"Last Stand in Singapore"*. Clayton has had an ongoing interest in military history from a very early age and as with most New Zealand families there is a tangible link with the military in one form or another. His maternal Grandfather, Francis James Graham, served with the 1st Auckland Battalion in France and Belgium, survived the First World War battle of Passchendaele but was later wounded in Amiens in 1918. He has two great uncles buried on the battlefields of Flanders, both killed on the same day on 12th October 1917 while serving with the New Zealand Rifle Brigade at Ypres. He has an uncle who served with the RNZAF in the Pacific in 1944. His Father, Bert Clayton survived the debacle of defeat in Singapore and the Allied surrender to the Japanese during the Second World War and went on to a 24-year career in the RNZAF. It was his story that was the catalyst for Part One of the 488 story. This led to the production of this, the second of the two-part historical narrative of No. 488 (New Zealand) Squadron of the Royal Air Force, the so called 'forgotten squadron' that was re-formed after being disbanded after the retreat from Singapore and took on the German Luftwaffe in the night skies over the UK and Europe.

Printed in Poland
by Amazon Fulfillment
Poland Sp. z o.o., Wrocław